RACIAL TERRORISM

RACE, RHETORIC, AND MEDIA SERIES
Davis W. Houck, General Editor

RACIAL TERRORISM

A RHETORICAL INVESTIGATION OF LYNCHING

Marouf A. Hasian Jr.
and
Nicholas S. Paliewicz

University Press of Mississippi / Jackson

The University Press of Mississippi is the scholarly publishing agency of the Mississippi Institutions of Higher Learning: Alcorn State University, Delta State University, Jackson State University, Mississippi State University, Mississippi University for Women, Mississippi Valley State University, University of Mississippi, and University of Southern Mississippi.

www.upress.state.ms.us

The University Press of Mississippi is a member of the Association of University Presses.

Photographs courtesy of the authors unless otherwise noted

Copyright © 2021 by University Press of Mississippi
All rights reserved

First printing 2021
∞

Library of Congress Cataloging-in-Publication Data available
Hardback ISBN 978-1-4968-3174-3
Trade paperback ISBN 978-1-4968-3175-0
Epub single ISBN 978-1-4968-3178-1
Epub institutional ISBN 978-1-4968-3173-6
PDF single ISBN 978-1-4968-3176-7
PDF institutional ISBN 978-1-4968-3177-4

British Library Cataloging-in-Publication Data available

CONTENTS

ACKNOWLEDGMENTS
VII

INTRODUCTION.
Understanding the Stakes Involved in the EJI's Lynching Remembrances and Historiographies
3

CHAPTER 1.
"The Blood of Lynching Victims Is in the Soil"
Reconstruction Horrors and Post-Reconstruction Peonage
19

CHAPTER 2.
The Progressives, Ida Bell Wells-Barnett, and the Multiple Racisms That Marked Jim Crow Segregation
39

CHAPTER 3.
"By Parties Unknown"
The Successes and Failures of Anti-Lynching Campaigns before World War II
61

CHAPTER 4.
Post–World War II Civil Rights Activism, Photojournalism, and the Domestication of Civil Rights Lynching Memories
87

CHAPTER 5.
Bryan Stevenson, the Formation of the Equal Justice Initiative, and the Fight against the "Stepchild of Lynching"
113

CHAPTER 6.
EJI Critiques of Confederate Statuary, Dixie Monumentalization,
and Charlottesville Legacies
137

CHAPTER 7.
Participatory Rhetorics at the National Memorial for Peace
and Justice and Legacy Museum
160

CHAPTER 8.
The EJI, the Legacy Museum, and "Postgenocide" America
184

CONCLUSION.
The Future of "Race-Conscious" Memorialization in
Twenty-First-Century America
203

Notes
218

Bibliography
258

Index
279

ACKNOWLEDGMENTS

This work would not have been possible without the support of several individuals from University Press of Mississippi and our respective universities at the University of Utah and the University of Louisville. We would first like to thank Vijay Shah for his sustained interest in our project, not to mention all of his encouragement, as former acquisition editor at UPM. Although Vijay is no longer with this press, there is no doubt that this text would not have been possible without him and his advocacy for this project. At UPM, currently, we are also grateful for all the assistance from such folks as Emily Bandy, Shane Gong Stewart, Todd Lape, and Jordan Nettles. We also could not have asked for a better copyeditor than Norman Ware. Norman's meticulousness and care truly enhanced the quality of this monograph. We are also grateful for the arduous work of our indexer, Kristin Kirkpatrick.

At the University of Utah, the authors thank everyone in the Department of Communication and Dean of the College of Humanities, Stuart Culver. The authors are also appreciative of all of the support from everyone in the Department of Communication at the University of Louisville and the interim dean of the College of Arts and Sciences, David Owen. We are particularly grateful for the financial assistance from UofL's Communication Department during critical times in the history of this project, which made possible both a pilgrimage to Montgomery in 2018 and, crucially, this book's index. We are specifically grateful to Al Futrell (chair), Kandi Walker (vice-chair and former interim chair), Keneka Cheatham (Program Coordinator, Sr.) and office staff—Katie Cross Gibson and Lauren May—in addition to Kamla Gant (UBM) for aiding this project in these ways and others.

Personally, there are too many people to thank, but a few of those that must be named for one of the authors include Steve Paliewicz, Lisa Fleet, and Cory and Ryan. The most important kind of support for that same author has come from Banrida Wahlang and sweet baby Amora.

RACIAL TERRORISM

─────── INTRODUCTION ───────

Understanding the Stakes Involved in the EJI's Lynching Remembrances and Historiographies

FOR MORE THAN A CENTURY, AMERICAN LEGISLATORS HAD TRIED, AND FAILED, TO pass federal anti-lynching legislation. All of this began to change when, on December 19, 2018, US congressional leaders finally passed the nation's first anti-lynching act—the Justice for Victims of Lynching Act. For the first time in US history legislators, representing the American people, were willing to classify lynching as a federal hate crime.[1] Introduced by Senators Cory Booker, Kamala Harris, and Tim Scott, this particular anti-lynching bill achieves what advocates such as the National Association for the Advancement of Colored People (NAACP) were unable to do for over a century. Between 1882 and 1968, Congress weighed in on nearly two hundred anti-lynching bills, and not one of them passed. In February 2019, the US Senate unanimously backed the anti-lynching bill,[2] and it was said that the bill stood a strong chance of "making it to President Trump's desk."[3] This particular federal anti-lynching bill contains language that recounts the brutal American history of racist lynchings, and then "makes injuring or killing someone because of race, color, religion, or national origin by two or more people a federal crime punishable by up to life in prison."[4]

However, in the middle of all of the celebration of how the nation seemed to be making headway regarding consciousness raising about historical lynchings, as evidenced by the bipartisan support of the Justice for Victims of Lynching Act, President Donald Trump, in October 2019, during heating argumentation preceding the House of Representatives' vote on impeachment proceedings, tweeted that all Republicans needed to remember that they were "witnessing his 'lynching.'"[5] Kamala Harris, who had cosponsored the bill and was still in the running for the 2020 US presidential election, responded to Trump's tweet by noting that lynching was a "reprehensible stain on this nation's history," and that the president's attempt to "invoke" the "pain and trauma of lynching" to "whitewash" his own corruption was "disgraceful."⁶ Cory Booker chimed in, arguing that lynching was "an act of terror used to uphold white supremacy" and that perhaps the American president needed to "try again."⁷

As the chapters of this book will demonstrate, this has not always been the case. The uncontested passage of this antifederal legislation by the House and Senate stands out even more when scholars and readers take into account the darkness of so many archival recordings of lynching incidents that can be found in tattered newspapers and in local libraries across the nation.

For years, organizations like the NAACP, led by activists like James Weldon Johnson and Walter Francis White, had done everything to try to convince the American nation that lynchings were immoral, illegal, and dehumanizing. The members of the NAACP, as Marlene Park explained, used many different tactics—press releases, publications, rallies, pickets, conferences, marches, lawsuits, and even art displays—to get across to audiences the graphic horrors of lynching.⁸

This book focuses attention on several key social agents who played vital roles in the public and legal consciousness raising that led to the passage of the Justice for Victims of Lynching Act in the Senate. We will argue that the labor of a lawyer named Bryan Stevenson, the work of an organization called the Equal Justice Initiative (EJI),⁹ and the efforts of curators at Montgomery, Alabama's new Legacy Museum all contributed to the formation of a "rhetorical culture"¹⁰ that helped set the stage for the serious consideration of this 2018 federal anti-lynching legislation. The EJI and their supporters, along with many interdisciplinary scholars who were worried about present-day carceral practices, would become twenty-first-century activists in the struggle for what some are now calling the "New Reconstruction."¹¹

That said, what would be the truths associated with the passage of the new federal anti-lynching legislation? Would they include calls for reparations, the need for truth and reconciliation commissions, or inquiries into the lingering aftereffects of lynching legacies?

As Kirk Fuoss, writing in 2002, explained: "[O]ne of the most significant aspects regarding the subjects of lynchings is precisely the way in which the true and complete story evades the truth-telling capacity of even the most able investigator employing the most insightful and uncompromising methods."¹²

This, we contend, is exactly why many visitors, investigative journalists, academics, and others are attracted to the activism of Stevenson, the EJI, and the Legacy Museum. The very important Justice for Victims of Lynching Act was supposed to do many key things, but it is the product of many, many negotiated compromises that have had to be negotiated with some who believe that we live in a postracial era and that the bill cannot exhibit the types of confrontational texts and visualities that can be provided by private activist organizations like the EJI.

The EJI helped with the passage of the Justice for Victims of Lynching Act, but this Montgomery-based group is also concerned with spreading the word across America about the need for more radical social change, and this book has been written with the intent of acquainting readers with the nature and scope of those demanded radical changes. We are convinced that the EJI serves as an organization that provides indications of harbingers to come, that the EJI's instrumentalist usages of lynching legacies are being mobilized for the purposes of drastically curtailing America's prison-industrial complex.

The EJI—the organization that opened both the National Memorial for Peace and Justice and the Legacy Museum in Montgomery in 2018—is increasingly being recognized for extending the prior work of reformers such as Ida B. Wells-Barnett, W. E. B. Du Bois, Walter White, and others who spent a major portion of their lives highlighting the terror of lynching performances.[13] A review of recent journalistic coverage of the passage of the Justice for Victims of Lynching Act shows that in almost every article detailing the historic passage of this bill, the EJI, the National Memorial for Peace and Justice, and the Legacy Museum are given credit for breaking down some of the walls of institutional racism and collective amnesia. For Louis Masur of the *Washington Post*, the inauguration of the National Memorial for Peace and Justice was "the most recent event to build momentum" for the passage of this type of congressional legislation.[14] Masur goes on to provide a typical summary of the suasory impact of the EJI when he avers that its National Memorial "is a powerful and potent memorial, spearheaded by EJI founder, Bryan Stevenson. It includes hundreds of jars of soil, retrieved from lynching sites, and steel monuments that dangle in the air."[15] All of these would be symbolic and material artifacts from the types of places that Kenneth Foote once called "shadowed ground."[16]

We will argue in this book that the hundreds of thousands of visitors who have traveled to Montgomery to see either the National Memorial for Peace and Justice or the nearby Legacy Museum—more than six hundred thousand by December 2019[17]—would be provided with pedagogical lessons from the EJI that characterized American lynching histories as times of "racial terror."

Although some journalists create the impression that the EJI introduced the term "terror" as a novel way of conceptualizing lynching pasts, since at least the end of the Civil War, African Americans have written about the special horrors associated with the act of lynching and the terrorists acts of the Ku Klux Klan and other organizations that tried to subjugate and terrify African American communities. Social activists like Ida B. Wells-Barnett also used the term "terror" (at times even "holocaust") to describe lynchings more than a century ago, and many others since that time have invited audiences to dwell on the trauma and terror of lynching. For example, Stewart Tolnay and E. M. Beck, in empirical research published in 2018, mention "racialized terrorism" and lynchings in the American South; they then try to provide academics with an "accurate record" of lynchings and attempted lynchings.[18] Tolnay and Beck don't need to reference the work of Bryan Stevenson or the EJI in an article that tells the conventional tale of how, after "peaking in the 1890s," the "annual number of Southern lynchings began a protracted decline," to the point where by the "early 1930s, lynching had become a relatively rare event."[19]

Yet few members of the public may be reading the academic work of writers like Tolnay and Beck, and it is fair to say that Stevenson, the EJI, and the Legacy Museum, within a few short years, may be given elite and public credit for helping popularize the phrase "racial terror" or "racial terrorism."

Not everyone may be in a hurry to confront these haunting terrorist pasts. When visitors take tours to places like the National Museum of African American History and Culture (NMAAHC), a Smithsonian Institution museum located on the National Mall in Washington, DC, they can learn about some lynching horrors, but the thousands of other artifacts that are displayed on the museum's many levels also include material on music, crowns of African Yoruba royalty, Chuck Berry's 1973 Cadillac Eldorado, materials from Whitney Houston, and many other items.[20] Some exhibits at the NMAAHC recall times of sadness during the African diasporas, but many of the affective states that visitors feel involve moments of celebration and pride in the ways that African Americans over the centuries have contributed to the US body politic.

We contend that the EJI's Montgomery sites of memory are very different. These are spaces and places for quiet contemplation and empathy but also for mobilized, collective activism. By many accounts, the National Memorial for Peace and Justice (sometimes referred to as the Lynching Memorial) and Legacy Museum are dark tourist sites.[21] Jane McFadden, for example, writing at the end of 2019, had this to say after her own trip to Montgomery:

> The EJI's memorial and museum take as their model other crucial sites of remembrance—the Holocaust, apartheid, genocide—to allow for "truth telling." Whether in the end they might cut through our national blindness is another question; the danger here, as for all sites of

remembrance, is that some visitors will come to pay homage and then return elsewhere unburdened by the reality of the ongoing injustice that others cannot leave behind.[22]

Those who visit these spaces and places can testify that often they are emotional visits, and in order to help individual visitors process the impact of the sites, the EJI hosts daily presentations and group meetings that help faith groups, corporate boards, students, and others grapple with what they have seen.[23]

Some historical lynching spectacles are so horrific and so symbolic that the photographs taken of them don't require the use of abstract, realistic, or surrealistic art to help represent their depravity, which defies all human understanding. In the visual registers of those who study the legacies of Jim Crow abuses, some of the most horrific reminders of the spectacle of Southern vigilante justice can be found in the photo archives of the lynching of Henry Smith.[24] Smith was ritually murdered in front of thousands of onlookers in Lamar County, Texas, in February 1893. Suspected of killing Myrtle Vance, a young white girl, seventeen-year-old Smith fled to Arkansas, but he was captured and forcibly returned to his hometown.[25] An eyewitness later recalled that, arriving at noon, the train that brought Smith back "was met by a surging mass of humanity 10,000 strong."[26]

Over the years, as interest was revived in studying lynching histories and public memories, Henry Smith's lynching was condensed into a symbol, an icon, a metonym for all types of American performative, public spectacles that would embarrass those who wanted to remember to forget. For some, the lynching was treated as a matter involving populist, retributive justice, where vendors sold food to children and photographers printed postcards so that those who were there that day would have some mementos. Known as America's first mass "public spectacle lynching," the murder of Henry Smith polarized many communities in Texas and across the country (fig. 1). Stories like Smith's, or the 1919 burning of Will Brown by a white crowd in September 1919 in Omaha, Nebraska, are used today to remind audiences of the indifference that contributed to the victimization of countless African Americans.[27]

For many years, at the place where Henry Smith lost his life lay an empty field, and some contend that the transgenerational absence of informational markers in places like this is telling. Yet the photographs that were taken of Henry Smith's hanging can serve as powerful reminders of a past that perhaps should be forgotten. Marita Sturken reminds us that some photographs serve as technologies of memory, mechanisms through which we can

Figure 1: The lynching of Henry Smith. The original caption noted "the avengers of Little Myrtle Vance, and the villain brought to justice—Parade around public square." Prints and Photographs Division, Library of Congress, LC-USZ62-115489.

construct the past and situate it in the present. Such images have the capacity to create, interfere with, and trouble the memories we hold as individuals and as a nation. They can lend shape to historical and personal stories, often providing material "evidence" on which claims are based.[28]

Remembering Henry Smith—and those masses who lynched him—reminds us that there are dark American lynching pasts that are occasionally rendered visible through the imagined photographic realism of images left in the lynching archives.

Yet what does this absence of markers at Smith's lynching site or of other commemorative devices truly communicate? Does it symbolize the attempt on the part of a local community in Texas to bury memories of Henry Smith, along with his body? The unwillingness of many Americans to admit the magnitude and the significance of extrajudicial acts that took, according to the EJI, the lives of more than 4,400 human beings?[29]

These are weighty questions, and more than a few realize the difficulties of finding the right communicative strategies to convey the horrors of American lynchings. Ed Pilkington of the British newspaper the *Guardian* used some of the language of truth and reconciliation advocates when he called for "atonement" for what Americans did to Henry Smith and many other people of color.[30] The corporate giant Google and the Brooklyn Museum in 2017[31] deployed traditional arts and new visual technologies to help broader audiences understand the horrors, and the trials and tribulations, of those who either helplessly watched lynchings, armed themselves, or became a part of the "Great Migration" north.

In this book, we are interested in studying how Bryan Stevenson, the EJI, the Legacy Museum, and the National Memorial for Peace and Justice are mobilizing stories about the lynching of Henry Smith and other victims to help raise consciousness about these legacies.[32]

Unlike other researchers who view the April 2018 opening of the Lynching Memorial as just another extension of neoliberal civil rights memorialization, we argue that these spaces are used by the EJI to rhetorically craft *more confrontational "race-conscious" messages*. While the vast majority of commentators in the years leading up to the memorial's opening have recognized how the EJI and the Legacy Museum have encouraged some eight hundred US counties to "master their past" (what the Germans call *Vergangenheitsbewältigung*) and admit that some of their county's residents were once involved with lynchings, what they have often missed are some of the more radical features of much of this monumentalization. As McFadden has recently observed, Bryan Stevenson, the EJI, and the Legacy Museum are all involved in a "broader project" intended to combat "racial bias in America's society and systems," and their attempts to render visible all sorts of evolutionary "reigns of terror" have included efforts to correct the "historical record" so that it would include data on the "12 million kidnapped bodies that were forcibly transported to the new world over the centuries."[33]

Attempting to revise America's lynching historiographies and public memories is no easy task. "Collective amnesia," argued Arvind Dilawar in 2019, "has long been the United States' default to its history of racial violence, but as questions of race continue to be at the forefront of national politics, more and more projects are emerging to properly memorialize that bloody past."[34]

EJI members like Bryan Stevenson want to "liberate" Americans so that general public acceptance of historical lynching legacies becomes a precursor to more probing and efficacious types of twenty-first-century activism.[35] As far as Stevenson is concerned, racialized lynchings did not "end" with the decline in the recording of public lynchings after World War II.

In the next subsection, we discuss some of the previous work that appears in communication literature on lynching pasts before we briefly outline our own critical, perspectival approaches to these race-conscious issues.

Previous Studies of Lynching in Communication Studies

Since at least the 1970s, studies of lynchings have garnered the attention of rhetoricians and other communication scholars. Some scholars, heavily influenced by the subfield of public address studies, have focused on either the discourse produced by single rhetoricians like Ida B. Wells-Barnett, broader discourses about the definitional scope of lynching, or personal debates that took place between several arguers in public spheres or legal fields.

For instance, in several publications, Jacqueline Jones Royster has examined the rhetorical actions of Wells-Barnett in her relentless efforts to confront the horrors of lynching before national and international audiences. In studying Wells-Barnett's eloquence, expertise, and leadership styles, Royster has contributed not just to the reclamation of women in the rhetorical tradition but to the struggles of women of color for social justice.[36] In doing so, Royster's work creates openings for drawing parallels between Wells-Barnett's rhetoric and contemporary rhetorics of social protest against lingering and emergent forms of injustice. As she notes in the preface of her edited volume of Wells-Barnett's work, *Southern Horrors and Other Writings: The Anti-Lynching Campaign of Ida B. Wells, 1892–1900*, this work continues to serve as an "excellent springboard from which to bring visibility to the dynamic interconnections among social justice movements—from abolition to the modern civil rights and human rights movements to the Black Lives Matter and Black Girls Matter campaigns." "When we connect these dots," Royster adds, "we highlight the importance of supporting exactly what Wells was advocating for: fairness and equity under the rule of law and keeping public sentiment attuned to the urgency of engendering peace and social justice for all."[37]

One of the most recent works on the living legacy of lynching, within the rhetorical canon, is Ersula Ore's powerful book *Lynching: Violence, Rhetoric, and American Identity*. Ore makes the compelling argument that the rhetorical significance of lynching has, sadly, always been attached to performances of American civic identity within the public imaginary of what it means to be constituted as part of "the people." At times the formation of American civic identity has unfortunately justified, if not necessitated, "state-sanctioned antiblack violence" as a form of epideictic, or demonstrative, rhetoric.[38] Understanding lynching as a performative act of American citizenship that involves violence against black bodies for the security of the "nation" allows Ore to draw important parallels to contemporary "lynchings" in cases involving undue police force—such as George Zimmerman's shooting of unarmed Trayvon Martin—and rhetorical performances such as the burning of effigies during the Barack Obama presidency. In this way, Ore presents contemporary audiences with the apt argument that lynching has always been about the "demarcati[on] of space for a certain kind of body."[39] Consistent with findings from others such as Ashraf Rushdy, who has traced the roots of lynching in America's dominant institutions since the seventeenth-century House of Burgesses,[40] lynching remains rhetorically embedded within the very ideas of American nationhood and civic identity. "The truly meaningful place to locate what is distinctively American about lynching," says Rushdy, "is in the political traditions Americans have formulated and the political myths they have held."[41]

Related approaches to lynching have focused on the activities of small groups of activists, on the NAACP, and on the efforts of those involved with lynching reenactments.[42] Kim Powell's study of the Association of Southern Women for the Prevention of Lynching (ASWPL) (1930–1942) helped communication scholars understand some of the rhetorical strategies that were used by coalitions of Southern women who theoretically helped bring "an end" to lynching in the South.[43] Many of these essays follow the conventional civil rights wisdom that the efforts of organizations like the NAACP, the Communists who helped the Scottsboro Boys, or the ASWPL changed minds and helped replace lynchings with lawful protections for African American communities. In 2009, Martha Solomon Watson used a more argumentative approach in studying how Mary Church Terrell battled Thomas Nelson Page over the need for anti-lynching legislation.[44]

Scholars such as Rushdy have also traced the discourses that led to what is generally for our purposes referred to as the "great forgetting" of lynching after important debates in the 1930s and 1940s within and among anti-lynching organizations. While some members of the NAACP were arguing for more expansive definitions of lynching to more fully account for the range of racial injustices, groups like the ASWPL may have contributed to the idea that lynching had ended by arguing for a more narrow conception of lynching restricted to particular kinds of killings.[45] Consequently, the "end-of-lynching" discourses that emerged from that time have stifled thinking about the effect of lynching on American cultural identities through national mythologies by seeing it as an aberration or a short episode rather than a systemic historical problem.[46]

Implicitly or explicitly, many of these studies adopted some of the fragments that would become part of "colorblind" ways of viewing neoliberal, progressive, civil rights activism.

Some communication scholars have chosen to focus on the use of visual argumentation or visual rhetoric as they provide academics and other audiences with more postmodern, poststructural, or postcolonial ways of viewing lynching afterlives and lynching legacies.[47] A fine example of this genre appears in studies investigating the nexus that exists between lynching histories, ethnic violence, and the role that some pictorials of victims have played in mobilizing civil rights activism. For example, Christine Harold and Kevin DeLuca published a 2005 essay in a special issue of *Rhetoric and Public Affairs* that was devoted to investigating the lingering persuasive power of representations of Emmett Till, Rosa Parks, and Martin Luther King Jr.[48]

In their own study of the Emmett Till case, Davis Houck and Matthew Grindy examined how the Mississippi press reacted to the 1955 murder of the fourteen-year old boy.[49] Surveying the coverage that appeared in various newspaper articles, letters to the editor, editorials, photographs, and other materials, Houck and Grindy argued that coverage of the attack "altered the discursive landscape."[50] The shapes of constantly evolving narratives in Mississippi were influenced both by the indifference that was shown by coverage of earlier black murders as well as by the rhetorical crafting of responses to what was viewed as outside interventionism and agitation by organizations like the NAACP.

Other types of rhetorical criticism that have studied lynching pasts have linked historical events to contemporary issues and public memories. While Susan Owen and Peter Ehrenhaus concentrated on investigations of the role that provincialism, religion, and spectacle played in lynching memories,[51] Jessy Ohl and Jennifer Potter critiqued the "post-racism" associated with medicated coverage of the famed *Without Sanctuary* photography exhibits.[52]

By 2011, Owen and Ehrenhaus, in an insightful review essay in the *Quarterly Journal of Speech*, could review studies of lynching as public spectacles that became entangled with contemporary acts of resistance. In their review of the work of Amy Kirschke,[53] Jonathan Markovitz,[54] and Amy Louise Wood,[55] they argued that although the interdisciplinary study of lynching has a "lengthy history of sustained investigation," contributions from rhetorical communities and critical studies communities were "modest" during many of these years.[56]

This has changed since around 2005 as interest has grown in studying not only lynching efforts but all types of restorative justice efforts. Rhoda Howard-Hassmann and Anthony Lombardo, writing in 2007, noted that "Africans interested in reparations from the West frequently ask why the Jewish movement for reparations for the Holocaust was successful, whereas Africans have been unable to obtain reparations for the slave trade, colonialism, and post-colonial relations with the West."[57] Jacqueline Bacon, writing in the *Quarterly Journal of Speech* in 2003, made a similar argument, commenting on the cultural memories and power politics that stood in the path of African Americans who sought reparations. She argued that polls showed that Americans were sharply divided on the question of reparations compensating African Americans for unpaid slave labor and suffering, with a majority of African Americans in favor and a large majority of whites opposed to payment of this type of restitution.[58]

Were the studies by Howard-Hassmann and Lombardo, and Bacon, providing us with clues as to why so many observers seem to want to avoid taking up some of the most radical challenges about racial terrorism that were advanced by Stevenson, the EJI, and the Legacy Museum?

We would argue that all of this renascent, communication interest in lynching and slavery studies is part of that same reservoir of arguments, or rhetorical cultures, that have influenced both the rise of the critical race theory movement and the growth of the EJI.

What we now need is a synthetic book that uses critical perspectival approaches to bring together some of these arguments about pasts, presents, and potential futures in one monograph, and the openings of the Lynching Memorial and the Legacy Museum provide that very opportunity.

The Heuristic Value of Critical Genealogical Studies of Lynching Pasts and Mass Incarceration Presents

Building on the work of poststructural writers, postmodernists, and critical genealogical scholars like Michel Foucault and Ann Stoler,[59] each chapter of this book contains examples of critical genealogical studies of some of the epistemes or Foucauldian "elements" that have provided the antecedent rhetorical fragments, arguments, and narratives that have gone into the production of what we will be calling "racial terror" *dispositifs*. A *dispositif* is a large assemblage, an organizational apparatus, or a major constellation of meaning that is made up of smaller rhetorical units that together render visible grids of intelligibility.[60] The jars of soil from lynching sites, the corten steel monuments that hang down from the rafters of the National Memorial for Peace and Justice, the web reports that are prepared by the EJI, the markers about discovered lynchings placed on highways, and so on, are all elements that go into the coproduction of the EJI's particular "racial terror" *dispositif*.

Often these epistemes or elements are reassembled in the historiographies or counterhistories or countermemories or other rhetorical figurations that are deposited in lynching archives, and those archives are some of the key rhetorical spaces and places that are critiqued by critical genealogical writers like Friedrich Nietzsche, Michel Foucault, and Ann Stoler.[61]

Within our own field of communication, Raymie McKerrow[62] and others have explained how "critical" perspective work differs from traditional social science research and conventional public address studies, and our work has affinities with humanistic studies that investigate the power/knowledge/discourse dimensions of debates over lynching legacies or mass incarceration histories. Unlike some other Foucauldians who may simply want to suspend judgment and merely describe the rhetorical efforts of the rhetorical work of the EJI, we are also interested in critiquing the prescriptive EJI efforts as well as the normative features of *audience receptions* of the work of Stevenson, the EJI, and the Legacy Museum.

That is why our book involves studies of the poststructural dynamics of the textual and visual arguments that are presented not only by the EJI but by audiences who react or don't react to their work. We do this by adopting a multimodal approach that combines critical genealogical studies of texts with participatory critical rhetoric (PCR) ways of recording experiential observations we made while visiting Montgomery spaces and places.[63] This involves analyses of several layers of epistemic knowledge formations, different conventional lynching histories, dissident histories, and competitive and multidirectional memories. It is the uses and abuses of lynching pasts, and the societal negotiations that take place during monumental disputation and memorialization argumentation, that interest us.

We recognize that our theoretical and perspective choices have political implications, and we will not be shy about critiquing even those narratives and other ideological formations that represent our own ways of viewing American political, social, economic, or legal affairs. If critical genealogists care about more than mere description, and if they go back to that story about the lynching of Henry Smith that we referenced in the introductory part of this chapter, they should not be satisfied with simply trying to piece together "what happened" at this 1893 event in Paris, Texas, in a positivistic historical sense. Critical genealogists who are willing to study both the descriptive and the prescriptive features of the representations of the Henry Smith lynching should be self-reflective as they review the *multiple* histories and the myriad countermemories that would be coproduced by many generations of social agents who were traumatized by what happened to Smith and other lynching victims.

In many ways, our critical genealogical approach has been influenced by the work of Walter Benjamin, who critiqued both historicisms and aesthetic reproductions of artistic works. In *Illuminations,* Benjamin noted in his justly famous "Theses on the Philosophy of History" that to articulate pasts historically involves seizing "hold of a memory as it flashes up at a moment of danger."[64] This reminds us that our archives are always filled with contingent, politicized, incommensurate, indeterminate, and partial reflections of a past that we only dimly see through a selective presentist lens.

Instead of ending our inquiry by documenting how many Americans gathered to watch Smith's lynching, and simply noting that this was a mass public spectacle, we want to use critical genealogical approaches to see how various other generations—since 1893—have left traces of their rhetorical reactions to that spectacle that reflected their own needs. For example, critical genealogists might study whether anything was done about vigilante justice after Texas journalists wrote newspaper articles that justified the hanging of Smith in 1893. Were any of the ten thousand spectators who witnessed Smith's lynching ever put on trial? Did the townspeople of Paris leave us their own histories or memories of what happened on the day of Smith's lynching? What did the national press, or decision-makers in Washington, do or not do when they read about Smith's lynching?

More detailed series of critical genealogical stories or vignettes could be provided by researchers, who might explain why pictorial copies of Smith's lynching ended up on Bryan Stevenson's wall, or how that lynching of Henry Smith was, or was not, contextualized in Montgomery's Legacy Museum. Critical scholars might provide further insights after reviewing how twenty-first-century digital copies of that same image were being interpreted and appropriated by average American bloggers as they posted blog pages on the horrors of racial terrorism.

These various generational or transgenerational types of an "anatomy" of a photograph[65] can be used by critical genealogists to complement the textual critiques and experiential insights that are provided by travelers to these sites, tourists who can use their visits to complement their critical rhetorical analyses of mediated journalistic coverage of these topics.

In order to evidence this book, one of the authors has taken a pilgrimage to these Montgomery sites of memory, and together the authors have collected thousands of newspaper accounts, popular press discussions, journalistic recollections, legal texts, photographs, and other artifacts on lynchings that circulated between the Reconstruction years (1866–1877) and the 2018 opening of the National Memorial for Peace and Justice. These types of artifacts contain the ideographs, the character types, the narratives, and the other archival elements that provide the units of analysis that help critical genealogists in their studies of EJI *dispositifs*.

The chapters of our book are organized to allow readers to follow us as we track, in purposive ways, some of lynching historiographies, the "competitive" and "multidirectional memories" that were coproduced by many of the social agents whose names are mentioned by Bryan Stevenson, the EJI, and the Legacy Museum.[66] In some cases, anonymous contributors, or those whose names are forgotten, left behind all sorts of private and public lynching archives.

At this point in our introduction, we also must note that our perspectival approach often blurs the mythic lines that positivists or formalists argue separate "primary" archival sources from "secondary" sources. In other words, we will not attempt to sift through the secondary "rhetoric" found in newspapers, journal articles, or popular press accounts so that we can get at some bedrock, apolitical historical knowledge that supposedly comes from arhetorical "primary" research on lynchings. We are convinced that the adoption of more "critical" ways of evaluating archival texts and contexts helps us see the constitutive nature *of all works left in lynching archives.*

While we do care what scholars have to say about lynching pasts or mass incarceration presents, we will not always privilege the arguments that come from the ranks of what Jacques Derrida called the "archons" who police convention archives.[67] Thus, readers will see how we also value the opinions of investigative journalists, the views of visitors to the Legacy Museum, and the perspectives of students who collect soil for jars that will be sent to Montgomery.

In a way, following Nietzsche, we are leaving readers with what he called some "untimely meditations."[68] Instead of taking at face value the claims that are advanced by Bryan Stevenson or the EJI or the Legacy Museum and viewing their efforts as contributing in apolitical ways to filling the "gap" of traditional historiography or archival work, we focus on the discourse/knowledge/power features of their constitutive efforts. For example, we are interested in seeing how the EJI uses lynching histories in strategic ways as they try to help the cause of millions of prisoners when they write and talk about lynching legacies or the lingering impact of the massive "Great Migration." We therefore adopt a more argumentative, "critical" approach to these controversies that treats these EJI commentaries *as contestable claims* that have everything to do with various audiences' perceptions, value systems, and constructed rhetorical situations. These make up some of the key epistemic fragments that must be studied by those who track any "critical genealogy of memory discourses."[69]

Are mainstream American communities suffering from "postracial" or "postgenocide" anxieties? Do visits to Montgomery's Lynching Memorial or

Legacy Museum provide performative opportunities to master contextual "racial terror" pasts in ways that remove some of the myopia that comes from averting our gaze from the more haunting parts of our racialized histories? Can Montgomery's lynching memorialization spaces and places—in the very heart of Dixie—provide artifacts that help with needed (re)territorialization of select multidirectional memories?

Or are EJI advocates going to run into some of the same institutional barriers or conceptual blockages that stood in the path of Ida B. Wells-Barnett's generation or frustrated the 1920s–1930s advocates of federal anti-lynching statutes? Do some go too far when they see connections between Confederate statuary and defenses of today's mass incarceration practices, or are they seeing important connections that are oblivious to others?

Conclusion: Acknowledging Dark Pasts as a Precursor to Mercy and Restorative Justice

Melissa Steyn has used the theoretical concept of the "ignorance contract" to explain what happens when governments and societies reach a "tacit agreement to entertain ignorance" as a way of dealing with the challenges that are posed by communities who are coping with complex pasts associated with postconflict violence that were "structured in racial hierarchy."[70] The ignorance contracts that Steyn studied that circulated in postapartheid South Africa bear a marked resemblance to American denials of racial terrorism that Bryan Stevenson and the EJI are trying to critique.

The chapters of this book will demonstrate why many African Americans and other US citizens seem unwilling to confront difficult and dark cultural heritages that may have something to do with today's carceral systems. These chapters will also outline some of the reasons why so many in places like Montgomery, Alabama, may have trouble coping with "epistemologies of ignorance."[71]

As we write this introductory section of our book, countless US citizens—including President Donald Trump—are engaged in heated debates about the tearing down, or the putting up, of countless Confederate road markers, statues, and memorials for those who died fighting for the "Lost Cause."[72] Others are worried about police brutality and how to make sense of what has happened in places like Chicago or Los Angeles or Manhattan. All of this is taking place while the nation's millennials use their social media skills to intervene in conversations about #Blacklivesmatter and #Bluelivesmatter.

At this point, we are led to wonder if others, especially those in the South, are willing to at least listen to those EJI members who contend that public lynchings did not end after World War II but evolved and went "indoors," that African Americans face unreliable verdicts, and that many today face the "same kind of death sentencing and the same kind of abuse of color in the courtroom that existed outside the courtroom during the lynching era."[73]

It would be a mistake to believe that EJI members and supporters are unaware of the emotional toil that might come from opening some old, traumatic American wounds. In 2014, Bryan Stevenson wrote that the "closer we get to mass incarceration and extreme levels of punishment," the more African Americans and others need to find ways of providing "mercy," justice, and "some measure of unmerited grace."[74] Elizabeth Alexander, a poet, hoped that the Lynching Memorial might "redeem America," but a less sanguine Sammy Feldblum opined in 2018 that, amid the "forest of hanging totems," the "task can feel impossible."[75]

The strategic ambiguity swirling around the ideograph "racial terrorism," and the graphic and authentic displays of mass attendance at lynchings like Smith's, seem to have facilitated several years of private fund-raising for the Legacy Museum and the National Memorial for Peace and Justice, but in many ways these efforts have raised as many questions as they have answered. Are these unique spaces, built in the "heart of Dixie," meant to provide visitors with a unique countermemorial that confronts both white silence and African American desire to forget about dark pasts, while future American generations credit the EJI with reopening conversations about African American reparations and "postgenocide" America?

These are the types of critical genealogical questions that we hope future readers and researchers will find to be provocative, and they have guided us throughout the rest of this book.

CHAPTER 1

"The Blood of Lynching Victims Is in the Soil"
Reconstruction Horrors and Post-Reconstruction Peonage

PREVIOUS GENERATIONS HAVE DEBATED WHETHER THE RECONSTRUCTION PERIOD should be remembered as a "dark and bloody" era that involved the foisting of Radical Republican ideals onto a prostrate and innocent South,[1] or whether this interventionism by Union troops was an enlightened experiment that aided the cause of those who wished to provide rights to former slaves. While the Dunning School of historiography produced generations of historians who complained about Northern "aggression" and unnecessary interference in Southern affairs, "revisionists" like Eric Foner rebutted these assumptions. In 1982, Foner averred that imperfect Reconstruction efforts, and the legacy of those efforts, deserved to "survive as an aspiration to those Americans, black and white alike, who insist that the nation live up to the professed ideals of its political culture."[2]

How we remember those post–Civil War efforts is not just a matter of knowledge retrieval. As Ron Eyerman has noted, there was a "distinctive gap" between the "collective memory of a reconstructed minority group and the equally reconstructed dominant group" who managed to control "the resources and had the power to fashion public memory."[3]

The archival inheritance of these conflicting historiographies ensured that by 2018 historian Michael Pfeifer, a specialist in lynching studies, could argue that "Reconstruction remains contested in local memory, and efforts to remember the achievements of Reconstruction are cancelled out by the seeming failure of the period to achieve lasting change."[4]

Critical genealogical readings of Reconstruction military reports, photographs, newspaper accounts, journal articles, and other rhetorical artifacts document some of the violence of this period. In 1868, for example, when African Americans tried to vote, or when they tried to openly show their support for Radical Republican allies who traveled south to places like Opelousas, Louisiana, they were met by hundreds of local whites who argued that a black rebellion was underway. When a small group of armed African Americans assembled to try to free one Republican reporter, they were accosted by an armed group of white men, who took 29 blacks to the local prison, where "27 of them were summarily executed."[5]

The lynching archives contain few systematic tallies of these unlawful acts of violence before the 1890s records of Gilded Age violence and Progressive Era lynchings (see chapter 2), but there is plenty of historical evidence that many Southern whites of various classes were convinced that Unionist post–Civil War support for former slaves was a costly venture, a zero-sum game whereby helping impoverished and disenfranchised blacks naturally meant taking power away from poor and middle-class whites. No doubt part of the animus that was directed at the Unionists by former Confederates and impoverished Southerners had to do with the fact that the Reconstruction Acts of 1867 "also granted voting rights to African American men while disenfranchising former Confederates, drastically altering the political landscape of the South and ushering in" what some EJI workers would call a "period of progress."[6]

As various nineteenth-century American communities debated about Northern "aggression" during the Reconstruction years, the rise of the Ku Klux Klan,[7] and the recognition of African American civil, social, and political rights, they came up with inventive ways of redefining the post–Civil War Thirteenth, Fourteenth, and Fifteenth Amendments so that most of those who benefited from these legislative reforms were whites and not people of color. These communities considered the meanings of these "rights" in labor, voting, land, and other contexts, producing competing historical fragments, epistemes, and racialized discourse/knowledge formations that could be configured in diverse ideological ways.

Twenty-first-century EJI workers have been able to chronicle some of the violent resistance to the Reconstruction, quoting materials from the archival volumes that were collected by congressional workers in the early 1870s who were trying to destroy the power of the Ku Klux Klan.[8] Other archival materials on post-Reconstruction violence appeared in the form of oral history reports on victims of lynchings that were collected from witnesses who were interviewed by New Deal employees during the Great Depression.

As we shall see elsewhere in this book, the EJI has done an admirable job of pointing out the petty, arbitrary, capricious, or horrific justifications that white supremacists contrived to legitimate so many lynchings or near-lynchings in the Reconstruction and post-Reconstruction years. The EJI's study of lynching pasts shows how people of color could be lynched for "minor violations of the racial caste system," like "failing to step off a sidewalk to make way for a white person."⁹ As Bryan Stevenson told young readers of *Teen Vogue*:

> The 13th Amendment ends involuntary servitude and forced labor but it doesn't say anything about the narratives of racial difference or white supremacy.... People would sometimes come to these lynchings, bring their children, bring their snacks, sip lemonade, eat deviled eggs, and create a carnival atmosphere while black men and women were being tortured and burned alive sometimes literally on the courthouse lawn.¹⁰

Stevenson's strategic historical (re)framing of these affairs jumps quickly from the passage of the civil rights amendments to summaries of some public lynchings that took place during the 1880s and 1890s, and all of this is then used to convey the magnitude and evolutionary nature of racial terrorism. Elsewhere, Stevenson explains that the "blood of lynching victims is in the soil."¹¹

A decoding of the EJI's arguments about lynching pasts and contemporary mass incarceration shows that Bryan Stevenson and his supporters, in their strategic narrations of Reconstruction and post-Reconstruction events, often use a blend of secular and sacred arguments that resonate with those who are skeptical about the exaggerated claims of neoliberal civil rights success stories. This strand of skeptical argumentation was passed down to later generations by those who faced daily abuse or even death during the nineteenth century when they tried to buy land, or vote, or marry someone of a different race.

Our critical analyses of the rhetorical fragments that circulated during the Reconstruction and post-Reconstruction years has convinced us that many social agents—including Unionists, members of the KKK, Southern Democrats, and others—played key roles in the shaping the contours of "Lost Cause" narratives. It was the coproduction of this thick *dispositif* that created so many difficulties for generations of African Americans before the rise of the EJI.¹²

The disempowered who had to face a variety of oppressive, post–Civil War social formations may have had their own "weapons of the weak,"¹³ and they may have produced what Ann Stoler calls "dissensus" archives,¹⁴ but those who want to read "against the grain" must simultaneously pay attention to the hegemonic materials that must be read "along the grain." If we are going to interrogate EJI claims about nineteenth-century "racial terror," then we need to keep an eye on the hegemonic tactics that were used by those who produced their own Reconstruction and post-Reconstruction narratives and other figurations.¹⁵

We begin our critique of some of the genealogical origins of the EJI's racial terrorism claims about Reconstruction legacies by explaining how talk of "Judge Lynch" entered American rhetorical framings of some post–Civil War violence.

Remembrances of "Judge Lynch," the Civil War, and Contested Histories of the Reconstruction Years

Many case studies and books that have been written on lynching contend that the word "lynching" comes from remembrances of the work of Charles Lynch, a Virginia planter and veteran of the American Revolutionary War. When Lynch was put in charge of an ad hoc court that was used to try and punish "loyalist" supporters through hangings, this was characterized as "lynch law." Since that time, many different communities in all parts of the United States before the 1950s disagreed about whether historical lynchings were legal or illegal forms of vigilante justice.¹⁶

Here we must note that we agree with Robyn Wiegman's assessment that in "the circuit of relationships that governs lynching in the United States, the law as legal discourse and disciplinary practice subtends the symbolic area."¹⁷ We will show that the very drawing of a mythic line between "legal" and "illegal" lynchings was a rhetorical act that had portentous consequences.

For many of those who lived through the halcyon Civil War years, one's reaction to talk of freedom for former slaves or to the violence associated with lynching had everything to do with how one defined the ideograph "redemption." While Northerners viewed their reconstruction efforts as redemptive, even spiritual acts that justified the sacrifices of the white and black soldiers who gave their lives during the bloody Civil War, many Southerners had different ideas with respect to the word "redemption." For them, redeemers were those who proudly wished to revive memories of romanticized antebellum ways of life. "Redemption," Carole Emberton opined, "should not be understood as a perversion of *true* Christian or democratic values" but as a word that signified how white Southerners were "ambivalent" about the violence that lingered after the carnage of the Civil War.¹⁸

Much of that ambivalence had to do with the experiences, and the memories, of those who had to witness the Union's occupation of the South, which began during the latter stages of the Civil War. The Radical Republicans, who worried about both the revenge that might be exacted by former slaves as well as the reactions of returning Confederate soldiers who had lost their possessions and their status, sent in Union troops to help redeem the South through Reconstruction efforts.

As we studied the discursive and pictorial representations of these lynching and Reconstruction archives, we were shocked to find the magnitude and scope of the violence that was witnessed during the Reconstruction years. Many black soldiers who had fought during the Civil War, who perhaps thought that they would be congratulated and thanked for their sacrifices, were not granted immediate citizenship for their efforts. Often, riots broke out in Southern districts that were occupied by victorious Northern troops. For example, Northern troops had been occupying areas in and around Memphis since 1862, and for years the city was a "magnet for runaway slaves."[19] It would also become the site of both physical and ideological warfare as various strategic, often temporary, alliances were formed between whites of different classes, who argued among themselves that they knew best how to cope with the rising power of former slaves.

Those of us today who read the short lines that appear in the Thirteenth, Fourteenth, and Fifteenth Amendments may have a difficult time understanding how Southerners often associated those few words with the alleged horrors that they believed victimized the losers of the Civil War. Critical rhetorical analysis of some of the rhetorical fragments that circulated after 1866 shows that some former Confederate soldiers and civilians contemplated the possibility that the Radical Republicans who pushed through post–Civil War amendments seemed intent on fueling what they regarded as a "race war" in the South. What was called the "hard war" (the Civil War) was supposedly followed by a period when foreign Carpetbaggers and local Scalawags helped Northern courts impose their will on recalcitrant Southerners.

While the Northerners who supported the Radical Republicans were convinced that the South had to accept their Reconstruction policies for free persons of color—especially black male citizens—many "unreconstructed" Southerners responded by attacking the very notion of "civil," "political," or "social" equality between the "races." The existence of these competitive worldviews made it difficult for organizations like the Freedmen's Bureau to help the Department of War carry out the mission of providing for the needs of emancipated blacks.

Lynchings were microaggressive acts that could be undertaken by returning Confederate soldiers and others who were convinced that the Radical Republicans were trying to punish the South for secessionism.

All sorts of political rationales could be found for Southern intransigence in the wake of occupation, but there were also other factors that impacted how one viewed these retaliatory measures. "During the Reconstruction era," noted Martha Hodes, "black male sexuality first became a major theme in white Southern politics, thereby commencing an era of terrorism and lynching."[20] To Ersula Ore, the sexuality of black men, particularly in relation to white women, was how lynching emerged as a constitutive form of "civic belonging" for whites that "reaffirmed communal spirit in the face of major social change."[21] Lynching was the "performative corollary" of white discourses of sexuality that dehumanized black men.[22]

It would be a mistake to argue that the Radical Republicans or other Unionists were egalitarians who viewed blacks as their equals. As many critical scholars have noted, racism appears in many shades, and former slaves were confronted by many different ideological figurations that rationalized their supposed inferiority. While Northerners treated images of beaten blacks, raped women, and "terrorized bodies" as "objects of pity,"[23] Southerners focused on their own post–Civil War problems and viewed the Unionists as interlopers.

Union generals like Clinton Fisk and Oliver Howard were put in charge of some of the Reconstruction districts, and they, along with many Northern preachers who supported the Radical Republicans in Congress, circulated texts about former slaves that conveyed a mixture of self-righteousness, genuine care for fellow human beings, and fear of those who might seek revenge in the absence of a Union military presence. As Emberton explained, popular publications like *Harper's Magazine* tried to elicit Northern sympathy for blacks living in the South, but in doing so they often cultivated the "political commodification of black bodies in pain."[24] These spectral, often voyeuristic visualities perhaps unintentionally contributed to the dehumanization of African American victims of systematic violence.

Many different societies and organizations were formed by white supremacists in the South after the Civil War, but it was the Ku Klux Klan that occupied the attention of the Radical Republicans. Later, in the years preceding World War I, national discussion of lynching and other forms of violence would be "voluminous," but some claimed that during Reconstruction, "southern whites had often tried to ignore" or "simply refused to acknowledge" the "existence of the Ku Klux Klan and other terrorist organizations."[25]

Supporters of the Radical Republicans tried to counter this Southern indifference. They constantly quarreled with the Southern Democrats in Congress, and they tried to render visible the attempts of the KKK to intimidate, or kill, former slaves. Political adversaries in Congress and disputants in broader American rhetorical cultures quarreled about whether the activities of the KKK actually represented the desires of the average Southerner after the Civil War.

Many of those in the North seemed to be convinced that white Southerners were unwilling to carry out the redeeming or reconstructive acts that were needed to help preserve the Union and afford citizenship rights to former slaves. After collecting many months of testimony about the KKK, congressional investigators who looked into the affairs of the "late insurrectionary states" filed a majority report concluding that "we see from Maryland to Mexico, the same general spirit of spite against the freedman, and determination to keep him down and use his labor without compensation."[26] Witness after witness explained to congressional leaders how the KKK used an assortment of tactics to undermine the efforts of the Freedmen's Bureau, including attacks on isolated rural communities at night, whippings, castration, rape, and even murder.

Some today, who look back on the origins of the KKK, characterize those who joined this organization as poorly educated whites who worried about competition from African American labor, but a review of the membership of the KKK shows that chapters were often led by former Confederate soldiers or well-to-do civilians. Their ranks included all classes of Southerners who believed in the importance of maintaining white supremacy. While President Ulysses S. Grant had been worried about the power of the KKK since the time of the 1868 elections, it took several years before he could muster enough political support to go after the organization.

The many congressional volumes found in the archives that were produced by those who wanted to chronicle President Grant's attacks on the KKK have bequeathed to posterity some of the most intriguing materials that we have on the extent of post–Civil War violence. The Radical Republicans used the congressional hearings as a rhetorical weapon that might help stamp out the power of the KKK. This makes sense, given that in effect, "the Klan was a military force serving the interests of the Democratic party, the planter class, and all of those who desired the restoration of white supremacy."[27]

When Congress first started to investigate the KKK in 1871, it was thought that "the Klan's actions represented the common concerns of Southern whites who wished to retain a racial hierarchy."[28] The congressional civil servants who were interested in Klan affairs listened to testimony that came from alleged victims and perpetrators of various crimes in the South. Some members of the Klan tried to evade congressional questioning and argued that they had never heard of the Klan, while others openly defended white supremacist activities.

Many of the blacks who testified before Congress during the KKK inquiries told congressional leaders about the terror they felt when dozens of masked riders would show up at their homes and take them to swamps and other places. Henry Lowther memorably testified that some twenty Klansmen on horseback arrived at his home and declared that he was working too hard for the Republican Party. Lowther was jailed on trumped-up charges, and when he got out of jail he was asked whether he "was willing to give up" his "stones" in order to save his life.[29] Two hundred riders may have witnessed his castration; Lowther recalled that his tormentors were all Democrats and that it had been KKK riders who had mutilated him. When asked by one of the investigators if he had ever "insulted any white woman," Lowther replied in the negative. Although Lowther admitted that he was "going to see a white lady," he pointed out that he was doing this because she had hired him to tend her land. After a Southern white Republican judge assured Lowther that he would not be compelled to incriminate himself, he admitted that "he had sexual intercourse with a white woman."[30]

Admissions like Lowther's put on display the precarious nature of rhetorical admissions during heated congressional debates that illustrated the intersectional nature of anxieties that confronted those who felt victimized by some of the parties involved in this Reconstruction disputation. Lowther's admission that he had engaged in sexual intercourse with a white woman could be used by Klansmen or their supporters to justify their racial terrorism and their repudiation of "social equality." In "the cases throughout the congressional testimony," noted Hodes, "white Southerners invoked charges of illicit sexual behavior toward or with white women together with accusations of Republican activism" or unwarranted agricultural successes.[31]

Not surprisingly, many Klansmen who were interrogated by congressional investigators insisted that emancipation had unleashed the beastly habits of the former slaves who were no longer restrained by the steady hand of their slave owners. Grand Wizard Nathan Forrest—one of the first leaders of the KKK—asserted: "Ladies were being ravished by some of these negroes, who were tried and put in a penitentiary, but were turned out in a few days afterward."[32] When pressed by investigators to provide specific names or instances of this to back up his claims, Forrest admitted that this was all hearsay and that he could not recollect the specifics.[33]

Just a few years before the EJI started making plans for the building of the Montgomery Lynching Memorial and Legacy Museum, Selma, Alabama, residents were embroiled in a heated controversy over the replacement of a stolen monument honoring Forrest, who has variously been described as a

"Civil War officer," "racist," "murderer," "Ku Klux Klan founder," and "savior" of Selma.[34]

The more that various witnesses during the nineteenth-century KKK hearings told congressional leaders their harrowing tales, the more obvious it became that one's race, as well as one's gender and one's class, influenced how one would be treated by the KKK and others who participated in or observed this Reconstruction violence. As Martha Hodes explained, poor white women could not count on the power of their whiteness to shield them from accusations that they had engaged in illicit sexual activities with former slaves. Congressional investigators and others who attended the KKK hearings heard stories of how a woman by the name of Griffin had been living with a white man, and she had been strapped across a log and then whipped.[35]

In cases when young girls or women were viewed as innocent victims of violence, they could escape the wrath of the KKK. In one 1866 case, Charles Clarke was accused of raping the white daughter of a Methodist preacher. After a judge found insufficient evidence for conviction, thirty-six "undisguised Klansmen" shot Clarke dead.[36]

While some who were accused of being KKK perpetrators of crimes argued that they were simply defending Southern women, others who testified before Congress told different tales. These different accounts of KKK activities were then linked to contentious ways of characterizing lynching.

During and after the congressional investigations of the KKK, all sorts of assertions and evidence were used to explain what should, or should not, be done to help various Southern constituencies during the Reconstruction years. Those who supported the passage of the post–Civil War amendments could frame these affairs in ways that tried to make sense of the intransigence of many Southerners who resented federal interventionism. For example, in 1873, Joseph Rainey, a black Republican from South Carolina serving in the US House of Representatives, linked the rhetoric of political rights and the discourse of black manhood during a heated congressional debate. Southern whites, opined Rainey, were trying to withhold citizenship rights from emancipated slaves because actions like suffrage "had a tendency to make him feel his manhood," and this, in the eyes of Southern whites, "is asking too much."[37] Observers like Rainey were convinced that white supremacists were demanding that black citizens accept their subservient station in life.

Documents produced by the EJI explain some of the features of the Reconstruction efforts that bothered some of these empowered Southern whites:

The newly elected and racially integrated Reconstruction governments took bold action at the state level, repealing discriminatory laws, rewriting apprenticeship and vagrancy statutes, outlawing capital punishment, and sharply reducing the number of capital offenses. African Americans also won election to law enforcement positions like sheriff and chief of police, and were empowered to serve on juries.[38]

We need to pause here to make several points. First of all, note how the EJI selectively frames these Reconstruction histories to make it seem as though their twenty-first-century "liberating" efforts with respect to current mass incarceration and capital punishment are simply carrying out the unfinished business of nineteenth-century African Americans and their Radical Republican allies. Note also the references to legal reformation that look very much like some of the prescriptive suggestions that appear in Bryan Stevenson's book *Just Mercy*.[39] Third, the provision of this type of information about the Reconstruction provides concrete examples of the cultural amnesia prevalent among today's American audiences, who have forgotten about some of the post–Civil War legalist reformist efforts that were soon to be dismantled by Southern whites who hardened racialized lines as they tried to rebuild the "New South."

This dismantling took place for a variety of reasons, including political changes in Washington, DC, and elsewhere, and the compromises and negotiations that were taking place among Southerners, Northerners, and other Americans who had reason to reconsider the perceived wisdom of having thousands of soldiers being stationed far from their own homes in far-flung regions of the South.

When President Rutherford B. Hayes agreed to finally end Reconstruction in 1877 in exchange for the support of white Southerners, many blacks feared for their lives and those of their loved ones. Many dreams of post–Civil War freedoms were quickly dashed when Southerners, and some of their Northern allies, found creative ways of using and abusing the post–Civil War amendments to legitimate everything from legal segregation to the attempted disarmament of black veterans.

The Post-Reconstruction Years, New Lynching Horrors, and the Racialized Features of Jim Crow Legislation

Many interdisciplinary scholars, when they study post-Reconstruction laws or politics, tend to lavish attention on the legalistic genealogies of "separate but equal" judicial formations, which can bracket out many tales of lynching violence from this period. For example, legal researchers who are in a rush to show linear or evolutionary American civil rights progress can track the chipping away at the discriminatory segregationist policies of the 1940s, 1950s, and 1960s in places like law schools, high schools, and public accommodations. Instead of dwelling on riots, lynchings, or other acts of violence, those who deploy these legalistic frames can implicitly or explicitly highlight the wisdom of the Earl Warren Court, the twentieth-century reduction of racism, the return of the rule of law, and the societal pressure that led to the filing of 1960s civil rights legislation. Using traditional race-neutral or "colorblind" rhetorics, various law review writers and traditional interdisciplinary scholars can trace the move away from the US Supreme Court's 1896 acceptance of the "separate but equal" doctrine and toward the legal cases leading up to *Brown v. Board of Education* (1954).[40]

Orthodox studies of these legal cases are important, but often they merge legal historicizing with American mythologizing as they downplay the failure to pass anti-lynching legislation or refuse to dwell on the horrific nature of the racial violence of the post-Reconstruction period. Those who want to speak about progressive or linear legal change in America must keep in mind that between "1882 and 1901, the number of lynchings per year in the U.S. fell below the one hundred mark only once."[41]

As we shall see in later chapters of this book, the American generations who lived after these years failed to pass hundreds of proposed state and federal anti-lynching bills. Was this failure another example of the "racial terrorism" that the EJI references?

Critical genealogists might argue that it is no coincidence that the removal of Union troops from the South took place during a period that also witnessed a rise in the number of recorded lynchings of people of color. By the end of the nineteenth century, there were so many newspaper reports about lynchings that anti-lynching advocates had difficulty chronicling all of these events (see chapters 2 and 3).

Moreover, in the same ways that KKK supporters during the 1870s could rationalize the mistreatment of recently freed slaves, whites during the post-Reconstruction years could come up with other social or scientific explanations for all sorts of lynching behaviors.

The Radical Republicans had tried to pass their own versions of anti-lynching laws, which were called "force bills," to help with the enforcement of the Fifteenth Amendment, but they were battling white supremacists who were "employing intimidation and bribery at the polls, arson, and murder."[42]

As readers might imagine, scientific racism and the growing resonance of eugenical ideas during the late nineteenth century influenced many contextualizations of post-Reconstruction lynching incidents. All sorts of animalistic, primitivist, Social Darwinian, and other rationales were used to justify everything from the poor schooling facilities that were provided to former slaves to the refusal to enforce voting rights. As if that were not discriminatory enough, millions of people of color lived in fear for their lives whenever there were any local incidents of violence that threated to turn into what nineteenth-century observers called "race wars."[43]

The strategic use of sociological and other social scientific ways of recording lynchings could be analyzed by lynching apologists as well as by critics of those apologists. Note, for example, that when James Elbert Cutler, in his book *Lynch-Law*, tried to explain the factors that contributed to the rising incidence of lynchings on "the frontier," he could dispassionately intone that there were basically two types of "frontier" lynchings—legal and illegal. He was convinced that while some lynchings were manifestly illegal, there were other acts that were "beyond the reach of human law."[44] Cutler then went on to explain that as time passed the justifications for lynchings changed, and those who rationalized their acts focused more on the "crime of rape directed against white women."[45]

Near of the end of the nineteenth century, a host of descriptive and prescriptive studies were published that tried to explain to readers why so many in the South seemed to support, or condone, the lynching of African Americans. There was no single class in the South that had a monopoly on the use of racialized and gendered rationales for lynchings. J. T. Winston, a letter writer from Bryan, Texas, responded this way when he heard some anti-lynching admonitions: "It may be bad to lynch, but is it not far worse for a demonized fiend, swelling with bestial lust, to lay his cursed hands on a pure, defenseless woman to satisfy his animal nature?"[46] Governor James K. Vardaman of Mississippi was willing to chastise a mob for burning, rather than hanging, an alleged black rapist, but his humanitarian sensibilities only took him so far. As Vardaman told one citizen in private, he would join a lynch mob if needed, and he didn't have much respect for a "white man who wouldn't."[47]

In theory, polite and respectable progressives in the South and elsewhere could find a variety of ways of discriminating between "legal" and "illegal" lynchings while assiduously avoiding the abolition of this type of behavior altogether.

Many African Americans were keenly aware of the political strategizing that was going on here, and black observers of post-Reconstruction lynchings argued that it was a mistake to take at face value the lynchers' claims that they were protecting Southern womanhood. W. E. B. Du Bois had this to say about some of the wordsmithing that took place during the post-Reconstruction years:

> The charge of rape against colored Americans was invented by the white South after Reconstruction to excuse mob violence. No such wholesale charge was dreamed of in slavery days and during the [Civil] war black men were often the sole protection of white women.[48]

Almost a hundred years later, EJI members would make a similar argument when they talked to reporters. These radical African American historical remembrances of the protection of women by blacks, alluded to by Du Bois, may have been selective and self-serving, but they put on display the inventive powers of Southerners who would not pass anti-lynching legislation.

As noted above, as critical genealogists we are concerned with the rhetorical production of ideological formations such as white supremacy as well as the historical critiques of these forms of racism, and we join the ranks of those who are suspicious of the claims that are circulated by those who raise the need for "context," and of explanations asserting that lynch laws were needed to protect Southern womanhood.

We do not doubt that some lynchings may have been motivated by rape allegations or similar claims, but there is also evidence that during the Reconstruction and post-Reconstruction periods economic factors also played some role in the rendering of this type of violence. In 2017, Bryan Stevenson explained:

> Leased black convicts faced deplorable, unsafe working conditions and brutal violence when they attempted to resist or escape bondage. An 1887 report by the Hinds County, Mississippi, grand jury recorded that six months after 204 convicts were leased to a man named McDonald, twenty were dead, nineteen had escaped, and twenty-three had returned to the penitentiary disabled, ill, and near death. The penitentiary hospital was filled with sick and dying black men whose bodies bore "marks of the most inhuman and brutal treatment ... so poor and emaciated that their bones almost come through the skin."[49]

Stevenson used this commentary on leased black convicts to provide historical, empirical, and legalistic evidence to support his twenty-first-century claim that while the "explicit use of race to codify different kinds of offenses and punishments" would be challenged and configured as "unconstitutional," this only led to the modification of criminal statutes, which were written in ways that avoided "direct racial references." The enforcement of these laws did not change, Stevenson averred, and black populations were routinely charged with a wide range of criminal offenses that many "whites were never charged with."[50]

This is an important lynchpin argument for EJI activists today because it becomes part of a larger narrativized claim that the legacies of lynching and carceral mistreatment were just a few of the events within a century-long pattern of abuse. Stevenson's is a race-conscious perspectival history that is filled with vignettes about violations of the equal protection principles of the US Constitution, and he emphasizes the links that can be made between economic, gendered, and racialized motivations.

Again, as we noted in the introduction, all of this EJI talk of the need to record the magnitude of historical lynchings is not taking place in a rhetorical vacuum.

Earlier generations also had their own motivations for selectively remembering the Civil War, the post–Civil War amendments, and the Reconstruction years. For those nineteenth-century social agents who sought to build the "New South," the development of the region's resources depended on capitalistic ventures that involved risks as well as potential rewards. The poverty of the immediate post–Civil War years had to be forgotten in order to demonstrate the redemption and opportunities afforded by scientifically managed Southern states.

Not everyone profited in equal ways from all the money that flowed into the "New South." By the 1880s, for example, the mortality rate among African Americans working in the mines of the South was incredibly high, due to brutal corporal punishment, chronic malnutrition, and studied indifference.[51] In some years, the mortality rate in Birmingham, Alabama, mines was estimated at ninety per thousand, and foreign observers compared this with the death rates experienced by Africans working in South African mines.[52] Jane McFadden has argued that, according to available data and photographic evidence,

> in 1898, 73 percent of Alabama's revenue was dependent on convict leasing, often founded on illegitimate and unjust charges. This period was marked by the use of terrorist tactics to keep racial divides intact. ... Remnants of the segregationist policies of Jim Crow remind us of the sickening pettiness of humanity dividing up space and privileges.[53]

Sadly, what looks petty to us may have looked like scientifically or socially justified discrimination during the late nineteenth century.

For some, the post-Reconstruction years were filled with the horrors of peonage, labor exploitation, and continued talk of white supremacy. Stories were told about how some black workers were punished by being placed in coffin-like boxes, and well into the 1920s Birmingham workers had to live in closed camps that were watched over by company guards. During some Jim Crow years, about one thousand convicts—including children between the ages of ten and sixteen—labored away in the Birmingham mines.[54]

Lynchings thus need to be viewed as just some of the means of social control that could be used in a racially stratified society that not only condoned but expected differential treatment of the "races." The post-Reconstruction segregationist practices that destroyed so many lives in places like the American South depended on both de jure and de facto discriminatory policies, and the perception that blacks need not strive so hard for "political," much less "social," equality.

More than a few Southerners were convinced that African American referencing of various equalities, including "social equality," were a prelude to greater threats like interracial marriage and the "commingling" of the races in all walks of life. A common Social Darwinian argument that circulated during these Jim Crow years was the claim that no laws could operate effectively if they were not based on the evolutionary nature of actual empirical and societal needs. For example, if society maintained that "races" existed and that "blood would tell," then Southerners believed that they were correct to rely on craniological, phrenological, anthropological, sociological, and eugenic studies to rationalize the separation of the races for the sake of preventing racial "friction."[55]

Those who talked about racial superiority and the need to prevent "race mixing" were often the same social agents who argued that no artificial laws passed by the Reconstructionists or deluded egalitarians could change societal attitudes or behavior. All sorts of legalistic and moralistic discourses centered around white supremacy and racial hierarchies could be concocted by those who demanded that civil rights interventionists admit the futility of their educational and reformist efforts. One white man from Mississippi tried to explain the inherent inferiority of African Americans by noting that "if every negro in Mississippi was a graduate of Harvard . . . he would not be as well fitted to exercise the right to suffrage as the Anglo-Saxon farm laborer."[56] Historian Edward Ayers remarked that "segregation became to whites" a marker "of sophisticated, modern, managed race relations."[57]

We will have more to say about the post-Reconstruction efforts of anti-lynchers in the next chapter, but for now we note how these segregationist views impacted the reception of anti-lynching legislation. We can readily understand the difficulties that were experienced by social agents like George H. White, a black congressman from North Carolina who introduced some of the first anti-lynching bills in the US House of Representatives in 1900.[58] This proposed legislation would be just one of many dozens of attempts to grapple with the violence of the Jim Crow years.

If Southern Democrats and other whites in the South were not interested in supporting anti-lynching legislation, then what types of Reconstruction or post-Reconstruction memories and histories resonated with these particular audiences? Would the residual, long-term effects of this kind of memory work later hinder the consciousness-raising efforts of Bryan Stevenson, the EJI, and the Montgomery Legacy Museum?

The Display of Confederate Statuary and Dixie Monumentalism

Above, we noted how some former Confederate officers and other Southerners during the 1870s congressional investigations of the KKK occasionally defended the antebellum way of life, and this rhetoric did not disappear. With the passage of years, some aspects of Civil War violence would be forgotten as the sons and daughters of rebels sought to preserve select memories. During the post-Reconstruction period, a type of nostalgia—which bordered on melancholia—made its appearance as observers noted new types of victimage campaigns.

It could be argued that many Southerners who wanted to preserve their own memories of the antebellum South felt threatened by people who sought civil rights for African American citizens. Kevin Levin of *Smithsonian Magazine*, who reviewed some of these American histories, has explained some of the ideological linkages that can be made between lynching pasts and the building of Confederate statuary. "The disenfranchisement of black Americans through legal means and the threat of lynching, throughout the Jim Crow Era," explained Levin, "allowed white southerners to frame their struggle as a 'Lost Cause'—a defiant and righteous stand against an illegal invasion by a corrupt federal government that sought to wipe out their peaceful civilization."[59]

New permutations of some older Reconstruction arguments started to appear in late-nineteenth-century and early-twentieth-century American novels and other texts by writers like Thomas Nelson Page[60] and Charles

Chesnutt,[61] who joined the ranks of those who wanted to tell Americans in all parts of the country that Southerners were having to deal with some complex societal causes for lynching. Once again, romantic stories of heroic defenders of Southern womanhood appeared on discursive horizons.

Often, this monumentalization and mythmaking went beyond the publication of books, as some Southerners enthusiastically collected the funds that were needed for the building of Confederate statues. Even during periods when those in the "New South" were financially strapped and many were trying to recover from the ravages of war or economic dislocation, they nevertheless prioritized the building of monuments that would celebrate the deeds of Robert E. Lee, Stonewall Jackson, Nathan Bedford Forrest, and Jefferson Davis. Some of these "Lost Causers" were even willing to construct fabricated tales of many "loyal" slaves. In 1895, for example, one cotton mill owner convinced members of the Jefferson Davis Memorial Association that they needed to put up a memorial in Fort Mill, South Carolina, that would honor "loyal" slaves. That memorial honored "the faithful slaves" who "toiled for the support of the army [and] with matchless devotion and sterling fidelity guarded our defenseless homes, women and children during the struggle for the principles of our Confederate States of America."[62]

Organizations like the United Daughters of the Confederacy (UDC) were some of the key social agents who helped with this Dixie monumentalization. After years of resistance, some nostalgic Southerners hired Moses Ezekiel, a Confederate veteran and a Richmond, Virginia, sculptor. Thanks to his work, on the grounds of Arlington National Cemetery now appears a thirty-two-foot-tall monument hovering over the graves of some 267 Confederate soldiers. Ezekiel's work was supposed to represent all of the different Southern communities who put aside their regional and class differences so that they could temporarily serve the rebel cause. Confederate colonel Hilary Herbert was chair of the executive committee of the Arlington Confederate Memorial Association when Ezekiel's monument was dedicated. Herbert told reporters that the statue showed "an officer, kissing his child in the arms of an old negro mammy."[63] No wonder that Karen Cox of the *Washington Post* would argue in 2017 that the "whole point of Confederate monuments is to celebrate white supremacy."[64]

Over the years, some who battled to preserve these types of Confederate memorials either were unaware of the contexts behind their dedication, or they simply ascribed new, supposedly innocuous meanings to these "Lost Cause" symbols. As we shall argue in later chapters, the EJI was one organization that would not remember to forget.

The Constitutive Creation of the "Lynching Archives" and the Evocative Power of Remembrances of Lynching Pasts

During the post-Reconstruction years, historiographical wars were waged by those who had different ways of configuring what we call the "lynching archives." As African American sociologists and other activists collected statistics to bolster their anti-lynching efforts, disputes broke out about how one categorized a "lynching." For example, if a white person died at the hands of a "mob," did that constitute a lynching? What if a black person was shot during an altercation? If a Southern court tried a person of color before that person was hanged, should that legalized incident be included in any sociological collection of aggregated statistics on lynching?

Such legal or academic disputations or archival contestations help explain the wide variety of statistics that present-day researchers and casual readers come across when they read newspapers, journal or magazine articles, books, or websites providing estimates of specific numbers of lynching victims. Ida B. Wells-Barnett, for example, used her own sociological methods to support her claim that some ten thousand blacks had been lynched. Other organizations—like the Association of Southern Women for the Prevention of Lynching,[65] the NAACP, and the EJI—came up with their own numbers. These statistics, in turn, provide rhetorical fragments that have been used in historical and contemporary debates about lynching legacies.[66]

Many would agree that lynching constituted a serious social problem during the post-Reconstruction years, but the motives of those who collected information about lynching incidents as well as the methods they used to determine what constituted a lynching incident impacted their tallying. Producing "the" historical or historiographic account of these lynchings has proved to be a difficult task, given the relative paucity of systematic studies of lynchings before the early 1880s. From a critical genealogical vantage point, it should also be viewed as a *politicized* task as well.

Few of these nineteenth-century lynchings were systematically recorded before the Tuskegee Institute in Alabama began investigating and archiving materials that helped aggregate and chronicle them.[67] Some of the major texts that were produced from these records were focused on reported lynchings between 1882 and 1901, but many interdisciplinary scholars have sought to go further back in time and discover earlier lynchings. By the fall of 2019, the EJI had provided information on at least eight hundred incidents of lynching that had been "forgotten," in some of the eight hundred counties that needed liberation and reconciliation.

As Michael Pfeifer noted in 2014, many "local" and "vernacular"[68] examples of lynching can be traced back to the "pivotal years that began with emancipation in the mid-1860s and ended with the return of white conservatives to power across the south by the mid to late 1870s."[69] "Substantial evidence," Pfeifer went on to explain, "suggests that whites collectively murdered several thousand African Americans during Reconstruction, sometimes through paramilitary organizations such as the Ku Klux Klan and sometimes in more routine, everyday enactments of brutal white supremacy in an era of continual contestation of racial boundaries and prerogatives."[70]

Note how this argument resembles the EJI's framings of some of these same historical periods.

Pfeifer is a scholar who realizes that the systematic study of lynching needs to do more than simply track the efforts of the KKK, and if critical interdisciplinary scholars are going to effectively assess the arguments proffered by the EJI about the longitudinal "legacy" of "racial terror," then they must acknowledge the suasory power of some of the competing epistemes that were produced by those who criticized, or who condoned, lynchings before 1900.

As we will argue in later chapters, some of those who were frustrated by the failure of federal anti-lynching efforts took solace in the fact that by the late 1940s there were fewer and fewer recorded illicit lynchings. Was this because of an actual decline in lynching incidents, or because of changes in how lynchings were recorded? Was this evidence of progress in what was then called "race relations," or was this wishful thinking?

On many, many occasions, Stevenson, the EJI, and the Legacy Museum raise the question of whether these lynchings actually "ended" or merely went underground, and that will be a topic that we take up later in this book.

Given the controversial claims made by the EJI regarding historical lynchings and the contemporary era of mass incarceration, it is imperative that critical genealogies look into some of the intersectional features of the lynching archives. We take the position that instead of trying to reveal some forgotten single "history" or solitary lynching "legacy," it makes more sense for readers to see the contentious nature of complementary and contradictory Reconstruction and post-Reconstruction histories and public memories of these eras.

This chapter has set the stage for some of these critical, perspectival investigations by highlighting some of the competing and complementary discursive formations that were produced during the post-Reconstruction and Jim Crow periods and that were used to rationalize all forms of peonage, convict release, lynchings, and other horrors that would later be discussed under the rubric of "racial terrorism."

Those who study the texts and visualities that are produced by Bryan Stevenson, the EJI, and the Legacy Museum will find that these social agents want to raise public awareness about the economic, social, political, and legal devastation that occurred before, during, and after the Reconstruction years. According to one of the texts produced by the EJI, this was a time when "vigilantes whipped and lynched black freedmen who argued with employers, left the plantations where they were contracted to work, or displayed any economic success of their own."[71]

One of the key issues, of course, is whether those Jim Crow lynching legacies can actually be tied to present-day discriminatory mass incarcerations. And, if this connection can be made, can mainstream American audiences be "liberated" in ways that allow them to see these same symbolic and material linkages?

CHAPTER 2

The Progressives, Ida Bell Wells-Barnett, and the Multiple Racisms That Marked Jim Crow Segregation

IN THE WEEKS LEADING UP TO THE 2018 OPENINGS OF THE NATIONAL MEMORIAL FOR Peace and Justice and the Legacy Museum, some observers sensed that these particular Montgomery spaces and places were not going to tackle "difficult histories" in the same ways the Smithsonian's National Museum of African American History and Culture (NMAAHC) in Washington, DC, chose to do.[1] Those who helped with the opening of the NMAAHC in 2016 did include gallery exhibits on lynching and the Reconstruction years, and many other topics in their eight levels and eight thousand square meters of space, but it could be argued that the Smithsonian's usage of visual, audial, and spatial materials served multidirectional purposes that did not always touch on some of the twenty-first-century topics that were of special relevance to EJI members and their brand of consciousness raising.

Critical scholars who follow Friedrich Nietzsche with his perspectival approaches and "untimely meditations,"[2] and researchers who extend the work of Foucauldians with their studies of countermemories and counterhistories, remind readers about all of the transgenerational presences and absences that swirl around any representations of fraught slavery pasts or lynching legacies. As Anne Rice explained in her essay "How We Remember Lynching":

> While propaganda and nostalgia in the press and popular culture screened slavery's traumatic past and rationalized its brutal aftereffects, the struggle against lynching operated as form of counter-memory testifying to African American suffering and drawing on centuries of resistance to white violence. The crossracial wounding and memory disturbances produced by lynching can only be understood in light of [the gap between dominant and minority group collective memories].[3]

The acts involved in remembering or forgetting lynching pasts were thus ideological decisions that had consequential aftereffects.

In the strategically selected EJI narratives that appeared on EJI websites and in Legacy Museum displays, it was individuals like Ida B. Wells-Barnett and W. E. B. Du Bois whose presence took center stage in EJI social dramas, and these and other radical, iconic figures became members of the EJI's pantheon of *parrhesiastes* (Michel Foucault),[4] activists who risked much in the name of immediate, and drastic, social change for aggrieved people of color.

We will argue in this chapter that many of the EJI's histories of the work of historical figures like Wells-Barnett are appropriated in race-conscious ways that allow ordinary American citizens to read about, or to visualize, the magnitude of the "racial terrorism" that has become the focal point of so many Equal Justice Initiative projects. As EJI staffers noted on their website in 2013, "[i]n 1900 African Americans constituted nearly a third of those living in Southern states and less than 2% in other regions. They occupied the lowest rung of the Southern racial caste system, relegated to sharecropping, discriminating Jim Crow laws, extreme poverty, and brutal racial violence."[5]

When the EJI attempts to raise consciousness about half-forgotten lynching pasts and underscores the activism of radical African Americans who refuse to forget the violence of slavery, the slave trade, Reconstruction, and the Jim Crow years, it does so in ways that postcolonial scholars would call the "decolonization" of American historical studies.[6] Rather than treating lynching incidents as isolated cases of American waywardness in an otherwise predictable path of linear progress for civil rights that begins with the passage of the civil rights amendments and carries through to the legalistic reforms of the 1950s and 1960s, the EJI's narrative trajectories resituate mass lynchings as key temporal events. The EJI's dissonant racialized histories work "against the grain" of conventional civil rights memorializing,[7] cutting and breaking up civil rights verities so that new assemblages, new imaginaries, can be formed to present visitors to Montgomery with inconvenient "regimes of truth" that are associated with all sorts of American economic, political, legal, and social forms of institutional discriminatory practices. The protagonists of the EJI's moral plays remind listeners and viewers that Ida B. Wells-Barnett and W. E. B. Du Bois lived at a time when a freed slave or their daughter or son "was socially an outcast, industrially a serf, legally a part of 'a separate and oppressed class.'"[8]

As we noted in chapter 1, few of those who lived in the post-Reconstruction period tried to keep accurate tallies of those who were killed by the KKK and other white supremacist organizations between 1866 and the removal of Union troops in 1877, but this started to change in the early and mid-1880s.

African Americans—who noted that the courts were controlled by whites who used and abused the post–Civil War amendments to avoid fulfilling the promise of Reconstruction—started to record, and to aggregate, the number of lynchings that were carried out by so many American lynch mobs.

Some who referenced these early tallying efforts chronicled how, between 1882 and 1944, there were nearly five thousand recorded lynchings. Infuriated witnesses to lynching started to combine graphic accounts of individual case studies of lynching with records of large numbers of similar incidents. For instance, individuals like Sam Hose, who was ritually murdered in 1899, was talked about and written about before, during, and after his lynching. Journalists for the *Atlanta Journal-Constitution* both described and contributed to the spectacular nature of some of these lynching performances, for example this particular visit by "Judge Lynch": "Fully 2,000 people surrounded the small sapling to which he was fastened and watched the flames eat away his flesh, saw his body mutilated by knives and witnessed the contortions of his body in his extreme agony."[9] Wells-Barnett argued that Hose's murder was a part of a "reign of outlawry," and she claimed that the *Atlanta Journal-Constitution* did little to prevent the carrying out of some twelve lynchings of African American men between March and April 1899. "Never a word for law and order," she lamented.[10]

Of course, given the polysemic nature of the phrase "law and order," those Southern populists, or reactionaries, who carried out the lynching of Sam Hose could argue that they were following the spirit of the law by defending the victims who allegedly suffered at Hose's hand. Wells-Barnett wrote that those who carried out lynchings "believed that virtuous white women should see their evil attackers punished quickly and with finality."[11] Ersula Ore later pointed out that some Americans seemed to be viewing all of this as "the physical embodiment of the nation."[12]

Did the *Atlanta Journal-Constitution*'s coverage of the lynching of Sam Hose reflect the views of only a few classes of people in Georgia and the rest of the South, or was this behavior typical of the broader public during the post-Reconstruction and Progressive years?

As many scholars and investigative journalists have noted, the Progressive Era was a time when the intersectionalities of race, class, gender, and nationality continued to influence the way people of color were treated in America.[13] By the early 1900s, the circulation of commentaries on the eugenical superiority of the "Anglo-Saxon" could be sutured together with all sorts of other political, scientific, legal, and cultural epistemes that could be used to deny rights to African Americans.[14] "Octoroons," for example, were considered to be deceptive, liminal figures, almost white, and yet because of Jim Crow hypodescent "one drop of black blood" rules they were still configured as degenerate and inferior beings.[15]

More than a few who wrote or talked about these lynchings during the Progressive Era still used the secular and sacred language of "redemption" in justifying this type of vigilante justice. Blacks accused of crimes like rape were said to have performed acts that illustrated the futility of providing irrational people of color with political rights, civil rights, and the ever dangerous "social equalities." As Leigh Raiford astutely observed, these intercultural performances produced interrelated forms of whiteness and blackness, and they became a part of the "truth apparatus" that structured the ethnic relations that contributed to "lynching's antidemocratic barbarism."[16]

Populist, reactionary American practices that were barbaric were justified by referencing the supposed barbarism of those lynched.[17] "Skipping the process of adjudication," noted David Squires, "lynch mobs" moved on the "presumption of guilt directly to the execution of a death sentence."[18] Note how these types of scholarly arguments about presumptions and legal lynchings helped set the stage for twenty-first-century EJI activism.

The repetitive, and predictable, nature of some of these rationales for lynching in the South and elsewhere did not mitigate the horror of these activities. During the Progressive years, organizations like the Tuskegee Institute and the newly formed NAACP (1909) recorded the number of reported lynchings. Often they also kept track of the rationales that were used to justify these acts, and the lynching archives are now filled with many records of these justificatory acts.[19]

Some of the most abusive types of rhetorics that were produced during this period supposedly put on display the fitness of the gallant and chivalrous lynchers, who were "forced" to take matters into their own hands when lax sheriffs,[20] or slow-moving American courts, did not protect "Southern womanhood."[21] Racist discussions of black "beasts" infantilized and demasculinized those who died in so many violent "riots" and other confrontations.

In this chapter, we will continue our critical analysis of EJI and Legacy Museum claims by focusing on the anti-lynching efforts of those who joined Wells-Barnett during her crusades. Although we personally applaud Wells-Barnett's bravery and agree with much of what scholars such as Jacqueline Jones Royster have said about her rhetorical eloquence and leadership, as poststructural critics we want to focus on the larger discursive formations that swirled around Wells-Barnett as she put together her famed "Red Record" of lynchings.[22]

We will argue in this chapter that when African Americans fought for anti-lynching reform during the Progressive Era and other periods, they had to struggle with more than just a few reactionaries, Southern Democrats in Congress, members of the KKK, and passive/aggressive observers of lynchings. Wells-Barnett, Francis Pauline Hopkins, Mary Church Terrell, and other African Americans who battled to end lynchings were confronting a deep, racialized *dispositif* that was composed of many layers of sedimented racialized, gendered, and class-based ideologies that could not be easily dislodged.

Our perspectival choice of topics in this chapter is necessarily selective, and we have, in part, been motivated by Wells-Barnett's central position before, during, and after the inauguration of Montgomery's Legacy Museum. In May 2018, Jamil Smith provided this typical contextualization of Wells-Barnett's significance for America's twenty-first-century "remembrance" needs:

> Lynching was a new kind of horror for the American descendants of kidnapped Africans. Ida B. Wells-Barnett, the Southern journalist who wrote critically about lynchings and was later exiled to Chicago after threats, wrote in her 1895 pamphlet The Red Record that "with freedom" for the newly emancipated, "a new system of intimidation came into vogue; the Negro was not only whipped and scourged. He was killed." Lynching was the most sustained campaign of domestic terrorism outside of slavery's holocaust. As Jesse Jackson noted last week [April 25, 2018] in Montgomery, there still is no federal legislation banning lynching. More than 4,400 deaths between 1877 and 1950 were tallied by the Equal Justice Initiative. These are just the ones that Stevenson and his EJI team were able to count.[23]

The EJI's efforts—and the journalistic support that came from Jamil Smith and others—could be viewed as twenty-first-century performances that carried on Wells-Barrett's radical legacy. Her works informed their own twenty-first-century confrontational, race-conscious advocacy.

Although scholars can appreciate why Bryan Stevenson and the EJI would place the work of Ida B. Wells-Barnett in the radical historical trajectories that link their respective efforts across the generations, we all need to be mindful of the fact that Wells-Barnett's work did not always resonate with members of the African American community, who had to worry about white backlash. Lori Amber Roessner noted in a 2018 academic essay that for a long time "the anti-lynching efforts of Wells-Barnett had been written out of the first official version of Black history" when "political tensions" led to the "omission of the militant social activist from the earlier narratives of the anti-lynching movement."[24] Conservatives and moderates had their own ways of dealing with varied forms of America's racisms.

Given the fickle nature of public memories, it is understandable that during generational periods when supporters of civil rights activism would rather see the promotion of moderate, "colorblind" ways of conceptualizing social change, the work of radical feminists like Ida B. Wells-Barnett mystically recedes from view. Yet when different generations, with their own presentist needs, want to identify, and advocate for, more radical or color-conscious ways of thinking about race, class, and gender issues, Wells-Barnett's work seems to take center stage.

Wells-Barnett's supporters crafted anti-lynching narratives that would respond to several different competitive memories of lynching pasts.[25] They not only had to deal with the open racism of those who revived the KKK, but they had to critique the efforts of conservative Southerners and liberal Northerners who argued that states, and not the federal government, should be put in charge of anti-lynching reform (see also chapters 3 and 4). At the same time, many whites were producing commentaries on the alleged causes of lynching that deflected attention away from labor abuses, peonage laws, economic discrimination, poverty, and related factors that were raised by African American feminist anti-lynchers.

Before moving on to our various subsections in this chapter, we suggest reviewing some of the discursive origins of the "colorblind" fragments that were reassembled by so many civil rights activists during the 1960s and 1970s. In 1896, in the case of *Plessy v. Ferguson*, the US Supreme Court, by a vote of 7–1, gave its warranted assent to the ideographic "separate but equal" doctrine.[26] Justice Henry Billings Brown led a majority of jurists who were of the opinion in *Plessy* that separate car laws in the state of Louisiana did not indelibly stamp African Americans with any "badge of inferiority." Justice Brown used this occasion to lecture his fellow Americans about the importance of having societies follow naturalized racial hierarchies, and he opined that if blacks considered Louisiana's separate car law to be discriminatory, then this was only the case if the members of the "colored race choose to put that construction up on."[27]

The prevention of social friction and the maintenance of racial harmony were reasonable goals. In theory, both the positivist rules of sociology and the legal premises of segregationist jurisprudential measures are apolitical and nondiscriminatory in nature.[28] This implies that those people of color in Louisiana like Homer Plessy who were objecting to the state's separate car laws did not understand either (1) the laws of nature or (2) the fact that the US Constitution does not contain provisions that contravene nineteenth-century Social Darwinian laws that have little to do with badges of servitude.

In a famous dissent, which many lawyers and judges have viewed as foundational and prophetic, Justice John Marshall Harlan responded to the rest of the Brown Court in the *Plessy* case, and he left us this pithy summary of a contrarian position:

> In the eye of the law, there is in this country no superior, dominant, ruling class of citizens. There is no caste here. Our constitution is colorblind, and neither knows nor tolerates classes among citizens. In respect of civil rights, all citizens are equal before the law. The humblest is the peer of the most powerful.... The arbitrary separation of citizens on the basis of race, while they are on a public highway, is a badge of servitude wholly inconsistent with the civil freedom and the equality before the law established by the Constitution. It cannot be justified upon any legal grounds.[29]

This legal archival fragment—which perhaps has antecedents that can be found in the briefs of Plessy's lawyers—would ideologically drift along and be cited countless times by those who tried to highlight the racist assumptions undergirding Brown's *Plessy* opinion. Justice Harlan would later be lionized by civil rights activists who fought to get rid of the "separate but equal" doctrine.

However, in the rush to embrace this colorblind stance, some modernists forget to tell members of the public that Harlan's words are not as egalitarian as they initially appear to be. In his same Plessy dissent, Justice Harlan went on to argue that while African Americans deserved to be treated as equal citizens in the United States, Chinese litigants and other foreigners were too racially different, outsiders who were not American citizens deserving of equal rights and constitutional guarantees.[30]

Brown's American audiences also understood that scientists and imperial or colonial administrators in places like the Philippines, Malaya, Cuba, China, or Africa were also trying to find various ways of drawing color lines, segregating the "races," and dealing with the threats posed by "race mixing" on the peripheries of empires.[31]

It was only later, after American and global audiences learned about the horrors of the Holocaust and the devastation that could be wrought by various "isms"—imperialism, racism, extreme nationalism, totalitarianism, and so on—that organizations like UNESCO produced documents discouraging racist thinking.[32] In the post–World War II world, which craved neutrality, peace, and scientific objectivity, the old, forgotten legal clichés that appeared in texts like Justice Harlan's dissent could be rediscovered and lifted from old, musty legal parchment papers that had been "scratched" over many times.[33] Harlan's—and Albion Tourgée's—words on colorblindness would be reappropriated by those who sought precedents and eloquent dissents that might aid the cause of the NAACP and other organizations that were trying to force Americans to live up to their constitutional promises and provide people of color with better schools and equal accommodations.[34]

Justice Brown's opinion—which in 1896 looked like cutting-edge legal science that followed the sociological, ethnological, and anthropological precepts of his day and time—would later be marginalized and ridiculed by those who rescued the Harlan dissent from oblivion. The seemingly fair and neutral principles of post–World War II legal colorblindness paradigms appeared to provide just the right tools to help moderate African American lawyers convince other Americans of the wisdom and legality of adopting nonviolent strategies to incrementally dismantle the racist Progressive ideologies that swirled around the old "separate but equal" doctrines.[35]

During this period, many whites did not have the same views regarding legal discrimination, and many supported lynching, viewing it as a matter that had little to do with the civil rights amendments. Some, like Hubert Bancroft, writing in 1887, justified lynch law as type of performative enactment of "the right of the governed at all times to instant and arbitrary control of government."[36] Characterizing some forms of popular justice as "friendly with the law," Bancroft went on to claim that vigilante committees fulfilled Americans' public expectation, "whenever they see the law ... trampled upon, distorted, or prostituted, to rise in their sovereign privilege and remove such unfaithful servants, lawfully if possible, arbitrarily if necessary."[37] As both Manfred Berg and David Squires have pointed out, Bancroft's commentaries on popular justice's "necessities" often papered over the fact that lynch mobs were just as interested in vengeance as they were in appearing as vigilantes.[38]

Some American writers, like Ray Stannard Baker, argued that while lynching violated both the letter and spirit of American jurisprudential principles, there were understandable reasons why upstanding citizens might take matters into their own hands. In his book *Following the Color Line*, Baker was adamant that a review of lynchings in both the North and the South showed that these excesses were caused by "corrupt politics, vile saloons, the law paralysed by non-enforcement against vice, a large venal Negro vote, [and] lax courts of justice."[39]

Although a vocal minority of Americans who read about the social agency of historical figures like Ida B. Wells-Barnett understood why some African Americans would continue to advance radical arguments in their anti-lynching and other civil rights campaigns,[40] many other Americans had no interest in tolerating those who would not accept the legality and legitimacy of US segregationist practices or laws aimed at preventing "race mixing."

We begin with a short summary of some of the ideological positions of Ida B. Wells-Barnett and other African American women who worked to pass federal anti-lynching legislation, and then we move in this chapter to a subsection that focuses on Wells-Barnett's supporters' encounters with America's legal structures.

African American Feminist Critiques of Progressive Racial Injustices

As Christopher Waldrep once wrote, there were "many faces of Judge Lynch" that could be used to justify the use of extralegal violence and other forms of punishment in America,[41] and nineteenth-century African American writers were well aware that they were fighting an uphill battle. Those who defended lynching, after all, often fused together the "rhetoric of emergency" with the "logic of popular sovereignty."[42]

Some members of Wells-Barnett's generation became familiar with her work when her essays appeared in New York's *New Age*, but others learned of her efforts after she delivered public addresses in Scotland and England.[43]

As noted above, during her lifetime Wells-Barnett explicitly characterized mass lynchings in America as a form of "terror," and she did not hesitate to tell her fellow citizens that there were occasions when one had to pick up a "Winchester" in order to protect one's home or place of business.[44] Influenced by the work of members of the Afro-American League, Wells-Barnett explained that she was convinced that there were times when only the adoption of militant civil rights activism could prevent even more mass lynchings.[45]

Unlike liberal whites, conservative African Americans, or others who were willing to wait on state lynching reform, Wells-Barnett demanded that members of her generation immediately pass anti-lynching legislation. She invited her readers to see "Lynch Law as a form of 'unrestrained outlawry' that depends on law enforcement's asymmetrical application across the color line."[46]

Some of Wells-Barnett's arguments were so radical for her time that they were rejected by members of the very organizations that she helped form, including the NAACP. It did not help matters when potential allies—people of color and whites—tried to undermine some of her efforts by espousing more conventional, less threatening paternalistic rhetorics that denied her social agency. Teresa Zackodnik noted in 2005 that for a time, when Wells-Barnett was traveling in Great Britain in 1893 and 1894, she was at the "center of British reform," which targeted "American atrocities," but later on she was "marginalized" or viewed as "a lone militant" by some anti-lynchers in America.[47]

At times, Wells-Barnett would write under the name "Iola" when she submitted contributions to the *Chicago Conservator* and the *Indianapolis Freeman*. Not only did her defenders battle outright postbellum apologists for "modern slavery" and peonage, but progressive Southerners and Northern liberals were bothered by the fact that Wells-Barnett had the temerity to question their alleged racial superiority or their protection of "Southern womanhood." She infuriated white supremacists when she dared to humanize lynching victims through her investigations of lynching contexts.

In the same way that the NAACP and the EJI would soon be pointing out the inherent contradictions, and the protean nature, of both extrajudicial and "legal" lynchings, Wells-Barnett used carefully chosen words and images to dismantle, "piece by piece," the "racist beliefs about African Americans perpetuated in the dominant press."[48] Armed with materials that were taken from her own investigations, or carrying with her copies of photographs that were taken from lynchers themselves, Wells-Barnett battled those who used both sacred and profane rhetorics to justify lynchings.

As critical genealogists, we note that many of these battles that were taking place between Wells-Barnett's supporters and her detractors were not only struggles about the necessitous nature of anti-lynching legislation but also contests about scientific authority, the facticity of racial sciences, and the social status of feminists like Wells-Barnett. White supremacists, for example, could argue that the "real" scientists of this era were those who had been trained at places like Yale, Stanford, or the University of Georgia who knew all about racial science, the need for segregation, and the like, and that Wells-Barnett could be configured, and dismissed, as a self-identifying researcher who used unscientific methods to reach predetermined and prejudicial conclusions about lynching cultures.

Wells-Barnett's radicalism thus needs to be understood as a type of counterhegemonic force that threated white supremacists in multiple ways, and her stances could be used to interrogate white supremacists' racial assumptions, their ways of configuring white womanhood, their manliness, and their scientific authority.

The American Public Culture Representations of the Deaths of Thomas Moss, Calvin McDowell, and Henry Stewart

Ida B. Wells-Barnett published in many different local, regional, and national venues, and her pamphlets and books were read by those who wished to challenge America's mythic color lines.

In some of the more conventional, less radical stories that are told about Wells-Barnett's contributions, it is not her mention of those Winchesters or her advocacy of defensive violence that garner attention, but her journalistic efforts that take center stage. Some researchers have highlighted the contributions she made to black journalism, gendered politics, class struggle in America, and anti-lynching efforts, and more than few trace these journalistic efforts back to when she edited the *Memphis Free Speech and Headlight*. This newspaper originally served as a church paper for publicity purposes but became an outlet for political activism, especially after the 1892 killing of three of Wells-Barnett's friends—Thomas Moss, Calvin McDowell, and Henry Stewart.

These three men ran into trouble in 1892 after a group of black and white youngsters, and their parents, started to quarrel about the results of a game of marbles. In a predominantly black neighborhood in Memphis called the Curve, the parents of these youngsters walked into a grocery store called the People's Grocery, which was owned by Moss, McDowell, and Stewart. These three African American business leaders had started a business venture, which they hoped would become a cooperative store, that directly competed with a white-owned store (Will Barrett's) in the vicinity.[49]

What began as a minor altercation between youngsters quickly turned into a deadly situation when Will Barrett threatened to "clean" out the owners of the People's Grocery. Various lynching archives are filled with conflicting information about whether Moss, McDowell, and Stewart armed themselves and stayed on their premises, or whether they paid some local neighbors to guard their store. Regardless, what seems to have taken place is that Will Barrett, accompanied by a posse of about a dozen men, surrounded the People's Grocery. This resulted in an exchange of gunfire that wounded three members of the posse—police officers—who eventually recovered from their wounds.

The Memphis police, using legalistic arguments about "conspiracies," then rounded up somewhere between thirty and one hundred African Americans, who were questioned about their involvement in the People's Grocery affair.

Some of Will Barrett's Memphis supporters sought to put Moss, McDowell, and Stewart on trial for the wounding of members of the posse, but before their cases could be litigated in a Tennessee courtroom, the three black men, who had been incarcerated, were taken out of their jail cells and shot to death in a field north of Memphis. Ida B. Wells-Barnett then wrote a series of articles in the *Free Speech and Headlight* that encouraged black citizens to leave Tennessee.[50] Wells-Barnett also argued that there was "no law on the statute books which would execute an Afro-American for wounding a white man, but the 'unwritten law' did."[51]

The lynching of Wells-Barnett's three friends would be remembered in the lynching archives as the "lynching at the Curve." As David Squires later noted, readers of Wells-Barnett's autobiography would learn that her friends' "lynching changed the course of her life."[52] Audiences in Tennessee and elsewhere read that those who had killed Moss, McDowell, and Stewart did not stop at killing these three but proceeded to ransack their place of business. The *Memphis Daily Commercial* reprinted some of the materials that had earlier appeared in Wells-Barnett's *Free Speech and Headlight*, although the *Daily Commercial*'s writers described how "obscene intimations" about consensual sex had brought prideful Southern whites to the "very outmost limits of public patience."[53] Just as problematic for these whites was Wells-Barnett's call for blacks to leave the area.

Wells-Barnett's lead editorial on these murders did more than just comment on the illegality and immorality of the arbitrary killing of the three store owners. She now took the radical step of asking African Americans to use their collective economic and political power and consider fleeing this part of Memphis. "There is only one thing left that we can do," she explained; "save our money and leave a town which will neither protect our lives and property, nor give us a fair trial in the courts, but takes us out and murders us in cold blood when accused by white persons."[54] Wells-Barnett went so far as to suggest that some blacks living in Memphis needed to pick up their bags and travel to Oklahoma, and this advocacy could later be configured as evidence of her involvement in the Great Migration.

Empowered whites living in Memphis must have felt that their honor was at stake, and perhaps they also sensed that they needed to publicly respond to Wells-Barnett's claims. Some of Memphis's business leaders met at the Cotton Exchange Building to organize the destruction of the *Free Speech and Headlight*'s office, and after ransacking the office they left a note threatening death to anyone who returned, after the local sheriff sold what remained of the business to pay off local creditors.[55]

In an uncredited editorial that appeared in the *Free Speech and Headlight*, Wells-Barnett argued against the outlawry that had led to the lynching of her three friends, and she implied that all of this was due to a type of reactionary populism that created bogus threats and "new alarms" by using the "old racket" of writing about the alleged raping of white women.[56] Using variants of arguments that would soon become familiar to her readers, Wells-Barnett went on to critique the economic motives of whites who did everything in their power to destroy African American businesses.

The uncredited author of the offending *Free Speech and Headlight* piece (Wells-Barnett) was vilified as a "black scoundrel" by writers for the *Memphis Daily Commerce*, and they blamed the black publisher who had allowed the publication of that editorial for "arousing the worst passions of their kind."[57] These same reporters were not shy about suggesting the proper remedies for those who would affront Southern sensibilities: "Tie the wretch who utters these calumnies to a stake at the intersection of Main and Madison Sts., brand him in the forehead with a hot iron, and perform upon him a surgical operation with a pair of tailor's shears."[58]

This referencing of actual castration would also be critiqued by generations of feminists after the 1880s, and more than a few would understand why a traumatized Wells-Barnett practiced what she preached by moving to Chicago. David Squires later noted that while "state laws in the South had prevented" Wells-Barnett from "riding in the first-class train car," other "municipal, state and federal laws had failed to protect her life and her property."[59]

From a poststructural vantage point, one could argue that Wells-Barnett had started to occupy several different, but related, subject positions. She had become a witness, a victim, and an advocate who refused to forget that she was the godmother of Thomas Moss's oldest daughter. Angered that the courts, the sheriffs, and other whites had refused to intervene to help her three friends, she was willing to critique the sacred and the profane features of systematic indifference to institutionalized lynching: "The Christian World feels, that while lynching is a crime, and lawlessness and anarchy the certain precursors of a nation's fall, it cannot by word or deed, extend sympathy or help to a race of outlaws."[60]

As Susan Owen and Peter Ehrenhaus have reminded us, many racialized lynchings had everything to do with how some Southerners performed their "Christian evangelicalism,"[61] and readers and scholars can just imagine the furor of those who heard Wells-Barnett reference Southern religious values and lynching practices.

Our critical genealogical readings also invite readers to pay attention to the power dynamics of the relationships that existed at the Curve. Wells-Barnett's critiques were not just addressed to the Southern reactionaries who killed her three friends. They also seem to be addressed to those African Americans who acquiesced and had misplaced faith in accommodationist efforts. Wells-Barnett was critiquing the apparent submissiveness of African Americans who refused to join her and who shied away from taking a more radical stance against empowered whites. In one passage of her chronicling of the deaths of Moss, McDowell, and Stewart, she averred that her friends' timidity had only emboldened their tormentors. She opined that her friends had thought that Jim Crow problems could be "solved by eschewing politics and putting money in the purse."[62]

Ida B. Wells-Barnett's Move to New York, Her Travels Abroad, and the Social Formation of More Nuanced Anti-Lynching Critiques

After having witnessed these Memphis murders, and after having read the threats that were sent her way following the recirculation of some of her essays in Tennessee and national newspapers, Ida B. Wells-Barnett must have realized that she would have to overcome many evidentiary hurdles that stood in her path as she advocated for anti-lynching legislation. She was going to be accused of condoning black male rape of white women, and her detractors would say that she was an ignorant interloper who knew little about the existential dangers that arose when poor whites and respectable middle-class citizens alike were not protected by local sheriffs from the bestiality of millions of uneducated, and lusty, African workers.

By 1892, and especially after her move north, Wells-Barnett likely no longer viewed herself as just the protector of her family or as a teacher, but as a social scientist, a sociologist, and an investigative journalist who now had to arm herself with more than the gun that she carried after the killing of Tom Moss and her other friends. Her adoption of each of these subjectivities made her into a major transgressive figure.

Both her contemporaries and future chroniclers of her activities took note of the way that, as she embarked on her highly visible anti-lynching career, she chose to "arm herself with photography as a weapon," and that her "larger truth apparatus" now included "statistics, dominant press accounts," and "investigative reports."[63]

To complicate matters, Wells-Barnett did not hesitate to name those white women who crossed the "color line" to engage in consensual sex, and she documented many examples of false rape allegations. She mentioned the case of a Mrs. J. Underwood, a white woman from Ohio who had confessed to falsely accusing William Offett of rape, and she referenced in some of her essays at least ten instances in which newspapers provided readers with details of consensual sexual encounters between white women and black men.[64]

Wells-Barnett joined the ranks of other African American intellectuals who recognized the material and symbolic importance of lynching for American "progressive" generations, and she began traveling across the South. With limited funding, she produced research reports and speeches that informed American readers and listeners about the public spectacle of hangings, the burning of homes, and the dismemberment of African American bodies.

Wells-Barnett learned to harness the evocative power of photography as she commented on some mass lynching spectacles like the hanging of Henry Smith. Her coverage of the lynching of Ray Porter in Clanton, Alabama, in 1891 became another "image event"[65] that helped launch her anti-lynching career. In both her essay "Lynch Law" (1893) and her pamphlet *The Red Record* (1895), she reappropriated drawings and photographic images from postcards that had once served as white supremacist trophies, souvenirs, or "I was there" images.

Given the polysemic and polyvalent nature of photographic representation, lynching communities in Alabama could use the image of Ray Porter to put on display the lynchers' prowess, their unwillingness to forgive slights against their womenfolk, and their ability to dispense vigilante justice with impunity when needed. This forced anti-lynchers to find inventive ways of repurposing these very same images. As Shawn Michelle Smith has argued, those who used the "photographic archive"—who wanted their representations to "resonate"—had to read "visual archives against one another to find photographic meaning in the interstices" so that these depictions could challenge dominant epistemic claims.[66]

In *The Red Record*, Ida B. Wells-Barnett used both a drawing from a photograph and a photographic postcard of the lynching of Ray Porter[67] to support her claim that lynchings were being carried out by ordinary Southern audiences. The photograph of Porter was presented to readers of her pamphlet near the end of a discussion section in which she commented on the innocence of many lynching victims. Wells-Barnett made the telling point that some people who witnessed Porter's murder were still questioning his guilt as others hoisted him up a tree.

This type of analysis prefigured Bryan Stevenson's later discussions of the loss of presumption of innocence for those who deserved tender mercy.

Like many horrific images, the postcard of Ray Porter that Wells-Barnett critiqued shows a crowd of many boys and men staring up at the corpse of an African American who supposedly deserved the brutalized punishment that he had received. "Porter's body" is no longer that of a "human being who once possessed a history and agency," but is rather an "object outside of time" in which "whiteness" and "blackness" are defined in relational ways that allowed those who came in their work pants and suspenders to believe that justice was being rendered.[68]

There were several plausible reasons why Wells-Barnett's critiques infuriated both advocates of open racism and supporters of more "liberal," covert ways of rationalizing lynching. First, she did not hesitate to talk about illicit, but consensual, sex between white women and black men, a taboo subject for those who presumed that all sex of this type must involve rape perpetrated by African American men. Second, she named those who she believed contributed to a "reign of outlawry." Third, she refused to accept the legitimacy of the mythic "color line" that was policed by so many who lived during the last part of the nineteenth century and the early part of the twentieth. At the same time, she did not confine herself to critiquing a few, supposedly ignorant white supremacists who engaged in barbaric lynching practices but instead implicated and indicted most, if not all, members of acquiescing Southern societies who did not put an end to lynching practices.

The vitriolic responses that Wells-Barnett received during the Progressive years seem to have galvanized the efforts of the dissidents, who realized that her unrelenting critique was having a persuasive effect. When Frederick Douglass read Wells-Barnett's *Red Record*, he had this to say about what should have been the mainstream public's reaction:

> If the American conscience were only half alive, if the American church and clergy were only half Christianized, if American moral sensibility were not hardened by persistent infliction of outrage and crime against colored people, a scream of horror, shame, and indignation would rise to Heaven wherever your pamphlet shall be read.[69]

Not all Americans, however, would express this type of reaction when they assessed Wells-Barnett's work.

If today's scholars wished to create a critical genealogical line, or a counterhegemonic lynching archive, that linked together more radical argumentation, that countermemorializing archive would include the work of abolitionists like Frederick Douglass and Ida B. Wells-Barnett, as well as the EJI and their supporters. It might begin by taking fragments of Enlightenment debates about the common traits of the human species, including materials from Anglo-American abolitionists, who fought to prevent the "extirpation" of "aborigines" on many continents, and other humanist strands of argumentation.[70]

More than a century before the EJI complained about the silences that swirled around American "race terror" legacies, Ida B. Wells-Barnett wrote openly about the unwillingness of US citizens to confront the magnitude of the problem of vigilante lynchings. The *Birmingham Daily Post* in May 1894 printed this rhetorical fragment from Wells-Barnett that seemed to critique America's sense of complacency:

> The pulpit and press in our own country remain silent.... [T]he voice of my race, thus tortured and outraged, wherever lifted in America in a demand for justice is stifled or ignored. It is to the religious and moral sentiment of Great Britain we turn. They can arouse the public sentiment of America so necessary for the enforcement of law. ... They can ... pray and write and preach and talk and act against civil and individual slavery; against the hanging, shooting, and burning alive of a powerless race. America cannot and will not ignore the voice of a nation that is her superior in civilization which makes this demand in the name of justice and humanity.[71]

The land that had seen William Wilberforce arguing in Parliament against slavery and the slave trade, the same Great Britain that had allowed British feminists to call for sugar boycotts, now welcomed a radical Wells-Barnett, who was fighting for different but related humanitarian causes.

Although Wells-Barnett left us archival missives indicating that she was sometimes disheartened when her anti-lynching protests did not lead to the formation of large-scale organizations, there is little doubt that her messages resonated with at least a few labor leaders, supportive newspaper editors, church members, and cosmopolitans living overseas. One of the most moving tributes that she received during her speaking tours came from an admirer who seemed to sense some of the personal burdens that she must have carried. The sender, an impoverished Mississippi sharecropper, included a dollar bill along with this message:

> The only thing to offer for you in your great undertaking [is] a prayer and this goes up from every lip. The words "God bless her" is written here on every acre of ground and on every doorstep and inside of every home. I don't know what is holding you up. I have been expecting you to break down for more than a year but have not yet seen any signs of your being discouraged. To note that you a woman (I might say a girl) and I a great big man and you are doing what I ought to do and have not the courage to, I think sometimes it's a pity that I am in existence.[72]

Is this not one of those forgotten shards of memory, long buried in the lynching or civil rights archives, that reminds all of us of the internalizing power of demeaning Jim Crow rhetorics?

It is telling that even though many of Wells-Barrett's colleagues openly wrote about how much they admired her work, they refused to follow her lead, and they questioned her leadership skills. After a few years of hard work in America she decided that perhaps she would have better luck traveling overseas, and that influenced her decision in both 1893 and 1894 to travel to Europe. Wells-Barnett journeyed to Scotland and England so that she could convince European elites and the public that they had a moral responsibility to try to put an end to these American lynching "atrocities."

Wells-Barnett's 1893 overseas presentations were so graphic and so detailed that some European ministers and other potential allies refused to believe what they were seeing and hearing. Yet apparently other Europeans realized that this iconic heroine, who spent so much time depicting African American victimhood, was telling the truth about "Southern Horrors." Victor-Ernest Rillieux compared her to Joan of Arc, and he wrote a poem entitled "Amour et Dévouement, A Miss Ida B. Wells."[73]

After years of public speaking, traveling abroad, and conversing with humanist writers, Wells-Barnett realized that she had struck a nerve with her discussions of the economic dimensions of lynching and her refusal to accept conventional white tropes that highlighted African male inferiority and black aggression. Note, for example, how she wrote about the archival records for lynching that she had produced by 1894:

> Not all nor nearly all of the murders done by white men, during the past thirty years in the South, have come to light, but the statistics are gathered and preserved by white men, and which have not been questioned, show that during these years more than ten thousand Negroes have been killed in cold blood, without the formality of judicial trial and legal execution. And yet, as evidence of the absolute impunity with which the white man dares to kill a Negro, the same record shows that during all these years, and for all these murders only three white men have been tried, convicted, and executed.[74]

Critical scholars, influenced by poststructural, postmodern, and postcolonial theories, might try to investigate how she arrived at that ten thousand figure, but from a Foucauldian "truth effects" standpoint what Wells-Barnett's supporters might have needed was a massive statistic that would shock them out of their complacency.

We would go so far as to argue that Wells-Barnett was helping produce the very archives that she might have believed she was merely describing.

Unwieldy Alliances and the Attempted Domestication of Radical African American Anti-Lynching Rhetorics, 1905–1930

Those who grew up believing in the inherent inferiority of black women must have had a difficult time accepting some of Wells-Barnett's arguments. When she traveled overseas, journalists for the *New York Times*, instead of applauding her efforts, treated her as a misguided member of an ungrateful race. In an article entitled "British Anti-Lynchers," the *Times* denounced her as a "slanderous and nasty-minded mulattress" who was unnecessarily stirring up trouble for law-abiding Americans.[75] The article went on to argue that scientific research indicated that blacks were especially prone to committing crimes, chastising Wells-Barnett and the members of the British committees who listened to her public addresses for not having the "scruple to represent the victims of black brutes as willing victims."[76]

Some white "progressive" women likewise refused to grant black women any constructive social agency. For example, Eleanor Tayleur, writing in the *Outlook* in 1904, accused African American women of having the "hand that rocks the cradle in which the little pickaninny sleeps."[77] Writing in an ethnographic or anthropological style that tried to get at the empirical root causes of black "social and moral decadence," Tayleur's hurtful essay argued that black women were the "Frankenstein product of civilization," creatures who lacked individual creativity and were a "great dark, hopeless mass ... leading lawless and purposeless lives in the cane and cotton fields, or herded together in the cities."[78]

The melding of cultural and scientific racism that appeared in the dense, sedimented epistemes produced by Tayleur and others was problematic enough, but imagine when potential allies, who should have known better, used more "liberal" ways of commenting on African American labor situations, criminology, or lynchings.

Note, for example, Ray Stannard Baker's usage of dehumanizing stereotypes implying that African Americans weren't ready to vote, or the ways that this framing placed the primary burden for social change on the shoulders of elite whites, who should have stepped up and enforced laws that were already in the books. As David Squires noted, Baker professed to be against lynch law, and yet in parts of *Following the Color Line* he insisted that there were times when mob violence worked to correct "delays and technicalities of the law" that allowed murderers to be set free.⁷⁹ This was simply one more reiteration of the familiar Judge Lynch lines of populist, vigilante justice.

Writers like Baker argued that segregationist policies should be managed by sympathetic whites who treated African Americans in paternalistic ways, and Baker demeaned or infantilized people of color in his valorization of his own class's responsibilities. In one passage in *Following the Color Line*, Baker suggested that unnecessary violence could be avoided if white leaders set an example of obedience to law for the black "wayward son." How, after all, could societies expect any racial regeneration if the "white man sets an example" of "non-obedience to law, of non-enforcement of law"?⁸⁰

Ray Stannard Baker conjured up a picture of how mass lynchings could be prevented in America by some "strong man" who stepped forward, assumed "responsibility and [became] a momentary despot" in order to subdue the "mob."⁸¹ This ignored the fact that so many supposed "strong men" in Southern communities were the very individuals who led manhunts and condoned lynchings.

Again, one wonders exactly how many Progressives during this period shared Baker's views. If he represented the mainstream of elite Northern public opinion, then readers can understand why so many members of Wells-Barnett's generation could tune her out and treat her as an un-American speaker who cared little for white victims' rights in the South. "The campaign of tireless activism that Wells pursued," averred David Squires, "offered a forceful counterpoint to the consensus between northern liberals and southern reactionaries that regarded mob violence as an issue that states had a right to resolve on their own terms."⁸²

No wonder, as we will note in later chapters, that until very recently, so few seemed to take much interest in the passage of restrictive federal anti-lynching legislation.

Conclusion: The EJI's Strategic Reframing of Ida B. Wells-Barnett's Lynching Archives

Interest in reviving memories of the more radical anti-lynching efforts of the Progressive years catalyzed black feminists like Angela Davis, who worked to make sure that at least some of the labor of the earlier radicals would not be forgotten. In *Women, Race and Class*, Davis wrote about the lingering influence of the "myth of the black rapist," and she credited Wells-Barnett for working to undermine the suasory power of those conventional racial stereotypes. David Squires opined that women like Wells-Barnett and Angela

Davis had contributed to the scholarship that "explained how the cultural logic of lynching placed white businessmen at the top of a social structure that idealized white femininity, maligned black men as savages, and left black women open to sexual abuse without any recourse."[83]

Recuperating the archival work of Ida B. Wells-Barnett has not always been an easy task, in part because contemporary interdisciplinary researchers have relatively few extant copies of her domestic and international speeches and pamphlets. We have her *Southern Horrors*, *The Red Record*, her autobiography, and a few other fragments that can be gathered from newspaper clippings, but we have perhaps lost forever some of her other works.

This failure to preserve some parts of the lynching archives provides just one more indicator of the marginalization, and the resentment, that Wells-Barnett must have faced as an African American woman who battled sexism, racism, and other intersectionalities. As noted above, not all members of her own generation agreed with how she wrote about consensual sex between white women and black men, or about the economic and political inequalities of her age.[84]

As poststructuralists and Foucauldians who are interested in the study of the rhetorical forces of anti-lynching memories and histories, we note that Wells-Barnett also helped coproduce the archival fragments that would be reassembled in later counterhistories and countermemories that ruptured and destabilized segregationist apologetics for "Judge Lynch." She continually inverted binaries, and her generation of radical African Americans gazed back at those whites who took their own children to watch horrific lynching spectacles. As Wells-Barnett explicitly noted in one of her publications, she was not going to accept white claims that the "horror of rape" constituted an "excuse for lawlessless."[85] Wells-Barnett's gendered analyses of the political, economic, cultural, and legal dimensions of systematic racial terrorism added a key dimension that was said to be "missing from many reparations arguments."[86]

Pictures of lynchings that were once circulated by lynching apologists are now reframed for pedagogical purposes as stories about Ida B. Wells-Barnett's radical civil rights activism and have been recontextualized to teach millions of US schoolchildren about the need to become involved in activist work. Writers like Lawrie Balfour could fairly note that Wells-Barnett was now remembered for her "commitment to truth-telling."[87] Others rediscovered her work so that they could talk about labor disputes, the limits of state redress, citizens' rights, or discrimination against immigrants.[88]

Readers can now understand why Wells-Barnett's work has been showcased so prominently in Montgomery's Legacy Museum.[89] She, and her supporters and allies, should be credited for coproducing rhetorics of social agitation that served as a "prolegomenon to militant civil rights activism."[90]

Some have argued that Wells-Barnett's critiques of the justifications for violence, which countered the commonly accepted notion at the time that violent episodes were an "exception" to the law, foreshadowed the work of Giorgio Agamben when he wrote about "bare life," and the sovereign decisionism that went into determining when "the law" would provide the ruling baselines and when deciders got to make exceptions to those normative regulations.[91]

While members of earlier generations fell prey to cultural amnesia when they "forgot" about Ida B. Wells-Barnett's radical activism, this would not be the case when twenty-first-century social agents applauded Bryan Stevenson's legal work and his Montgomery advocacy efforts. Lori Roessner took comfort from the fact that the *New York Times* decided to finally print an "overlooked" obituary of Wells-Barnett and that the EJI's Montgomery sites of memory paid her tributes that offered America "hope for truth to combat cultural amnesia and future reconciliation."[92] DeNeen L. Brown, writing for the *Washington Post*, noted that the opening of the new Legacy Museum involved the honoring of the "fearless" Wells-Barnett.[93]

Patricia Williams, one of the founders of the critical race movement in US law schools, wrote an article for the *Nation* in which she argued that the National Memorial for Peace and Justice was "extraordinary."[94] Williams opined that it was in "recognition" of Wells-Barnett's "determined advocacy" that the "newly opened National Memorial for Peace and Justice in Montgomery, Alabama, has dedicated a space to her."[95]

All of the varied ideological fragments and rhetorical tropes that Ida B. Wells-Barnett's generation produced over a forty-year time span aided members of later generations, who readily understood why she once wrote about the need to have a "Winchester" by one's side.

CHAPTER 3

"By Parties Unknown"

The Successes and Failures of Anti-Lynching Campaigns before World War II

IN THE PREVIOUS CHAPTER, WE NOTED HOW IDA B. WELLS-BARNETT AND OTHER anti-lynching activists collected their own statistics on "Southern Horrors," and yet it took time before these arguments gained traction and resonated with American audiences in various regions of the country. The EJI and the Legacy Museum later applauded and spotlighted Wells-Barnett's efforts, and they extended her arguments as they wrote about how the alleged rape of women by those accused of lynching served as only one of many rationales for the perpetration of racial terrorism.[1]

As we show in this chapter, all chroniclers of US lynching horrors, including the EJI, have inherited many competing and multidirectional racialized histories, historiographies, and public memories of lynching pasts, and there are many plausible explanations for why so many American generations may have "forgotten" lynching legacies. We will argue that the very defining, recording, and chronicling of lynchings were rhetorical acts that preoccupied many Americans between 1900 and 1945.

These definitional and chronicling acts, in turn, impacted how members of several American generations responded to calls for the passage of state or federal anti-lynching legislation. As Christopher Waldrep noted in 2000, representatives of these anti-lynching organizations during the interwar years were "sniping at each other over whether particular murders" of people of color "should be classed as lynchings or not."[2]

In this portion of our book, we extend many of Waldrep's arguments, and we claim that there were times when anti-lynching organizations had a vested interest in utilizing expansive, or restrictive, definitions of lynchings, depending on social agents' ideological orientation or their organization's needs. For example, there were times when Jessie Daniel Ames and the

Association of Southern Women for the Prevention of Lynching (ASWPL) touted the efficacy of their own campaigns by advocating for the use of restrictive definitions of lynchings. As Ashraf H. A. Rushdy argued in *The End of American Lynching*, this made it easier for ASWPL members to show reporters that the South was gradually "ending" lynching practices, and that the ASWPL had played a major role in that achievement.[3]

Other subsections of this chapter will highlight how organizations like the NAACP—which relied on lynching campaigns and the dissemination of horrific visualities to attract donors—finally decided to advocate for expansive definitions of lynching, which helped rationalize more NAACP interventionism in Southern affairs.[4] We will also show how the *Chicago Tribune*, the Tuskegee Institute, and the International Labor Defense (ILD) among other organizations circulated their own definitions of lynching, using their own preferred definitions when collecting lynching statistics.

As each of these organizations tried to tell the American public about the "parties unknown"—a "phrase commonly used when lynchers, however well-known, were unidentified and unpunished"[5]—they produced massive amounts of raw data and statistical information that appeared in many different, constitutively created, lynching archives. Instead of bequeathing to posterity a single, rational, mammoth, modernistic, comprehensive lynching archive, previous generations left us many complementary and contradictory lynching narratives filled with residual traces of how they wanted future generations to think about lynching pasts.

It mattered a great deal how collectors of lynching statistics conceptualized murders, near-lynchings, rioting, and the number of lynching perpetrators that needed to be present in order for a hanging or death to qualify as a lynching. In the "long struggle against racial violence," explained Christopher Waldrep, the "word *lynching* became an important battleground between rival reform efforts" (emphasis in the original).[6] In 2019, Stewart Tolnay and E. M. Beck were sure that "accurate" and "true" studies of "racialized terrorism" had to take into account "three elements" for "quantum" studies of these lynchings: (1) those cases in which initiated lynchings were completed; (2) the times when lynchings were threatened but not carried out; and (3) instances when "nonlethal violence was directed at Southern blacks."[7]

Americans living during the first four decades of the twentieth century seemed to be genuinely torn when they read the circulated statistics that had been collected by the Records Office of the Tuskegee Institute showing that some 4,732 individuals had been lynched altogether, including whites.[8]

In spite of the circulation of these statistics, it is possible that many US politicians living during the first four decades of the twentieth century—and their constituents—failed to support state or federal anti-lynching measures because they realized that if federal authorities were provided with the legal tools to go after *all* lynchers, *this might lead to the jailing of thousands of supposedly law-abiding citizens.*

The interwar American failures to pass federal lynching legislation did not escape the attention of Bryan Stevenson, the EJI, the Legacy Museum, and their supporters. In May 2018, Professor Nina Silber visited the National Memorial for Peace and Justice and concluded that the EJI was setting out "to document this little-known" history of "racial terror lynchings."[9] The title of Silber's essay in the *Washington Post* implied that the new monument in Montgomery was going provide a corrective revisionist "history" that would help with the "unraveling" of "historical lies."

Some of the lies that Silber critiqued for millions of *Washington Post* readers had to do with the traditional stories that circulated during the heated legislative debates on lynching during the interwar years. The memorial, she averred, "exposes how both Southern and Northern politicians used nostalgia and false history to preserve the system of white supremacy that stood at the core of their political power."[10] She elaborated by noting that nowhere was this clearer than the "fight over the anti-lynching laws," and she observed how, during the 1930s debates over the Costigan-Wagner bill (discussed below), "Senate opponents explained their hostility by reminding listeners of the purported horrors of Reconstruction."[11]

We continue our genealogical critiques in this chapter with a rhetorical history of some federal anti-lynching efforts before 1935.

Federal Anti-Lynching Efforts before 1935

In previous chapters, we considered how Ida B. Wells-Barnett and many other observers noted some of the economic, political, and cultural factors that impacted the rising numbers of lynchings during the Progressive years, and media framings of these lynchings clearly played a role in how society debated them. "Southern newspaper editors," noted Waldrep, "generally defined lynching as a community's proper response to heinous crimes against neighborhood values."[12] Lynching, in other words, could be characterized as a local policing matter that had nothing to do with either American institutional racism or potential violations of constitutional rights.

The power of Southern editors before World War II often created major difficulties for Progressive reformers and interwar anti-lynchers, and those who were opposed to lynchings had to come up with their own rhetorical arsenals that might aid them as they talked to decision-makers in the halls of Congress and other forums.[13]

Since at least the post-Reconstruction years, there had been those who "permanently associated lynching studies with social science positivism," and this explains why writers like Ida B. Wells-Barnett could use large aggregates of statistical information to blame "entire white communities for lynchings."[14] As noted in chapter 2, her *Red Record* provided vital, empirical ammunition to her supporters, who, thus armed with collections of lynching statistics, no longer had to rely exclusively on the emotional appeal that came from detailed case studies of single, but horrific, lynching incidents.

Those who conducted this type of aggregational statistical research were perhaps aware that these collections were important symbolic devices for people who battled lynching apologists. By 1905, sociologist James Elbert Cutler, in his *Lynch-Law* investigations, was sure that there was sociological "evidence that there is usually more or less public approval, or supposed favorable public sentiment, behind a lynching."[15] "Popular justification," Cutler went on to explain, "is the *sine qua non* of lynching," and he was convinced that populist justification distinguished particular lynching acts from legally recognizable assassinations, insurrections, and murders.[16]

In theory, if sociologists like Cutler could explain how lynching was a separate crime that had its own identifiable characteristics, then other sociologists who were properly identifying lynchings were helping anti-lynchers put together prima facie cases for anti-lynching legislation. Years later, the NAACP's Walter White, following the lead of writers like Wells-Barnett and Cutler, in his book *Rope and Faggot* argued that between 1890 and 1900 more than 1,600 individuals had been lynched.[17]

Sociological statistics on lynchings could therefore be used as swords or shields, depending on one's views on lynching definitions, the causes of lynchings, and the solutions to these problems. In Alabama, for example, delegates to a state constitutional convention in 1901 blamed lynching on the "moral sentiment of the community," and delegates assumed that when societal sentiments evolved, then communities would turn against lynching, and "the thing practically ceases."[18] Societies would change—without the help of federal governmentalities—in much the same way that scientific paradigms changed when scientists engaged in the self-correcting process of scientific inquiry.

Depending on their motives and methodologies, those who collecting lynching statistics could use broad or narrow definitions of lynchings. Monroe N. Work, a minister and 1898 graduate of Chicago Theological Seminary, obtained two degrees in sociology. He "came out of the sociological tradition launched by Wells and endorsed by Cutler," and he "sought an objective, empirical definition of lynching."[19] For many years, Work complained that some anti-lynchers were going too far when they sought to include in their compilation of lynching statistics cases in which the police had killed blacks in their jail cells, a single individual had tortured an African American, or a labor dispute had led to an exchange of gunfire.

From a poststructuralist vantage point, these competing definitions of lynching were part of larger discourse/knowledge/power formations. How one defined lynching, and how one chose one's sociological, theological, anthropological, or political science evidence on lynchings, influenced one's contestable, contingent rhetorical framings of lynching. Argumentative clusters of statistical materials on lynchings that were taken from strategically selected archives could be adopted by people who either expanded, or contracted, the number of reported lynching victims.

The *Chicago Tribune* was one newspaper that kept tallies of those who were lynched, and the Tuskegee Institute, the ASWPL, the NAACP, and the ILD all began keeping records that tracked the numbers of lynchings, as well as the "social" features of lynching.

What inevitably happened during the Progressive Era and the interwar years is that these various organizations started to quarrel with each other about lynching definitions, the accuracy of particular statistical methods, and the question of whether it was local opinion or national sentiment that should determine success or failure in measuring changing attitudes toward lynching. In 1919, for instance, the NAACP came out with a tally of lynchings for that year that differed from Monroe Work's tally, and there were disagreements about whether the murders of Elihu, Louis, Gibson, and Leroy Johnson near Elaine, Arkansas, should be recorded as "lynchings" or "murders." Work, who believed that local newspaper designations should be dispositive in these definitional debates, finally convinced the NAACP that these Johnson deaths should be categorized as lynchings.[20]

On many other occasions during the 1920s and 1930s, the NAACP defined lynchings in a broad, inclusive manner, while Tuskegee's Monroe Work argued for narrower definitions.

At first glance, these definitional or typological disputes may seem to involve arcane, scholarly, or legalistic disputation that would have no political import, but this was not the case. During the 1870s and 1880s, the US Supreme Court had ruled in several judicial cases that the federal government could only interfere when wrongs may have been committed by "states" and not by individuals.[21] This is part of the reason for people's focus on documenting the "social" dimensions of lynching. The more that lynching could be configured as a rare, individual problem and not a "social" problem, the less state or federal legislators had any reason to pass contentious anti-lynching legislation.

The "social" in Social Darwinian thinking was there for a reason, and in order for organizations like the NAACP to make any headway in congressional or state corridors, they had to be able to argue in front of American lawyers and judges who were not predisposed to believe that lynching was a matter that involved any *communal* or *"societal"* failure to treat citizens equally.[22] After all, wasn't there plenty of evidence that educated progressives in the South also despised lynching, and wasn't this evidence of changing societal views having an impact on lynching statistics?

These ideological problems for anti-lynchers were exacerbated when NAACP members disagreed among themselves about how best to define or prevent lynching, and it took time before more radical members of this organization were able to persuade their more moderate colleagues that effective lobbying for anti-lynching required the use of explanatory frames that would appeal to broader, national constituencies. In 1919, the NAACP published one of their most influential archival chroniclings of lynching—*Thirty Years of Lynching in the United States, 1889–1918*.[23]

As we reviewed many of the texts and arguments that circulated in academic circles, we could not help noting how this particular 1919 NAACP publication was cited over and over again. *Thirty Years of Lynching* helped produce the discursive template, and the antecedent genres, that would be used by many of those who attended anti-lynching meetings, conferences, picket lines, marches, and courtroom proceedings before World War II.

NAACP leaders like James Weldon Johnson and Walter Francis White spent years publicizing the efforts of the NAACP, and when they approached empowered legislators they carried with them the statistical information from the *Thirty Years of Lynching* report as they worked to convince decision-makers that drastic measures had to be taken.

The NAACP would join Ida B. Wells-Barnett and many others who realized that the Great Depression would only place more hurdles in the path of those who fought the ravages of Jim Crow segregation. *Thirty Years of Lynching* mentioned how "being disrespectful," "insulting women," "self-defense," and even "window peeping" could be used as illogical rationales for the lynching of blacks.[24] The NAACP was thus following the lead of African American women who had on many occasions pointed out the inventive ways that lynching apologists rationalized so many lynching spectacles.

This expansion or contraction of definitions of lynching had to be done while combating pernicious ideological representations. Martha Solomon

Watson noted how anti-lynchers had to come up with inventive ways of countering "the mythology that incorporated images of African American men as violent sexual predators," because this was the "greatest challenge" that they faced.[25] As Ersula Ore observed, tropes of black men as violent sexual predators are centered on the idea that white women are the "embodiment of the nation" who must be protected by white men. "Metonymically constructing white women as America's national body," Ore wrote, "figured white men as the ultimate citizen-savior while at the same time casting lynching as a performance of virtuous citizenship."[26]

No doubt the revival of the Ku Klux Klan after World War I took advantage of this virtuous citizenship performativity. In 1915, William J. Simmons helped oversee the reorganization of the KKK. Inspired by D. W. Griffith's cinematic *The Birth of a Nation*, this Atlanta native traveled to Stone Mountain, Georgia, with fifteen other men (in a rented bus) so that they could light a massive wooden cross and proclaim the rebirth of the Knights of the Ku Klux Klan.[27] Vilified by some and admired by others, members of this revived KKK were said to have flogged Mexicans, organized the lynching of blacks, terrified "prostitutes, bullied Jews, and lashed young women found riding in cars with men."[28] All of this, for sociologists, lawyers, and others interested in the "social," provided much-needed empirical evidence that lynching violence was not an individuated problem.

Those who fought for anti-lynching legislation in the decades before World War II often cited the work of the KKK, but Joshua Rothman has more recently argued that this revival of the Klan did not resonate with most Americans. "A century ago," Rothman averred, "millions of Americans banded together in defense of white, Christian America and traditional morality," and "most of their compatriots turned a blind eye to the Ku Klux Klan."[29]

Yet if this was the case, then why didn't the majority of Americans whom Rothman is referencing repudiate the racial, white supremacist arguments used by the KKK, and why didn't mainstream Americans immediately pass state or federal anti-lynching legislation? If so many Americans were opposed to the white supremacist claims of the KKK, then how did the KKK manage to have members win local, regional, and state elections?

Granted, many Americans did ridicule some KKK activities, but this did not prevent KKK members from arguing that they represented true "Americanism." On August 8, 1925, more than fifty thousand KKK members paraded down the streets of Washington, DC, and many of their leaders were wearing satin robes. These marchers agreed to walk unmasked, because government officials had insisted that they would only sanction the parade if participants refrained from wearing their traditional masks.[30]

Members of the KKK during the interwar years were only one facet of the continuing lynchings and interracial violence. Many African Americans could not help noting the contradiction between the democratic rhetoric of "Americanism" that was used to recruit soldiers to fight against the imperialism of the German kaiser during the Great War, and the treatment of those same soldiers when they returned home. As William Pinar noted in 2001, "'the law' did not even try to keep" whites from lynching blacks, and during "1917 and 1918, while 300,000 black soldiers served their country, a tenth of them in Europe, lynch mobs murdered over 100 African Americans at home."[31] The *Chicago Defender*, in commentary typical of the nation's black presses at the time, wondered: "With tens of thousands of our race fighting for civilization in France under the American flag, how much longer are the American people going to tolerate lynching?"[32]

Given the protean nature of the Americanization "Anglo-Saxon," and the eugenic rhetorics that were circulating in so many circles during this time, readers can understand why returning black soldiers, and their families back home, were not going to be treated as equals. Winfield Collins, a Southern apologist for segregation, noted that as "the world is to be made safe for democracy, so ought the South to be made safe for white women."[33] James Harmon Chadbourn, in a survey of 1920s state legislation, noted that "lynching is often interpreted as a protest against the inefficiency of courts as agencies for the punishment of crime."[34]

Newspapers during these interwar years carried numerous stories about real or imagined "race riots," but it was the notorious "Red Summer" of 1919 that put on full display an array of various material and symbolic factors that contributed to the rise of recorded lynchings. In places like Chicago and Washington, DC, African Americans fought back when they felt threatened,[35] and this violence in turn was configured by whites in ways that allegedly showed the immaturity of the "colored" race.

Given the scope of this violence, why did it take so long for members of the NAACP to begin filing anti-lynching legislation? George Rable provided an early assessment of these efforts when he noted that, although the NAACP had spent years preparing drafts of anti-lynching legislation, it "had encountered difficulty mustering support in Congress."[36]

Some elements of this needed support finally arrived in 1918, when Republican representatives Leonidas Dyer of Missouri and Merrill Moores of Indiana were convinced by members of the NAACP that lynching was a "social" problem that warranted federal legislative efforts. What became known as the Dyer Anti-Lynching Bill had provisions that allowed for federal intervention when there was evidence that state officials were not providing all citizens in a given state with their "equal" rights to be protected.[37]

The Dyer bill would be a lightning rod for heated disputation for at least five years. Many of the bill's provisions seemed to be specifically targeting the very groups that many lawyers and prosecutors were hesitant to go after. The bill also contained provisions that provided indemnities to the families and heirs of lynching victims.[38] Today, these might be called reparations for historical racial terrorist practices.

A critical, close textual analysis of some of the specific provisions of the Dyer bill, and critiques of the responses to that legislative measure, help critical researchers and readers gain an appreciation of why it became such a contentious text. Defining a "mob" as "five or more persons acting in concert for the purpose of depriving any person of his life without authority of the law as a punishment for or to prevent the commission of some actual or supposed public offense," the bill's authors made participation in any lynching a felony that was punishable by a minimum five-year prison sentence.[39]

In many ways, the requirement that entire communities had to "pay for murders committed by crowds meshed with the definition of lynching prevailing at the beginning of the twentieth century: murder by community."[40] This had huge political and social implications, because it meant that police officers, judges, local sheriffs, and community elites could all be tried if they participated in, or condoned, some of these lynching practices.

No specific region was mentioned in the Dyer bill, but that did not prevent Southern Democrats and others from viewing it as an attack specifically targeting Southern lynching behavior. Even though the bill received the endorsement of President Warren G. Harding, it was a measure that was so radical that even the NAACP had a difficult time keeping together coalitions in the House of Representatives who would support it.

Today, many of those who visit Montgomery's Legacy Museum or read materials on the Equal Justice Initiative's web pages understand perfectly well why the Fourteenth Amendment serves as some of the legal underpinning for the Dyer Anti-Lynching Bill, but in the decades before the 1920s members of Congress and jurists in courts had gutted some of the rhetorical power of those post–Civil War amendments. As noted in the previous chapter, conservative American legislators and members of the judiciary had interpreted the amendments narrowly in racial civil rights cases but expansively in cases that involved the alleged "rights" of corporations and businesses engaged in interstate commerce.[41]

Inverting some of the arguments of the African American opponents of lynching, some Southern whites and their allies in Congress tried to argue that federal anti-lynching bills victimized Southerners. Those who opposed the Dyer bill, for example, argued that if this measure passed it would turn the states into "vassals" of the federal government. Citing the *Slaughter-House Cases* of the 1870s and other court decisions that had interpreted the Fourteenth Amendment as a protector of all Americans' civil "liberties" and as a bulwark against federal interference, Southern whites argued that the Dyer anti-lynching measure could not be used to check "individual" behavior.[42] This set the stage for those who argued that these types of bills were unconstitutional because they provided too many "police powers" for federal authorities, who should not be interfering with local state powers and individual rights.

Again, at first glance this legalese sounds apolitical and fairly tame, but it was often followed up with intersectional commentary and dehumanizing observations that brought to the surface many latent racialized, gendered, class-oriented, and nationalist ways of framing these lynching debates. It is telling that Finis Garrett of Tennessee argued that the Dyer Anti-Lynching Bill would "encourage rape." Other Southerners conjured up memories of the alleged horrors of what happened when Saint-Domingue, and later Jamaica, were emancipated, and congressional audiences had to listen to quoted materials from newspapers that mentioned savage assaults by blacks on white women.[43] Huge inferential leaps made from accounts of Caribbean slave revolts and rebellions provided cautionary tales for those who might listen to the siren calls of African American anti-lynchers.

Postcolonial scholars would have a field day decoding or decolonizing some of the linkages made by Southern legislators who connected Caribbean slave rebellions with Southern anxieties, but for our purposes, we agree with those who noted that the speeches made by Southern congressional leaders on the "southern social order of the twentieth century bore striking similarity to" earlier representations of the "antebellum South."[44]

Throughout the 1920s and the 1930s, a familiar legislative dynamic would take place in which members of the House of Representatives would support an anti-lynching measure that would then be defeated during Senate debates. For example, in 1922, the Dyer bill passed the House by a vote of 231 to 119, but it had trouble getting past the persuasive efforts of Democratic Southern senators.

Anti-lynchers tried not to be disheartened by these setbacks. James Weldon Johnson argued that even though the Dyer Anti-Lynching Bill did not become law, the 1920s nevertheless witnessed a drastic decline in the number of lynchings. He opined that activist efforts had "served to awaken the people of the Southern States to the necessity of taking steps themselves to wipe out the crime."[45]

Some, like Walter White, tried to "fetch good out of evil" after the defeat of the Dyer bill by treating this as an ongoing process or a structural issue rather than a single event.[46] In his own autobiography, White opened up about his personal reactions to some of the violence that he had witnessed over the years, and part of this text explained to readers how he became an empirical investigator who once "passed" as white so that he could mingle with white crowds and investigate actual lynching cultures.[47]

Walter White's autobiography and other books describe how White began working for the NAACP after he learned about the Tennessee lynching of Jim McIlherron, a black sharecropper who was "slowly burned to death by a mob for defending himself from a beating by his employer."[48] During his investigation, White learned that McIlherron had been lynched because "anytime a nigger hits a white man, he's gotta be handled or else all the niggers will get out of hand."[49]

In order to combat this type of racist rhetoric, the NAACP, by 1926 or 1927, started to "dramatically loosen its definition" of lynching so that the organization would no longer need to argue that "community support" was the "key to distinguishing lynching from murder" of people of color.[50] Now they would argue that lynchings could be carried out *either by individuals or by social groups*. In 1927, NAACP investigators puzzled their colleagues at the Tuskegee Institute when they changed some of their metrics by characterizing the killing of a prisoner in a Los Angeles jail as a lynching, as well as the killings in Tennessee and North Carolina of blacks during manhunts.[51]

NAACP members felt even more pressure to broaden their definitions when organizations like the Associated Negro Press argued that a lynching should be defined as "any death to an individual or individuals inflicted by two or more privately organized citizens, who impose such violence with correctional intent."[52] A writer for the Baltimore *Afro-American* provided self-serving reasons for this type of broadening when he opined: "Inasmuch as this mob of white outlaws is organized for the purpose of murdering all Negro firemen on Southern railroads, why shouldn't it be termed a lynching?"[53]

One of the contributions that black laborers, Communists, and others made to this "war of words" was the notion that declining numbers of reported lynchings by newspapers—especially in the South—may have only meant that white lynchers were becoming more *secretive* in how they dispensed vigilante justice.[54] In 1935, the Sharecroppers' Union reported on how whites in Alabama had covertly lynched Joe Spinner Johnson; the union accused the NAACP of deliberately downplaying some of this violence by white ruling classes as they conspired to deceive the "Negro Masses."[55]

Is it possible that the ideological drift through various generations of radical claims like this—about hidden lynchings—became a part of the reservoir of archival epistemes that were available for EJI arguers who wanted to later write and talk about the "evolving" nature of lynching terrors?

The Activist Work of the Association of Southern Women for the Prevention of Lynching and the Attempted Narrowing of Lynching Definitions

One of the organizations that was bothered by this broadening of definitions of lynching was the ASWPL, which was led by Jessie Daniel Ames. The ASWPL was formed in 1931 when women in church groups and women's clubs came together because they believed that they could no longer stand by and watch the perpetration of these lynching horrors. For some ten years, Ames served as the executive director of the ASWPL, and many in the South respected how this Texan fought for state anti-lynching legislation. Ames realized that the ASWPL was going to encounter all sorts of hurdles, in part because lynching, unlike murder, was a crime in which the guilt was so widespread.[56]

Ames worked as both a suffragist as well as a civil rights activist, and from her base in Texas she tried to rally white women across the South so that they could see how lynchings destroyed not only black communities but white communities as well.[57] While Kimberly Powell has argued that the ASWPL successfully brought an end to lynching in the South,[58] we contend that this either takes at face value the claims that Ames and her supporters made, or presents the hagiographic treatment of this type of ASWPL work that later appeared in "colorblind" genealogies of these efforts.

As noted above, the ASWPL had a vested interest in trying to document fewer and fewer lynchings in the South as they defended the need for state, but not federal, anti-lynching legislation. Moreover, as Tessa Brown observed in 2018, some of the discourse that praises ASWPL efforts obscures "how Black women were used as tokens and as source material for the group."[59] It is also possible that the ASWPL's attempts to focus on the need for Southern, state reform of lynching laws hindered the efforts of the NAACP and other groups who were asking for federal anti-lynching legislation.

Jessie Daniel Ames, like many other anti-lynchers, stayed in contact with potential allies, but that did not mean that these anti-lynchers saw eye to eye when it came to the ways that victims, perpetrators, and bystanders in lynching contexts were characterized. For example, when the NAACP counted as a lynching the burning of an African American who had died *before* a mob burned him, Ames was bothered by the way the act was configured. "There is nothing in the provision" of the "federal anti-lynching bill," noted Ames, that would have allowed for the counting of that type of an incident as a lynching.[60] Later on, the ASWPL refused to characterize some violence in Atlanta as "lynching" activities, and this bothered NAACP lawyers like Thurgood Marshall.

However, in many Southern regions the arguments of the ASWPL resonated with those who could not identify with the NAACP's theories and practices. In June 1934, in Charlottesville, one journalist noted how in Virginia the "Council" of Southern Women for the Prevention of Lynching had spent several years circulating literature that was "designed to educate the masses about a brutal custom that has taken 4,751 lives since 1882 in Southern States alone."[61] Charlottesville's *Reflector* argued thus in an article entitled "Lynchers in Congress":

> It has been the opinion of the public for years that the illiterate whites of the South are the blood-thirsty mobsters who had repeatedly disgraced this Republic with this savage method of punishment. But attention should be directed now to Washington and to that other type of mobster who filibusters and uses all sorts of tricks to give his voters the unmolested privilege of burning, shooting and killing at will.[62]

Using metaphoric allusions to images of Depression gangsters, the radical writers for the *Reflector* went after the elite decision-makers in Washington, DC, who had thus far escaped censure in the mainstream press. This was a not-so-veiled reaction to some of the arguments coming from the North that targeted Southern lynching.

We are convinced that the ASWPL is one of many anti-lynching organizations that were responsible for the constitutive crafting of the discourse about the "end" of American lynchings during the late 1930s and early 1940s, and that the referencing of this "end" had strategic consequences.

1930s Attempts to Pass Federal and State Lynching Legislation

Many members of the KKK, Southern Democrats, and other critics of federal anti-lynching legislation had hoped that the defeat of two different versions of the Dyer Anti-Lynching Bill would discourage the ASWPL and the NAACP from carrying on their crusades.

Regardless of which definition anti-lynchers used, many Americans realized that in the 1930s huge audiences across the country still attended lynching spectacles. Two to three thousand people often participated in mass lynchings. Arthur Raper, writing in 1930, estimated that in his study of almost two dozen lynchings the "mobs" collectively totaled about "75,000" members, including men, women, and children. After reviewing these massive numbers, he could not help mentioning that these "so-called onlookers" were morally and legally culpable.[63]

Imagine the difficulties that would attend any legal attempt to prosecute the tens of thousands of participants in the lynching spectacles that Arthur Raper documented. Raper, who represented the Southern Commission on the Study of Lynching, visited some twenty-one lynching sites, and he produced what many critical scholars might call a moderate, progressive tract on lynching reform. While parts of his book *The Tragedy of Lynching* are filled with arguments based on statistical information, other portions touch on the psychological and social facets of lynching.

As noted above, people who have written articles and books on lynching have left us with a variety of competing and multidirectional commentaries on possible causes and solutions to the lynching "problem," and Raper is no exception. He argued that mob lynchings could be eliminated if economic, cultural, educational, and welfare reforms helped improve the lives of "irresponsible population elements."[64] This type of New Deal framing did not single out any individual or any particular small group who might be blamed for leading horrific lynchings. Instead, this materialist approach focused on some of the more macro, institutional, and societal aspects of these problems.

Readers of Raper's book get the textured feeling that he was often seeing a parallel between life during the Great Depression and the labor competition that might have impacted the formation of lynching cultures in the South before the 1930s.

In some ways, Raper's book is an optimistic text in which the author conjured up egalitarian visions of an America that might soon modernize in ways that would cut down on the number of incidences of racial and class violence. In theory, the provision of "great economic opportunities" for both blacks and impoverished whites might help reduce friction and bring racial harmony.

Some of Raper's ideas reflect the views of whites and people of color who were living in an age when many had high hopes that the New Deal would help improve race relations. Many African Americans, including members of the NAACP, were hopeful that the election of Franklin D. Roosevelt in 1932 would finally bring an end to lynching. After all, it seemed axiomatic to some that the efforts of Mary McLeod Bethune, Walter Francis Wright, and other African American campaigners against lynching had helped catapult FDR into office.[65] Wasn't America's new president obligated to reciprocate and show his gratitude by supporting federal anti-lynching legislation?

Some of those who hoped that FDR would join their ranks may have underestimated the political clout of Southern Democrats in the US Senate.

In an intriguing attempt to harness the power of visual images for anti-lynching causes, Walter White and the NAACP in early 1935 put together a sophisticated art exhibit. A year earlier, White explained in a letter to Julius Block that he was planning to find a major New York City gallery that would allow dozens of artists to present "paintings, cartoons, drawings, etchings, and sculptures dealing with the subject of lynching."[66] The exhibit would be called "An Art Commentary on Lynching." White characterized this as an "indirect approach" to the topic of lynching in which "the hand of the N.A.A.C.P. will not be evidence."[67]

One satirical drawing in the exhibit, Richard Marsh's *This Is Her First Lynching*, showed a frightened, young, and "fascinated girl of about 8 hoisted up by her mother above the heads of the mob to get a better view of the gala proceedings."[68] Isamu Noguchi's Monel Metal contribution, *Death (Lynched Figure)*, described as a "gnarled chromium victim" that was "moving under the wind-swayed rope," presented such a horrific image that if there was "anything to make a white man feel squirmy about his color," this was it.[69] Winston Burdett of the Brooklyn *Daily Eagle* was one of many who reviewed these and other artworks in White's exhibit, and this was his overall assessment:

> It includes sentimental glorifications of the martyred Negro, symbolic analogies between the Negro and Christ, scenes of lust-ridden mobs at lynching parties and a number of cartoons. The pictures are particularly good when they satirize less the act of lynching than the state of mind which makes it possible.[70]

The New York City press as well as national opinion were divided on whether White's art exhibit would help the cause of the NAACP and the other anti-lynchers, but many were convinced that it was a worthwhile effort.

In the next section, we critique what happened in places like Washington, DC, when American legislators were faced with the next group of federal anti-lynching proposals.

Elite and Public Responses to the 1935 and 1936 Attempts to Pass Costigan-Wagner Congressional Legislation

Many of the rhetorical histories and genealogies about lynching that have been produced by traditional historians, critical race theorists, and other academics identify the Costigan-Wagner bill as coming closest to becoming America's first official federal anti-lynching legislation before 2018. Robert F. Wagner and Edward Costigan sought to draft legislation that was as radical as some of the other New Deal initiatives that had been proposed by those who were seeking to overcome conservative intransigence. Specifically, Wagner and Costigan proposed congressional legislation that would have allowed for the prosecution of any law enforcement officers who had learned about a lynching attempt and failed to exercise their responsibility to stop it.[71]

While many supporters of the Costigan-Wagner bill thought that this was exactly the type of remedial measure that was needed to combat the magnitude of lynching horrors, skeptics on the other hand articulated a variety of legal, political, and social reasons why the bill was a well-intentioned but misguided effort.

As an example of the varied arguments that were used to avoid joining supporters of the Costigan-Wagner bill, note the response of Maryland senator Millard Evelyn Tydings. Thurgood Marshall, then the solicitor general, urged Tydings to support the bill. Marshall, playing on the senator's identity as a "champion of fair play and justice," hoped to convince the senator that he needed to act, but Tydings had other ideas. Tydings explained to Marshall that he had a number of legal objections to the Costigan-Wagner bill, including the fact that the proposed legislation interfered with "states' rights."[72]

Marshall responded to Tydings's claim in a way that underscored how talk of "states' rights" could be interpreted as a coded way of avoiding the criminalization of an activity that might penalize more than a few American police officers, judges, and others who were a part of institutional lynching efforts. Marshall sent this missive to Tydings:

This bill does not deprive the states of a single right which they have now. When the officers of the state either act on behalf of the mob or fail to use reasonable means to prevent them from acting, as was done in the lynching of Claude Neal in Florida, when daily newspapers told of the proposed outrage and invited all to attend, and when the lynching was over, the lawless element with the sanction of officials of the state continued to spew their venomous wrath upon innocent, law abiding tax-paying Negro citizens.... How in the name of justice and decency can anyone talk of protecting the rights of such a state when it has forfeited all rights to be classed as a state because of open treason and rebellion?[73]

All types of competing versions of criminal and constitutional arguments could be used in these anti-lynching debates to talk about state adherence to or violations of federal constitutional principles or laws.

Marshall was advancing an incredibly radical idea—that entire *states*, like Florida, could be accused of committing treason and rebellion if state residents continued to carry out systematic lynchings, which were in contravention of the letter and spirit behind the passage of post–Civil War legislation. Marshall wanted to highlight the innocence of the disempowered, tax-paying African Americans who approached Florida state officials who were doing little to protect them in the wake of the lynching of Claude Neal, a farmhand who was murdered by a mob near Greenwood, Florida, on October 26, 1934.

Lack of sufficient congressional support was bad enough, but what were anti-lynching activists supposed to do when the nation's president would not join them? Many African American activists, members of the NAACP, and other supporters of federal anti-lynching legislation were shocked to find that political considerations impacted FDR's refusal to speak out against lynchings.

Did FDR sense that many of those who carried out lynchings, or were bystanders at these lynchings, were members of the classes who helped put him in office?

Many conventional writers on lynching histories try to compensate for FDR's noninterventionism by focusing on the social agency of Eleanor Roosevelt. In the wake of the mass media coverage of the Claude Neal lynching in 1934, Eleanor Roosevelt informed Walter White that her husband hoped "very much to get the Costigan-Wagner Bill passed in the coming session."[74] She regretted the unwillingness of the Justice Department to acknowledge that the transportation of some lynching victims from one state to another might justify the use of federal authority to prevent these types of lynchings.[75] In spite of her best efforts, many African Americans felt as if the Roosevelts had abandoned them.

By the mid-1930s, many Southerners in Congress were unwilling to recycle the same apologetic arguments for lynchings that had been used during the post-Reconstruction years and during the earlier Dyer bill debates. Embarrassed by the very subject, some tried to argue that lynching was a national problem and that it was unfair to single out the South for particular attention. For example, a few Southerners in Congress mentioned that Senator Wagner came from New York City, which had many gang murders, and they contrasted images of a "cold, impersonal, and violent North" with the "paternalistic paradise" of the South.[76]

Throughout 1935 and 1936, there were renewed calls for anti-lynching legislation, and whenever newspapers publicized the graphic nature of a recorded lynching, the story was then put forth as one more reason why supporters needed to back the passage of the Costigan-Wagner bill. For example, one of the major events that spurred many 1930s anti-lynching discussions was the coverage of the lynching of Rubin Stacy. Investigative journalists learned that six deputies had been escorting Stacy to Dade County Jail in Miami on July 19, 1935, when Stacy was taken away by a white mob and hanged by the side of the home of Marion Jones, a woman who had accused Stacy of frightening her.

Those who lynched Rubin Stacy clearly wanted American audiences to know why he had suffered this fate, but not everyone agreed with their argument. A journalist for the *New York Times* later reported that "subsequent investigations revealed that Stacy, a homeless tenant farmer, had gone to the house to ask for food" and that Jones "became frightened and screamed when she saw Stacy's face."[77]

The recirculation of stories of what happened to Rubin Stacy would not only become a part of the Costigan-Wagner bill debates, but they would also become some of the rhetorical fragments that would be placed in the lynching archives as future generations also referenced this particular incident.

In order to stave off federal interference during these federal anti-lynching debates, many crafty Southern politicians came up with a novel way of handling calls for congressional legislation. Some, instead of denying the need for any improvement in "race relations," put together *their own commissions*, tasked with improvising more local solutions to difficult problems. Southern liberals, for example, helped form the Commission on Interracial Cooperation, whose members then campaigned to convince Southern whites that unnecessary lynchings and other forms of violence hurt everyone, regardless of race. This commission went on to argue that only state and local officials had the ability to eradicate lynching evils.[78]

Those who refused to listen to all of this talk of Southern state reform, who dared hold out hope that the authors of the New Deal were also interested in lynching reform, placed their faith in promoters of the Costigan-Wagner federal anti-lynching bill.

In order to combat the NAACP's stories about Rubin Stacy and other lynching victims, Southern leaders conjured up images of a prostrate South that need not suffer again from the ravages of post–Civil War Reconstruction. Hugo L. Black—before he joined the US Supreme Court—warned his congressional colleagues about a time when federal troops had supposedly occupied private homes.[79] During a 1938 deliberation about one anti-lynching proposal, Senator Ellison "Cotton Ed" Smith from South Carolina recalled a time when "strife and contention" ran "rife during the dark period subsequent to the war known as the period of reconstruction."[80] Senator Smith characterized the Costigan-Wagner bill as an "effort to bring in the very identical same element, reopening the chasm that once divided the Confederate States from the other States for the sole purpose of getting the vote of a certain race."[81] Why did Costigan or Wagner want to divide the ranks of whites in the name of helping that "certain" race?

These 1930s Southern Reconstruction narratives were sometimes linked to calls for more domesticated ways of viewing African American racial issues. For example, Senator John Bankhead of Alabama accused Costigan and Wagner of "consulting sociologists, theorists, economists, highbrows among the colored race and the white race" when the Senate should have been hearing from leaders like Booker T. Washington.[82] Accommodationists like Washington were supposed to provide the models for those in the South and the rest of America who wanted to see incremental social change led by the "white race."

Congressional leaders from the South were not the only social agents who were involved in the constitutive formation of all of these nostalgic narratives that were used to make it appear as if blacks and other supporters of anti-lynching legislation were troublemakers who did not know their American history. Newspapers across the country helped spread the word about the perceptual dangers associated with another federal reconstruction era. A Georgia senator cited a *Washington Post* editorial claiming that lynching only "became a serious problem in the South" when "stupid 'reconstruction' policies" were "foisted upon that section following the Civil War," allowing

"Carpetbaggers" to impose "a reign of terror on the South."[83] Did legislators in the 1930s want to forget Reconstruction lessons and make those same interventionist mistakes?

Note the rhetorical beauty of this strategy. Those who opposed the anti-lynchers must have realized the affective power that came from the circulation of photos and stories about actual lynchings, so they had to come up with equally emotive textual arguments and visualities that dwelled on other imagined horrors. Discussing the Reconstruction years provided a way to discuss racial politics that did not look overtly racist, and it allowed congressional leaders to make it appear as if Southerners were potential victims of traumatizing Northern aggression that came in the form of anti-lynching legislation.

Professor Nina Silber, in her analysis of the demystifying work of the National Memorial for Peace and Justice, explained the coherence and the resonance of the Reconstruction narrative that circulated during these interwar anti-lynching debates:

> The false historical narrative they put forth went something like this: In the years after the Civil War, the federal government, having assumed the bad intentions and rebellious spirit of white Southerners, had come to the aid of "negroes" with disastrous results. The story of vengeful carpetbaggers, working in concert with ignorant and sometimes malicious blacks, squelching the honest efforts of Southern whites to rebuild after the Civil War, was, by the 1930s, one of the most hardened myths about the American past.[84]

Given the racial stereotypes of the times, a Southern politician could produce an enthymeme—a truncated syllogism—that mentioned Carpetbaggers or the Scalawags but did not have to mention black terror. American audiences during the interwar years could fill in the missing part of the argumentative syllogism on their own.

Countless numbers of popular novels, as well popular films, took advantage of this most recent wave of Lost Cause nostalgia and interest in post-Reconstruction mythologies. Those who went to see the movie *Gone with the Wind*, for example, were expected to identify with the plight of characters like Scarlett O'Hara and Ashley Wilkes. "'Whatever sentiment there was in the South for a federal anti-lynching law,' NAACP leader Walter White supposedly said, 'evaporated during the "Gone with the Wind" vogue.'"[85]

Some of the most interesting—if largely forgotten—anti-lynching arguments came from the ranks of those who blamed the NAACP for colluding with the lynchers' supporters. Members of the Communist Party's John Reed Club lashed out at the elitism and moderation of the NAACP. US Communist Party members were convinced that capitalists, liberals, and members of organizations like the NAACP were responsible for promoting ineffective lynching legislation. In one pamphlet, entitled *Lynch Justice at Work*, Communist writers argued that members of white middle classes had joined those across the color line who shared similar capitalistic interests.[86]

Some African Americans, like A. Philip Randolph, used outlets like the *Messenger* to argue that the NAACP was handling racism and economic disparities the wrong way, because black communities that were terrorized by lynching did not need organizations that appealed to "white benefactors in a defensive posture."[87]

The NAACP and other anti-lynchers had to be satisfied with celebrating a few small victories in what looked like a protracted ideological struggle. For example, newspapers between 1932 and 1935 could carry stories of how the Supreme Court had overturned the wrongful conviction of the Scottsboro Boys based on readings of the due process and equal protection clauses of the Fourteenth Amendment.[88]

Some activists were so frustrated by the entrenched, sedimented nature of these racialized discourses that they refused to accept the idea that the NAACP's moderate campaigns were going to have much impact on altering material conditions for blacks living in America. W. E. B. Du Bois—who once supported many NAACP initiatives—grew despondent after years of watching how lynchers in the South made a mockery of justice, even taking their children to see the burning and mutilation of African Americans. All of this radicalized Du Bois, to the point where he averred that the police were a part of the mobs and the "courts are lynchers."[89]

During these turbulent interwar years, a familiar figure returned to the ramparts of those who battled the segregationists. After learning about some Arkansas riots, sixty-year-old Ida B. Wells-Barnett returned to the South. In 1922, Wells-Barnett visited the cells of twelve African Americans who were accused of rioting, and she had them write down their own stories about the numbers of acres of land that they tilled, the cotton and corn that they raised, and their treatment at the hands of jailers in Helena, Arkansas.[90] This effectively weaponized, and turned into lawfare, some of the peonage stories that we referenced in chapters 1 and 2.

Wells-Barnett's militant admirers characterized her absence on the center stages of civil rights activism as thirty years of banishment, and now she was returning so that she could help twelve African Americans who were incarcerated in a penitentiary. Wells-Barnett told the interwar press about a time when thousands of African Americans had fled Arkansas due to white violence, and how there had been a time when she tried to raise money for those who were said to have been terrorized with threats of electrocution and other abusive police behavior.[91] After sending materials to the *Chicago Defender* and asking about what the NAACP was doing about this situation, Wells-Barnett decided to carry out her own investigations.

After investigating the Arkansas prison, Wells-Barnett reported to journalists that she had discovered what amounted to what she called a "terrible indictment of white civilization and Christianity."[92] Arkansas whites had done exactly what they had accused of their black neighbors of doing, namely murdering others and then stealing crops, stock, and household goods.[93] Wells-Barnett argued that after committing these crimes, local whites were able to "put the seal of approval on their deeds by legally executing those twelve men who were found guilty after six minutes' deliberation."[94] Adopting some interwar permutations of her inverting techniques and graphic depicting of racial terror horrors, she did her best to help new victims of segregation as they fought to overcome social, legal, and economic impediments.

Eventually the NAACP, Ida B. Wells-Barnett, several lawyers in Arkansas, and their supporters were able to win the case involving those twelve jailed defendants—called *Moore v. Dempsey*—and these activist allies were ultimately able to obtain freedom for some seventy-nine defendants. Twelve of these defendants had been on death row, and sixty-seven had been serving either life imprisonment sentences or very lengthy prison terms.[95]

We would argue that part of the "truth effects" that helped achieve these successes in Arkansas had everything to do with activists' evolutionary efforts to study "legal" as well as "illegal" lynchings. Wells-Barnett referenced the law's involvement in the case of the Elaine, Arkansas, rioters in 1919, and this would provide some of the discursive prefigurations of what would later be called "legal lynchings," whereby illegal lynching performances were replaced with punitive American laws that were used to persecute of persons of color.

Ida B. Wells-Barnett passed away in 1931, but others continued to recruit crusaders for anti-lynching campaigns. While the NAACP received the support of many members of the "talented tenth," others looked for organizations that they felt represented their own pragmatic needs. Many African Americans, living in places like Harlem or the Chicago suburbs, realized that it had been the efforts of the Communist-led International Labor Defense (ILD) that had gained control of the Scottsboro case, as the ILD battled the NAACP as well.[96]

The Scottsboro Boys, the International Labor Defense, and Radical Interpretations of Segregationist Violence

NAACP members—who viewed themselves as belonging to the premier civil rights organization in the United States—were both embarrassed and surprised when the families and friends of the Scottsboro Boys turned to the International Labor Defense for help. The ILD's approach—which took "the battle against Jim Crow justice into the court of public opinion"—"struck a chord with a population the NAACP had not been able to reach."[97] As one scholar noted, the competition between the NAACP and the Communists was over the "hearts and minds of the black public."[98]

The Communist Party of the United States of America gained the attention of many African Americans when it led the legal defense efforts of those involved in defending the Scottsboro Boys. On March 25, 1931, a group of young hoboes got off a freight train at Stevenson, Alabama, and told local authorities that they had been beaten and thrown off the train by a "bunch of Negroes."[99] When deputies searched the train, they found nine black boys, one white boy, and two young white girls. While they were being loaded onto a truck, one of the white girls allegedly told a deputy sheriff that the two girls had been raped by the nine black youths.

All of the black youngsters who had gotten off that freight train were then taken to nearby Scottsboro, Alabama, and eventually the governor of the state sent in National Guard troops in order to stop any potential lynching. In trials that were marked by arbitrary decisions, contradictory information, and discriminatory practices, eight of the black youths were sentenced to death.[100]

The Scottsboro trials entered the annals of famous American public trials as well as the lynching archives. Some death sentences were commuted to life, and the US Supreme Court overturned the Scottsboro convictions by a vote of 7 to 2. While members of the NAACP used these trials to illustrate the problematics of legal responses to segregationist prejudices, members of the Communist Party treated the Scottsboro trials as an opportunity to highlight how moderate, middle-class activists were not addressing the real causes of lynching "terror." Harry Haywood, for example, summarized the feelings of many when he wrote an essay entitled "The Scottsboro Decision: Victory of Revolutionary Struggle over Reformist Betrayal."[101] Although the eight black youths were not lynched, they spent years languishing in jail, while the Communist Party took credit for rallying the legal forces who helped the working classes fight against the Southern "ruling" class.

This would be one of the few victories for civil rights activists who were still bothered by the lack of any federal anti-lynching legislation, but it wasn't until 1976 that the last of the Scottsboro Boys would be exonerated.

Declaring the "End" of Southern Lynching, 1937–1945

For a few years, Southern politicians congratulated themselves for having twice defeated the Costigan-Wagner anti-lynching bill, but it soon became apparent that they may have been trapped by some of their own rhetoric. Southern Democrats had prevented federal interventionism by making many, many promises, and they had gained allies when they argued that states would be the governmentalities that would soon pass anti-lynching legislation. When state reform stalled in 1937, "several leading newspapers blamed state inaction for making federal intervention necessary."[102]

Even before the "end" of Southern and national lynching was declared, efforts were made to make it appear as if the interwar and World War II–era American public had progressed to the point where they had no interest in following the lead of the KKK. Much was made of two Gallup polls that showed that, in the South, a majority of citizens favored making lynching a federal crime, but this apparent shift in public opinion did not lead to any major, vernacular, proactive efforts to end these lynching horrors.[103] Some commentators, like George Rable, were convinced that although "demagogic spellbinders no longer encouraged racial vigilantism," there were still "political" barriers that stood in the way of passage of federal anti-lynching legislation.[104] President Roosevelt still feared that these lynching debates might derail his New Deal legislative efforts.

By the late 1930s and early 1940s, as American audiences witnessed the rise of the Nazis, they were still not sure what to do about anti-lynching legislation. James Harmon Chadbourn's studies of the enforcement of lynching laws found that there were already state laws on the books that punished participation in mob violence, fined counties where lynchings took place, and allowed for the firing of law enforcement officers who neglected their duties or permitted the use of state militia where necessary. However, there was only sporadic enforcement of these laws that were already on the books.[105]

What explains this reticence to openly support the NAACP's anti-lynching efforts? The supposed "end" of attempts to pass federal anti-lynching measures—which many have claimed happened near the beginning of World War II—may have been influenced by the fact that the NAACP was receiving so little support from those who were supposed to be helping eliminate formal and informal structures of racial discrimination. Josephus Daniels, for example, was a journalist who opposed lynchings, but at the same time he "inadvertently promoted the practice by reporting black criminality."[106]

Before the days when those who believed in "colorblind" justice celebrated the legal victories of Thurgood Marshall and other members of the NAACP in cases like *Brown v. Board of Education*, it was the lynching campaigns that enhanced the NAACP's reputation. Robert Zangrando, writing in 1980, opined that "lynching became the wedge by which the NAACP insinuated itself into the public conscience, developed contacts within governmental circles, established credibility among philanthropists, and opened lines of communication with other liberal-reformist groups that eventually joined it in a mid-century, civil rights coalition of unprecedented proportions."[107]

Yet, if this was the case, then why were these civil rights coalitions unable—after more than half a century of activism—to pass federal anti-lynching legislation? Why wasn't this "coalition of unprecedented proportions" capable of forcing congressional leaders to pass these controversial bills?

As we noted in previous chapters, the EJI's position assumed that lynching "evolved" instead of ended, and that illicit lynchings were replaced with other means of social control, involving everything from the redefinition of "legal" lynching to the promotion of capital punishment and other ways of preserving white superiority.

Were they wrong?

If we move away from modernist conceptualizations of "truth" that assume the existence of one lynching "history," then it becomes easier for us to see some of the myriad rhetorical constraints that were placed in the path of anti-lynchers between 1900 and 1940. We can see how Southern Democrats and others opposed to federal interventionism had their own strategic ways of responding to the collection of statistics by the *Chicago Tribune*, the Tuskegee efforts of Monroe Work, the suasory efforts of the Association of Southern Women for the Prevention of Lynching, the lobbying of the NAACP, and the legal aid provided by the International Labor Defense.

These groups left us all types of multidirectional and competing historiographies and public memories, and critical scholars and others who study their efforts will not find a single, coherent, monolithic lynching archive but instead many different lynching archives.

Later generations who were soon writing about "colorblind" and "race-conscious" ways of viewing ethnic relationships produced their own genealogies, which were based on selective, contingent, and motivated ways of reading the lynching debates that took place between 1900 and 1945. Those who were attracted to the nonviolent efforts of social agents like Martin Luther King Jr. or Rosa Parks were not always interested in circulating memories of the work of radicals like Ida B. Wells-Barnett or the Communists who rallied to help the Scottsboro Boys. In the hagiographic stories that could be told about valiant NAACP anti-lynching efforts, there was little room for discussing the now forgotten efforts of socialists and other radicals who defended more militant ways of viewing the lingering influences of Jim Crow segregation.

If the EJI makes a good case about all of the forgetting that took place that required "liberation," "truth," and "reconciliation," then perhaps it should be noted that many seem to have forgotten the interorganizational infighting that led to the formation of different definitions of lynching and that "war of words." The involvement of so many in these interwar lynching debates who did not join the Ku Klux Klan—mainstream American voters—continues to bother those who have a difficult time explaining the lack of success during four decades of activism before World War II. Researchers—perhaps enamored with the later successes of the NAACP or with FDR's support for New Deal legislation—have managed to avoid harshly critiquing those who could, and should, have done more.

The consequences of congressional and executive branch failures still linger. For example, one can follow the arguments of Hillary Coker in a 2015 essay that she wrote for *Jezebel* after following the *New York Times*' coverage of some Southern lynching histories. She noted how this representative mainstream media outlet had trouble naming exactly who was doing the lynching during those earlier periods that witnessed so much debate over lynching legislation.[108]

If the EJI is right about averted gazes and cultural amnesia, then it behooves all of us to remember the motivations of those who tried, and failed, to pass anti-lynching legislation.

In December 2018, when Senators Kamala Harris and Cory Booker took to the Senate floor to ask for unanimous consent to pass the bipartisan Justice for Victims of Lynching Act of 2018, they could look back on the earlier efforts of other activists. "From 1882 to 1986," argued Senator Harris, "Congress failed to pass anti-lynching legislation when it had an opportunity 200 times."[109] Senator Harris, like Bryan Stevenson and the EJI, characterized the earlier failure to pass federal anti-lynching legislation as a failure to "recognize lynching for what it was: a bias-motivated act of terror."[110]

Did this achievement represent the mainstreaming of the radical nature of historical anti-lynching rhetorics or the domestication of earlier activist efforts?

CHAPTER 4

Post–World War II Civil Rights Activism, Photojournalism, and the Domestication of Civil Rights Lynching Memories

AS NOTED IN OTHER CHAPTERS, MEMBERS OF THE EQUAL JUSTICE INITIATIVE AS WELL as their supporters have not forgotten the efforts of the NAACP, which worked tirelessly before World War II to try to convince state and federal communities in the United States that they needed to pass anti-lynching laws.[1] In June 2016, EJI members traveled to Brownsville, Tennessee, so that they could help commemorate the lynching of Elbert Williams, an NAACP activist who was lynched in 1940.[2] This was one more example of the EJI's community outreach projects, which involve the participation of many other communities outside of Montgomery, Alabama.

Elbert Williams was the first known member of the NAACP to be killed for his activist work. Three days after he was abducted, his body was pulled from a river, and he was buried in an unmarked grave. Prosecutors ran into difficulties when a jury of six refused to return any indictments, and to this day there is no official recording of any cause of death. In the aftermath of the Williams lynching, other NAACP workers and their family members fled Brownsville, including Williams's wife and one of his sisters.[3]

In this chapter, we use our critical genealogical tools to investigate the question of when, and why, Americans started to forget about the deaths of individuals like Elbert Williams. We also want readers to understand some of the material conditions and rhetorical situations that contributed to the intentional or unintentional marginalization or containment of the more radical ideological formations that had been coproduced by Ida B. Wells-Barnett, the NAACP, the Communists who worked to help the Scottsboro Boys, and others who at one time did their best to craft radical and dissident stories about lynching terrorism.

We do not agree with those who take a progressive, neoliberal, linear stance and argue that it was only the declining number of recorded lynchings that contributed to post–World War II amnesia. The conventional wisdom that appears in many colorblind tales and progressive civil rights narratives is that those living in the US mainstream—especially white Americans—began to realize the errors of their ways, and that discriminatory, segregationist violence that manifested itself in forms like lynching drastically decreased. There is no shortage of researchers who contend that with the passage of time "lynching itself virtually disappeared."[4]

If Montgomery's EJI workers and others who share their views are right about how many Americans have forgotten about systematic lynchings and racial terrorism, then there must have been key events or rhetorical influences—those "flashes" that we mentioned in our introduction—that contributed to these cultural amnesias, or what Michel Foucault in his *The Order of Things* called "atopia" or "aphasia."[5] What if these violent events were only partially forgotten, or what happens when lynching memories are temporarily overshadowed by other discourse/knowledge/power formations?

One plausible theory might be that the perceived "end" of mass-spectacle lynching changed some civil rights movement prioritization. "After World War II, when Civil Rights legislation became the main priority," noted Marlene Park, "images of lynching continued primarily in the works of African American artists."[6] She went on to argue that "in these later works, lynching became the prime symbol of American racism, springing from a black perspective rather than from political campaigns or from contemporary experience."[7] That said, what about the memories, and the visual registers, of those who were not artists?

In this chapter we argue that it was during the post–World War II years that Americans decided to stop listening to those who wished to continue to prioritize anti-lynching efforts. A crisis of representation occurred when the NAACP and other anti-lynching organizations realized that compromises would have to be made about the type of confrontational or nonconfrontational strategies that would be used in trying to dismantle US segregation theories and practices. Cold War audiences, tired of conflict, were ready to hear about improved "race relations," and civil rights activists did not want to offend the sensibilities of those who might be willing to hear critiques of the "separate but equal" doctrines.[8]

This does not mean that artists, NAACP activists, and other members of civil rights movements totally "forgot" about historical lynchings during the 1940s and 1950s. As Park has noted, "it was not until 1965 that there were four years in a row without a lynching. In all, nearly five thousand people were lynched, of whom 72.7 percent were African Americans."[9]

That said, why do so many scholarly works on anti-lynching efforts focus on *pre–World War II reformist efforts* and not on Cold War anti-lynching campaigns? Did the civil rights activists simply decide that it was futile to continue calling for anti-lynching measures, so they devoted their efforts to winning legal cases about schools and public accommodations? Did these researchers not see the causal links that could be made between the declining numbers of reported lynchings and rising numbers of capital punishment and carceral cases?

Moreover, when, during the twentieth century, did some African American and other US communities start taking renewed interest in revitalizing lynching studies?

Our readings of various post–World War II texts and visualities have led us to conclude that while pictures of lynchings and stories about these horrific acts still circulated in African American newspapers and other journalistic outlets, there were a host of other visualities and narratives that caught the attention of NAACP members, who did not always agree with each other regarding how best to try to dismantle the enduring legacy of the Jim Crow years. Some members of the NAACP focused on "due process" and legalistic approaches to social reform, while others, using consciousness-raising methods, wanted to take a more aggressive approach in dealing with white supremacy, the "separate but equal" doctrine, and the discrimination that weighed so heavily on those living in impoverished and marginalized communities.

As Beth Bates noted, during World War II, a "new crowd" was challenging the "Old Guard in the NAACP," some of whom resented that some leaders were not engaging in grassroots activism or forming alliances with groups like the Communist Party and the Brotherhood of Sleeping Car Porters.[10] Roy Wilkins, the assistant secretary of the NAACP, pointed out that his organization had been "refusing to adopt any suggestion for mass appeal with the single exception of the anti-lynching buttons."[11] Some members of the "talented tenth" (W. E. B. Du Bois) still preferred to operate behind Washington, DC, closed doors in order to achieve incremental civil rights reform.[12]

Instead of working with more radical activists—like Communists, labor reformers, and others who pushed for more aggressive measures—most of the NAACP leadership seemed to place their hopes in the appeals that were made "in courts on a case-by-case basis."[13] This, along with providing social scientific information about deteriorating race relations and racism to local, regional, and national government officials, was supposed to gradually help end the ravages of Jim Crow segregation and societal inequalities.

As we explain in more detail below, this would drastically change as more and more people of color and their allies who were involved in civil rights activism realized the importance of grassroots support for antidiscrimination activities. The type of boycotts that Ida B. Wells-Barnett had recommended, which had seemed so radical to American progressives, were now viewed as essential tools for Cold War struggles for justice.[14]

While we recognize that some academics have argued that a "more militant impulse galvanized black communities by World War II,"[15] we would qualify these remarks by noting that during the Cold War years African American communities were not always sure what to make of those more radical impulses as they were operationalized in disputes over private golf courses, bus systems, public accommodations, law schools, "race-mixing" laws, and so on. Colorblind rhetorics still resonated with many black communities.

One of the contributions that we will make in this chapter is to show how these Cold War contests between American moderates and radicals added more layers of signification to those parchments found in lynching archives, and how these evolving contests set the stage for the racial terror arguments that would be used by race-consciousness advocates.

With the benefit of hindsight, we now know that not everyone was willing to go along with the notion that "race" was simply a social construct. Although some members of the NAACP and their supporters during the post–World War II years argued that UNESCO reports showed that fewer Americans and others believed in racial superiority, many of the social scientists who helped produce UN reports in 1951–1952 insisted that "races" were genetic essences. Moreover, population geneticists, physical anthropologists, and "reform" eugenicists who studied mental and physical racial differences claimed that they were not racists.[16]

During World War II, African Americans who contributed to the war effort in the European and Pacific Theaters were demanding that the American public rethink its support for discriminatory segregationist practices. After failing to garner the attention of congressional leaders, A. Philip Randolph proceeded to help organize a march of one hundred thousand blacks who traveled to Washington, DC, in June 1941.[17] Randolph would be one of the rhetors who inherited some of the more radical strands of civil rights advocacy.

Moderate Americans were willing to pay greater attention to the legalisms of the NAACP, whose legal teams sought more active federal court interventionism. President Harry Truman, often remembered for presenting listeners with conflicting and ambivalent rhetorics on civil rights, nevertheless appointed a Civil Rights Committee that issued a report calling for the "elimination of segregation based on race, color, creed, or national origin, from American life."[18] This eliminationist language seemed to echo previous moves toward a colorblind America. Truman also famously issued an order integrating the armed forces. No wonder that some who reviewed these activities could conclude that the "NAACP abandoned the seemingly hopeless fight for an anti-lynching bill."[19]

What caused this abandonment, and is it part of the American amnesia that the EJI often references?

As critical rhetoricians, we are mindful that others before us have commented on the need to pay attention to post–World War II material conditions as well the contradictions that came from fighting Nazi racism abroad but not at home.[20] These types of Cold War sensibilities must have catalyzed the efforts of those who shared the views of the more radical members of the NAACP. August Meier and John H. Bracey have explained that while racial prejudices still hindered postwar social justice efforts, the American political landscape had changed. After having defeated Hitler's minions, Meier and Bracey argued, "race riots no longer took the exclusive form of pogroms," blacks were "better able to defend themselves," and African Americans could "inflict casualties on whites" or attack "white property in predominantly black areas."[21]

With this in mind, the first major subsection of this chapter provides readers with a textured sense of how lynching and anti-lynching efforts were viewed during World War II, followed by a critical reading of the Emmett Till legal case.[22] The third portion of the chapter explains why so many between 1950 and the end of the twentieth century appear to have forgotten about lynching pasts, while the fourth subsection explains how some members of the critical race theory (CRT) movement helped revive interest in lynching studies in law schools and the academy. The fifth subsection notes how all of this was happening during a time when the American public was confronted with James Allen and John Littlefield's evocative photography book *Without Sanctuary*, and the exhibits that followed, in 2000.

We anticipate that this chapter will provide readers with a better understanding of why the EJI might be justified in arguing that both African Americans and other Americans had their reasons for "forgetting" about traumatic lynchings and unsuccessful federal anti-lynching efforts.

Fighting Racism at Home and Abroad during World War II

During the 1930s, several schisms could be found within the ranks of the unwieldy alliances that had temporarily been formed by many local, regional, and national anti-lynchers (see chapter 3), and the advent of World War II magnified them. Some of these schisms had to do with disagreements about whether moderate reformers should join radicals like A. Philip Randolph, and others had to do with quarrels about whether fighting the poll tax or registering eligible voters in the South made more sense for civil rights activists after the loss of so many anti-lynching battles.

This did not mean that all NAACP workers were willing to give up their anti-lynching crusade. More than a few members of the NAACP and other civil rights organizations sensed that the rise of the Nazis might lead to the development of helpful international critiques of American indifference to domestic racism. Arthur Spingarn mentioned during the interwar years that authors of newspaper articles in Germany, Italy, Japan, the Soviet Union, and several Latin American nations were now writing about lynchings in the United States. Among these sources was an article published in the *Völkischer Beobachter*, a Nazi Party publication, that characterized the American treatment of its black citizens as worse than the Nazi treatment of Jews![23] As Robert Zangrando would later argue, these types of interwar arguments would become even more convincing after the war, when international communities had to cope with both Cold War tensions and "decolonization" in the so-called Third World.[24]

Leaders in Washington, DC, already facing many competing segregationist and desegregation narratives, were now having to cope with many different "isms"—Nazism, totalitarianism, Stalinism, capitalism, militarism—and they were caught between the need to placate powerful Southern Democrats and the need to acknowledge the rising power of black soldiers, required for service overseas. After heated exchanges about managing these competing pressures, Franklin D. Roosevelt, on June 25, 1941, signed into law a seemingly innocuous measure, Executive Order 8802, that would forbid racial discrimination by defense contractors and agencies of the federal government.[25]

In the short term, this executive measure would do little to help stop the everyday racism that black soldiers experienced, but in the long term it did help thousands of African Americans who were looking for better jobs than had been available to them before. The passage of Executive Order 8802 marked the first time that whites had ever had to worry about federal interference in unjust employment practices, and this set the stage for later, more substantive federal legislation.[26]

The grammatological changes that were taking place in several military and executive branch forums would impact how radicals and moderates argued about the progress and speed of civil rights reform. Fewer Americans had qualms about discussing "social" equality as they listened to talk of "political" equality and "civil rights."[27]

By the beginning of World War II, those who supported the passage of Executive Order 8802 were convinced that a massive campaign for the prevention of mass lynchings was no longer a major priority, but during the war politicians were constantly bedeviled with reports of more lynchings taking place across the country. For example, in January 1942, in Sikeston, Missouri, Cleo Wright was arrested for allegedly assaulting Grace Sturgeon with a knife. While being transported in a police car, Wright stabbed a night marshal, and then gunshots riddled Wright's body. After he received medical treatment for his gunshot wounds, Wright was taken to his home, then back to city hall; then, an impatient mob took him from his cell, hooked him to the bumper of a car, and drove the car around, before finally dousing his body with gasoline and burning him to death.[28]

Many black Missourians who heard radio broadcasts or read news reports on the Cleo Wright lynching demanded that local, state, and federal officials investigate the incident. Dominic Capeci Jr. contextualized the wartime atmosphere that impacted how people processed information about the Cleo Wright death: "Already anxious over the recent bombing of Pearl Harbor and U.S. entry into World War II, they grasped for resolution to the black brutalities that rubbed raw their white nerves. Some believed that it lay in still more bloodletting. How could public order be restored abroad, if not first at home?"[29] Activists linked Cleo Wright's death to recent attacks on black soldiers in Alexandria, Louisiana, but all of this brought mixed responses. While some Missouri journalists expressed dismay that the coverage of this event continued to "go on and on," the *Washington Post* referred to the Cleo Wright lynching as an "act on par with the diabolical murders perpetrated by Nazi and Japanese gangsters."[30] In a very unusual move for the times, President Roosevelt ordered his attorney general, Francis Biddle, to lead an FBI probe into what had happened that had led to Wright's lynching. Coming so soon after Pearl Harbor, few members of the nation's executive branch could politically afford to look the other way.

Even after the war ended, some people realized that, in spite of the rhetoric about the "end" of American lynching, studies of material reality showed that lynching had not ended. Occasionally, anti-lynching activists did see some signs of change, as evidenced by how the FBI reacted to the killing, on July 25, 1946, of two black couples in Walton County, Georgia. At that time, Walter

White suggested to President Harry Truman that he needed to reconvene Congress in order to enact federal anti-lynching legislation, but this fell on deaf ears. The NAACP had to be satisfied with being able to offer financial rewards for those who supplied information that would lead to the arrest and conviction of the lynchers.[31]

Exasperated Cold War writers sensed that far too many social agents were contributing to the creation of rhetorical cultures that still condoned lynching. Lillian Smith, in her *Killers of the Dream* (1949), remarked that while "politicians" were the ones who "dished out most of the racial hog slop," the "preacher and editor have done their fair share, too."[32] After 1942, the FBI became more involved in lynching cases, but they were battling local and regional agents who were shocked by the aggressive federal interference, which they chalked up to outside agitation.

Critical scholars who review the archival chronicling of these events can readily understand why post–World War II audiences may have had ambivalent feelings about both the need for anti-lynching legislation as well as the speed of desegregation. A host of contradictory interpretations of what democratic governance actually meant were circulated by those who disagreed about the need to desegregate, the application of federal police powers to Southern issues, and the perceived benefits of US government interference in "private" affairs.

Among the many social scientists and humanists who have studied American lynching pasts, there seems to be little disagreement that post–World War II generations at least acted as if they thought the lynching "problem" had been solved. W. Fitzhugh Brundage, writing in 1993, argued that "by the end of the 1930s, the demise of lynching was irreversible," and that "the combination of the continued efforts of antilynching activists and profound changes in the southern economy delivered the decisive blows to the tradition of mob violence."[33] William Pinar, who used a different but related interpretative lens as he looked back at these postwar decisions, argued that while the NAACP "refused to accept the indifference with which most Americans regarded the practice of lynching," by the 1950s "lynching was no longer a national issue."[34]

Again, this all provides even more support for the EJI's assertions about how America came to forget about those fraught lynching legacies.

One of the key questions for us in this chapter is whether anti-lynching should have remained a national issue, or whether it was acceptable after World War II for many social agents to strategically decide to move on to other civil rights issues. Are twenty-first-century observers willing to critique the actions of organizations like the NAACP, whose members at times may have been more interested in fighting winnable battles, like protecting the right to an education in cases like *Brown v. Board of Education* (1954), rather than tackling more difficult battles over lynching and the institutional nature of segregationist violence?

In most traditional legal histories and reformist civil rights chronologies, it is the victories, and not the defeats, that tend to take center stage in neoliberal tales of "colorblind" advocacy successes. For example, the NAACP Legal Defense and Educational Fund (LDF) is given credit for being the arm of the NAACP that led to several key judicial decisions, including the 1944 case of *Smith v. Allwright*,[35] which outlawed exclusionary white primaries; the LDF is also credited with helping win the *Brown v. Board of Education* decision a decade later. While the NAACP continued to work on its original 1909 goal to secure the basic rights guaranteed by the Fourteenth and Fifteenth Amendments, the growth of the organization allowed it to become involved in efforts that eventually aided the passage of both the Civil Rights Act of 1964 and the Voting Rights Act of 1965.[36]

Did all American communities who celebrated these civil rights and voting achievements choose to remember to forget about federal anti-lynching efforts?

Critical Genealogies of the Emmett Till Case

With the passage of years after the war, it seems as though there were fewer and fewer sustained regional and national discussions of lynching and related crimes in the mainstream press, but occasionally some image events would come along that forced Americans into the challenge of once again dealing with such a crime. In 1955, Mamie Elizabeth Till-Mobley made a momentous individual decision that had symbolic communicative consequences. Till-Mobley decided that she wanted to have an open-casket funeral for her fourteen-year-old son, Emmett Till, who had been tortured, and then murdered, by several white assailants. Emmett died in August 1955 for allegedly showing disrespect toward a white woman, Carolyn Bryant, during a visit to a small rural store in Money, Mississippi.[37]

Throughout the first two decades of the twenty-first century, Emmett Till's death, and Till-Mobley's subsequent decisions, have captivated more and more activists, researchers, and members of the public who are still trying to determine whether certain iconic photographs have the rhetorical power to help bring about substantive social change. Dennis Parker of the American Civil Liberties Union, after hearing in 2018 that the US Department of Justice had just reopened this old case, wrote:

The sight of Emmett's body, mutilated beyond recognition, spread throughout the world in photographs published in Jet Magazine and other outlets. The shocking sight so outraged people in the United States and other countries that it helped spark the civil rights movement of the 1950s and 60s. That outrage did nothing to assure accountability for Till's death—no one was ever found guilty in spite of confessions in Look Magazine by one of the murderers.[38]

From critical genealogical vantage points, was this a critique of the deployment of voyeuristic photographic images in an attempted consciousness-raising effort? Was this an indictment of America's unwillingness to accept the photographic realism of the Till images, which symbolically represented many other terrors?

Both the killing of Emmett Till and the brazen manner in which his murderers escaped the hands of justice horrified many people of color and other Americans who had heard about the supposed progressive nature of Southern race relations. Was this horror filtered through racial or moderate frames of analysis?

Since the publication of the *Jet* magazine article and the essay in *Look* magazine, hundreds of essays and books have been written about Emmett Till's murder. Petula Dvorak wrote for the *Washington Post* in 2018 about the people who lined up to "file past the open, butternut-brown casket at the Smithsonian's African American Museum" and "silently" pay tribute to his memory as "men remove their hats" or "mothers wipe at tears as Mahalia Jackson's voice fills the room."[39] Dvorak wrote convincingly that Till's funeral "unfolds every day in the nation's capital," so that few would forget that Till had been "lynched in 1955."[40]

By now many scholars, journalists, and others interested in civil rights have at least heard some version of the contentious and multidirectional stories that would be told about Till, a Chicago native who traveled to visit relatives in Money, Mississippi. One day, Till, along with several other black teenagers, entered Bryant's Grocery Store, and Carolyn Bryant would later testify in front of a jury that Till grabbed her by the waist and uttered obscenities in her direction.[41]

Carolyn Bryant's husband, Roy Bryant, and his brother-in-law, J. W. Milam, would eventually be accused and prosecuted for Emmett Till's murder. Scholars and investigative reporters of several different generations have chronicled how it took an all-white jury only about an hour of deliberation before they decided to acquit the two. Both Roy Bryant and Milam died without ever being convicted of any crime. For decades, federal investigators tried to find new evidence or novel leads that might justify new prosecutions, but in 2007 the case was closed.[42]

Till's relatives, activists, journalists, and others worked to reopen the case, but most attempts failed. Some investigative journalists have noted that in the town of Money, Mississippi, fewer and fewer remember Emmett Till's death or his legacy,[43] but these reports of local amnesias need to be juxtaposed with commentaries on rising national interest in this case. In 2004, for example, the Justice Department was asked to consider prosecuting some of those who may have been involved in Till's murder—mysterious individuals who may have occupied the back seat of Roy Bryant and Milam's vehicle.

The FBI reopened one Till investigation, and agents eventually decided to exhume Till's body, hoping that that performative act might encourage others to provide needed evidentiary clues. Officials, however, stopped working on the case when they decided that they did not have legal jurisdiction because the statute of limitations had expired on any potential federal crimes. The case, in 2007, was then referred to the state prosecutor for Mississippi's Fourth Judicial District, but a grand jury in that district declined to issue new charges.[44]

The polysemic and polyvalent nature of the case perhaps ensured that Emmett Till histories and memories would proliferate, evolve, and be revived for strategic purposes. In 2017, Timothy Tyson published *The Blood of Emmett Till*, which included what many regarded as the first interview with Carolyn Bryant, now known as Carolyn Donham. She reportedly told Tyson that Till had not come on to her sexually, and that nothing "that boy did could ever justify what happened to him."[45]

Those interested in purveying colorblind ways of viewing civil rights activism could situate the reopening of Till's story as more proof of the inexorable march of civil rights reform or an illustration of the self-correcting nature of legal science, while those who advocate color-conscious ways of viewing civil rights reform could point to the aphasia of those who could not find the right language to explain why no one was ever convicted for Emmett Till's murder.

The Great Forgetting, 1950–1990

Given the nature of critical genealogical studies, no scholar can pinpoint an exact date or single image event that can be credited with empirically changing societal attitudes in ideological contexts, but textual and contextual analyses can be used to note paradigmatic as well as traumatic changes in elite or public argumentation. As David Eng and David Kazanjian argued, those who study past memories of historical emergencies often have to cope with the "tension between the past and the present, between the dead and the living," in order to establish some type of dialogue over losses and remains.[46]

For our purposes, some key questions that have to be asked involve whether the EJI can evidence the existence of any major American forgetting about legal lynching legacies, and whether it is feasible for critical scholars to trace that forgetting.

After all, as we noted above, during World War II there were still highly publicized instances of lynching that embarrassed those who fought the Nazis or the Japanese. So is it plausible to argue that what we will call the "great forgetting" *dispositif* must have been formed sometime between 1950 and the early 1990s, when critical race theorists helped revive interdisciplinary interest in lynching studies?

Our review of diverse rhetorical fragments has convinced us that a number of societal factors during and after the Cold War years contributed to this "great forgetting" of lynching legacies. No doubt one factor that came into play was that the announcement of the *Brown v. Board of Education* decision in 1954—unlike the old *Plessy* decision—made front-page news. Although the Earl Warren Court's very readable decision did not technically overturn all of the legal precedents that were based on the "separate but equal" doctrine, legions of legal realists and supporters of "neutral principles" doctrines were taught that *Brown v. Board* for all practical purposes spelled the end of separate but equal doctrines in federal venues. Legal teams led by the likes of Charles Hamilton Houston and Thurgood Marshall were winning cases that made it appear as if the NAACP's earlier abandonment of some anti-lynching efforts had been a wise decision. These African Americans had overcome the earlier efforts of Southern legislators, who would now spend decades trying to undermine the work of the now recognizable "civil rights movement."[47]

Another factor that may have influenced the "great forgetting" of lynching pasts was that newspapers were recording fewer and fewer reported lynchings during and after the 1940s. For example, in May 1940, a *New York Times* article was entitled "South Goes Whole Year without Single Lynching."[48] Written by a reporter working out of Atlanta, this article noted that this was the first twelve-month "lynchless period" since tabulations had first been taken. Instead of focusing on the radical activism of the NAACP or the efforts of Northern lawyers, the reporter highlighted the work of Jessie Daniel Ames, the leader of the Association of Southern Women for the Prevention of Lynching. Readers learned that Ames's organization represented some forty-one thousand Southern women. Ames was quoted as saying that the "modern South" had ended this first year without a lynching because of effective education and the swift work of police radio patrols.[49] The reporter seemed to assume that it had been the labor of the ASWPL—and not the NAACP or the looming threat of federal intervention—that could be empirically linked to that decline in lynching statistics.

The implicit message was clear—liberal or reformist Southerners, on their own, were fighting racial prejudice and should be given credit for having effectively worked to eliminate the ghastly phenomenon of lynching without federal interference. Didn't this show that segregation policies were reducing friction, and didn't this demonstrate that Southerners could end lynching horrors without having to listen to those radicals who sought "social equality" or immediate desegregation?

We are convinced that critical genealogical studies of these World War II and Cold War rhetorics illustrate how a confluence of factors created ruptures, domestications, and containments of the thick racial terror *dispositif* that had been crafted by audiences following Ida B. Wells-Barnett and four decades of federal anti-lynching activist work.

Fewer and fewer audiences during and after the Cold War saw those graphic images of the 1893 lynching of Henry Smith (see this book's introduction) or other lynching victims, and until the early 1990s the lynching statistics and photographic collections that had been collected by Wells-Barnett, the Tuskegee Institute, and the NAACP were only occasionally taken out of the archives for the purposes of helping with the formation of radical critiques.

However, as noted above, not everyone was willing to participate in this "great forgetting." Activists like Mary McLeod Bethune—who occasionally sympathized with the efforts of Jesse Daniel Ames and the ASWPL—still wanted to see the passage of federal anti-lynching legislation.[50] W. E. B. Du Bois, who grew increasingly disenchanted with the assimilationist visions and moderate reformist tactics of so many, continued to avoid the use of an American exceptionalist lens as he reviewed lynching horrors. After visiting Warsaw in 1949 and seeing firsthand the destruction left behind by Nazi Germany's invasion of Poland, Du Bois began to write about the parallels between America's management of the so-called Negro problem and the Holocaust. In an essay he wrote after returning from his trip to Poland, Du Bois explained some of the intersectional and international features of dehumanization that crossed borders of time and space that had forced him to rethink some of what he had earlier written in *The Souls of Black Folk*.[51] In "The Negro and the Warsaw Ghetto," published in *Jewish Life*, Du Bois reflected on his Poland trip and commented:

The result of these three visits, and particularly of my view of the Warsaw ghetto, was not so much a clearer understanding of the Jewish problem in the world as it was a real and more complete understanding of the Negro problem. In the first place, the problem of slavery, emancipation, and caste in the United States was no longer in my mind a separate and unique thing as I had so long conceived it. It was not even solely a matter of color and physical and racial characteristics, which was particularly a hard thing for me to learn, since for a lifetime the color line had been a real and efficient cause of misery.... [T]he race problem in which I was interested cut across lines of color and physique and belief and status and was a matter of cultural patterns, perverted teaching and human hate and prejudice, which reached all sorts of people and caused endless evil to all men.[52]

To Michael Rothberg, this transition is evidence of the multidirectionality of memory—particularly of memories of the Holocaust—that has left "tracks on all forms of knowledge."[53] For us, it shows how genealogies of racial terrorism and lynching jump time and space, creating what John Durham Peters, drawing from Walter Benjamin, calls "wormholes," which inflect public memories of the past—even when those memories seem most stable and chronological.[54]

Du Bois and his revisiting of the color line, and his discussions of physical and racial characteristics as well as his referencing of "cultural patterns," anticipate the ways that Bryan Stevenson and the EJI would refuse to individuate lynching evils.

Those like Du Bois who refused to participate in the "great forgetting" were gesturing toward the phonological existence of a mnemonic tension over how to remember, or forget, lynching pasts and what to do about it moving forward. While some commentators during and after the Cold War focused on the legalistic need to pass more colorblind legislation, many conservative Americans tried to respond to the growing power of the civil rights movement by arguing that federal legislation could never legislate morality. Dr. Martin Luther King Jr. risked offending the colorblind moderates when he responded to one journalist's question by noting that while the "law may not be able to make a man love me," it did "keep him from lynching me."[55]

Perhaps King recognized that lynchings could be prevented by motivated police who did not need the backing of federal anti-lynching measures to stop these types of violent acts, or perhaps he had a faith in legal and other restraints that was not shared by individuals like Ida B. Wells-Barnett and W. E. B. Du Bois.

Academics still wrote books about lynching during the 1950–1989 period, but they were usually for the purpose of setting the lynching archival "record straight." Michael Pfeifer argued that, by 1990, the "history of mob violence was obscured into oblivion."[56]

Many ordinary citizens may have forgotten about lynching victims, but that was not the case when members of the critical race theory (CRT) movement started writing for law students and other audiences about fraught lynching pasts.

CRT Discussions of Lynchings and Lynching Legacies

While CRT advocates have written about the general problematics of colorblindness and postracial rhetorics, they have also written on topics related to historical lynching and lynching legacies. Some of their essays cover the legal histories of lynchings that were produced during the Jim Crow years,[57] while others critique the NAACP's anti-lynching efforts, the use of lynching metaphors, and the links that some have made between lynching legacies and today's prison industrial complex. One of the founders of the CRT movement in law schools, Richard Delgado, has written about the "law of the noose," and he investigated how those who once used these tactics for social control have now seen them replaced with "a different set of practices, notably police profiling, imprisonment, and the death penalty."[58] All of these activities, argues Delgado, are meant to "remind African Americans of their precarious position."[59]

Drawing from the work of critical sociologists, members of the critical legal studies (CLS) movement, poststructuralists, postcolonial scholars, and others CRT writers supplemented their analyses of legal cases with broader studies of lynching cultures. For example, Anthony Alfieri studied both trial records and public reactions to lynchings; he was interested in the "rhetorical" features of these public spectacles. In a law review article entitled "Lynching Ethics," Alfieri opined:

> [T]he rhetorical structure of criminal defense stories of black-on-white racial violence incorporates competing narratives of deviance and defiance that engraft an essentialist dichotomy of good-bad moral character on the racial identity of young black men. The distillation of male racial identity into objective, universal categories of black manhood distorts the meaning of racial identity and the image of racial community. Moreover, the tendency of criminal defense lawyers to

privilege deviance narratives and to subordinate defiance narratives in storytelling magnifies the distortion, inscribing the mark of bestial pathology into the texture of racial identity and community.[60]

Note how Alfieri connected historical image making about "bestial pathology" with the contemporary viewpoints of criminal defense lawyers and prosecutors.

Extending the work of both CLS commentators and CRT scholars, Jeannine Bell, writing in the *Harvard Civil Rights–Civil Liberties Law Review* in 2011, examined the lingering influences of lynching cultures as she decoded what had happened in Jena, Louisiana, in 2006. During August of that year, during a school assembly for Jena High School that was meant to set forth the rules and policies for the upcoming year, one black student asked the assistant principle whether black students were going to be allowed to sit under a tree in the center of campus.[61] The next day, nooses were found hanging from that tree, and a group of black student athletes held a silent protest under the tree. After three white students were identified as the culprits who had put up the nooses, a debate ensued about how to punish them. A school committee decided that those who had put up the nooses would spend nine days at an alternative facility, followed by two weeks of in-school suspension, some Saturday detentions, and time spent attending a disciplinary court. The school committee also recommended that the white students who had put up those nooses should undergo psychological evaluations. Yet when that same school committee ruled that there had been "no racial motivation" behind these acts, this catalyzed the efforts of Jeannine Bell and other CRT scholars, who argued that the series of events exemplified the legal difficulties of showing how the display of a noose could be criminalized as an example of hate speech.[62]

All of this underscored the point that issues of white supremacy, power, and privilege, and the rhetorical functions of lynching, have not disappeared. They have just changed form, and without color-conscious critiques and interventionist acts, micro acts of blatant racism reminiscent of the lynching era are less likely to be recognized, let alone redressed.

These are the arguments that CRT theorists have been making for decades. Some of these scholars have drawn from NAACP histories, poetry about lynching, and the work of Ida B. Wells-Barnett and others to advance the argument that the Ku Klux Klan were not the only social agents involved in perpetrating mass lynching performances.[63]

The late twentieth-century work of CRT advocates and their admirers helped set the stage for interventionists like James Allen, who in 2000 revealed some of the manifest and latent tensions that exist in moderate and radical contestations when, with three coauthors, he released a powerful book—*Without Sanctuary: Lynching Photography in America*[64]—and a traveling exhibit that altered the historiographies and memoryscapes of past lynchings in powerful ways.

It would be the work of advocates like James Allen's supporters that would help set the stage for the race-conscious activism of Bryan Stevenson, the EJI, and Montgomery's Legacy Museum.

The Rhetorical Force of Without Sanctuary: Lynching Photography in America

Featuring hundreds of lynching representations, postcards, warning signs, and notes from white majorities, *Without Sanctuary* is said to have broken the silence that had settled over America. Due to the grotesqueness of the crimes depicted, Allen's book and the traveling exhibit were provocative shards of memory that raised all sorts of questions about whether it is ethical to see, or not see, such graphic and horrid photographic images. Was viewing this exhibit an act of voyeurism that did little to help the cause of moderates or radicals, or was reading Allen's coauthored book or seeing the *Without Sanctuary* exhibit a defiant, performative act of vicarious twenty-first-century witnessing?

Regardless of how one answers such questions, one cannot help noticing how Allen's interventions, as well as those of his supporters, became the type of disruptive moves that provide critical genealogists with clues about the timing of evolutionary epistemic changes and shifting rhetorical influences. The post-2000 debates about viewing, or not viewing, *Without Sanctuary* provided a test run of how audiences might view the sculptures and hanging steel panels of the EJI's National Memorial for Peace and Justice, as well as the visualities that appear in the Legacy Museum.

Allen's efforts reminded many scholars of Walter White's 1935 exhibit, which attempted to raise public consciousness about lynching in New York City (chapter 3).

James Allen, like Du Bois before him, was willing to make multidirectional arguments about the parallels that might be found between the abuse of African Americans and the victims of the World War II Holocaust. To Allen, *Without Sanctuary* is a documentation of "one of the darkest and sickest periods in American history," which "make[s] real the hideous crimes that were committed against humanity" through photographs that "bear witness to the hangings, burnings, castrations, and torture of an American holocaust."[65] Against a troubling history of failed anti-lynching laws and a culturescape in which many refuse to "believe" that these "atrocities happened in America not so very long ago," Allen set out to show to the world, through his exhibit, what actually happened, as it was.[66]

What was Allen's objective? To help posterity by exploring some of the contexts and motivations of these lynching evils. "What is it in the human psyche that would drive a person to commit such acts of violence against their fellow citizens?" he asked. Advancing arguments that resemble some of the claims that appear in Bryan Stevenson's book *Just Mercy*, Allen stated: "It is my hope that *Without Sanctuary* will inspire us, the living, and as yet unborn generations, to be more compassionate, loving, and caring. We must prevent anything like this from ever happening again."[67]

Allen, who has collected lynching items in an antique shop outside of Atlanta, used photography to capture not just the visualized representation of the person who was lynched but also the mood of the crowd who performatively carried out what Peter Ehrenhaus and A. Susan Owen describe as a "constitutive" act "of the perpetrator's Christian faith."[68] It might be said that at least in some cases lynching performances were characterized as acts of justice that had everything to do with the fervor of Christian evangelicalism. Those who participated in these rituals were said to have experienced feelings of purity, redemption, and rebirth through suffering and eventually death.[69]

As ghastly as the corpses of the identified and unidentified victims are in these photos, it was more the portraits of those white persons whose faces express pride, enjoyment, and judiciousness that bothered those who came to see *Without Sanctuary*.

In some of these photographs collected by Allen, spectators of the lynchings appear standing next to their victim—many of them, mostly men, in formal attire, with their hands on their hips, as they seem to be reflecting on the justness of their crime. The hysteria, awe, and zealotry of the others depicted tell the true horror of lynchings: white jouissance. Common white folks maniacally performed what they saw as American or Southern "citizenship" by ritualistically torturing and killing blacks in the most dreadful ways possible in order to enforce popular, perhaps reactionary, notions of "justice" that commodified the act as spectacle.[70]

Allen's work could be used by radical critics of lynching who point to the systematic nature of performative acts that unified, at least for a time, those who might otherwise be divided by other motivations and interests. Some who helped organize lynchings in Kentucky sold tickets for five cents (to view the performance) or fifty cents (for the right to shoot the dead body, also part of the ritual).[71]

The potential heuristic value of *Without Sanctuary* is a talking point that was mentioned by many mainstream and alternative press journalists. To Vanessa Gregory of the *New York Times*, the debut of *Without Sanctuary* in New York exposed the jubilance of "white crowds" that forced a reckoning. "Among the most disturbing images," she noted, "were those of white children in the crowds, some with expressions of smug delight on their faces."[72] This echoed Walter White's interwar concerns.

Vermont teacher Gaen Murphree tried to assess how high school students might react to the pictorial depictions of lynchings that were attended by children in *Without Sanctuary*. After giving tenth graders one of the photos to review, Murphree recalled that "what they noticed most—aside from the unspeakable brutality of the act itself—were the kids, boys and girls, just like them, smiling and posing for the camera, as if at a picnic.... If we can keep remembering and asking why, maybe we can bring our 'dream deferred' of a better nation just a little bit closer."[73]

We can readily appreciate the contentious nature of these *Without Sanctuary* images, and critical genealogists can try to explain why, as with the Emmett Till case, the use of graphic images is the most rhetorically effective way to facilitate social change.[74] To Ersula Ore, "*Without Sanctuary* encoded values of equality and humility onto lynching victims in ways that shifted the signification of the victim from the abject object worthy of scorn to the citizen-neighbor worthy of compassion and justice."[75]

Regardless of whether we have radical or moderate leanings, the *Without Sanctuary* images bring to the fore questions about the limits of pictorial representations of such abject horror. Consider one photo of a limbless, headless person who appears to be hanging from thin air. The caption reads, "The charred torso of an African American male. 1902, Georgia," but there nothing left of the body that even remotely resembles human form. No arms. No legs. No head. And scorched. While a group of white men wearing fedoras and slacks huddle, smoking pipes, this dehumanized body dangles from the air, in an open space, like some sort of trophy. The horror of this sight is beyond words. And it was made into a postcard, which reads: "*Warning*. The answer of the Anglo-Saxon race to black brutes who would attack the womanhood of the South." Stamped: Wrights Kodak, Savannah, GA.[76]

Every photo in the *Without Sanctuary* collection shows a similar portrait of inhumanity in gruesome detail. Calling to mind what Roland Barthes calls the "punctum," these images forcefully evoke the irreducibility of photography and the chilling darkness of crimes unpunished.[77] Mostly, to Allen and others, the images reveal the macabre way in which lynchings were received by common white persons, who apparently took pleasure in the ritualistic performance of torturing and killing black persons in tragically spectacular fashion. While the maimed, burned, tortured, abject bodies limply swing from trees or lie in the dirt, dressed-up white persons bear ear-to-ear smiles, stoically stand in pride, or point and laugh.

Some of these images would become iconic markers symbolizing the brutality and inhumanity of lynchings. Consider a postcard of Jesse Washington, who was dragged six miles from Waco to Robinson, Texas, to be lynched before an audience of fifteen thousand people eager to "relish the torture of the day." The charred man hangs from a telephone pole by a chain around his neck. The only thing human about this figure is the loincloth wrapped around his waist.

The disturbing nature of these images was intended to ensure that viewers would not forget these victims of racialized lynching pasts. In an interview with National Public Radio spokesperson Terry Gross, Allen described the postcard depicting Jesse Washington's death as "particularly disturbing," and not only because of the masses who came to "relish the torture of the day." While the postcard depicted a victim who "was tortured and burned alive at the stake," this was a particularly haunting image because of a note that had been "written by the owner of the prized post card."[78] A man by the name of Joe Myers had purchased this card; put an X over his own head appearing in the mob of onlookers; written on the back, "This is the barbeque we had last night. My picture is to the left with a cross over it. Your son, Joe"; then sent it home to his mother.[79] Allen noted that this postcard had been used as an advertisement for the photographer, Katy Electric Studio, Temple, Texas, H. Lippe Proprietor.[80]

It is the banal use of these lynching photographs, postcards, and other visualities that is so maddening to many twenty-first-century viewers.

When asked about the main "function" of these photographic postcards, Allen agreed that they were "supposed to ... commemorate the hanging." He adds that, besides the obvious function of sensationalism and the profitable nature of these images for photographers, many of them were also sold on the streets, in drugstores, and through the mail.[81]

Sadly, from all sorts of perspectival vantage points, they served to bond the white communities who came to these spectacular lynching events in their pursuit of the evidencing of white supremacist power and terror.

Allen explained that these types of lynchings were also major news events, and he told reporters that they were well publicized. Some images that appear in *Without Sanctuary* were printed in local newspapers just after the events occurred, so that people could send the newspapers to their relatives and say, "This is what happened in our hometown."[82]

How can viewers of these lynching photographs and postcards ignore these extreme acts of inhumanity, given their rhetorical force? It is no surprise, then, that from a critical rhetorical perspective, *Without Sanctuary* triggered widespread discussion about lynchings in twenty-first-century America and the haunting specter of impunity that comes from acknowledging the recovery of unaccounted-for crimes against humanity.

Some critics of *Without Sanctuary* objected to the open display of these horrific images, but others explained why societies needed to see these particular lynching visualities. To Sherrilyn Ifill, president and director-counsel of the NAACP Legal Defense and Educational Fund—and also the author of *On the Courthouse Lawn: Confronting the Legacy of Lynching in the Twenty-First Century*—it was the complicity, and the displays of outright affective pleasure, of swarms of whites participating in lynchings that was key. Ifill averred that American communities needed to know that, during lynching spectacles, "hundreds or thousands of white witnesses . . . might stand beside and fail to stop this. . . . This is powerful to unpack the complicity of those who remained silent and stood by and attached. That always has to be reckoned with, and we have to deal with that today."[83]

Here, we need to make several points. First of all, note how in earlier chapters we saw the general reluctance that prevented the passage of hundreds of proposed anti-lynching bills, and how some of those involved in debates about lynching during the interwar years sought to narrow definitions of lynching at the same time that they tried to minimize the magnitude of lynching horrors (chapters 2–3). Contrast this with the way that Ifill is willing to mention "hundreds of thousands" who could be characterized as either bystanders or perpetrators of these acts of what the EJI calls racial terrorism.

Allen's defenders have argued that rediscovering and showing the public graphic images like these aids the cause of civil rights activists who do not want us to forget the horrors of lynching performances, but not everyone is convinced that this is the best way to promote consciousness raising. Brent Staples, in a reflective essay ("The Perils of Growing Comfortable with Evil"), argued that while *Without Sanctuary* indeed contributed to conversations about "the nature of violence," as Allen had hoped, there were limits. Staples elaborated by noting that there is "an unbearable measure of horror here that I have no interest in learning to endure."[84] The re-presentation of these atrocious photos risks recommitting, even redeeming, those crimes visually, by placing viewers in the subject positions analogous to those of the white mobs who were spectators. "With these horrendous pictures loose in the culture," argued Staples, "the ultimate effect could easily be to normalize images that are in fact horrible."[85]

Staples is not alone in advancing a skeptical critique of Allen's project. In his book *Legacies of Lynching*, Jonathan Markovitz worried that Allen's project might desensitize audiences to the "horrors" of lynching at the same time that it reproduced the spectacle of lynching and its racial violence.[86] When the exhibit arrived at Emory University in Atlanta in 2002, it stirred some discussion and controversy about how to respond to seeing these image events. Archivist Cynthia Wilson said: "If I have to spend much time in those files," it "makes me want to leave here and kill every white person within five miles."[87] While the expression of such sentiments can be readily understood given the horridness of these forgotten crimes, they led Emory religion professor Theophus Smith—who was also on the exhibition committee—to offer a more tempered response. "If you walk away from here hating white people, you've been had. You're part of the mob," Smith said. "What we're trying to do is reclaim and humanize these people."[88]

Was this asking for a more moderate critique of lynching, or a different radical rendering?

Defenders of *Without Sanctuary* wanted to focus on the pedagogical lessons that could be taught by having to cope with the visceral nature of these representations. Commenting on the memorialization of these atrocities, another exhibit organizer aptly observed: "It's been a powerful experience. ...I think a lot of communities could benefit from facing up to the past like this. The only problem is we're half a century too late."[89] Two communication scholars, A. Susan Owen and Peter Ehrenhaus, have argued that some of the challenges posed by these horrific images can be faced by fostering "ethical relations of looking," akin to the way we have also "fostered ethical relations of speaking and writing," and of studying such troubled artifacts.[90]

These are obviously issues that have everything to do with the circulation of lynching photographs, postcards, and other visualities from the "Heart" of Dixie, and we are also convinced that they have everything to do with the rhetorical frames that twenty-first-century observers wish to use as they cope with the "great forgetting" that we referenced earlier in the chapter. English professor Wendy Hinshaw, in an interview with the *Montgomery Advertiser*, acknowledged the dangers of voyeurism, but then she went on to explain that seeing these historical artifacts was worth the risk, because it ensured that "we're held accountable for our acts of looking."[91] "I was really struck when I attended the exhibit when you look at the postcards in person, it's a much deeper experience," she commented. "You have to walk up and look at it in person. You're aware of being there, looking. You're self-aware of your own position."[92]

Allen took this a step further, arguing that there is a sort of moral obligation to witness these crimes and confront this dark reality, which is also why he turned his work into a traveling exhibit that appeared on many college campuses throughout the United States.[93] Allen has also made these photos publicly accessible on his website, which includes a five-minute video.[94]

The shocking photographs that Allen has collected, much like Walter White's 1935 exhibit of lynching artworks, have been met with a mixed reception. Anne Rice, writing in 2006, contended that the "photographs in Allen's collection place us at the crossroads of memory and forgetting, where the moral imperative to mourn intersections with the historical burden of willful amnesia."[95]

We are not the first to argue that parallels can be found between Allen's efforts and those of the Equal Justice Initiative, which uses Montgomery's National Memorial for Peace and Justice and Legacy Museum to grapple with similar questions having to do with radical effectivity, the nature and scope of lynching imagery, and perceived crises of representation. In a *New York Times* article entitled "A Lynching's Long Shadow," Vanessa Gregory argued that the EJI "stems from earlier scholarship and activism," which, among other things, followed Allen's efforts and attempted "to foster lasting conversations about lynching and puncture popular myths about the practice, like the notions that lynchings were isolated aberrations, pioneer justice or the work of social outsiders like the Ku Klux Klan."[96]

Perhaps in the same way that the collection of statistics revealed the magnitude of lynching horrors for radicals who supported Ida B. Wells-Barnett or NAACP activists, exhibits like Allen's *Without Sanctuary* prevent denialism or revisionism that tries to narrow the number of perpetrators of these horrors. While there were periods of silence about past lynching crimes after the Cold War, *Without Sanctuary* was a visual "mind bomb" that sparked rampant discussion and debate about memories of lynching. Even the US Senate took note while Allen was engaged in his traveling exhibit by passing the national apology bill in 2005.[97]

Jessy Ohl and Jennifer Potter, in their journal article "United We Lynch: Post-Racism and the (Re)Membering of Racial Violence in *Without Sanctuary: Lynching Photography in America*," contend that part of the suasory power of these images comes from their ability to "collapse the distinction between spectators and mob" as a way of creating a "countermemory" that challenges traditional memories of lynching.[98] "By framing lynching as a constitutive ritual of community and citizenship," Ohl and Potter argue, "*Without Sanctuary* displaces dominant public memory's therapeutic effect on contemporary audiences fearful of guilt and responsibility for previous injustices."[99] This, in other words, is the rupturing effect that Christine Harold and Kevin DeLuca discuss in "Behold the Corpse."[100]

From a poststructural, critical genealogical vantage point, is it possible that Allen's collection of images is not just for "remembering" historical social change, but is also a form of interventionism that facilitates social change itself? As Bryan Stevenson—whom Allen praises as "absolutely awesome"—said: *Without Sanctuary* "for some people ... created this optic that was shocking, and we were less interested in shocking optics.... We really wanted to create a narrative that is in some ways even more shocking. That it wasn't the Klan. It was the teachers and the lawyers and the journalists and law enforcement officers cheering as a man was brutalized."[101]

Some academics are willing to make very large claims about the effectivity of these lynching photographs, and they seem to be following Ehrenhaus and Owen when they suggest that instead of averting our gaze we instead need to adopt particular ethical stances as we view collections like Allen's *Without Sanctuary*. Wendy Hinshaw, of Florida Atlantic University, explained that what she really appreciated about this memorial exhibit was how it "forces us to participate and feel implicated as spectators," to the point that the collective activity that we see in the photographs is depicting an "American Holocaust."[102]

Even those who do not characterize these mass lynchings as genocidal acts can still underscore the point that Allen's *Without Sanctuary* has much to tell us about atrocity remembrance and forgetfulness. To Ehrenhaus and Owen, "the atrocities of lynching cannot be understood apart from the historical trajectories of peoples brought together in that moment. Safely contained by the distance of that historical past, we both construct and confront the possibility of memory."[103] In this way, the visual artifacts that display such performances reveal the historical "scale" of these collective traumas through their present/past historical "collisions."[104]

Part of the reason for the radicalness of some receptions of Allen's *Without Sanctuary* has to do with the fact that some were willing to adopt what we would view as "color-conscious" approaches to race or ethnicity when they viewed these optics. As Ohl and Potter argued, *Without Sanctuary* "interrupts post-racial sensibilities" by providing an exemplar of what bell hooks called the type of "counter-memory" that allowed subjugated persons to "know the present and invent the future" through visualizations of the past.[105]

In other words, for many radicals who wanted to redeploy the archives left by known rhetors like Wells-Barnett, Du Bois, and Allen, the visual force of these lynching photographs created spaces for challenging dominant white narrations of fraught lynching pasts. The visualized "Other" did not have to accept the domestication or the containment of those who tried to individuate lynching guilt. The "Other" could take back what had been denied: acknowledgment and commemoration for the whitewashed historicity of racial terrorism.

As we show in the next chapter, Bryan Stevenson's commentaries, as well the remarks of his supporters, provide us with epistemic clues that the stated goals and methods of the National Memorial for Peace and Justice and the Legacy Museum bear marked resemblance to some of the competitive and multidirectional memories that once swirled around Allen's *Without Sanctuary*.

Conclusion

In this chapter, we have argued that the post–World War II era was a crucial time for lynching memoryscapes, as various social agents worked to advance competing moderate and radical visions for how to best cope with lynching legacies and civil rights futures.

While some kept asking the NAACP to quit prioritizing their anti-lynching campaigns, vocal dissenters refused to stop campaigning for federal anti-lynching measures. For example, James Weldon Johnson complained that the Americans' "moral position in international relations" was compromised when many international observers noted that human beings, in the "presence of men, women, and children," can be "burned at the stake or done to death in defiance of the courts and with the connivance or actual assistance of officers sworn to uphold the laws and protect the public."[106]

Others seemed willing to move away from apparently losing battles as they sought evidence that members of US civil rights movements could achieve some demonstrable victories. These social agents left us archival materials that linked these lynchings to other civil rights efforts, including the celebration of the Supreme Court's decision in *Brown v. Board of Education* (1954), the mediated coverage of the Emmett Till case, and the passage of the 1964 Civil Rights Act.

Our own research supports some of the EJI's claims regarding the post–World War II forgetting of horrific lynching pasts. While the EJI may have underestimated the rhetorical power of consciousness-raising efforts, like those of the CRT movement or James Allen, there is nevertheless plenty of anecdotal and other evidence that dense ideological formations were put in place by those who shared Southern state desires to show the progressive nature of "race relations" through decreased lynching statistics.

Although there is plenty of evidence that scholars and investigative journalists after the Cold War occasionally showed an interest in preserving lynching memories, some of the public reactions to Allen's *Without Sanctuary* underscore the point that more than a few were uncomfortable with preserving lynching pasts when that involved confronting the photographic realism provided by authentic pictures of mass-spectacle American lynchings. This discomfort may have been going on for generations, and it could have contributed to the great forgetting.

Given the radicalness of some of the arguments presented by the EJI and the Legacy Museum, we found it intriguing that the Montgomery EJI facilities do not seem to be interested in openly displaying gruesome lynching photographs in their own visual assemblages. While these images of the torturing of black bodies are readily available to visitors who travel to Montgomery, they are stored in an interactive computer screen that requires visitors to consent before they can see some of them.

Could this act of self-censorship be a postvisual way to present race-based arguments? Is this an ethical or political decision that comments on the same sort of academic arguments about "how to see" that have surrounded *Without Sanctuary*? Or is this one of the compromises that Bryan Stevenson and the EJI had to make in order to appeal to a broader audience in Montgomery, Alabama?

CHAPTER 5

Bryan Stevenson, the Formation of the Equal Justice Initiative, and the Fight against the "Stepchild of Lynching"

AS WE HAVE NOTED THROUGHOUT THIS BOOK, IT WOULD BE A MISTAKE TO THINK that the building of the Legacy Museum and the National Memorial for Peace and Justice only involved the formation of spaces and places that would help American audiences recover forgotten lynching pasts. In order for some of these lynching histories to come alive, and order for them to have presentist meanings for twenty-first-century visitors and admirers, these Montgomery sites of memory need to tell narratives, and they need to provide pedagogical information in ways that resonate with readers who come from all walks of life. The dry, statistical collections of lynching information that were distributed by researchers like Monroe Work of the Tuskegee Institute during the federal anti-lynching campaigns were needed during the 1920s and 1930s, but they, alone, may not be that persuasive for visually oriented twenty-first-century audiences who support the EJI and are interested in being presented with interactive, technologically sophisticated ways of reading about race consciousness and traumatizing pasts.

We have also mentioned in passing the characterological role that Bryan Stevenson has played in the debates about the Montgomery Legacy Museum and the National Memorial for Peace and Justice, and in this part of the book we want to reassemble some of those rhetorical fragments in novel constellations of meanings. We do this so that readers can understand what seems to motivate not only Stevenson but those African Americans and other critics of postracial politics who sense that this may be just the opportune time to consider how studies of Stevenson's life might help recontextualize Ferguson, Charlottesville, police targeting of black youths, and the ethnic tensions that still exist across the United States.

Even before the publication of his book *Just Mercy*, Bryan Stevenson was garnering a great deal of legal acclaim and media attention for his legal representation of the downtrodden.¹ As poststructural critics, we argue that, among the EJI's race-conscious narratives that were starting to appear, Stevenson occupied a variety of subject positions that allowed him to connect with a wide range of audiences. Religious Americans could identify with the ways that he wrote and talked about mercy, atonement, redemption, the need to heal, and the spiritual side of providing help to even the guilty who were on death row. Nonreligious readers of his work could relate to the radical ways in which he consistently tried to undermine the operative logics of late capitalism and white supremacist rhetorics.

Given the mass-mediated suturing together of fragments about his various efforts, it is not always easy to tell the difference between Stevenson the person and Stevenson the persona, the twenty-first-century activist who followed the lead of larger-than-life figures like Frederick Douglass, Ida B. Wells-Barnett, W. E. B. Du Bois, Thurgood Marshall, Rosa Parks, Martin Luther King Jr., and perhaps even Barack Obama.

In a host of ways, what Stevenson seemed to specialize in was a unique ability to take complex, provocative ways of conceptualizing carceral processes and explain these evolving lynching legacies in ways that made sense to audiences who may not be familiar with the radical work of critical sociologists or critical race theorists. When Bryan Stevenson, for instance, wrote about the American people being "broke," he was not simply referencing the characteristics of those who still exhibited racial animus against people of color, but all humans. Visitors to Montgomery could understand the frailties and vulnerabilities that Stevenson mentioned in his textual accounts of US carceral systems.

Since at least 2010, Stevenson has played key roles in helping produce some of the EJI's epistemes and memes. He and other EJI workers have circulated law review articles, books, newspaper commentaries, video materials, and blog commentaries that provide critical genealogists with all sorts of Foucauldian archival parchments that contain clues about how to decode the discourse that swirls around both Stevenson the person and Stevenson the persona.

In July 2017, Stevenson published an essay in the *New York Review of Books* that used the story of his own encounter with police officers in Georgia as an entrée point for discussions of the daily struggles of many nonwhites:

> People of color in the United States, particularly young black men, are often assumed to be guilty and dangerous. In too many situations, black men are considered offenders incapable of being victims themselves. As a consequence of this country's failure to address effectively its legacy of racial inequality, this presumption of guilt and the history

that created it have significantly shaped every institution in American society, especially our criminal justice system.²

The personal had become political for Stevenson.

Stevenson's referencing of the American "criminal justice system" only hinted at the radical nature of his, and the EJI's, ambitious plans for changing the status quo. During an interview in February 2018, Stevenson explained that in today's America, African Americans were five times more likely to be incarcerated than whites.³ How would changing America's rhetorical culture, acknowledging fraught lynching pasts, help alleviate this problem?

In order to see the "backstories" behind these Stevenson quotations, we must see how critical genealogists can decode some of repetitive ideographs, narratives, and other discursive units of analysis that have been cobbled together out of the lynching archives to suit the presentist needs of Stevenson and the EJI. Many EJI archival commentaries on lynching legacies and racial terrorism are crafted by those who write in universalist language, but this hides the selectivity and partiality of the particular stories that often symbolically and materially link Stevenson's particular subject positions and the larger discursive and visual assemblages that are produced by the EJI. Critical rhetorical analyses of dozens of Stevenson's rhetorical missives render visible the ways that the EJI wants to highlight the trials and tribulations of black veterans returning home, or the mistreatment of black women in prisons, or the discriminatory nature of capital punishment regimes. The textual productions and visual registers that appear in outlets like Stevenson's book, his TED Talk, and the artifacts in the Legacy Museum are intended to be provocative in radical ways that would not garner the universal approval of everyone, especially those living in places where residents still defend what we have called Dixie monumentalism.

From a critical vantage point that focuses more on the coproduction of large, discursive formations than on any individual social agency, it could be argued that Bryan Stevenson, the person, could only do so much, but Stevenson, the persona, could accomplish much more. By 2020, several documentaries and films about Stevenson had transformed him into a twenty-first-century model activist who showed people of color how those living in the post-truth, Trumpian world could overcome incredible odds and help reform the US criminal justice system.

The EJI's Legacy Museum also participates in what we would call the coproduction of "New Reconstruction rhetorics," and it not only puts on display some of Stevenson's most famous sayings—it also embodies, through style and substance, Stevenson's and the EJI's unrelenting critiques of mass incarceration practices. While some EJI personnel have provided needed legal representation for those on death row and other victims of racial discrimination living in legal spheres, the Legacy Museum helps tourists and others who visit these Montgomery spaces see a specific race-conscious "history" in a more radicalized public sphere. In Montgomery, the EJI hoped to revive interest—and perhaps to mainstream—the radical ideas about racial terror that were once commented on by other activists whose haunting memories swirl around these hallowed grounds.

To be sure, Bryan Stevenson and the other members of the Equal Justice Initiative were interested in extending the work of those who had historically toiled away at tallying the lynching dead, in the same way that Ida B. Wells-Barnett, the Tuskegee Institute, the NAACP, Stewart Tolnay and E. M. Beck,[4] and others had worked on the establishment and preservation of these evolving lynching records.[5]

These are key efforts, and those who have written about some of the other lynching memorials and acts of memorialization—like the commemorations at Moore's Ford, Georgia, or Duluth, Minnesota, or Tulsa, Oklahoma—are aware of the challenges that come with this monumentalization. Anne Rice, writing in 2006, noted:

> The process of building memorials and writing histories represents the first tentative step toward acknowledging the sites on our haunted landscapes, where so many people, both individually and collectively, have been harmed. Yet alongside the movement toward reconciliation and reparation exists the impulse to ignore past injustice and violence.[6]

Those who helped craft Stevenson's persona were going to do their best to resist that ignoring of past racial injustice.

In Montgomery, the word and the image come together as the EJI monumentalizes some of Stevenson's claims. If, for example, Stevenson is going to note that lynching did not "end" in the 1930s, 1940s, or 1950s, then the Legacy Museum displays and EJI website need to show viewers that this is indeed the case. If Stevenson is going to argue that lynching evolved, and that legal discriminatory practices shackled both black victims and their racist oppressors, then visitors to Montgomery need to *be able to see and feel that need* for "liberation" that Stevenson references (more on this in chapters 6 and 7).

Stevenson does more than his fair share in ensuring that the mainstream and alternative press know about these emancipatory needs. During one interview, for example, he argued that when it came to restorative justice issues that were related to America's capital punishment regime, the question was "not whether these people deserve to die for what they did" but rather "whether given our history, we deserve to kill them."[7] In Foucauldian terminology, Stevenson was suggesting that America replace its vengeful thanatopolitics with more merciful biopolitics.

Stevenson and the EJI are interested in many aspects of what they view as the search for a more accurate "legacy" of lynching that begins with colonial slave trading and brings us to the present, and often when Stevenson covers this wide array of topics he adopts grammatologies that appear to come directly from the mouths of the downtrodden. That is exactly how the EJI's personification of the death penalty, as the "stepchild of lynching," became one of the key tropes in the strategic racial terror histories that have been rendered visible by Stevenson and the Legacy Museum.[8]

In other parts of this book, we have deployed different critical tools in our studies of various competitive histories and multidirectional memories, and here we use what interdisciplinary scholars call a "critical biographical" approach as we provide readers with critiques of both Stevenson the person and Stevenson the persona.

Many social agents need time to craft identifiable personas, and that is certainly the case here with the crafting of Stevenson's activist persona. Several years before the opening of the National Memorial for Peace and Justice, Tim Adams of the United Kingdom's *Guardian* reported that Archbishop Desmond Tutu had called Stevenson "America's Mandela," and Adams pointed out how this African American EJI activist had devoted his entire life to exposing racial prejudice in America's legal system.[9] Stevenson's TED Talk, entitled "We Need to Talk about an Injustice," was viewed by millions.[10] To our knowledge, by early 2020 Stevenson had received at least twenty-nine honorary degrees, and he is still in great demand as a public speaker. Just about every year, a major filming company or documentary production crew produces some type of visuality about the EJI that brings together materials on Stevenson's life, his legal efforts, and his current quest to recover forgotten lynching pasts. These filmmakers and documentarians become coproducers of the New Reconstruction rhetorics that are presented to growing numbers of American viewers.

In many of the articles that have been written about Bryan Stevenson, journalists recite similar facts as they craft recognizable narratives about this iconic figure for their readers. For example, authors often mention how Stevenson grew up in impoverished neighborhoods, attended Harvard Law School, and then traveled from there to Montgomery, where he founded the Equal Justice Initiative in 1989. At various times, Stevenson has been characterized as a lawyer, a human rights activist, a recipient of a prestigious

MacArthur Fellowship, and the author of the best-selling book, and now a major motion picture, *Just Mercy*.[11]

An aura has formed around Stevenson the persona, as various writers move from describing his background to talking about his twenty-first-century crusading efforts. For instance, one writer explained that Stevenson, who grew up "black in segregated Delaware," finished law school so that he could "offer his services as the pro bono defender of inmates on death row in Alabama."[12] As the story goes, when he started realizing that these societal and legal problems were too big to be solved through legal advocacy alone, Stevenson decided to build his own organization, the EJI, and through this he started working away at changing American hearts and minds about mass incarceration reform.

Given the pushback from conservative whites and others who used postracial and colorblind arguments to complain about affirmative action, political correctness, the influence of liberals in academic hallways, and so on, during the Barack Obama and Donald Trump administrations, Stevenson and the EJI provided some much-needed dissident spaces and places for African American communities and radical whites who still wanted to hear social justice messages.

Stevenson, the person, often supplied the rhetorical fragments that went into the production of these epistemes about Stevenson, the persona. In Stevenson's narration of what he did after law school, he traveled to Mississippi, had not planned on staying, but then met someone by the name of Stephen Bright who convinced him that he was just the right type of person who should work at helping the helpless who had landed in prison.[13]

To elucidate some of the motivations behind Bryan Stevenson's legal efforts and the strategic crafting of this radical persona, this chapter begins with an explanation of Stevenson's select historicizing of what happened during Reconstruction and the Jim Crow years, and after the Great Migration. This is followed by a praxiological segment that illustrates how representations of Stevenson's legal practice could be synthesized with representations of some of his, and the EJI's, theorizing.

The third part of the chapter supplies readers with a close-textual, critical biographical reading of Stevenson's *Just Mercy*, while the fourth part explains the diverse reactions of audiences when they learned about Stevenson's legal efforts, his book, EJI advocacy, and the building of the Legacy Museum.

No one who listened to even one or two of Stevenson's presentations could doubt his sincere conviction that America needed to be awakened from its dogmatic slumber, and in the name of reflexivity we need to admit that we often can relate to many of his messages.

Bryan Stevenson's Historical Explanations of the Parallels between Lynching Pasts and Capital Punishment Presents

Unlike many of the orthodox histories of lynching that we referenced in chapters 1-4, Stevenson's narratives of what happened after the Civil War include references to labor abuse and the local policing efforts of communities in the South that were intent on maintaining white supremacy. Stevenson, like Ida B. Wells-Barnett and the Communists who helped the Scottsboro Boys, refused to see lynching as only a matter that involved black criminality and the rape of white women. He shared the interest of his radical predecessors in highlighting some of the more structural, functional, or materialist linkages that could be found between capitalist competition and societal excuses for lynchings.

Ironically, Bryan Stevenson often begins his historical tales for readers by providing a type of moderate "legislative intentions" view of the passage of the Thirteenth, Fourteenth, and Fifteenth Amendments that focuses on the possibilities, but lost promises, of these constitutional fragments. He explains that the passage of these amendments did bring some measure of "black autonomy," but this may have only provided a temporary reprieve for those people of color who had to witness the undermining efforts of white supremacists, who became adept at getting state legislatures to pass the Black Codes that paved the way for convict leasing and the control of black labor.[14] These historical fragments are then used by Stevenson to narrate a story of continued exploitation, which has manifested itself in different forms during the twenty-first century.

Stevenson has written about how Southern states established their own local and regional systems of criminal justice, and in his telling of the tale Southerners used ideographic terms such as "vagrancy" and "loitering" to get around the letter and spirit of what the Radical Republicans and others had intended with the passage of the post-Civil War amendments. Instead of enforcing constitutional provisions that were meant to help protect the political and civil citizens' rights of former slaves, inventive Southern politicians reappropriated some of the language of the amendments in order to promote white control of black labor. After all, fragments of the Thirteenth Amendment indicated that there would be a prohibition of slavery and involuntary servitude, "except as punishment for crime," and this qualification opened up a Pandora's box of potential abuse in the late nineteenth and twentieth centuries. Southerners could argue that their sharecropping rules that were put in place during and after Reconstruction had everything to do with the deserved punishment of lawbreakers and the survival of Southern farms, and little to do with slavery.

Stevenson critiqued white Reconstruction mythologies, and he pointed out in some of his essays and public addresses that when Union troops left the South after Reconstruction in 1877, this emboldened Southern lawmakers who sought to exploit, with impunity, the labor of African Americans in what Stevenson called private lease contracts or "state-owned farms."[15] Plans for peonage accompanied disenfranchisement and the passage of other discriminatory laws. The older auction blocks and slave systems that had been banned by the Radical Republicans and their vaunted Civil War amendments were replaced during the Jim Crow years with a variant of what some called "modern slavery."

Stevenson, like many critical race theorists, invited readers to focus on the intersectionalities of class, race, and gender as he cobbled together a legal narrative that linked illegal lynching to legal forms of oppressive white practices. For example, in an essay titled "A Presumption of Guilt," Stevenson cited the work of Jennifer Rae Taylor, who noted that while "a black prisoner was a rarity during the slavery era," the solution after the emancipation of slaves involved the "criminalization" of many activities of free black populations. She elaborated by noting that it did not hurt state coffers when black convicts were sold as forced labor for "the profit of the state."[16]

In this strategic narration of Southern racialized pasts, the rise of lynching would be paralleled by the growing use by Southern states of black convict leasing practices. Stevenson noted in 2017 that, "beginning as early as 1866," states "like Texas, Mississippi, and Georgia" started to use convict leasing, and this spread throughout the South.[17]

This focus on exploitative labor is usually omitted from moderate critiques of the "end" of lynching, but for the EJI's arguments about the enduring legacies of lynching and Jim Crow labor abuses, it was important that readers of Stevenson's work see the connections that could be made between historical peonage and today's carceral practices.

All of this could be used by Stevenson to underscore the point that the prosecution of "racial terrorism" included more than just illegal lynchings. Yes, this terrorism included the dread that individual blacks must have felt when, one day, masked KKK riders might ride up to their family's home. But this form of racial terrorism was also collective and structural, and it had everything to do with the daily micro- and macropolitics that were practiced by those who believed in the policing of the American "color line." This included labor exploitation.

In Stevenson's telling of the tale in "A Presumption of Guilt," the refusal of many blacks to accept these abuses during the Reconstruction and Jim Crow years did not lead to any removal of formal or informal discriminatory laws, but it did bring about the hardening of many American hearts. White supremacists sought ways to channel their feelings of frustration, and this led to provocation and agitation. In the words of Bryan Stevenson, these tensions "led to an era of lynching and violence that traumatized black people for decades."[18]

In many of his writings and interviews, Stevenson explains that the EJI has provided new research that has built on the efforts of those who recorded the more than four thousand lynchings that were carried out between 1877 and 1950. He explains how the EJI defines "racial terror lynchings" in ways that distinguish these activities from the hangings or mob violence that followed in the wake of some sort of criminal trial, or lynchings that were "committed against non-minorities."[19]

These are important commentaries, because they implicitly reference some of the issues that plagued members of earlier anti-lynching organizations, who argued among themselves about how to define and how to chronicle lynchings and nonlynchings (see chapter 3).

Many generations of Southern writers—dating back to the slavery era—have associated blacks with criminality, and it is these social knowledge formations, produced by racists, that have been directly challenged by the EJI. In a nice summary of the EJI's agenda, Stevenson noted some of the complexities of these racial terror memoryscapes:

> [R]acial terror lynchings were directed specifically at black people, with little bearing on an actual crime; the aim was to maintain white supremacy and political and economic subordination. We [the EJI] also distinguish terror lynchings from other racial violence and hate crimes that were prosecuted as criminal acts.... [T]he lynchings we documented were acts of terrorism because they were murders carried out with impunity—sometimes in broad daylight.[20]

Stevenson may have thought that this type of commentary brought definitional clarity, but for critical academics who are familiar with some of the earlier "wars of words" that took place during twentieth-century anti-lynching debates, his commentaries might be viewed as raising as many questions as they answered. Was the EJI including "murders" of African Americans who were killed in broad daylight in their lynching statistics, even if no rope was involved? What specific criteria were being used to determine when a violent act of "murder" warranted labeling as a "terror lynching"? Was the EJI including the lynchings of other people of color, who were not African Americans, in their lynching statistics? What if a single individual attacked and killed a black victim? Did that constitute a recorded lynching, even though the killing did not involve a group of three or more who conspired to commit the act?

Regardless of how the EJI was answering these types of queries, the key point here is that Stevenson appeared to want readers of his "Presumption of Guilt" article to be cognizant of the magnitude of racial terror. He drove home the point that public lynchings were meant to put on display the hegemonic powers of white supremacy and were directed against the entire black population.

This point had been alluded to by Ida B. Wells-Barnett, Walter White of the NAACP, W. E. B. Du Bois, and many interdisciplinary writers active since the Cold War years.

Some of the archival records produced by the EJI emphasized the wide variety of ideological forces that motivated those who carried out racial terror lynchings. Bryan Stevenson, in "A Presumption of Guilt," mentioned how distorted fears of interracial sex, "casual social transgressions," allegations of murder or other series crimes, and "retribution for sharecroppers, ministers, and other community leaders who resisted mistreatment" could all lead to lynchings or similar abusive acts.[21]

This underscored the point that Wells-Barnett had made (chapter 2)—that talk of alleged rape of white women by blacks was often a rationale that hid many other personal, social, cultural, and economic motives for lynchings.

As readers might expect, the EJI's chronology needed to account for some postlynching afterlives—"legacies"—and Bryan Stevenson's narrations accomplish this by noting that even those who were not lynched, who may simply have heard rumors of lynchings, were victims of institutionalized racial terrorism. In one typical rhetorical fragment, Stevenson explained:

> Thousands of people fled north for fear that a social misstep in an encounter with a white person might provoke a mob to show up and take their lives. Parents and spouses suffered what they characterized as "near lynchings" and sent their loved ones away in frantic, desperate acts of protection.[22]

We may never know precisely how many African Americans feared for their lives, but the migration of millions provided ample testimony that these fears manifested themselves in observable ways.

Stevenson's way of framing lynching pasts magnified the numbers of potential victims who experienced traumatic fear, and it also raised the question of the transgenerational transmission of lynching trauma. Although Stevenson does not cite much of this work, for decades interdisciplinary scholars interested in Holocaust research, trauma studies, memory studies, genocide studies, and related areas of interest have been debating whether or not relatives, or those who actually experienced horrific events—the "first" generation—could "transmit" or "transfer" those traumas to the sons, daughters, other relatives, or members of second or third generations who shared particular affective feelings.[23]

These would be important issues for people who might seek acknowledgments, apologies, reparations, or other forms of restorative justice for past lynching abuses.

This commentary on "parents and spouses" who suffered was a crucial way of creating discursive bridges that the EJI was willing to build as they linked historical acts of lynching to today's discriminatory societal and carceral practices.

Mediated Representations of Bryan Stevenson's Involvement in Court Cases

In this section, we argue that journalistic commentary becomes a crucial factor in the rhetorical creation of the Stevenson persona.

One key subtheme in the mediated coverage of Stevenson's legalistic narratives of racial injustice is that Southern authorities, after the reported "end" of illegal lynchings, simply moved matters "indoors" into courtrooms. For example, in front of reporters, Stevenson argued that during the Scottsboro trials some whites living in the town of Scottsboro—who wanted to congratulate themselves for getting authorities to intervene to prevent the lynching of these youths—had difficulty processing the negative reactions they were experiencing. Stevenson was not impressed by the appearance of legality whereby the nine Scottsboro defendants were given a trial instead of being lynched in extrajudicial fashion. "In reality," Stevenson noted, "many defendants" of that era "learned that the prospect of being executed rather than lynched did little to introduce fairness into the outcome."[24]

As noted earlier, American moderates and others could point with pride to declining lynching statistics, but what they failed to mention was *the rise of executions*, which Stevenson referenced. This rhetorical linkage of lynchings and executions that appears in Stevenson's narrative of the 1930s Scottsboro trials thus serves as the politicized gateway for critiques of twenty-first-century trials, which Stevenson hints may be just as problematic as historical lynching or legal lynching.

At this point in our critique of Stevenson's discussion of the "rule of law," we invite readers to pause and think about the ideological nature of his claim. As we noted in the introduction, some audiences may be completely on board with the EJI's efforts to recover forgotten lynching pasts, and they may applaud Stevenson's followers for their plan to invite contrite counties to remove parts of the temporary exhibit at the National Memorial for Peace and Justice and relocate them to their respective counties. EJI workers can also be thanked for getting countless visitors, students, amateur historians, and many others interested in revisiting lynching pasts, then returning home to see if their own counties have acknowledged these fraught pasts.

Will some of those same audiences push the envelope and accept Stevenson's tethering of lynching pasts to the history of America' capital punishment apparatus? Will they leave Montgomery and join social movements that campaign for the abolition of capital punishment?

Conservative African Americans, for example, may be willing to support efforts to mark lynching sites, but they may not agree with what Stevenson (or the EJI) are saying about the causes of racialized violence or the politics behind drug laws. Neoliberal politicians, or their constituents, may be willing to defend the study of historical lynching without taking the next step and abolishing capital punishment. These same social agents may see no need for any drastic change in the ways that America's laws are used to confine some Americans to life in prison without parole. Conservatives could argue that, in theory, African Americans and other people of color are imprisoned in disproportionate numbers because they commit a disproportionate number of crimes (see chapter 8).

However, the EJI's supporters might respond to such disassociation of lynching pasts from mass incarceration horrors by arguing that this is one more example of "forgetting" that shows that America truly needs "liberation." For many who identify with Stevenson's legal work, twenty-first-century American defenses of death row policies only underscore the point that a variety of denials, deflections, and equivocations manifest themselves whenever mainstream US audiences are asked to reevaluate the supposed "end" of twentieth-century lynching.

No doubt a great deal of Bryan Stevenson's interest in encouraging pedagogical discussion of capital punishment involves his own practical experience as a lawyer and public advocate. Stevenson has argued several cases in front of the US Supreme Court, and he has petitioned the nation's highest appellate court to end the legal incarceration of children who have been sentenced to lengthy sentences without parole. By 2015, the Equal Justice Initiative could take pride in the fact that they had been involved in saving some 115 persons from the death sentence,[25] and some of those who attended the opening of the Legacy Museum in 2018 were Stevenson's Harvard Law School mentors.

Many of Stevenson's diatribes are directed against the arbitrary, capricious, and unreasonable nature of various capital punishment schemes that often try to bracket out the racist elements that would be an inherent part of lynching legacies. Stevenson argues that the decline in the number of recorded lynchings simply indicates the evolution of social controls, as the American public accepted, or perhaps even demanded, that the use of capital punishment be accelerated. "By the end of the 1930s," Stevenson noted in one chronology of these events, "court-ordered executions outpaced lynchings in the former slave states for the first time."[26]

No doubt Stevenson was hoping that his readers would agree with him that many of those court-ordered executions were carried out after defendants had suffered through cases that had encountered either procedural or substantive due process problems.

These linkages between lynching pasts and capital punishment presents should not be read in a political vacuum. They resonate with like-minded critics of America's judicial system who agree with Stevenson when he argues that something has broken down when a democratic country like the United States incarcerates so many millions.

Once again, when we move into a discussion about the abolition of capital punishment, the lines between Stevenson the person and Stevenson the persona are blurred. Now, instead of simply being the astute organizer who raised funds for the building of the National Memorial for Peace and Justice and the Legacy Museum, he occupies the subject position of the seasoned lawyer who has witnessed more than his fair share of racial discrimination and is demanding the abolition of capital punishment.

The formation of any persona relies on the work of many coconstituents, and in this particular case it is sympathetic journalists who have helped craft and shape the contours of Stevenson's persona. Liliana Segura, for example, commented on the opening of the National Memorial for Peace and Justice, and we would argue that she used the occasion to provide her own incisive critique of America's infatuation with maintaining death rows for prison inmates. In her praxiological reading of Alabama's death row politics, Segura links Montgomery's monumentalism with broader debates about capital punishment reform. She presents readers with analyses of everything from the veins in the bodies of those who are about to die to the technological makeup of electric chairs. She can barely repress her anger as she considers the convoluted rhetorics of people who try to normalize state death penalty policies.

Segura contextualizes some of the work of the EJI in ways that allow her to tell stories about those who are executed, who watch executions, or who listen to Department of Corrections commissioners defend the use of this or that particular method for carrying out capital punishment.

As we read some of Segura's work, we could not help reflecting back on our own readings of 1920s and 1930s federal anti-lynching debates, in which so many Southern politicians in Congress either defended the need for lynchings or argued that, over time, state lynching reform would take care of the lynching problem.

Segura's work also reminds us that interrogating twenty-first-century debates over capital punishment will unearth a few generic elements that have been around since the supposed "end" of lynching. Those who defend capital punishment might argue that the use of lethal injections does not violate constitutional proscriptions against "cruel and unusual" punishment, or that defendants on death row have access to plenty of lawyers. Others might respond to Segura and the EJI by noting that federal and state courts have constantly monitored these practices to ensure that America's implementation of capital punishment is humane in nature. In these colorblind capital punishment tales, authorities spend an inordinate amount of time making sure that those involved in the process don't stray too far from strict criminal justice rules, or constitutional limitations, or other governmentalities that have been imposed by Supreme Court rulings.

Segura situates the growing interest in the EJI's work providing legal representation for needy defendants in ways that underscore the almost Kafkaesque nature of Alabama's capital punishment practices. She ridicules the state's "nothing-to-see-here posture" as a "façade," and she argues that instead of admitting that the system has broken down, Alabama prison officials launch campaigns of obfuscation and misinformation.[27] Much of Segura's writing connects anxieties about lynching pasts with contemporary complaints about what she calls Alabama's "lethal injection regime."[28]

Segura explains that the denialism that is apparent in Alabama can be found in other American states and penal institutions. States like Arkansas, for instance, ignore the horrific nature of lethal injections and other methods of carrying out capital punishment. At one point, Segura notes that after hearing all of this "brazen denialism," she could not help reflecting on the words of "an anti-lynching activist I read before arriving in Alabama," who had written that a "lynching makes a lot of otherwise good people go blind or lose their memories."[29]

This very line, which Segura took out of the lynching archives, appeared in chapter 3 of Arthur Raper's book *The Tragedy of Lynching*, published in 1933.[30]

At this point in her telling of the tale, Segura sees some light at the end of the tunnel when she critiques the work of the Equal Justice Initiative, a "famed legal nonprofit" organization founded in 1989 by Bryan Stevenson. She argues that Stevenson "has made it his life's work to transform how Americans think about our criminal justice system, by tracing its origins and making them visible."[31]

Segura applauds these EJI efforts, and her own investigative journalism lends support to those trying to abolish state capital punishment regimes, which she views as carrying out reprehensible practices that are tantamount to torture. She fights the dismissive nature of the Alabama Department of Corrections' missives, which try to create the public impression that all is well.

The invisible carceral world that Segura renders visible is populated by people who are drugged, placed in "eerie crucifix" positions, and prepared for leaving this world as hundreds of other death row inmates watch, or listen. She conjures up a world where court decisions might temporarily block this or that particular execution, but she describes the judicial process as a machine that drives executions to continue apace.

Liliana Segura is accustomed to visiting state corrections facilities, and when she described in writing the April 2018 opening of the National Memorial for Peace and Justice, she reminded readers not only about sites of lynching but about *places where capital punishment is being meted out*. For example, when Segura read some of the names found on the 805 steel panels at the Lynching Memorial, she could not help noticing the name of Lincoln County, Arkansas, where Kenneth Williams was executed in 2017. She noted how Butts County, Georgia, was not only the site of two recorded lynchings—it was also the home of the Georgia Diagnostic and Classification State Prison in Jackson, the county seat. She recalled a time, years earlier, when a man named Kenneth Fults was executed at that prison, despite the fact that one of the jurors at his trial had allegedly said: "I don't know if he ever killed anybody, but that nigger got just what should have happened."[32]

In an insightful reading of a 1947 US Supreme Court case—which revised the constitutionality of the conviction of a black teenager named Willie Francis—Segura exposed the porous boundaries that theoretically separate lynching rhetorics and capital punishment defenses. Willie Francis had gone to Louisiana's electric chair and somehow miraculously survived, and the obvious legal question was whether punishment had already been meted out, or whether Francis needed to suffer through another round of having electricity flow through his body. The majority of the members of the US Supreme Court, in their eternal wisdom, decided that having Francis endure another electrocution attempt did not violate his Eighth Amendment rights. "Accidents happen," the court decision explained, "for which no man is to blame."[33]

How could readers of Segura's essay doubt that these spaces and places that were now used for carrying out executions were some of the same geopolitical places where lynchings had been carried out "at the hands of persons unknown"?[34]

This last phrase—carried out "at the hands of persons unknown"—had been ridiculed by members of the NAACP and other anti-lynchers during the 1920s and 1930s, but it obviously continued to ideologically drift in the public memories of those who disagreed with the claim that imperfect American laws were to be preferred over lawless lynchings.

Liliana Segura, the investigative journalist—with her epistemic knowledge of capital punishment pasts and her presentist usage of death row politics—was able to see facets of EJI rhetorics that seemed to be ignored, or at least marginalized, by many other visitors to the National Memorial for Peace and Justice. She seemed to truly understand that Stevenson and the EJI wanted to do more than simply add more materials to the lynching archives. Near the end of one of her essays, Segura noted:

> Stevenson calls the death penalty the "stepchild of lynching." At the Legacy Museum, the parallel is starkly drawn. Yet historians who have probed the precise connection have been hamstrung by an absence of reliable data. The federal government never bothered to count the thousands of lynchings that terrorized black communities across the country; and it did not start keeping track of legal executions until 1930.... A data base of early executions exists because of the work of Watt Espy, an Alabama researcher who died in 2009. Nevertheless, the link is unmistakable in the South, where both lynchings and early executions were lawless forms of racial control. Public executions looked a lot like lynchings—and the justifications for both were often the same.[35]

Segura seemed to be aware of some of the historical and argumentative linkages that rarely appeared in more mainstream accounts of the work of the Legacy Museum and the EJI. It was journalistic essays like Segura's that helped transform Stevenson into a heroic, iconic figure among people who wondered, in this age saturated with postracial commentary, if there were any selfless lawyers around who were willing to battle institutional evils.

Some of Segura's work gets at the darkness of mass incarceration, providing insights into the intransigence of states, but Bryan Stevenson—at least in some of his public commentaries—seemed optimistic that, over time, some of this denialism could be eradicated. In the next section, we provide a close-textual reading of some of the key arguments that Stevenson presented in his best-selling book, *Just Mercy*.

A Close-Textual, Critical Reading of Bryan Stevenson's *Just Mercy*

Those who have read *Just Mercy* often comment that it makes them feel sadness, anger, or melancholy. The book is a page-turner, filled with anecdotes that expose the prejudice, indifference, ignorance, and wrongheadedness of those who supervise America's carceral system. In one key passage of *Just Mercy*, Stevenson pulls no punches as he outlines the litany of problems that he has observed after more than three decades of work:

> This book is about getting closer to mass incarceration and extreme punishment in America.... It is also about a dramatic period in our recent history, a period that indelibly marked the lives of millions of Americans.... Today we have the highest rate of incarceration in the world. The prison population has increased from 300,000 in the early 1970s to 2.3 million people today. There are nearly six million people on probation or on parole.... We've institutionalized policies that reduce people to their worst acts and permanently label them "criminal," "murderer," "rapist," "thief," "drug dealer," "sex offender," "felon"—identities they cannot change regardless of the circumstances of their crimes or any improvements they might make in their lives.[36]

Here, it is retribution rather than reform that takes center stage in the defense of American carceral practices. The older lynching mythologies have been replaced with new mass incarceration mythologies populated by the figurative, and racialized, threats that Stevenson identifies in today's drug wars and other campaigns.

Like many successful best-selling authors, Stevenson uses narrative genres to help readers of *Just Mercy* get a textured sense of the racial traumas associated with lynching and other acts of discrimination. He organizes his book to highlight stories about Walter McMillian, a black owner of a timber business who was wrongfully convicted of murdering an eighteen-year-old by the name of Ronda Morrison in Monroeville, Alabama. Stevenson provides us with an "over-the-shoulder" way of following his interactions with McMillian as he explains his initial meetings with McMillian and describes the lengthy appeals process as it worked its way through the justice system. Readers also get an inkling of how Stevenson felt about McMillian's return to society.

In Stevenson's telling, McMillian was blamed for a crime he did not commit. McMillian had an alibi: dozens of witnesses could attest that at the time of Morrison's murder, McMillian was at a home barbecue. McMillian was no angel, and as Stevenson notes in *Just Mercy*, he was accused of infidelity and of carrying on a love affair with a married white woman. Stevenson argues that these types of facts contributed to the guilty verdict that eventually placed McMillian on death row.

Stevenson's defense of McMillian was his first case and would be the highest-profile case of his career. Although it led to a death row acquittal, Stevenson makes the point that before the acquittal McMillian served seven years in prison.[37] Stevenson uses McMillian's case as a representative anecdote, and other parts of *Just Mercy* are filled with similar stories of how the guilty and the nonguilty alike were not provided with the due process rights that they deserved.

One of the many ironies of Stevenson's book is the fact that Monroeville, Alabama—the home of Ronda Morrison—is also the hometown of Harper Lee, author of *To Kill a Mockingbird*, and the model for Lee's fictional town of Maycomb. As in so many other situations, life became entangled with art, and Stevenson's defense of McMillian would be compared with the trial work of the fictional Atticus Finch, the lawyer in Lee's novel. During McMillian's trial, some of the state's key witnesses finally broke down and admitted that that they had totally fabricated the supposed eyewitness statements that they'd filed against McMillian.

Elsewhere in *Just Mercy*, Stevenson uses other narrative devices to help readers understand just why he wishes to abolish capital punishment. He explains that when "a conservative majority took power in Congress in 1994, legal aid to death row prisoners became a political target," and most of "the capital representation resource centers around the country were forced to close."[38]

What Stevenson does not mention in *Just Mercy* are many of the racial, class-oriented, gendered, and other political stances behind the conservative majority decision-making that he alludes to in his book. We will have more to say about that in our conclusion.

While the first half of *Just Mercy* provides background materials pertaining to Stevenson's motivations for going to Harvard Law School, the second half of the book is framed in ways that allow the author to tackle a variety of mass incarceration issues—from the treatment of the mentally disabled to the wrongfully convicted to the lack of mercy for guilty prisoners who have changed their ways. For example, addressing the problematic nature of trying African juveniles as adults and placing them in horrific prison situations, Stevenson notes that two of the Scottsboro Boys in the 1930s, Roy Wright and Eugene Williams, were "just thirteen years old when they were wrongfully convicted of rape and sentenced to death in Alabama."[39]

Here, we should note that in Montgomery's Legacy Museum visitors are presented with a massive, blown-up picture of a mother tearfully saying goodbye to a fourteen-year-old youth who is about to be executed.

Stevenson's book situates these types of historical miscarriages of justice by placing them in a much broader racialized genealogy when he references South Carolina's 1944 execution of "a fourteen-year-old black boy," George Stinney. In Stevenson's chronicling of Stinney's predicament, Stinney had been playing with his siblings in his hometown of Alcolu, South Carolina, while search teams were looking for two young white girls who had gone missing. The naïve Stinney just happened to mention that he and his sister had seen the two missing girls earlier in the day. The next day, after the bodies of the two dead girls were found, Stinney—in the presence of his parents and an attorney—was subjected to withering interrogation, because it was assumed that he was the last person who had seen the girls alive.[40] The sheriff tried to strengthen the case against Stinney by claiming that he had confessed, and when a lynch mob formed outside the jail, Stinney was moved to a facility in Charleston, South Carolina.

One can almost sense Stevenson's feelings of disbelief and anger as he retells Stinney's tale in *Just Mercy*. We read about how the proceedings of the trial convened in a South Carolina courtroom required the fourteen-year-old defendant to sit all "alone in front of an estimated crowd of fifteen hundred white people who had packed the courtroom and surrounded the building."[41] When the judge, Philip H. Stoll, sentenced Stinney to death, Stinney's lawyers announced that there would be no appeal because his family didn't have the money to pay for it. "Years later," Stevenson notes, "rumors surfaced that a white man from a prominent family confessed on his deathbed to killing the girls," and this information has recently been used to try to posthumously exonerate Stinney.[42]

The following passage serves as an illustrative example of how Stevenson sees symbolic and material connections between past racial terror events and present legal shortcomings:

> The Stinney execution was horrific and heartbreaking, but it reflected the racial politics of the South more than the way children accused of crimes were generally treated. It was an example of how politics and norms once directed exclusively at controlling and punishing the black population have filtered their way into our general criminal justice system. By the late 1980s and 1990s, the politics of fear and anger sweeping the country and fueling mass incarceration was turning its attention to children. Influential criminologists predicted a coming wave of "superpredators." ... Panic ... led nearly every state to enact legislation that increased the exposure of children to adult prosecution.[43]

By the time proponents of this "superpredator" theory realized the error of their ways and recanted, it was too late, resulting in the "adultification" of youths.

Throughout *Just Mercy*, Stevenson moves back and forth in time, developing his argument that, in spite of generational differences, some structures and societal attitudes toward blacks remained the same.

When Walter McMillian was released from prison, and when he started to travel with Bryan Stevenson to legal conferences to talk about his experiences, Stevenson chronicled how his story "was a counternarrative to the rhetoric of fairness and reliability offered by politicians and law enforcement officials who wanted more and faster executions."[44] Aided by the publication of Pete Earley's book on McMillian's case, *Circumstantial Evidence*,[45] Stevenson and McMillian were able to tell many legal students and decision-makers about the problematic nature of America's capital punishment system.

By the time readers get to the end of *Just Mercy*, they have been presented with depictions of dedicated EJI workers who are constantly flying to places like South Dakota or Missouri or California so that they can argue cases on behalf of indigent defendants, prisoners with disabilities, those who have been unjustly accused, or even the guilty who are nevertheless suffering from excessive punishment.

From a critical rhetorical vantage point, the very act of reading *Just Mercy* becomes an invitation to readers who may wish to join the ranks of the EJI "stonecatchers," who take on the Sisyphean task of trying to ameliorate conditions in America's prison industrial complex. The "stonecatchers" stand "between those who 'cast stones' and those who are daily injured by a politics of hate and violence" in the age of Trump.[46]

Reactions to the Formation of Stevenson's Persona and Responses to His Commentaries on Capital Punishment

Reading *Just Mercy* may be an enlightening or liberating act in and of itself, but as critical genealogists we are also interested to taking up the question of whether his treatment of legal lynchings and other problematics resonates with other Americans in legal or public venues. One way that critical scholars might gauge this is by seeing how American and international audiences have reacted to the ways investigative journalists and others have adopted certain perspectival positions on his work.

In November 2015, Stevenson was interviewed by Oprah Winfrey for *SuperSoul Sunday*. Trumpeting one of his favorite themes—that America's system of justice "treats you better if you're rich and guilty than if you're poor and innocent"—Stevenson went on to elaborate on how "wealth, not culpability—shapes outcomes."[47] Abolishing the death penalty, argued Stevenson, would "liberate us from the worst parts of our history. . . . You can't be in counties and communities where people have been lynched and threatened and menaced and terrorized, and then have a person of color taken to death row."[48]

Obviously, given the polarizing nature of the topic of capital punishment, not all Americans are going to accept Stevenson's reasoning, his evidence, his warrants, or his framing of criminality. That said, growing numbers of journalists seem genuinely interested in helping the EJI cause. Robert Siegel of National Public Radio explained to listeners how the EJI staff, by 2015, had won "cases for 130 people who had been wrongly condemned."[49] Siegel then mentioned that some 2017 executions in Arkansas (four in eight days) were the first there in more than a decade, and that perhaps they were coming at a time when public support for the death penalty was on the decline.[50]

The exchange that took place after this seemed to provide both Siegel and Stevenson with a political platform for critiquing capital punishment in general and these Arkansas executions in particular. Stevenson responded to Siegel's comments by noting that the state of Arkansas didn't carry out those executions because the "process had worked to completion with the kind of reliability that we tend to want," but rather because of concerns over a "drug expiring." Stevenson then suggested that while the statistical figure of 49 percent public support for capital punishment indicated a dramatic decrease in such support from decades earlier, listeners needed to keep in mind that lawyers had now seen "158 people released from death row after being proved innocent." This meant that, extrapolating from the total numbers, for every nine people who had been executed, one of them might have been an innocent person.[51] Had the circulation of such information changed American attitudes toward capital punishment?

International audiences have also had the opportunity to listen to some of Bryan Stevenson's pithy remarks. For example, during a visit to Australia, the director of the EJI asked, as quoted in the title of a *Guardian* article: "If It's Not Right to Rape a Rapist, How Can It Be OK to Kill a Killer?"[52] Stevenson took the opportunity to argue that capital punishment dehumanizes everyone who is involved in the carrying out of death penalties, and he expressed his sense of the surrealism that surrounded the execution of one of his clients, Herbert Richardson. After the courts denied Richardson a stay of execution, guards had to physically separate this newly married man from his family before he was strapped into the electric chair. During his interview with the *Guardian*'s Brigid Delaney, Stevenson recalled his last conversation with Richardson:

> It was impactful for me to witness that. I was standing with this [condemned] man and he was saying, "Bryan it's been such a strange day—all day long people, the guards have been saying, 'What can I do to help you? Can I get you something?'" . . . More people said, "What can I do to help you?" in the last 14 hours of his life than the last 19 years of his life when he really needed it—when he returned from Vietnam drug addicted and traumatized—where were they? . . . Seeing people moving around this man in his last hours, shaving the hair off his body so he would be a more efficient conduit for electricity that would kill him and watching these people try to do that—it was so clear that everyone there knew what was happening was wrong.[53]

Stevenson's *Guardian* interview—like the statues outside the National Memorial for Peace and Justice, the displays in the Legacy Museum, the EJI's commentaries, and the text of *Just Mercy*—serves as a vehicle for bringing together those who would abolish capital punishment in the same way that earlier generations abolished slavery.[54]

Make no mistake that there are many who listen to, and learn from, Stevenson's interviews, lectures, and speeches. When Jeffrey Toobin of the *New*

Yorker heard about the famous *Sullivan* case that Stevenson argued in front of the US Supreme Court, he cared enough to track down Joe Sullivan, a mentally disabled prisoner who now lived in a remote part of northern Florida. Sullivan told Toobin that he was "just with the wrong people at the wrong time," and that the crowd that he was with claimed that Sullivan was a mastermind who committed sexual battery. Toobin then proceeded to write an essay that begins with Stevenson's opening remarks during his 2009 presentation in front of the nine justices of the Supreme Court.[55]

Is it possible that, in the coming years, if enough American citizens decide to abolish capital punishment, Stevenson will be remembered as one of the iconic figures who made that happen? Will more stonecatchers help universalize Stevenson's radical message?

Throughout this chapter, in presenting our critical biography of Bryan Stevenson, we have purposely selected commentaries from journalists and others who often sympathize with the radicalism of the EJI. That said, we also recognize the challenges that Stevenson may face in future years when supporters of anti-lynching efforts find that he is also advocating the abolition of capital punishment and unfair prison sentencing. Stevenson may have become a heroic public figure for some, but we hazard the guess that others may soon be viewing him as a polarizing figure—once they realize that the EJI is asking for more than just setting the record straight about historical numbers of lynchings.

We are not alone in arguing that not everyone will be interested in reading *Just Mercy*, listening to Stevenson's 2012 TED Talk, or parsing the words that he uses as he contextualizes mass incarceration presents and lynching pasts. Tim Adams, for example, noted how reviewers of Stevenson's book seemed to have "stopped short of confronting the magnitude of what he writes," and more than a few seemed to treat some of the epistemic materials that he presents in his book as "an examination of certain miscarriages of justice." What they were missing, opined Adams, was that this was also intended to be an "indictment of the system as a whole."[56]

Yet, those of us who study the various subject positions of Bryan Stevenson, and those who investigate the responses to those rhetorical constructions, may want to take solace from the fact that Stevenson is not toiling alone. Already, several empowered decision-makers, including justices, have changed their minds or spoken out about the problematic nature of America's death penalty regime. In 1994, for example, Justice Harry Blackmun wrote in *Collins v. Collins*:

> From this day forward, I no longer shall tinker with the machinery of death. For more than 20 years, I have endeavored—indeed, I have struggled—along with a majority of this Court, to develop procedural and substantive rules that would lend more than the mere appearance of fairness to the death penalty endeavor. Rather than continue to coddle the Court's delusion that the desired level of fairness has been achieved ... I feel morally and intellectually obligated simply to concede that the death penalty experiment has failed.[57]

Note how much stronger this message might have been if Blackmun had gone on to point out that some of those death penalty delusions *had everything to do with ethnic or racial discrimination.*

CHAPTER 6

EJI Critiques of Confederate Statuary, Dixie Monumentalization, and Charlottesville Legacies

SOME OF THE MOST CONTROVERSIAL TEXTUAL AND VISUAL ARGUMENTS THAT HAVE been presented by Bryan Stevenson, the Equal Justice Initiative, and the Legacy Museum have to do with the attempts to dismantle the Confederate statuary that appears in so many American landscapes. As an example of how some members of the EJI contextualize efforts to build, maintain, and guard Confederate memorials, note how the EJI's website discusses some of these issues in an essay entitled "Alabama Lawmakers Protect Confederate Memorials":

> In a move to prevent communities from addressing racially insensitive memorials, symbols, and monuments, the Alabama legislature passed an unprecedented bill that prohibits the "relocation, removal, alteration, renaming, or other disturbance of" any Confederate or other monument that is at least 40 years old. Alabama Governor Kay Ivey signed the Alabama Memorial Preservation Act into law.... The new law also prohibits renaming buildings and streets with historical names that have been in place at least 40 years, and requires approval from a new commission to change or rename buildings, streets, schools, or other monuments that are between 20 and 40 years old.[1]

The essay went on to explain that Alabama senator Gerald Allen had introduced the legislation to "shield Confederate memorials" after the state had decided to remove the Confederate flag from the capitol grounds in 2015, following coverage of the killing of African American worshippers in a Charleston, South Carolina, church by a young white man "who embraced Confederate iconography."[2] In spite of the fact that an "88-foot-tall Confederate monument" remained on the capitol grounds, the EJI reported that hundreds of white Alabamians had gathered in Montgomery to protest the flag's removal, "alleging cultural genocide and holding signs proclaiming that 'Southern Lives Matter.'"[3]

All of these activities that linked the preservation of Confederate memorialization to allegations of "cultural genocide" can be viewed as examples of participatory acts that have been carried out by members of far right, the alternative right, white nationalist groups, and others in places like South Africa, Australia, Canada, France, and elsewhere who complain about the "Great Replacement" of the white race or "white genocide."[4] The proclamation "Southern Lives Matter" is an example of the inversions and appropriations made by Alabamian whites of "leftist" arguments about the World War II Holocaust and indigenous genocides that have been forwarded since at least the early 1960s.

The EJI symbolically and materially linked local, urban disputation in Montgomery to more regional arguments about monument preservation when they noted that across the South, "132 Confederate rallies took place within six weeks of the Charleston shooting, including a Ku Klux Klan rally at the South Carolina statehouse demanding the flag's return."[5]

Although the EJI argued that the Alabama legislature's monument preservation act was unprecedented, there are in fact many historical and contemporary precedents for the passage of these acts. Some Southern states passed Confederate memorial preservation acts during the early decades of the twentieth century, and other states in the South during the twenty-first century either amended those older statutes or passed new ones.[6] The Alabama law that the EJI was critiquing was just one of many Southern Confederate monument preservation acts that would be proposed in these localized skirmishes in what Kirk Savage characterized as the larger "monument wars."[7]

The EJI's interventions in these monument wars become performative events that have everything to do with related arguments about the acknowledgment of past lynching horrors, presentist efforts to defend white supremacy, and the need for eventual reconciliation. On the same weekend that the National Memorial for Peace and Justice was opened to the public, the Southern Poverty Law Center reported that as "Confederate monuments are going down, lynching memorials are going up."[8]

But what about situations in which new Confederate memorials and other types of monumentalization *were also going up* in these symbolic battles over memoryscapes, landscapes, and hearts and minds?[9]

Some academics who observe these local or regional monumental feuds, or who are studying the nature of racial terrorism, or who are investigating lynching histories, may view some of these memorial debates as matters that involve "misunderstandings." W. Fitzhugh Brundage, for example, writing in 2018, opined:

> The contemporary commemorative landscape in the United States is dense with Confederate memorials. Although the national tolerance for these monuments that honor sedition, rebellion, treason and white supremacy has waned in some communities, there is still widespread misunderstandings [sic] about their origins and intended meanings.[10]

Brundage assumes that if most members of the mainstream knew about the origins of these monuments, or the racism associated with these "Lost Cause" memorials, they would not be that tolerant of Confederate monument preservation acts.

We are not so sure. What if many of the audiences who defend this Confederate statuary have no misunderstandings about the Jim Crow origins of these older Confederate memorials that are being preserved, and what if they are aware of the symbolic significance of these monuments? Brundage may be right, that some Americans may be genuinely horrified to learn of the white supremacist origins of some of these memorials, but others may know all about their "intended meanings" and may be trying to mobilize those very resources in today's culture war confrontations.

We shall see in this chapter that, often, Southern cities that have newly formed publics—made up of coalitions of economically empowered blacks, immigrants, and others who want to see more municipal expressions of intercultural tolerance—try to pass Confederate statue removal regulations, only to have lawsuits filed by proponents of the statues seeking help from state legislatures. As one newspaper noted in 2019:

> Two years after the Charlottesville march and its aftermath, states, cities, and citizens all across America continue to struggle with how to handle and interpret the artifacts of the past in the present day. In that struggle, different narratives clash with modern distributions of power. Conservative Southern state legislatures have passed laws protecting historical monuments, including Confederate statuary. More liberal local jurisdictions are trying to rethink and reframe the meaning of these relics by surrounding them with context, including explanatory material such as signs and plaques.[11]

William Ferris, a University of North Carolina professor, contends that the "statues are markers along the way of how we address both the past and the future as a people," and that change is in the air because "in the 21st century" we are witnessing "an interesting turn as the country is becoming predominately nonwhite."[12]

One's views regarding this entanglement of local-state relations, cultural clashes, and disagreements about multiculturalism and heritage impact how one assesses these Southern state statutes that are passed in order to prohibit the removal of older Confederate statues and other Lost Cause memorialization.

This political wrangling between cities and states has not dampened the spirits of EJI workers, who place Confederate monument removal on their agenda. In the same ways that critical race scholars once used arguments about hate speech to try to change hearts and minds about the limits of freedom of expression, now EJI members are joining those who are asking Americans to reconceptualize how they think about Confederate statuary. For example, in an interview with *Vox*, an alternative press outlet, Bryan Stevenson explained to Ezra Klein what it was like to "grow up black amid Confederate monuments."[13] When Campbell Robertson of the *New York Times* commented on how the National Memorial for Peace and Justice was going to be dedicated to "victims of white supremacy," he could not help commenting on the symbolism of Confederate statuary.[14]

As critical poststructural scholars, we are interested in understanding the power/discourse/knowledge dimensions of this variant of the monument wars.[15] Rather than adopting a priori, neoliberal positions on these disputes, which assume that attempts to preserve Confederate monumentalization can be explained by historical ignorance and misunderstandings, we want to see how these monumental disputes involve local and regional power struggles as well as epistemic contestations.

As we have noted in previous chapters, the National Memorial for Peace and Justice was placed in Montgomery, Alabama, for strategic reasons. Montgomery was the original capital of the former Confederacy (before that was moved to Richmond, Virginia), and it was a major hub for the trafficking, sale, and purchase of slaves. Tangible and intangible traces of this dark history—or difficult heritage—are located throughout a city, which, to reporter Chris Flood, remains "the heart of the Confederacy."[16]

While some defenders of Confederate statuary might argue that these monuments are apolitical and arhetorical in nature—like the legal "neutral principles" or the "colorblind" rhetorics we critiqued earlier—we beg to differ. There are no shortages of American communities who believe that white

CONFEDERATE STATUARY, DIXIE MONUMENTALIZATION, AND CHARLOTTESVILLE LEGACIES 141

Figure 2: Lurleen B. Wallace Office Building, Montgomery, Alabama. Photo by the authors.

supremacy is etched into the very stones of Montgomery buildings. "These statues of metal look like mute monuments," contends Jalane Schmidt, "but as we found out they are distilled hate."[17]

Keep in mind Schmidt's critique in realizing that the state of Alabama has 121 monuments to the Confederacy, and that relics of this Confederate past are located in schools, public buildings and offices, and memorials and museums.[18] This is one of the reasons why in chapter 5 we underscored the point that Bryan Stevenson's and the EJI's historicizing is not the only "history" of fraught Southern pasts.

When one travels to the National Memorial for Peace and Justice and the Legacy Museum, one cannot help noticing this surplus of Confederate symbolism, and the surfeit of memories, that have become indelible parts of the cityscapes of Montgomery and the state of Alabama. Observable from the apex of the Lynching Memorial, for instance, is the Alabama State Capitol, a structure glossed with white paint and surrounded by memorials to former Confederate soldiers. Across the street is the Lurleen B. Wallace Office Building, named after the forty-sixth governor of Alabama, who succeeded her infamous husband, George Wallace (fig. 2).

It is also hard to miss the eighty-eight-foot-tall Confederate Monument, mentioned above, which commemorates the fallen Confederate soldiers who fought the "War of Northern Aggression." From an interpellation standpoint, how can visitors avoid being "hailed" as they walk up and down a grand

Figure 3: Jefferson Davis statue, Montgomery, Alabama. Photo by the authors.

Figure 4: Jefferson Davis statue, Montgomery, Alabama. Photo by the authors.

staircase that appears directly in front of the capitol? In these politicized webs of signification, to be Southern, or to be American in this part of the country, is to be immersed in Dixie life. The EJI's works must sense that visible and invisible inclusionary and exclusionary boundaries are being constructed through bricks and mortar and these Confederate ideological assemblages.

Figure 5: James Marion Sims statue, Montgomery, Alabama. Photo by the authors.

Figure 6: Plaque for James Marion Sims statue, Montgomery, Alabama. Photo by the authors.

Tourists and others who view these grounds, whether they are aware of it or not, are traversing spaces and places that are constructed in ways that not only represent histories and memories but *produce them as well*. On the grounds of the Alabama State Capitol are larger-than-life statues of Jefferson Davis and James Marion Sims—the "father of gynecology," who conducted surgical experimentation on slave women without anesthesia and who has been dubbed "Father Butcher" and even "Frankenstein" due to allegations of medical malpractice, which have been considered precursors to the Tuskegee syphilis studies (figs. 5, 6).[19]

And just down the street from the National Memorial for Peace and Justice is the First White House of the Confederacy.

The Confederate battle flag, of course, is another visual icon that appears throughout this region. As a symbol with its own Southern genealogy—one that has unfortunately been used to promote anti-desegregation efforts, intimidation tactics, white supremacy rallies, and Southern "Lost Causes"[20]—the flag has come under recent scrutiny in the wake of racialized hate crimes such as the tragic deadly shooting at the Emanuel African Methodist Episcopal Church in Charleston, South Carolina, by Dylann Roof, who claimed the lives of nine African Americans. Roof was an outspoken white supremacist who once posed for a glorified selfie in front of the Confederate flag at the South Carolina State Capitol.[21]

No longer can visitors to the Lynching Memorial or the Legacy Museum look at those Confederate flags and say that they have nothing to do with race or ethnicity because we live in a postracial age. Events in Charlottesville, Virginia, in August 2017, discussed below, also make that clear. But how can one resolve, or at least come to terms with, seemingly irreconcilable monumentalization issues when so much is at stake?

The fact remains that, regardless of multidirectional motivations, the South is peppered with Confederate monuments and memorials. Speaking about the impact that all of this memorialization has on identity formation, Bryan Stevenson noted that many in the South have "created the counternarrative that says we have nothing about which we should be ashamed."[22] "Our past is romantic and glorious," he continued. "In my state of Alabama, Jefferson Davis's birthday is a state holiday. Confederate Memorial Day is a state holiday. We don't even have Martin Luther King Day in Alabama. We have Martin Luther King/Robert E. Lee Day. Our two largest high schools are Robert E. Lee High and Jefferson Davis High. They're both 90-some percent African American. If we don't think it matters, then I think we're just kidding ourselves."[23]

Here, we would like to make several points about Stevenson's framing of these monumental contests. First, note the way that Stevenson characterizes the Confederate memorialization in Alabama as a "counternarrative," implying that the EJI's shaming storytelling provides the real "history" and essential "narrative." Second, his referencing of twenty-first-century recollections of glorious antebellum memories in the South provides one more piece of evidence that America does indeed need to be liberated from its failure to master difficult racial terror pasts. Third, his commentaries on Jefferson Davis High School and Robert E. Lee High School do more than imply that all of this Confederate naming of buildings is an example of what Friedrich

Nietzsche during the nineteenth century called antiquarian, ossified histories that are in need of "critical" historical contextualization.[24]

Bryan Stevenson contends that he sees all of this symbolic contestation in Alabama and the rest of the South as evidence of the continued legacy of slavery, which, we might add, adds extra potency to place-based rhetorics at places like the Lynching Memorial and the Legacy Museum.[25]

While academic visitors to the Lynching Memorial might argue that the memorial does not directly challenge Confederate monumentality, it is also clear that the EJI prepares reports that include critiques of Confederate statuary and monuments. The EJI organization insists that it is seeking "the truth" about this historical "legacy of racial terror" for more "thoughtful and informed" commitments to justice in the present.[26] "If you read the 13th Amendment," Stevenson notes, "it talks about ending involuntary servitude and forced labor, but it doesn't say anything about the narrative of racial difference, the ideology of white supremacy." That is why, he contends, "slavery didn't end in 1865; it just evolved. We had decades of terrorism and violence and lynching. The North won the Civil War, but the South won the narrative war. There was no actual accountability. There was no reckoning. There was no acknowledgment that slavery was wrong at some fundamental level."[27]

What would Stevenson see as "actual accountability," a "reckoning," or "acknowledgment"? Would these abstract ideographic terms be concretized or operationalized by acts of removal of Confederate statuary? Is Stevenson calling for the formation of US truth and reconciliation commissions? Is his own storytelling in this "narrative war" being deployed by those who are demanding reparations or other forms of restorative justice? Is Stevenson right, or is he exaggerating when he contends that many Southerners saw nothing fundamentally wrong with slavery? What would his brand of the New Reconstruction look like in places like Montgomery?

We will work at answering some of these questions in later chapters, but for now we want to underscore the point that Stevenson seems to be convinced that when the white South won its "narrative war," this led to the formation of many absences, including the lack of acknowledgement that the civil rights movement had only been partially successful.

In his book *Just Mercy*, Stevenson talks about Southern monumentalization as well as some of the granular features of what happened after the white supremacists in the South "won" the post-Reconstruction narrative war. Stevenson uses his book as a vehicle to show readers what life was like in Montgomery—or what he calls the "Old South"—during a time when he was legally representing a mentally challenged individual for the Equal Justice Initiative. His client, who suffered from brain damage after a car accident, was accused of killing a police officer when a gun accidentally went off after the officer, who had "a reputation for being aggressive," forcefully removed the individual from a house that he confusedly thought was his. Pulling into the prison parking lot to meet his client, Stevenson saw some of the Confederate flag decals, bumper stickers, and images that are commonplace in this region. One bumper sticker read, "If I'd Known It Was Going to Be Like This, I'd Have Picked My Own Damn Cotton."[28]

Here, in one section of *Just Mercy*, Stevenson manages to suture together commentaries about Dixie monumentalism with talk of labor abuses along with critiques of police harassment and societal presumptions of guilt. For Stevenson, Confederate remembrances provide some of the ideological grammatologies and rhetorical influences that contribute to racial tensions and feelings of retribution and revenge that stand in the way of the dispensation of mercy.

Stevenson's *Just Mercy* is filled with references to the Confederate statuary and memorialization that serve as reminders of the ossified nature of the racial terrorist ideologies that helped create the inequitable world he has to deal with. In portions of his book, Stevenson talks about how his grandmother—the daughter of enslaved persons—told stories about how Confederate symbolism was used to scare blacks into submission during the Reconstruction years. His grandmother made him aware, in his words, that "the recently emancipated black people were essentially re-enslaved by former Confederate officers and soldiers, who used violence, intimidation, lynching, and peonage to keep African Americans subordinate and marginalized."[29] After talking with her, Stevenson could realize that "any sign of black progress in the South" was susceptible to being undermined by white reactionary performances that used signs and symbols of the Confederacy to help spark "talk of resistance."[30]

Stevenson's book thus provides one more rhetorical weapon in the arsenal of twenty-first-century academics, Antifa activists, and others who defend multicultural ideologies at the same time that they work feverishly to either take down Confederate statuary or prevent the building of new Confederate markers or monuments. For African Americans who view themselves as members of second- or third-class generations who are also traumatized by this Dixie monumentalization, trying to liberate America from Confederate nostalgia becomes a moral imperative.

The state governments of both Alabama and South Carolina eventually removed the Confederate flags that once flew over their respective state capitols, but those symbols remain part of the very identity of those who believe in mythic "Lost Cause" ideologies. While many decision-makers have also removed, banned, or outlawed monuments to the Confederacy, thousands of other monuments have been preserved, and they continue to become lightning rods for controversy throughout the United States. To Rick Hampson, writing in an essay entitled "Confederate Memorials Turn Up Faster Than They Can Be Removed," those who try to remove these Confederate symbols face difficult tasks. The registry of Confederate memorials, according to the Southern Poverty Law Center, is currently at 1,740—237 more than in 2016.[31]

Obviously, something is going on that has to do with more than just the preservation of the older Confederate memorials that were put up during the Reconstruction or post-Reconstruction years. In this return of the repressed, in the same ways that African Americans and their Radical Republican allies once faced backlash after the end of the first Reconstruction in 1877, now "New" Reconstructionists like EJI workers who try to combat Confederate statue preservation acts have to deal with other forms of recalcitrance.

Is it possible that some in the South seek to win yet another battle in the evolving Lost Cause transgenerational "narrative" wars that Bryan Stevenson mentioned in one of his essays?

In Alabama, Confederate Memorial Day was revived when white Southerners formed the "Dixiecrat" coalition to oppose desegregation efforts. Perhaps anticipating that African Americans returning home from World War II would no longer tolerate certain working arrangements or carceral practices, whites in Alabama sought to let everyone know that little would, or should, change in their state. "Massive resistance" was in the air during the turbulent Cold War years, and we must contextualize Alabama's passage of Confederate Memorial Day by adding that some of these events were transpiring after the US Supreme Court in *Brown v. Board of Education* ruled that racial segregation in public schools was unconstitutional.[32]

Alabama's state constitution to this day can be interpreted in epistemic ways that seem to continue to mandate that persons of color ("coloreds") and whites attend separate schools.[33] Consider also how, in a 2018 federal appeals court case, judges struck down a lower court ruling allowing Alabama to continue its segregationist practices in public schools in Birmingham, concluding that schools were making racially motivated enrollment decisions that, essentially, "kicked out" black students from predominantly white suburban schools.[34]

Is this more evidence of the failures of "colorblind" contextualizations? In a 2018 *Slate* article entitled "How Did an Alabama County Just Open Its First Integrated School," author Molly Olmstead explains how, "nearly 65 years after the *Brown v. Board* ruling," these racial practices are made possible through redlining, racialized political scheming, and "segregation academies" that have allowed Southern states to evade federal mandates for integration. Even though these court-ordered schools have begun to integrate, many Southern public schools "remain overwhelmingly white and feed into a system of education inequality that persists to this day."[35]

The invisibility of these racial inequalities might explain why many people of color argue that they lost "the narrative" after the Civil War. Hence the importance of providing American publics with the in situ counternarratives of racial terrorism that can be found at the National Memorial for Peace and Justice and the Legacy Museum.[36]

During times when so many can witness these renewed debates over the status of Confederate memorials and monuments—and see the impact of hate crimes that are committed in places like Charleston, South Carolina; Louisville, Kentucky; and Pittsburgh, Pennsylvania[37]—these places of public memory in Alabama present some of the most compelling counterarguments against the forgetting of the legacy of slavery and racial terrorism.

The National Memorial for Peace and Justice is not a hermetically sealed container of meaning that exists only to remove conceptual blockages about slavery pasts and lynching legacies in Montgomery; it is a living, didactic, participatory, vernacular public place of memory that powerfully speaks against the glorification of Confederate pasts through monumentalizations of the "Lost Cause." Supporters of the EJI's efforts to demystify these Lost Cause rhetorics could say that the EJI is needed precisely because the Lynching Memorial generates a countercultural historicity—or what James Young calls a countermonumentality[38]—that critiques the romanticized and glorified features of Dixie monumentalization.

We wonder, then, how this place of memory creates or contributes to the stasis of debates about the role of Confederate monuments throughout the United States. How are locals responding to the EJI's arguments in Montgomery? Are people who tend to defend Confederate monumentality also those who tend to be more critical of the National Memorial for Peace and Justice and the Legacy Museum? Is this an example of what Michael Rothberg called a "competitive" or "multidirectional" memory?[39]

We argue that some of the cultural resistance to the National Memorial for Peace and Justice and the Legacy Museum has everything to do with what V. William Balthrop once described as the mythic ideology of the Lost Cause.[40] While we acknowledge the continued resonance of these Lost Cause ideologies in the perpetuation of Dixie monumentalization, we also recognize that the EJI's Lynching Memorial and Legacy Museum provide cultural provocations in Montgomery that remind us all of the revelatory potential of countermonuments.

The Cultural Challenges Posed by Confederate Memorialization

If the Unite the Right rally in Charlottesville, Virginia, in August 2017 made one thing clear, it was that Confederate monumentality and paraphernalia are more than cultural tokens to an innocent Southern past in a "postracial" American era. Confrontation erupted after a group of about 250 Unite the Right marchers—including neo-Nazis, members of the KKK, and members of the alt-right—assembled at the University of Virginia campus and began a march to protest plans to remove both the Robert E. Lee statue in Emancipation Park and a nearby statue of General Stonewall Jackson. Chants could be heard throughout the campus as the marchers yelled "Blood and soil!," "You will not replace us!," "Jews will not replace us!," and "White lives matter!"[41]

Matters got completely out of hand in Charlottesville. As the confrontations escalated, expletives were exchanged between protesters and counterprotesters. "Go the f— home!," yelled a black women as she passed the protesters.[42] "Go the f— back to Africa," a white supremacist yelled back. "Dylann Roof was a hero!" shouted another. And then someone threw a torch at Joe Heim, a *Washington Post* reporter.[43] One of the counterprotesters, Heather Heyer, was killed by a white supremacist who plowed his vehicle into a crowd of people.

After these violent clashes, President Donald Trump said that there were "very fine people on both sides" of the Charlottesville dispute; and scholar James Sanchez was convinced that Trump had emboldened the national supremacists when he did not distance himself from the rhetoric and actions of the KKK.[44] Some critical scholars might go so far as to argue that Trump's populist way of defending members of Unite the Right resembles the tactics of others on the far right, including David Duke and other members of the KKK, who recirculate ideologies that exhibit the *rhetorical versatility* and heterogeneity that can render such racialized discourses "palatable for a general audience."[45]

Depending on one's political views and one's multidirectional memories, some or all of those who clashed in Charlottesville could be viewed as culpable social agents who were contributing to spirals of violence. The antifascists argued that they were simply trying to counterdemonstrate and curb the excesses of the white supremacists and their Unite the Right allies, while their detractors argued that they, too, were acting as if they were domestic terrorists.[46]

What happened in Charlottesville galvanized the efforts of many Americans, who began discussing some of the very same issues regarding the recruitment of youths by white supremacist groups that were already being addressed by those who were putting up the National Memorial for Peace and Justice and the Legacy Museum.[47]

As we write this chapter, both the Lee and Jackson statues in Charlottesville remain in place as court cases are appealed.[48] Some judges, lawyers, and legislators in Virginia are arguing that the statues are war memorials that are protected by both long-standing and contemporary Virginia state preservation laws.[49] Many Confederate monuments throughout the country, however, have been removed, including the Stonewall Jackson and Robert E. Lee monument in Baltimore (in addition to numerous others in that city), the Robert E. Lee monument in New Orleans, the Monument to Confederate Soldiers on the University of Louisville's Belknap Campus, and "Silent Sam"—a statue of an anonymous Confederate soldier on the campus of the University of North Carolina at Chapel Hill.

Perhaps, given the heated nature of the twenty-first-century culture wars, it was inevitable that municipalities, states, and other entities would get caught up in these monument disputes. New Orleans mayor Mitch Landrieu took down four monuments in one jurisdiction and had this to say regarding to the need to confront this dark part of American history: "These statues are not just stone and metal. They're not just innocent remembrances of a benign history. These monuments celebrate a fictional, sanitized Confederacy—ignoring the death, ignoring the enslavement, ignoring the terror that it actually stood for."[50]

Again, the EJI was not the only social agent using racial terror grammatologies.

These types of contextualizations did not go unchallenged. President Trump, who opposed the removal of Confederate statues and monuments from public spaces, argued: "You can't change history, but you can learn from it. Robert E. Lee, Stonewall Jackson—who's next, Washington, Jefferson? So foolish! Also the beauty that is being taken out of our cities, towns and parks will greatly be missed and never able to be comparably replaced!"[51] Trump portrayed an American culture that was being "ripped apart" by removing Confederate statues and memorials.[52]

Representative Karl Oliver, of the Mississippi House of Representatives, advancing similar claims, wrote this in a Facebook post:

> The destruction of these monuments, erected in the loving memory of our family and fellow Southern Americans, is both heinous and horrific. If the, and I use this term extremely loosely, "leadership" of Louisiana wishes to, in a Nazi-ish fashion, burn books or destroy his-

torical monuments of OUR HISTORY, they should be LYNCHED! Let it be known, I will do all in my power to prevent this from happening in our State.⁵³

Notice how the representative does not mention anything about the horrors of racial pasts for people of color in Louisiana but nonetheless explicitly invokes the dark thanatopolitics of lynching in order to tell a different victimage tale. Here, talk of the preservation of Lost Cause memorialization is used to configure white descendants of those who put up these Confederate memorials as the real victims in these heritage disputes.

Meanwhile, Confederate memorials still keep popping up. "Some of the newly listed memorials were in plain sight," writes Rick Hampson, "such as a monument to Lee in downtown Fort Myers, Florida.... But who knew that Winnie Davis Hall at the University of Georgia is named for the daughter of the Confederate president? That Graceville, Florida, pop. 2,200, 'Where the Living is Easy,' is named for a Confederate officer? That there's a Jefferson Davis Highway marker in Las Cruces, New Mexico, or a monument in Monterey, California, to an officer who left the U.S. Army to serve the Confederacy?"⁵⁴ Other places such as Richmond, Virginia—the final site of the former Confederacy—adds Hampson, remain bold, "open-air argument[s] for 'The Lost Cause.'"⁵⁵

This "Lost Cause" *dispositif* has deep roots in the American South. As Professor Balthrop once observed, these sentiments speak to the "relations between culture, myth, ideology, and public arguments" that have given form to a "model of appropriate behavior" that was developed in response to federal mandates for racial integration and new standards for racial equality.⁵⁶ Highlighting the conjunctival nature of these racial mythologies, Balthrop called for the critical appraisal of argumentative, ideological, and cultural "enjoinments" that orient one to past remembrances that are placed in the service of presentist worldly affairs.⁵⁷

International critics have also noted the symbolic significance of this Confederate monumentalization as well. To Tyler Stiem of the *Guardian*, the "Lost Cause narrative shaped white Americans' understanding of slavery and racism." Originally, he notes, for "southern segregationists at the turn of the 20th century, it was a way to reassert their identity within the union and recover a measure of dignity. For northern abolitionists, it was a bargain to be struck for the sake of national unity: let them have their statues and their Confederate flags if it brought them back into the fold." At the same time, Stiem avers, "it did something else too" by giving "comfort" to those who believed in a sort of false narrative that was rooted in racist ideologies. Quoting Ibram Kendi, Stiem continued that these ideologies ultimately denied "how fundamental racism has historically been to America."[58]

This is why, as Balthrop notes, citing the work of Charlie Willard, ideology reveals rhetorical and argumentative motivations. In Willard's own words: "People are apt to reveal the most about their thinking when they are pressed to give reasons, to account for themselves, to justify their claims."[59]

Those who wanted to preserve Dixie monumentalization did not hesitate to provide the types of justificatory arguments that Balthrop was referencing. Many defenders of Confederate memorialization argue that the taking down of Confederate monuments are in fact blatant efforts to "sanitize the past."[60] Preserving Confederate heritage can be framed as apolitical work, while the tearing down of Confederate memories is treated as politicized identity politics.

Some participants in these Confederate preservation or removal disputes demonstrate that they are aware that this "identity politics" involves the existence of different perceptual frames and disagreements about whether statuary has anything to do with "emblems of brutal oppression."[61] Margot Patterson, writing a month after the Charlottesville clashes, opined:

> The bitterness of symbolic battles lies in inverse proportion to their substance. Dismantling a Confederate monument will not do anything about curbing police brutality or reforming a criminal justice system riddled with racism or reducing bias in the workplace. It is an unproductive debate. Whatever satisfaction comes from purging Confederate monuments from public spaces will be fleeting, and possibly counterproductive if it stokes resentments among white Americans that, however specious, fuel racial bigotry. Under pressure, local communities are making rapid changes. Let us hope they make decisions about historical monuments thoughtfully and on a case-by-case base.[62]

The multivocal nature of statues was used as an argument for the preservation of Confederate statuary.

That said, certain members of the American public are willing to openly challenge those Dixie monumentalist claims. For example, Quess Moore—leader of "Take 'Em Down in Louisiana"—argues that the "real sanitization of history" occurred when those memorials were originally erected in the wake of the Civil War to construct a "false" narrative and "trickledown mythology of slaveholder success."[63]

One does not need to be an openly avowed white supremacist to be a constituent in Alabama or Louisiana or elsewhere who silently or vocally supports legislators who campaign promising to help preserve Confederate statuary. Vered Vinitzky-Seroussi and Chana Teeger have written of how "unspoken silences" can also be a part of critical studies of public remembering and forgetting.[64]

The EJI perhaps senses that vocal as well as silent white majorities support the passage of state Confederate preservation acts. When asked about the difference in the "collective consciousness" between the United States' unaccounted historicity of racial terrorism and that of other countries that have come to terms with those terrors, Bryan Stevenson directly addresses the problematic of Confederate memorialization:

> What we do in the memorial spaces says a lot about who we are. The American South is littered with the iconography of the Confederacy. We are celebrating the architects and defenders of slavery. I don't think we understand what that means for our commitment to equality and fairness and justice.[65]

Stevenson reinforces this point, as he has done elsewhere, by making comparisons between American and foreign monumentalization practices. "If there were Hitler statues all over Germany," he said, "I couldn't go there. I just couldn't. I would not able to make peace with the nation that was still comfortable with the era of German history where Nazis were responsible for the death of millions of Jewish people in concentration camps."[66] "But if you go to Berlin," he explained, "the Holocaust memorial is extraordinary. You can barely go a hundred feet without seeing a monument that's been placed at the home of a Jewish family that was abducted."[67]

As Susan Neiman observed, "the stumbling stone project"—in which four-inch squares recall the loss of ordinary human lives during the Judeocide—has been "laid across Europe, from Poland to Spain," and artist Gunter Demnig's efforts continue to garner rave reviews.[68] Newman argues that Bryan Stevenson "was profoundly affected by the stumbling stones."[69]

German local and regional monumentalization is not the only topic that garners Stevenson's attention. After other visits to places like Rwanda, he noted:

> [Y]ou are required to hear about the genocide. You can't go to Rwanda and spend a few days without someone talking to you about the damage and despair and the hurt and the pain created by that horror. In

the genocide museum there, there are actually human skulls; that's how powerfully people want to express their grief. And in South Africa, you are required to see the consequences of apartheid. There are places where camps and prisons have been turned into visiting sites where people can reflect on that legacy.[70]

Was Stevenson implying that Alabama needed some slavery holocaust monuments or genocide museums? Was he arguing that, even if one took down Confederate statuary, this did not suffice?

If the EJI's efforts can be viewed as examples of multidirectional memory work, does that also mean that the continued, twenty-first-century promotion of Dixie monumentalization and fascination with Confederate statuary preservation provide more evidence of what Michael Rothberg called "competitive" memories? After all, the very existence of the "Lost Cause" dominant ideological frame—and its postracial fragmentary epistemic units—may create challenges for those who advocate coming to terms with the enduring memory of institutionalized American racial terror, which was often carried out by Confederate insurrectionists.

This leads us to wonder how tourists—particularly white visitors—respond to the EJI's involvement in the monument wars.

In the following section, we continue our investigation of these lynching claims by relating them to people who visit the memorial and justify their own views of the EJI's argument. We then conclude with a few reflections about the possibilities of this site to create spaces for thinking differently about Confederate monumentality.

"Let Sleeping Dogs Lie": The Cultural Challenges of Place-Based Countermonumentality at the National Memorial for Peace and Justice and the Legacy Museum

While many public figures, local residents, and out-of-town visitors have given the Montgomery Lynching Memorial and Legacy Museum much credit for confronting an ugly and largely forgotten past, others—namely some vocal white Southerners—have responded with anxiety and defensiveness over the fate of Confederate monuments, which they see as under threat of attack from "left-wing" activists. For instance, Alabama's own governor—Kay Ivey—was among several prominent politicians not present at the Lynching Memorial's commemorative service; instead, in the apparent context of her campaign for the Republican gubernatorial primary, she disseminated a thirty-second political video that emphasized the continued importance of preserving Confederate monuments, given Alabama's recent passage of a bill intended to do just that. With an "old-time" dramatic museum in the background and visual elements that displayed Alabama's Confederate monuments, Governor Ivey, in a strong, thick Southern accent, opened with: "Up in Washington, they always know better . . . Politically correct nonsense, I say."[71] After defending her successful political initiative to prevent Washington from "tear[ing] down our historical monuments," she said: "We can't change or erase our history . . . but here in Alabama, we know something Washington doesn't: to get where we're going, means understanding where we've been."[72]

More than a few understood the symbolic importance of these types of gestures, which on the surface appeared to have nothing to do with race or power. The NAACP's president, Benard Simelton, replied via e-mail at AL.com: "Just when we thought Alabama was beginning to turn the corner in race relations, we see our governor wanting to continue to remind African Americans and people of color where Alabama stands when it comes to race relations. . . . Not on her watch will Alabama move to be a more inclusive state."[73]

Foreign correspondents recognized how the EJI's efforts seemed to be bothering those who had an interest in preserving Dixie monumentalization. In an essay in the *Guardian* entitled "Lynching Memorial Leaves Some Quietly Seething," Sam Levin reported on how locals such as Bob Wieland supported the Legacy Museum but also felt strongly about the historical importance of Confederate memorials and landmarks while the "sleepy old cotton south falls away."[74] Speaking from the old front porch of the Confederacy's first White House, Wieland clarified that he wanted to find some means of "keeping this museum [the first White House] just to have a positive taste, an old south taste, as the new one comes up."[75]

Why, some argued, wasn't there room in Alabama for all sorts of historical monuments and museums? Why not be tolerant and accept the need for both lynching memorials and Confederate statuary?

While some commentators defended the position that all parties concerned should be allowed to erect their own monuments, others wanted to discuss the taking down of what they viewed as offensive symbolic displays. Speaking directly about the possibility of the first White House "whitewashing" slavery, Wieland admitted: "[W]e could certainly tone down the celebration [of Jefferson Davis], but . . . it is part of civil war history," since it is "more of a political military history" and less of a "social history."[76] Others were more direct in expressing "anxiety" about the "impact" of the Legacy Museum, and Levin noted how they were "reverting to racist stereotypes of African American rioters."[77] Tommy Rhodes, a member of the Alabama Sons of Confederate Veterans, thought that someone could bring "that stuff to light, and let it be there, but don't dwell on it. . . . We have moved past it. . . . You don't want to entice them and feed any fuel to the fire."[78] Another member of the Sons of Confederate Veterans, Randall Hughey, also gave a nod to the new Legacy Museum but "repeatedly questioned the veracity of its facts," noted Levin. "They have every right to have the memorial, if it's accurate," said Hughey, who also expressed doubt about the reports of more than four thousand lynchings. "That seems pretty incredible to me that there would be that many documented lynchings. . . . That was not the norm."[79] Mary Massey showed open contempt for the EJI's lynching project: "We didn't have nothing to do with that," she said. "I think they just need to leave it alone. It's just stirring up something." Mary's husband, Jim, showed support for the memorial, but he was sure that lynchings were "gone and won't happen again," and he felt that the general Montgomery sentiment was: "Let sleeping dogs lie."[80] Another interviewee indicated that she would not visit the Lynching Memorial and "worried [that] it would exacerbate 'racism' in Montgomery," according to Levin. "It ain't gonna change that. It's going to get it started more," she said.[81]

These expressions of ambivalent feelings toward the Lynching Memorial and Legacy Museum show the deep-seated ideological attachments that many still have to extant Confederate monumentality. While nearly all of these individuals in some way, at least discursively, showed Levin that they were willing to offer some sort of qualified support for the building of the Lynching Memorial, they were unwilling to join those who wished to tear down Confederate statuary and other monumentalizations of the Old South. Still clinging to a version of the Lost Cause mythology, locals in Montgomery and in other parts of the South want to avoid stirring up trouble—a euphemism for avoiding radical critique from EJI workers and others.

It is also intriguing to see how, consciously or unconsciously, some of these commentators were using twenty-first-century permutations of older arguments that had been used to originally put up the Confederate statues, or to prevent the passage of federal anti-lynching legislation.

What we do know is that from a perceptual standpoint, the National Memorial for Peace and Justice and the Legacy Museum are "rebranding" Montgomery by "confronting its past" and opening new possibilities for tourism.[82] In an Associated Press piece entitled "Lynching Memorial May Be Game-Changer for Montgomery Tourism," Beth Harpaz noted that the Lynching Memorial had ten thousand visitors in its first week and was projected to bring in one hundred thousand more the following year (in 2019).

Brian Major, a New Yorker, was reconsidering visiting the Deep South. "As a black man, I'm not crazy about the idea of driving down streets named after Confederate generals and averting my eyes from Confederate flags. ... But reconciliation and peace-making has to begin somewhere."[83] Major went on explain that, given the importance of the Lynching Memorial, he was "willing to make the trip."[84]

Might others feel the same way? With time, might the National Memorial for Peace and Justice and Legacy Museum even bring back many of the descendants of those who fled persecution during the Great Migration?

At this stage, we pause and wonder if these individuals realize the radicalness of Stevenson's argument at the Legacy Museum—a musing that we will return to in later chapters. If so, how might that change their opinions?

Margaret Renkl is one person who has acknowledged that she began to see the world differently after visiting the Legacy Museum. "Heading back toward Nashville on Interstate 65," she said,

> I noticed a giant battle flag of the Confederacy flying on the side of the highway outside Verbena, just north of Montgomery. I could swear I'd never seen that flag before, though I grew up in Alabama and though I've driven the length of that state during each of the past four summers. I wondered if the flag's flagrant placement, so close to Montgomery, was an in-your-face rebuke to the presence of the Legacy Museum and the National Memorial for Peace and Justice.[85]

Commentators who write in support of the Legacy Museum and the National Museum for Peace and Justice rarely mention the kind of pushback that Renkl is referencing.

Some of this pushback can be configured by the EJI in other ways. Such testimonial evidence, for example, gives credence to Bryan Stevenson's claim that this counternarrative compels a sort of cultural "awakening" of the symbolic signification in the Deep South that gets at the (in)visibility of these memorials. For many, it is our habits that reveal and conceal what we take for granted and don't always question. As Tyler Stiem observed,

> There was a time not long ago (though it feels like forever) when a kind of blindness was possible as you moved through your city—any city. . . . This is the blindness of the everyday. We grow used to the spaces we inhabit. We stop seeing them. And we grow used to the ideas around us until we can't see them either. Not long ago it was possible to believe the past was irrelevant—that history had no

purchase on the postcolonial, post–cold war, post-everything present. With the horrors of the 20th century behind us, the free market would deliver us into a future where democracy and prosperity were available to all.... Little by little, that narrative began to fray.[86]

The competitiveness of this lynching memorializing narrative, then, is thus not only found in the discursive but is also deeply rooted in a visual optic politics that competes for what Nicholas Mirzoeff has called "visuality"—a regime of truth and power that gives form to the "commonsensicalness" of visible everyday life experiences.[87]

In this way, what the EJI and others are attempting to do is dare to "look back" by forcefully creating a new, albeit competitive, visuality that "sees" the world through the lens of the oppressed. Hence, the importance of finding visual rhetorics at the Lynching Memorial and Legacy Museum that serve as aesthetic vehicles for the formation of a new, more empathic community.[88]

This new way of gazing, or looking back, on contentious racialized pasts impacts more than just Montgomery memoryscapes. In Abbeville, South Carolina, locals engaged in a similar cultural battle over the memorialization of forgotten lynching pasts when the town decided to put up a memorial for one many who were lynched—Anthony Crawford, lynched in 1916. Crawford had been described in the *Abbeville Press and Banner* as a "negro of wealth"—who got into trouble when he became involved in a heated verbal exchange with a store owner about selling cotton seeds. Crawford's great-great-granddaughter, as she recalled the plight of her ancestor, told one reporter: "You have all of this Confederate memorabilia, but nothing that talked to the black experience. So we wanted to do something big and bold and outdoors."[89]

Others feel differently and yet recognize the importance of having vernacular as well as elite sites of memories in these monumental wars. Consider the activities of Robert Hayes, who once sold "Confederate memorabilia" at the Southern Patriot Shop, which occupied space near Crawford's memorial in Abbeville.[90] The store sold Confederate flags and bumper stickers that included messages like, "If at first you don't secede, try again." For Hayes, all this lynching memorialization only tells a partial truth that denies history. He just wishes that the lynching memorial "told what he considers the whole story."[91] Demonstrating the observed competitiveness between lynching memories and Dixie monumentalization, Hayes, bizarrely, said: "I submit there were a lot more blacks killing blacks, and possibly blacks killing whites."[92]

The archival records that are kept by the Tuskegee Institute and the NAACP indeed record that more than one thousand whites lost their lives to lynching violence during the decades when lynchings were condoned (see chapters 1 and 2), but these were nowhere near the numbers that Robert Hayes speculated must have existed. Was he reading the past through the lens of twenty-first-century racial violence and American ethnic strife?

As reactions to lynching memorialization continue to percolate with the passage of time, we wonder how these sites of memory in Montgomery and elsewhere will be situated in both competitive and multidirectional ways in the future with respect to the cultural challenges of "Lost Cause" mythic ideology. For now, critical genealogists might argue that the conventional memories of the civil rights movement, with their focus on nonviolent protests and legal reforms, have not helped that much in the dismantling of vestiges of "Dixie" and their glorification of Confederate pasts. Modernists interested in putting up classical, traditional civil rights memorials rarely show an interest in taking down Dixie monumentalism.

As times, we wonder if those who are fighting these competitive monumental wars have any interest in leaving room for multidirectional memoryscapes, and we worry about the immediate, short-term prospects for meaningful reconciliation in the Deep South.

CHAPTER 7

Participatory Rhetorics at the National Memorial for Peace and Justice and Legacy Museum

AT THIS POINT IN OUR BOOK, WE WISH TO INVESTIGATE THE WAYS IN WHICH THE National Memorial for Peace and Justice, during and after its opening in 2018, strategically commemorated the victims of racial terrorism in Montgomery, Alabama. This memorial uses brick and steel to etch into twenty-first-century memory "acts of violence that were done with complete impunity."[1]

Work on collecting funds for the building of the memorial began in 2010, at about the same time that the Equal Justice Initiative staff was putting together some of the first comprehensive twenty-first-century archival accounts of recorded lynchings in America.[2]

Bryan Stevenson and the EJI used private funds to build the Lynching Memorial,[3] and in myriad ways this national site of memory etches into stone and metal some of the ideologies that have been circulated by the EJI and its supporters. MASS Design Group, the Boston firm that was contracted to design the memorial, sought to create a facility that would aid those who wanted a space for critical reflection. EJI leaders admitted that they were bothered by the surfeit of Confederate memorials that left generations "burdened" by the iconography that we discussed in the previous chapter.[4]

As we explain in more detail below, MASS Design Group used a combination of affective displays, dispassionate textual materials, statistics on recorded lynchings, and narratives based on oral transcripts as strategic rhetorical devices that, in theory, would allow visitors to experience an entire range of visceral responses, from anger to critical reflection.

One of the features of this memorial that is of particular interest to us as critical rhetoricians and fieldworkers is its *participatory dimension*, whereby it not only functions as an agent of cultural change but also, quite literally, participates in the expansion of racialized public memory-work throughout America.

In a move that provides evidentiary support for our claim that "racial terrorism" is becoming a widely deployed ideography, the Georgia commission that would be involved in the lynching commemorations in Decatur, Georgia, described America's lynchings as "racial terrorism" that had lasting consequential effects, echoing the EJI's rhetoric.[5] The EJI was now showing that some five thousand African Americans had been lynched, and their efforts ensured that visitors would remember someone like Mary Turner, who in 1918 had been lynched for making what a newspaper called "unwise remarks" when she objected vociferously that her husband had not been involved in a murder.[6]

As we noted in the introduction, some of our critical rhetorical analysis of these Montgomery lynching sites of memory involves reviews and critiques of journalistic articles as well as personal reflections of tourists, while elsewhere we would utilize the perspectival heuristic known as *participatory critical rhetoric* (PCR).

PCR is a branch of critical rhetoric within the field of communication that provides a heuristic way of studying the affective, visual, and embodied appeals of these Montgomery places, spaces, and objects. As Michael Middleton and colleagues explain, PCR is a perspectival type of rhetorical criticism that suggests that one's body moving through a museum or memorial space facilitates the production of texts in situ, so that a critic can highlight the more immanent, affective, and antagonistic components of the materiality of some spaces.[7]

While PCR has been used to study protests, national parks, and a few museums, it is just beginning to be used in the study of contentious statues, monuments, and other forms of monumentalization. Of course, over the past several decades, many critical rhetoricians have studied the materiality of memorials, such as the Vietnam Veterans Memorial in Washington, DC, and the Civil Rights Memorial in Montgomery,[8] but we submit that such studies can be supplemented by more pointed poststructuralist critiques that note how there are times when *memorials are themselves* turned into interventionist assemblages that complicate critics' very ability to "observe" them as objects that help with the formation of counterpublics.[9]

If we study the agentic nature of the National Memorial for Peace and Justice, we find that the performative aspects of memorialization are especially salient due to the memorial's own, sometimes nonhuman (perhaps "posthuman") participation in the historical struggle for racial justice.[10]

While the Lynching Memorial's textual features are dark and melancholic—an example of what John Lennon and Malcolm Foley would call a site of "dark tourism"[11]—the memorial does much more than simply ask that we remember some forgotten victims' names. After subjectivizing visitors as witnesses, the memorial creates race-conscious actors who are better equipped to address racial injustice in the present.

In what follows, we provide an illustrative PCR tour of the National Memorial for Peace and Justice that invites readers to focus on the more experiential features of these Montgomery discourse/knowledge/power formations. We begin with what might be described as a typical pilgrimage tour of the Lynching Memorial,[12] based on the experience of one of the authors who traveled to this "site of memory" (Pierre Nora)[13] in May 2018. We then discuss the performativity of the Lynching Memorial at this Montgomery monument park. We conclude with a discussion of what we call the participatory rhetorical culture of the memorial and speculate about whether the memorial will help "liberate" Americans in the ways that have been envisioned by Bryan Stevenson and the EJI.

A Typical Tour of the National Memorial for Peace and Justice

Sitting on top of a small hill on a six-acre site, the National Memorial for Peace and Justice is poised to provide visitors with a performative space for remembering Dr. Martin Luther King Jr.'s statement—written on the wall of the memorial's entrance—that "true peace is not just the absence of tension, but the presence of justice." As readers will soon see, that strategic phrase is used as a warrant to help explain to visitors why they are about to be surrounded with materials and haunting images that will make them reflect on the bodily experiences of those who did not receive any justice.

One's experiential journey at the Lynching Memorial begins by finding and following an angular walkway, which slowly guides the visitor up what we consider to be a melancholic hill. Along the way, tourists encounter a sculpture by Kwame Akoto-Bamfo, the *Nkyinkyim* installation. This sculpture depicts enslaved persons of color held captive in neck shackles, manacles, and fetters that symbolize the plight of those bound by the grip of white tyranny (fig. 7). The memorial's program pamphlet, available to all who take this pilgrimage, explains that this installation symbolizes the horrors experienced by persons "searching for humanity in a foreign land."[14]

This way of thinking about "foreign" subjectivity is intriguing to us, especially given how critical interdisciplinary scholars have recently argued that some of those who were lynched were considered by nineteenth-century Southerners to be members of African labor pools who were threatening the

Figure 7: *Nkyinkyim* installation, by Kwame Akoto-Bamfo. Photo by the authors.

livelihoods of poor whites, prompting the latter to join vigilante lynching mobs (see chapters 1 and 2).

One of the slave figures in the *Nkyinkyim* installation is shown gasping in desperation for freedom while holding a baby in her left arm. Her right arm is extended outward toward another, who is looking downward while standing upright and revealing his entire body. This installation, by itself, is a postmodern form of critique of slavery that underscores the objectification and dehumanization of African slaves. Some of the installation's figures look sorrowful, symbolizing the collective suffering of millions who lived short and troubled lives in a distant past.

Other figures in the *Nkyinkyim* installation are crouched in a squatting position, silently weeping or screaming. All of their faces are in a state of extreme suffering in raw form. Meanwhile, the weathered chains that bind them leech onto their naked bodies as tears, or more accurately, blood, is spilled. The abstract and the concrete come together to let visitors know that this particular journey is likely to be emotive and provocative.

In the same way that the nearby Legacy Museum chronicles racial terror histories by putting on display abject slavery objects of memory (see chapter 8), the Lynching Memorial provides a parallel chronicling for tourists by allowing them to affectively respond to the emotive *Nkyinkyim* installation, which makes it difficult to forget the horrors of the transatlantic slave trade.

When the sculptor, Kwame Akoto-Bamfo, was asked about the ideological, affective features of the *Nkyinkyim* installation, he told one interviewer:

> I want black people, especially people of this generation, to know that this work was not done by an American. It was done by an African person who feels their pain and who is also connected. African Americans in particular should understand that we also know their pain. We empathize. I want white people to see [the sculptures] as human beings and not black people. That is the realism that I tried to put in the work. I want them to feel the pain that these people felt and the emotions from the hands through their feet.[15]

Participatory critical rhetoricians can also feel this same type of pain if they visit, and interact with, those who express their emotions while viewing the *Nkyinkyim* installation and other Lynching Memorial objects, spaces, and places.

It is telling that an evocative and realistic object like Akoto-Bamfo's sculpture provides some of the first visceral challenges to visitors who walk the pathways of the Lynching Memorial, because this provides both a chronological and a topical way for the EJI to set up some of the race-conscious, visual arguments that will be made later on during the tour about the nature and scope of slave horrors.

Who, after all, who has seen Akoto-Bamfo's sculpture, walked by it, and observed the tears of others passing by, can question the possibility that some traumas and traumatic memories can be passed down through the generations? Or are these new traumas that are part of the requisite memory work of those who convey the need for a "New" Reconstruction?

While some visitors to the Lynching Memorial may be satisfied with the consciousness-raising efforts that are primarily aimed at the retrieval of needed historical insight into past lynching injustices, others will be in a position to appreciate the more contemporary—perhaps more abstract—EJI lessons that are proffered during these experiential tours about twenty-first-century societal concerns. To Atlanta-based mixed media artist Masud Olufani:

> The work [the Akoto-Bamfo sculpture] is a literal interpretation of the "institution" that laid the groundwork for what was to come. Conceptually, it represents the starting point, the ideological fissure that objectifies and dehumanizes, making lynching in our recent past, and the disproportionate rate at which black people are murdered

by the police in our present, not only possible, but in some sense, inevitable. It's an important and sobering point to make—poignant and deeply moving.[16]

Clearly, there are some who visit the Lynching Memorial who understand the radical nature of the EJI's memorializing messaging.

PCR tours keep track of temporal or thematic coherences and ruptures; after visitors move past the *Nkyinkyim* installation, they are about to be presented with an embodied chance to get a feel for the nature, scope, and magnitude of mass-spectacle lynchings. A narrow V-shaped path directs visitors to a cascade of rusted steel monoliths at the top of a small hill. By the time academic visitors reach the middle of the memorial, they realize that the builders must have used these six acres to produce a type of counterhistory, beginning with iconic images of transatlantic slave trading and moving toward aesthetic, more abstract representations of nineteenth-century mass-spectacle lynchings that complement the more realistic *Nkyinkyim* installation.

Continuing down this directed path, visitors walk among and underneath more than eight hundred corten steel monuments that hang from the ceiling. To Philip Kennicott of the *Washington Post*, this memorial space is made up of "coffin-shaped boxes of oxidized steel hanging from a square canopy."[17]

At one point during this typical tour of the Lynching Memorial, visitors find themselves standing on a wooden platform—which bears passive resemblance to the false bottom of a gallows—and encounter the clusters of corten steel panels at eye level. Weathered like the memory of time, each of these panels for PCR observers is an architectural representation of a hierarchical power relationship. They are all engraved with the names of some of powerless thousands of known victims of Jim Crow violence perpetrated by empowered communities who wanted to remind those being lynched—and those African Americans who witnessed these hangings—that American courts would not prosecute the thousands of people who watched these lynching spectacles.

Walter Fitzhugh Brundage, using Georgia and Virginia case studies, argued in 1993 that "mass" lynchings were defined as involving crowds of sixty or more, and, using that criteria, he determined that there must have been at least 1,100 black individuals who died at the hands of mass lynching mobs.[18]

The Lynching Memorial, in the middle portions of the tour, enables visitors to get an experiential feeling of the arbitrary nature of the "allegations and charges" that were used by those involved in these mass lynchings, including claims that lynching victims violated vagrancy or trespassing laws.[19]

Captions on the hanging corten steel panels provide those who walk by with some needed contextual information to help them process what their bodies are experiencing. One hanging monument, for instance, reads "Shelby County, Kentucky," and provides a list of names of those who were racially terrorized in this county, and visitors can see the exact dates when these crimes occurred: Reuben Dennis, 2.15.1878; Sam Pulliam, 7.20.1891; Clarence Garnett, 10.02.1901; Eugene Marshall, 1.15.1911; Wade Patterson, 1.15.1911.

Visitors often comment on the evocative power of actually seeing the names of those who were lynched—especially in their own home counties—and several parts of the Lynching Memorial document and commemorate in different ways the thousands of African Americans who died between the end of Reconstruction and the post–World War II years. Bryan Stevenson said in an interview with CNN reporter Nia-Malika Henderson: "If I asked the question, 'Name one African American lynched between 1877 and 1950,' most people can't name one person. . . . Thousands of black people were lynched. Can't name one. Why?" Answering his own question, Stevenson replied, "Because we haven't talked about it."[20]

Remembered names, then, for activists like Stevenson serve the function of humanizing those who were lynched in ways that begin a national conversation about the inhumanity of those practices within a shared moral framework for understanding.

The typical tour of the Lynching Memorial allows PCR scholars to see how this radical space and place will serve as an agentic force in national conversations that will take place about lynching pasts. Consider the pedagogic value of the memorial for Robert M. Franklin Jr.—a James T. and Berta R. Laney Professor in Moral Leadership at Emory University's Candler School of Theology, who visited the Lynching Memorial with a group of 150 students, faculty, staff, and alumni in December 2018. Franklin had visited the memorial earlier with his wife, and during that earlier tour he was able to acknowledge the fate of a lynching victim who happened to be a relative of his wife, who is commemorated at the memorial. For Franklin, this personal journey began when he came across a monumental fragment from Washington County, Texas, with his wife's maiden name on it. The name was James Rogers, and he and his wife discovered from Gladys Goffney—Franklin's mother-in-law—that James was her cousin, and that he had been lynched based on allegations of "befriending" a white woman rumored to be pregnant (later found to be not pregnant). To Franklin, this experience created a "personalization of the anguish [he] was already feeling," and it became a powerful opportunity to ask his theology students big questions such as, "How does a loving God allow this kind of suffering? How could people who identified themselves as Christians participate? What role did the church play?"[21]

The hundreds of reddish-brown rusting steel panels that are suspended from the ceilings of the Lynching Memorial thus do more than just help aggregate statistics for those who wish to emphasize the magnitude of these lynching horrors. That would be a noble goal in and of itself, but the memorial also creates genealogical spaces betwixt and between lynching histories and contemporary social conditions so that visitors on pilgrimages like Professor Franklin can ask weighty theological questions.

The hanging monuments that one passes at the Lynching Memorial are also *materially* performative. When it rains, the rainwater that falls onto the panels turns a copper color, and the dripping of the water helps bring together material objects and people, as both weep as the people walk among the panels. Designers who helped plan these affective materializations explain that the dripping that accompanies the rain is intended to remind visitors of the terror of lynching. High lynching scaffolding was "lifted up over communities to taunt and terrorize."[22]

On the wall of one corridor of panels, visitors are informed that there were thousands of "African Americans" who were "unknown victims of racial terror," whose "deaths cannot be documented," and they, too, are honored by the EJI and the National Memorial for Peace and Justice.

Seeing row after row of corten steel helps visitors understand the institutional nature of condoned local and regional lynchings, and some architects aver that these rows recall the grids of concrete slabs that can be found at Berlin's Memorial to the Murdered Jews of Europe.[23] Philip Kennicott commented similarly that the "descent into this space [the Lynching Memorial] explicitly recalls the experience of Peter Eisenman's sunken concrete jungle near Berlin's Brandenburg Gate, in which the outside world disappears, replaced by a disorienting landscape of unyielding, funereal, boxlike forms."[24] Rabbi Michael Lezak, who traveled from San Francisco to visit the memorial, said that "he felt like he'd been to the 'American Auschwitz.'"[25]

For us, all of the darkness we might experience during a typical tour is a critical component of the memorial's transformative potential. The performativity of this journey begins from the start, when the visitor encounters these monuments at eye level (fig. 8) while descending to the wooden platform. As the visitor walks farther along, they must weave in between the monuments, which interrupt their walk; also, the hanging panels are organized in such a way that there is no single clear path to the other side of this edifice. Each one of these hanging monumental objects seems to jump out in front of the visitor, like a ghostly apparition, forcing the visitor to acknowledge the

Figure 8: Monuments at eye level. Photo by the authors.

horror(s) that took place in the county whose monument they are observing. In theory, the visitor's individual awakening advances collective American race consciousness.

As the visitor weaves through the reticulate maze of monuments, the steel panels slowly become levitated above the ground as the plank begins to give way. As the monuments rise, visitors experience the performativity of the memorial, which, in a way, changes each visitor's subject position from anxious observer to historical witness who, by becoming part of the memorial's assemblage, is compelled to look, to encounter, and ultimately to act.[26]

What PCR scholars might call a transvaluation of values takes place as the visitor becomes a voyeur, forced to look up and gaze at the haunting colonnade of monuments.[27] As the visitor walks, the monuments also appear to be moving—elevating themselves high above the head of the visitor to the point where the names are no longer legible (fig. 9). Each one hangs from the air as a body would during a lynching spectacle, situating the visitor as a possible perpetrator of the memories of racial injustice, haunted by ghosts from the past.

As visitors continue to walk down the corridor, they find themselves slowly descending as the colonnade of monuments rises to their ankles, knees, waist, chest. The second corridor is a memorial in transition from participant to voyeur. The gradient monuments appear to still be moving as visitors continue their descent (fig. 10).

Figure 9: Monuments levitating as the visitor descends. Photo by the authors.

Figure 10: Monuments ascending. Photo by the authors.

As light pierces through narrow spaces created between the tripartite angles of the visitor's position, the top of the cement walls, and the hanging panels, there is enough visibility to read, in short texts presented on the peripheries of the corridor, the stories of dozens of persons of color who were lynched for minor social offenses:

"Grant Cole was lynched in Montgomery, Alabama, in 1925 after he refused to run an errand for a white woman."[28]

"David Walker, his wife, and their four children were lynched in Hickman, Kentucky, in 1908 after Mr. Walker was accused of using inappropriate language with a white woman."

"Horace Duncan and Fred Coker were lynched in Springfield, Missouri, in 1906 by a mob of 5,000 people."

"Fred Rochelle, 16, was burned alive in a public spectacle lynching before thousands in Polk County, Florida, in 1901."

"William Donegan was lynched in Springfield, Illinois, in 1908 for having a white wife."

When the visitor reaches the concrete floor of the memorial, and as they take one of two descending corridors on the peripheries of the memorial, they may feel as though they have entered the crypts of America's lynching past, or that they are encountering the subconscious of the dark memories that have been repressed from the national consciousness and stored here, at the sepulcher that lies below (fig. 11). Only the bottoms of the monuments can be discerned: Woodford County, Kentucky; Humphreys County, Mississippi; Gaston County, North Carolina . . .

Observers need not be reminded that to arrive here, at this point in the tour, they have subjected themselves to conditions whereby their bodies have helped them occupy the subject positions of the spectator/mourner/audience. To *New York Times* columnist Campbell Robertson, at this stage in the memorial journey the visitor is put "in the position of the callous spectators in old photographs of public lynchings."[29]

As the visitor continues through the Lynching Memorial, multilayered ledges span outward and wrap around into the final corridor of this catacombic space. Encouraged to sit, contemplate, mediate, visitors can pay their respects to those who experienced the injustices of the past while they read the words written on the wall:

> For the hanged and beaten. For the shot, drowned, and burned. For the tortured, tormented, and terrorized. For those abandoned by the rule of law. We will remember. With hope because hopelessness is the enemy of justice. With courage because peace requires bravery. With persistence because justice is a constant struggle. With faith because we shall overcome.

Figure 11: Cascade of elevated monuments. Photo by the authors.

One hears the soft and tranquil sound of water that gently rolls over an epitaph on the adjacent cement wall: "Thousands of African Americans are unknown victims of racial terror lynchings whose deaths cannot be documented, many whose names will never be known. They are all honored here" (fig. 12).

Figure 12: The waterfall at ground level. Photo by the authors.

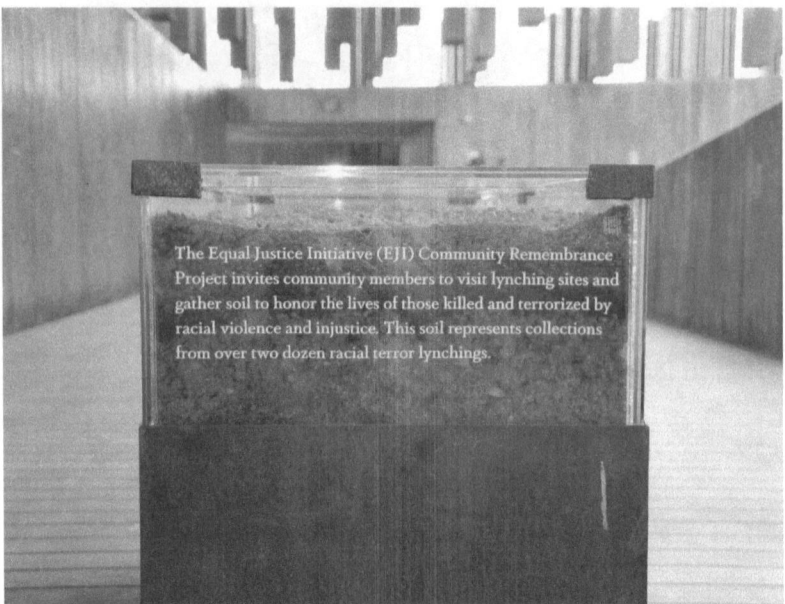

Figure 13: The aquarium of soil. Photo by the authors.

Those deaths are forensically documented within a glass aquarium, holstered by a weathered steel base, at the end of this final leg of the memorial journey. Inside are stratified layers of soil, which have been taken from over two dozen sites where "racial terror lynchings occurred" by the EJI Community Remembrance Project (fig. 13).

The performativity of the memorial takes on added value at the epicenter of the memorial, called Memorial Square, which lies at the heart of the arcades of monuments. The space is accessible only at the end of the journey; the visitor ascends a small grassy knoll by way of a small set of wooden steps and an angular pathway that leads to the apex of the hill (fig. 14).

From this vantage point, visitors can see the colonnade of monuments that circumscribe the entire square. This spatial positioning is like a Foucauldian panopticon, in which the visitors/objects are seen without being seen, but the performativity of the memorial is even more radical than that. Because, while taking in the monumental scene and while becoming aware of one's spatial position in it, visitors realize that they are the ones, not the visitors on the periphery, who are being watched. And in a flash it is made clear that they are reenacting the scopic regime of a lynching ritual. But this time around, rather than being spectators, these visitors are *the objects* of the public gaze, in the same way that helpless lynching victims were gazed on by so many children and adults before their death (see chapters 3 and 4).

Figure 14: Memorial Square. Photo by the authors.

Few visitors to the Lynching Memorial can avoid discussing how objects at the memorial are used to convey the magnitude of these human losses. To Jonathan Capehart of the *Washington Post*, occupying this liminal space in Memorial Square was one of two moments that revealed to him the "enormity" of what he saw at the memorial (the other being Monument Park, described below). To him, "[a]s our guide ... pointed out, we were having the *inverse* experience of the lynched. Instead of the victim being in the center, the visitors are in the place of the lynched, who are now standing in judgment. The brown oxidized monuments that reflect the array of skin tones of African Americans compound the symbolism."[30]

To us, one plausible PCR reading would be that the visitor is the victim who is subject to the judgmental gaze of onlookers. In fact, upon closer examination, the center of this open space features a wooden platform that in many ways resembles the false bottom of a gallows. At this point, then, the visitor goes from observing to being observed, becoming the object of the subjective gaze of the monuments themselves. Call it a way of allowing the victims to reclaim agency, or "justice," but no longer can it be said that visitors are mere spectators, because now they are the objects of humiliation on the lynching stage.

This transformative, or liminal, space reveals the performative nature of this memorial and its potentiality for subjective change. Far beyond the Kantian subject, the visitors' subjectivity is thus, in a way, deconstructed, and, if they are willing, they can now move forward as an extension of the memorial itself as both subject (visitor/spectator) and object (monument/victim).

This participatory critical rhetorical reading seems to have some merit when we read the words that appear on a small plaque that tells the visitor about the symbolic significance of Memorial Square:

> Hundreds of racial terror lynchings took place in front of thousands of onlookers in public squares and on courthouse lawns. These public spectacle lynchings transformed community spaces where the rule of law should have been sacred into sites of terrorism and violent injustice. This Memorial Square honors all victims of racial terror lynchings; acknowledges the unconscionable horror of being tortured and killed while thousands watched and cheered; and seeks to address this history of violence with a new commitment to eliminate racial injustice.

Note, significantly, how all of this was accomplished without the memorial having to circulate any of the modernist photographs or lynching postcards that were critiqued by individuals like Ida B. Wells-Barnett and Walter Francis White.

This powerful space at the Lynching Memorial creates new possibilities for acting. To Jennifer Arnold, a student at Emory University, the "memorial re-imagines a public square, where the ghosts of history are there looking back at you, judging you. What are you going to do with your own life once you feel those eyes upon you?"[31] To Robert Franklin Jr., a professor at Emory discussed above, "[w]hat we've seen prompts an inner search for empathy and for courage. Part of the courage is asking 'What would I have done then, observing this, being aware of the violence and horror?' And then, 'What am I prepared to do now?'"[32]

As the visitor continues this typical journey through the Lynching Memorial, it becomes clear that the reconstruction of this performative displacement of subject/object occurs in what is called Monument Park, which consists of "a vast, open-air morgue, outside the memorial structure," where visitors are invited to "claim their monuments" and take them home.[33] It is here where the visitor is called upon to act.

The Participatory Dimension of Monument Park: Memorials as Assemblages

As visitors walk outside to Monument Park, they witness the other half of the Lynching Memorial, which consists of some eight hundred monument doubles that await relocation to the counties in which the lynchings recorded on each respective monument occurred. Monument Park contains replicas of the monuments that are hanging, and that visitors have already passed by, in the permanent part of the Lynching Memorial.

Each lynching monument in Monument Park is intended to be (re)claimed by those counties in the United States whose residents are willing to come forward and admit that their county has a remembered or forgotten history of lynchings. For example, in January 2019, the *Atlanta Journal-Constitution* could tell its readers that Georgia's DeKalb County had taken a "forceful step to reckon with the legacy of racial terror in the county" when county commissioners approved the placement of a historical marker to lynching victims near town square in Decatur, the county seat.[34] This was an important milestone in the EJI's plans, because there are almost six hundred verified cases of Georgians who were lynched in the state between 1877 and 1950.

This portion of the Lynching Memorial also encourages those in Georgia and elsewhere to act as genealogists or lynching archivists or activists who are willing to work with the EJI and local communities in putting up markers to once-forgotten lynching victims. These performative acts at the same time encourage local newspapers to carry human interest stories on these efforts, applying political pressure on legislators, who are asked to help those studying lynching in local homes, libraries, universities, and government agencies.

With time, Monument Park will inevitably change as counties claim and remove their respective monuments; in fact, visitors will be able to see which counties nationwide have decided to confront their past by expressing an act of contrition and taking back their monument double. In this way, the National Memorial for Peace and Justice is a sort of "living memorial" that will expand its territorial influence throughout the United States, much like a network, or what Gilles Deleuze and Félix Guattari called an "assemblage."[35] American counties that are willing to confront their fraught pasts thus become the EJI's strategic partners, who help facilitate even more consciousness raising.

Those redeemed thus become EJI allies, unlike the unreconstructed Southern redeemers of the nineteenth century.

Figure 15: Monuments for claimants at Monument Park. Photo by the authors.

For visitors, Monument Park is the participatory arm of the memorial. During an interview with *Montgomery Advertiser* reporter Andrew Yawn, Bryan Stevenson described the park as a place that served "as a real-time 'report card,'" and this led Yawn to say that it was "a tool of atonement for a culture of killing that could have been labeled genocide if the murders were not so individual and scattershot."[36]

The EJI has no interest in allowing Americans to treat mass lynchings as individuated, scattered incidents that cannot be traced and linked together in coherent "New Reconstruction" memorialized metanarratives. This gets at some of the genocidal arguments that commentators are making about America's racial terrorist acts, which involve horrors dating back to the time of the transatlantic slave trade. But Yawn seems to focus on the aggregation of lynchings when he makes his statement about cultural genocides. This is perhaps why Yawn mentions the twelve million souls who were transported across oceans during the centuries of the slave trade.

Some PCR researchers can get at the sense of hesitancy to discuss these fraught lynching pasts without having to go so far as to frame it as genocidal in nature. Philip Kennicott, for example, averred that "counties that refuse to collect their 'monument' will be shamed by the presence of the unclaimed coffin form on the grounds of the national memorial."[37] Figure 15 shows the monuments that are waiting to be picked up by contrite county claimants.

Consider a few of the communities that are already taking action. Organizers in Birmingham, Alabama (Jefferson County), for instance, hope that their county will be one of the first to claim their monument to remember those who were lynched on their soil, and discussions about the significance of place and space are already under way regarding where to place the retrieved monument.[38] The organizing group, called the Jefferson County Memorial Project, has already decided that Linn Park (the old Central Park) would be the perfect site for a monument, given the fact that that was the place where the county's first known lynching occurred when a man named Lewis Huston was murdered by a mob in 1883. One of the key organizers, Abigail Schneider, explains that Huston "was specifically taken from the jail on Fourth Avenue North and dragged to Central Park to be lynched as a way to claim this as a white space and show that we can do this in the public and have the government's support behind it and they're not going to stop us."[39] The park was also the location where witnesses observed protests against the poll tax during in the 1930s.

While the temporary monuments in Monument Park overwhelmingly "belong" to Southern counties, it is also important to remember that citizens of Northern states were also culpable in this history of racial terrorism. Duluth, Minnesota, for instance, in St. Louis County, is one such place; it has struggled to come to terms with the memory of the high-profile lynching of three individuals—Elias Clayton, Elmer Jackson, and Isaac McGhie (fig. 16). These three men were charged with the rape of a nineteen-year-old woman, even though her claims were never really believed and were eventually disproved by a medical examiner.[40]

Before the National Memorial for Peace and Justice opened, Duluth, in many ways, set the standard for bringing communities together for reconciliation, given its own memorialization of these victims on East First Street in downtown Duluth. There was regional and national coverage of the matter, including a 2003 article in the *New York Times* entitled "Letter from Duluth: It Did Happen Here; The Lynching That a City Forgot."[41] A great-grandchild of one of the lynchers, Warren Read, wrote a book entitled *The Lyncher in Me: A Search for Redemption in the Face of History*,[42] in which he apologized to the survivors of the victims on behalf of the great-grandfather he never met.[43]

It was no surprise, then, that when the Lynching Memorial opened in Montgomery, thirty-four individuals from Duluth traveled ninety-eight hours by bus to represent their county after receiving over $12,000 in donations for their historic trip, which also included pit stops at sites of racial struggle such as in Memphis and Birmingham. "We're going to claim our

Figure 16: The Clayton Jackson McGhie Memorial in downtown Duluth, Minnesota. Courtesy of Cory Paliewicz.

pillar," said Heidi Bakk-Hansen, the board secretary for the Clayton Jackson McGhie Memorial Incorporated.[44] Until St. Louis County's monument came home, Brady Slater of the *Duluth News Tribune* noted, it "lay like a coffin alongside all the rest in what appeared as bars of a xylophone—their music played out but still ringing all the same."[45]

Of course, not all counties with lynching histories can muster the impetus to follow the lead of communities like Birmingham and Duluth—and not all have residents as proactive as James Yamakawa, who is collecting dirt from lynching sites for the Legacy Museum (see chapter 8).

With time, the National Memorial for Peace and Justice will, hopefully, continue to expand horizontally across the American nation as community leaders and publics decide to take the road toward social/historical justice and possibly atonement. The fact that more than a few communities are already talking about the Lynching Memorial in relation to their own county's history of racial terrorism is evidence that this memorial is beginning to create a race-conscious rhetorical culture through its own material performativity.

This is not to mention, as we noted in the introduction, that the US Senate in 2018 passed the nation's first anti-lynching bill, thereby taking ownership of its own part in perpetrating, and condoning, racial terrorism. To P. R. Lockhart of *Vox*, that "acknowledgement fits into a larger demand for a racial reckoning in America, a demand that is also seen in calls to remove

Figure 17: Monument Park. Photo by the authors.

Confederate monuments and expand teaching about the legacy and impact of slavery."[46] Lockhart also quoted an EJI member as saying that the National Memorial for Peace and Justice forces "the nation to confront and understand its history."[47]

In this way, that the National Memorial for Peace and Justice is a "living memorial" that participates as an actor with agency in the shaping of the kind of rhetorical culture Bryan Stevenson has in mind. While all memorials, in some way, can be said to be performative in that they change in texture and meaning with the passage of time,[48] this memorial literally moves (fig. 17). Not only are visitors encouraged to claim their home county's monument and discursively engage their community in a discussion about how to remember their own racialized "truth," but visitors themselves may be classified by newspapers as amateur historians, even archivists, forced to read the past "against the grain."[49]

Equipped with new resources, visitors become social and historical agents who help with the unearthing of, and coming to terms with, the forgotten historicities of racial terrorism.

That said, do these same activists who care about lynching pasts also apply this genealogical sensibility when they hear what the EJI has to say about today's criminal justice system?

Our reading of the National Memorial for Peace and Justice as a participatory actor in this race-conscious rhetorical culture formation has been informed by what Michael Middleton and colleagues call a participatory epistemology during the critical act.[50] While memorials such as the Vietnam Veterans Memorial and the Korean War Veterans Memorial can be, and have been, read as performative spaces that change with time,[51] they nonetheless often remain beholden to researchers'—and society's—dominant gazes.

On another level, the National Memorial for Peace and Justice's Monument Park is also plainly a visual resource for safety. For persons of color who continue to struggle against the injustices of racial terrorism and all of its "colorblind" codes and implicit biases in public and institutional arenas, Monument Park provides them with a "map" of counties that have, for various reasons, failed to confront their past—thus, possibly, providing a guide to which counties they may wish to avoid. We are reminded of other historical maps that have served communities of color in similar ways, such as *The Negro Motorist Green Book* (which allowed relatively affluent persons of color a way to navigate through the territorial milieu of racism in towns that had laws and curfews for persons of color, called "sundown towns"), and, a century earlier, the Underground Railroad.[52]

Maps, in many ways, have always been sites of struggle and resistance (*topos*) for persons of color living in the legacy of racial terrorism. Since racial terrorism has changed form in the twenty-first century, it makes sense that such a map exists today.[53] At the very least, the visuality of this "map" provides social actors with a legend of the nation's pressure points with respect to places that choose to continue to remember a cultural forgetting.[54]

As visitors complete their journey down the striated path back toward the memorial's entrance, they encounter more sculptures, such as Dana King's *Guided by Justice*, which features three iconic women of color, including Rosa Parks as she struggled for justice during the Montgomery bus boycott (fig. 18). To King, these women "walked everywhere, everyday: to the doctor's office, grocery store, church, work, hairdresser, school, to pay bills, etc.," and these three particular women

> represent the range of a woman's life: a young mother to be, a middle aged school principal and a grandmother . . . who were constantly harassed, spit at, cussed out and threatened with disfigurement and even death, yet they walked every day. They honored the call and persevered by walking, rain or shine, in blazing heat or bone chilling cold weather. This sculpture represents the quiet constancy of women determined to make a difference in ways available to them at the time, doing what needed to be done, one step at a time.[55]

Figure 18: *Guided by Justice*, by Dana King, National Memorial for Peace and Justice. Photo by the authors.

Adjacent to this sculpture is a space for reflection dedicated to Ida B. Wells-Barnett.

This part of the memorial encourages visitors to think about the gendered nature of radical civil rights activism, and the women who often served as leaders of bus boycotts and other acts of resistance.

The focus of attention in these politicized Montgomery spaces is not primarily on the epic exploits of the Reverend Martin Luther King Jr. or Malcolm X or the Kennedy brothers or Lyndon Johnson, in his efforts at passing civil rights legislation. Instead, the spotlight is on the anti-lynching activities of Ida B. Wells-Barnett and other women who spoke out against reactionary, populist Jim Crow racism or who fought against dehumanizing segregationist practices.

As visitors continue to walk along the final leg of their journey, they encounter Hank Willis Thomas's *Raise Up*, which displays a line of persons of color with their arms held in the air—not in celebration of emancipation, but as a memorial to those slaves who were deloused when they were kidnapped and brought to America (fig. 19). Thomas, a sculptor, re-creates photographer Ernest Cole's rendering of the horrors of South African apartheid in his famous late-1950s image, *Miners' Physical Check*. To Kerr Houston, "the outstretched arms of Cole's miners cease to become signs of industry's power to control the body of the worker. Rather, they are converted into a sign of

Figure 19: *Raise Up*, by Hank Willis Thomas. Photo by the authors.

insurgence; they are given covert agency. A debasing procedure yields to an exhortation to rebellion."[56]

Can PCR critics be forgiven for pointing out the parallels that can be found with purveyors of representations of #Blacklivesmatter movements?

We would add that, like the *Nkyinkyim* installation, Thomas's sculpture speaks to the transnationalism of racial terrorism and in doing so opens doorways for new solidarities to be forged through these shared histories of suffering. By confronting the true legacy of slavery, and also by appropriating historical artifacts such as Cole's photography, the Lynching Memorial's artists not only connect their subjects to a genealogy of racial terror but empower them to dissent as well. In their doing so, the memorial's performativity is once more carried out through the visitor, who, like the memorial itself, turns orthodox American historicity against itself.

Altogether, as PCR visitors piece together the mosaic of textual and visual arguments that are materially on display at the National Memorial for Peace and Justice, they find that this type of countermonument is a powerful place of genealogical memory that forcefully brings to the surface all the suppressed memories of systematic US racial terrorism. By the time that visitors come to the end of their pilgrimage through the memorial, they have gained a sense that another implicit argument is being advanced—that some type of willful repression has contributed to forms of collective amnesia.

Acknowledging the magnitude of historical lynching thus becomes just one-half of the EJI's place-based arguments, for the companion to the Lynching Memorial, located less than a mile away—and inside a former warehouse that once imprisoned slaves—is the Legacy Museum (see chapter 8). And if the visitor looks carefully, she or he can see the Alabama State Capitol and the eighty-five-foot-tall Confederate statue in its front yard.

The affective, visual, and embodied appeals at Montgomery's Lynching Memorial help turn these sites of memory into participatory spaces that allow visitors to join the ranks of those who are willing to work at lynching remembrance long after they leave Alabama. Statuary, walkways, hanging panels, and other material objects create haunted spaces that not only recall the absence of public memory about lynching pasts but bring to life the genealogical components of the EJI's stories about racial terrorism that we have discussed so far. As one journalist for the *New York Times* noted when the memorial was inaugurated, the "country has never seen anything like it."[57]

While other, more traditional memorials to the civil rights era—many of them in Alabama—have been erected by those who wish to recall triumphal outcomes to historical struggles, few have attempted to create a site of rupture, of open wounds, of haunting traumatic lynching memories. While visitors to orthodox, modernist, classical civil rights museums are invited to celebrate how far we have come, tourists who travel to Montgomery learn how far many of us still need to travel.[58]

Rather than pausing and reflecting on how far "we" have all come, the Lynching Memorial provides a dark tourist countermemorial, a place that asks visitors to reflect on how much more still needs to be done in the civil rights struggles for truth and reconciliation.[59] Visitors are invited to participate in the political reclamation of memory, history, and mourning so that they can help the EJI counter the forgetfulness found in sanitized versions of civil rights histories.[60]

The following chapter continues our genealogical investigations by focusing on the rhetoricity of the counterpart of this lynching memorial, located just a few blocks away: the Legacy Museum.

CHAPTER 8

The EJI, the Legacy Museum, and "Postgenocide" America

AS WE NOTED IN EARLIER CHAPTERS, WHEN THE LEGACY MUSEUM OPENED TO THE public in April 2018 in Montgomery, Alabama, it was met with mixed reactions from locals, journalists, and visitors. Many of those who were interviewed by reporters were clearly excited about the prospects of having a new race-conscious place of memory in the heart of the former Confederacy. Philip Kennicott of the *Washington Post* was among those who recognized the more radical message of the Legacy Museum, and he argued that the EJI's ambitious Montgomery project "will force America to confront not only its wretched history of lynching and racial terror, but also an ongoing legacy of fear and trauma that stretches unbroken from the days of slavery to the Black Lives Matter Movement of today."[1]

Critics complained that it was this very attempt to leverage lynching pasts that was so problematic. Paul Kersey of the *Unz Review* (a controversial outlet) averred that all of this demonstrated the EJI's sites of memory's "potential for racial indoctrination."[2] He elaborated by asserting that while it was "common to describe lynching as mobs of howling whites hunting down and killing blacks for trivial reasons," such "lynchings were rare," and he further asserted that the EJI was ignoring lynchings of whites. As if this wasn't problematic enough, Kersey had to go on and say that most victims of lynchings were "probably" guilty.[3]

The Southern Poverty Law Center has responded to these types of commentaries by noting that mythic views regarding black-on-white crimes, and white perceptions of "some quiet race war," have had a "very long history in America."[4]

Other observers who may have little in common with far-right white supremacists nevertheless seem to advance postracial arguments that the South in general, and Alabama in particular, is now a place markedly different from the violent, segregated, Reconstruction South of yesteryear. Why, some complained, after all the therapeutic healing that has taken place since the 1960s civil rights era, would anyone want to stir up trouble? For instance, to Montgomery resident Mikki Keenan, all this Equal Justice Initiative memorialization was "going to cause an uproar and open old wounds."[5] "It keeps putting the emphasis on discrimination and cruelty," said her friend.[6]

It was much more comforting to dwell on civil rights successes and improved ethnic relationships in Alabama than to see the failures and amnesias that the EJI was referencing. More than a few, it appeared, wanted Montgomery to be remembered as a progressive, neoliberal part of the South that had already mastered its difficult, dark past.

The stance that Alabama should avoid putting up any provocative edifices that focus on violence and lynching hauntology is a reflection of the modernist views of those who wish to see "history" as a linear progression of time that is both preconstituted and taken for granted rather than constructed through constellations of meaning. Michel Foucault, and countless followers of his work, often talk about the need to critique this essentializing by paying attention to "cuts"[7] in time, and many interdisciplinary scholars have extended his critiques of traditional historicism as they discuss the building, and the tearing down, of libraries, archives, and other depositories of preserved knowledge formations. Ann Stoler, for instance, has written about debris and dissident archives,[8] while others still call for counterhistories or countermemories.[9]

The mixed reactions to the EJI's Legacy Museum, as well as the commentary on the need to preserve some Dixie monumentalism, suggests that those who critically investigate these tensions in Montgomery may view contests over "history" as part of a complicated genealogical struggle wherein time, as Walter Benjamin would say, "is full of ruptures and shortcuts."[10]

From a critical genealogical vantage point it could be argued that the Legacy Museum has become embroiled in a dialectical and ongoing museological struggle over the question of whether America is an exceptional nation with generations who have "lessons learned" who don't deserve to be straddled with fraught and haunting pasts. EJI defenders respond that this denialism of the systematic and enduring nature of lynching legacies is myopic, and that those who don't understand the structural nature of America's discriminatory carceral practices are wearing blinders.

Is it possible that the EJI's workers are right, that we moved on *too quickly* from the pedagogical lessons that were taught by Ida B. Wells-Barnett, W. E. B. Du Bois, Walter White, and others?

With the 2018 opening of the Legacy Museum, all of these unresolved cultural tensions come to the surface, and they allowed Bryan Stevenson and the EJI to bring to a few spaces and places in Montgomery the argumentative, epistemic fragments that would go into the constitutive production of a large, race-conscious *dispositif* on difficult "truths" and "reconciliation," which would emulate South Africa's Ubuntu (a Bantu word meaning "humanity toward others"). However, instead of forming a truth and reconciliation commission, such as those that have helped nations like South Africa resolve postconflict issues, the EJI cobbled together rhetorical materials that were reassembled in uniquely radical and Afro-American assemblages.

At this juncture in our book, we return to some of the seminal questions that have guided our critical genealogical and PCR work all along. Have mainstream American communities, which many believe suffer from "postracial" maladies, indicated that they also have "postgenocide" anxieties?

By "postgenocide," we are referencing some different but related claims that have been made about mass-spectacle lynchings. Sometimes, as we hinted in chapter 5, the term "genocide" was used in reference to the war on drugs, as a way of carrying out the genocide of blacks. At other times, the phrase "postgenocide" was used by the EJI to punctuate time by noting the period after the reported "end" of mass lynchings. Other applications of postgenocidal notions involved representations that situated mass lynchings in the midst of lengthy "legacies," in which the word "genocide" was used to remind readers or viewers of the hundreds of years of slavery, slave trading, segregation, and so on, that are sometimes configured as facets of a massive "African American Holocaust."[11]

The polysemic and contentious nature of the term "postgenocide" is one more reason why we have continually cited materials by Stevenson and other EJI representatives who realize that it is not always easy for American audiences to believe that slave legacies can be compared with the Holocaust or the Rwandan genocide.

Extending some of the arguments that we made in the previous chapter about the participatory rhetoricity of the National Memorial for Peace and Justice, this chapter argues that the Lynching Memorial's counterpart, the Legacy Museum, thematically and chronologically picks up where the National Memorial for Peace and Justice left off. While the Lynching Memorial focuses on providing emotive displays that show the magnitude of lynching pasts, the Legacy Museum focuses on how those same lynching histories have impacted American legal and social acceptance of capital punishment, mass incarceration, and other legal inequalities.

By including labor and prison issues in conversations about racial terrorism, Reconstruction, the post-Reconstruction era, and civil rights movements, the EJI can use the Legacy Museum as a twenty-first-century venue for inviting visitors to join them in working to help indigent blacks, improve the lives of African American juveniles, protect those with disabilities, bring back presumptions of innocence, and abolish capital punishment in America.

While a few investigative journalists and academics have noted how the EJI is focusing on mass incarceration, what we add to this conversation is the possibility that the Legacy Museum is positioning itself to be the type of agentic museological "advocate" that might—just might—be able to get visitors to Montgomery and other US citizens to rethink their views regarding the need for slave-trading acknowledgments, apologies, reconciliation, or African or African American reparations.[12] Some EJI writers and Legacy Museum curators might even be able to pave the way for contemplating the existence of an African American genocide or a black holocaust.

Granted, given postracial American stances, these are all difficult tasks, but can we fault the EJI for trying to use brick and stone and memes and epistemes as they try to accomplish those missions?

We firmly believe that in the coming years, just as the US Holocaust Memorial Museum (USHMM) is often used as a place of research and commentary on the acknowledgment, study, and prevention of other modern genocides around the world, the Legacy Museum in Montgomery may serve as a nodal point for discussions about the African American holocaust and other indigenous genocides. The EJI may, in the very near future, be leading efforts to recognize "forgotten" mass murders of people of color that are not conventionally called "genocides" by traditional Holocaust or genocide scholars.

At the present time, EJI members confine themselves to only occasionally presenting members of the public with a few sporadic genocidal references, spending the bulk of their time talking to reporters and visitors to the Legacy Museum about the lingering, discriminatory effects of racial terrorism in the nineteenth, twentieth, and twenty-first centuries. That said, Bryan Stevenson sparks interest whenever he compares the Legacy Museum's focus on racial terrorism with other dark tourist sites, such as the USHMM's displays of Nazi horrors and the National September 11 Memorial and Museum's depictions of what happened during that terrorist attack. EJI members also travel to sites of memorialization abroad, and when they return home they write and talk about how their travel inspired them to prepare for the pilgrimages of visitors to Montgomery's Legacy Museum.[13]

To develop our arguments about the politicized nature of Stevenson's and the EJI's "postgenocide" claims, in this chapter we extend our critique by providing a subsection that describes a typical tour of the Legacy Museum. As mentioned in the introduction to this book, one of the authors took a tour of these Montgomery spaces and places during the summer of 2018, and in the first subsection below we use the framing of a typical tour to point out curatorial presences and absences.

In the second subsection of this chapter, we briefly explain how the EJI uses the Legacy Museum to focus on present-day carceral abuses in the United States. This allows readers intending to visit the museum who might not have read Stevenson's book *Just Mercy*, or who may not have seen his TED Talk, to get a visual introduction to his perspectival ways of viewing issues such as the need to provide mercy to the guilty and the best ways of going about reforming disparate sentencing practices.

The final subsection of the chapter concludes with a brief but speculative discussion of how Americans might react when they eventually learn more about the radical nature of the EJI's claims regarding America's "postgenocide" society.

A Typical Tour through the Legacy Museum

What is unstated, or possibly implied, at the National Memorial for Peace and Justice is made explicit at the Legacy Museum, which is where the EJI traces the ongoing history of racial terrorism in the United States "from enslavement to mass incarceration." As an advocacy museum, the Legacy Museum chronicles the horrors of specific lynchings, the banality of Jim Crow segregation, and the traumas that are experienced by today's African Americans who are incarcerated in US prisons. These events are viewed as historical events that are linked together in material and symbolic ways.

Place matters when it comes to arguments and social change,[14] so where else to put a national memorial museum that traces the dark legacy of racial terrorism "from enslavement to mass incarceration" than in Montgomery, Alabama, a place that we have previously noted is inundated with Confederate and civil rights monuments. The monuments and places of commemoration include the First White House of the Confederacy, the Rosa Parks Museum, the Civil Rights Memorial, the Dexter Avenue King Memorial Baptist Church and Museum, and the Freedom Rides Museum. Not to mention the infamous Edmund Pettus Bridge in Selma, where civil rights protesters were brutally beaten and shot in 1965 on their march from Selma to Montgomery; the Sixteenth Street Baptist Church in Birmingham, where four girls were killed during a Klansman attack; and the Birmingham Civil Rights Institute—all cartographic places on the civil rights geopolitical map that are an easy drive from the Legacy Museum.

If some exhibits at the Birmingham Civil Rights Institute, the Rosa Parks Museum, and the Civil Rights Memorial give the impression that civil rights struggles were successful in dismantling the power of white supremacy and racial segregation, the Legacy Museum implies that mainstream Americans' views on civil rights may be too focused on school segregation or busing histories and not enough on labor exploitation, capital punishment, and other forms of lingering social injustice.

Visitors to the Legacy Museum are invited to mull over these in situ arguments as soon as they enter the museum doors. Painted on the brick wall is this line: "You are standing on a site where enslaved people were warehoused." Here, before visitors even get a chance to enter the main exhibit area, they can read about the slave trade routes along the Alabama River, follow the massive migrations of slaves from the western shores of Africa to the fertile Black Belt region of Alabama, read about the massive fatality rates of slaves on slave ships, and learn that, by 1860, Montgomery was the capital of the slave trade in Alabama—and one of the two largest slave trading centers in the United States. Even visitors may have had doubts about the quality of antebellum life for slaves, they can read on a Legacy Museum wall a quotation from Harriet Tubman: "Slavery is the next thing to hell." This undermines some contemporary arguments that have been advanced about how slaves were treated well during the slave years, and that radical civil rights activists have misrepresented the antebellum South.

Visitors are then guided to a dark antechamber that features five holding cells, or "slave pens," where former slaves waited to be bought or sold. This eleven-thousand-square-foot site, then, is not just a slave warehouse but also a symbolic place that provides evidentiary proof—or what Eyal Weizman might call "forensic architecture"[15]—that incarceration has always been a dark element of slavery wherein persons were held against their will until others decided their fate. Each pen has a hologram of enslaved victims behind bars dressed in nineteenth-century garb. One cage features an elderly woman singing a gospel song. Another has children in raggedy clothes crying for their "Mama." "Have you seen our mother?," one of the children asks. And yet another pen is empty, leading the visitor to assume that the person who was once in there was bought, sold, or died.[16] Once again palpable absences can be used to make visual arguments about present suffering.

This brings to mind the horrors that were witnessed by those who watched as French children were sent on trains to ghettos like Warsaw, or the death camps of Auschwitz or Treblinka during the World War II Holocaust. Only the Legacy Museum's historical focus is on the familial and cultural destruction that was wrought by American institutional slavery.

As visitors exit this dark room filled with critiques of the slave trade, they enter the main exhibit, which is spatially organized by a timeline that chronicles the legacy of racial terrorism. There are four sections that use bold text and black-and-white photos to document the evolution of slavery: "Kidnapped," "Terrorized," "Segregated," and "Incarcerated." Each section includes an adhesive banner that sprawls across the floor and demarcates the section from the rest of the museum. As visitors walk along this timeline, they encounter a very different kind of historicity that doesn't resemble the traditional periodization that can be viewed at the nearby Civil Rights Memorial.

Rather than document the accomplishments of 1960s civil rights leaders, which cover a relatively short time span in American historiography, the Legacy Museum invites visitors to envision a much longer periodization of racial terrorism, beginning with the kidnapping of people or color from their homes in the seventeenth century and lasting for centuries.

Kidnapped

Visitors to this section are invited to trace the origins of racial terrorism back to the seventeenth century, when so many were forced into a life of bondage. Twelve million souls were kidnapped during this period, reads a bold streamer that unfurls itself onto the wooden floor, and visitors learn that an estimated two million people died on the journey to the United States. Despite the 1808 abolition of the slave trade and proscriptions against the importation of slaves to the United States, the cruel practice of slavery, and the holding of racialized persons against their will, persisted as cultural practices throughout the land.

It is at this point that visitors who may be familiar with colorblind ways of conceptual constitutional rights and civil rights reform may start to realize how EJI framings of the post–Civil War years differ from conventional American historicizing. In this "Kidnapped" portion of the Legacy Museum, curators have provided sectional texts noting that even after the passage of the Thirteenth Amendment—which prohibits slavery, "except as punishment for crime"—slavery continued for "another century." This statement differs from most civil rights accounts that contend that the Civil War, and the passage of the post–Civil War amendments, "ended" slavery in the 1860s.

Here, the Legacy Museum states that slavery was justified by "false notions of black inferiority" that were grounded in the logic of eugenics, which sought to prove this "necessary" hierarchy of race relationships with evidence from racialized "science."[17]

Terrorized

As visitors proceed down the EJI's visitor timeline at the Legacy Museum, they enter the "terrorized" period of postslavery. Here, viewers learn that nine million persons of color were terrorized by threats of death within a "racial caste" system that was met with "brutal violence." Does the mention of such a large number signify more than just a recovery of past archival lynching facts?

One of the precedents for extrajudicial terrorism by white supremacists and dominant white majorities was established in 1875 in the case of *United States v. Cruikshank*, in which the US Supreme Court, in a 9–0 decision, failed to interpret constitutional provisions in ways that would have mandated federal intervention against racial terrorism. Instead of interpreting the post–Civil War amendments in ways that challenged white hegemony in the South and elsewhere, the Supreme Court reinterpreted those same amendments so that they could be used in other ways.

In this "Terrorized" portion of the Legacy Museum, audiences are informed that during this "lynching era," persons of color who were accused of violating white social codes were subjected to heinous rituals of persecution, mutilation, and death. Seeking to preserve a legal system of disenfranchisement and Jim Crow laws, white mobs would take some black victims from jail cells and administer extrajudicial "justice"; other victims endured trials before all-white juries whose outcomes were essentially predetermined. Illegal lynchings and legal lynchings were not that different for those who suffered the consequences of these carceral practices.

Visitors to this second section are thus presented with some of the same information—and some of the same photographs—that we presented in chapters 2, 3, and 4. Graphic displays show how lynching victims were burned, mutilated, or shot, and visitors to this Montgomery museum are informed that these pictures were often taken by perpetrators and turned into postcards.

Importantly, this museological periodization also notes that nearly six million refugees attempted to flee the "threat of racial terrorism" from the Deep South by migrating north. This six million figure may be an accurate representation of the magnitude of the movement of blacks during the Great Migration, but the polysemic nature of this statistic allows visitors to also infer that perhaps—just perhaps—this might be yet another dimension of some forgotten genocide or African American holocaust. To our knowledge, the Legacy Museum's curators do not explicitly articulate that position, but some online admirers of the EJI are willing to making those huge claims.

In the latter decades of the twentieth century, some critical race scholars and interdisciplinary writers concerned about reparations advanced similar claims, and readers need to keep in mind the countless interviews in which Bryan Stevenson has said explicitly that the builders of the Legacy Museum were deeply inspired by the US Holocaust Memorial Museum (and other genocide museums).[18]

If you begin to add up the millions who are referenced in two or three subsections of this part of the museum—those enslaved, those who died from transatlantic crossings, those who were lynched, and those who migrated north—you have little trouble seeing how you might be invited to view all of this as part of a cultural genocide *dispositif*.

Are these memories of tragedy, death, and terrorism multidirectional, or are they competitive? We discuss this point in further detail in the following section of this chapter; however, we want to point out the possibility that the Legacy Museum wants visitors to recontextualize the Great Migration in novel ways.

Segregated

As visitors continue their performative journey following the prescriptive EJI timeline, they enter the period of segregation wherein the Jim Crow "separate but equal" laws reigned throughout the South and impacted ten million persons. What made these segregation laws so nefarious was how they institutionally warranted the dispensation of extrajudicial punishment against African Americans for transgressing social conventions that had been established by the dominant white majority. This was the age when members of the US Supreme Court and other jurists believed in Social Darwinian ways of conceptualizing not only "servitude" but "equality."

Many portions of this "segregated" part of the Legacy Museum look very much like typical civil rights historicizing. Here, visitors learn that during the period following *Brown v. Board of Education* (1954), activists participated in boycotts, sit-ins, and marches, and backlash against perceived federal interference led to increased threats of attack by the white majority.

The Legacy Museum does not pull any punches, however, in showing that during the 1950s and 1960s churches were bombed, black children were humiliated and killed, police dogs were ordered to brutally attack African Americans, and persons of color throughout the South were presumed to be guilty in criminal contexts. Highlighting the power of Southern mythologizing, the Legacy Museum notes that George Wallace once declared: "Segregation forever."

Incarcerated

The final portion of this temporal journey brings the visitor face-to-face with the present-day inequities of mass incarceration. This is where the Legacy Museum, through the work of the EJI, displays its place-based arguments by showing how the legacy of racial terrorism now manifests itself in new twenty-first-century iterations, whereby eight million persons of color are incarcerated in America's prison industrial complex.

Notice once again the tallying of figures, the magnitude of these horrors.

For EJI supporters, this portion of the historical tour not only shows the fruits of historical racial terrorism—it also shows that mass incarceration *is an underappreciated form of racial terrorism*. Capital punishment and the unfair sentencing of juveniles, for example, can be categorized by the EJI as twenty-first-century examples of racial terrorism.

In their writings, members of the EJI note the politicized, arbitrary, and problematic nature of the rationales that were once used to justify lynching, and the curatorial displays in the Legacy Museum convey the related message that many, if not most, of those incarcerated today are incarcerated for reasons that make little sense.

Those who travel to Montgomery to visit the museum are informed that slavery, evidently, has simply mutated. For example, as one display reads, the operative logic of white supremacy remains the same, wherein "a presumption of guilt and danger ... [is] assigned to African Americans." The evidence to support these claims appears in the referencing of policies such as Richard Nixon's ideographic "law and order," the backing of mandatory minimum prison sentences, and the declaration of the "War on Drugs." These policies not only play on the tropes that we discussed in prior chapters—they are now explicitly linked in a race-conscious symbolic work in which the activities of persons of color are criminalized for a host of seemingly irrational reasons.

In the same way that Bryan Stevenson's book *Just Mercy* explains the problems with the "adultification" of the trials of young blacks, the Legacy Museum chronicles the stiffening of penalties—and the lack of mercy and compassion—as represented by the "superpredator" discourses of the 1990s. What is left in the American mainstream consciousness is a "black community" that is allegedly full of "deviant" and "delinquent" adults.

From a critical participatory rhetoric vantage point, this timeline is not merely an arhetorical, depoliticized "history" of lynching legacies. It is a selective chronology that has no place for the white supremacist arguments that were popularized during the Reconstruction and post-Reconstruction periods. At the same time, this select genealogy presents the visitor with a powerful argument about the legacy of racial terrorism throughout the United States, a legacy that would not be halted by talk of the legal victories for equality, such as the Civil Rights Act of 1964 or the Voting Rights Act of 1965.

Thus, the curators of the Legacy Museum argue that the involvement of the police and courts in carrying out repressive responses to nonviolent social protest shows the impoverished nature of colorblind rhetorics. This museum—unlike many other civil rights museums—demonstrates that white supremacist thinking has infiltrated every corner of social, legal, and cultural life in America.

Some of the very same arguments that appeared in the writings of Bryan Stevenson and other EJI members at least a decade before the opening of the Legacy Museum now (re)appear in vernacular forms that can be understood by laypersons and other visitors. "The United States has the highest rate of incarceration in the world," states the museum pamphlet that is distributed to visitors. The authors of the pamphlet go on to note:

> One in three black male babies born today is expected to go jail or prison during his lifetime. Black women and girls are disproportionately targeted in schools, and discouraging racial disparities can be found in virtually every metric evaluating the quality of life in America. Understanding these issues requires a deeper, critical examination of American history, which is the purpose of the Legacy Museum.[19]

Note how this stance assumes that this type of "critical examination" cannot be found in mainstream newspapers, on the National Mall in Washington, at other civil rights museums, or even at other memorializing spaces that may be devoted to US lynching histories.

Words and images are brought together at this evocative place of memory. In a powerful yet perturbing way, the Legacy Museum highlights the stories of those who have been incarcerated for life. These stories are told through the handwritten letters of people who were wrongfully committed, who may be serving life sentences, or who may be sitting on death row. The museum also provides opportunities to hear interactive phone conversations with those incarcerated who share their narratives with listeners, as well as documentary films that feature those who have survived years of incarceration and are attempting to reintegrate themselves back into society. This visually allows visitors to see the "mercy" and rehabilitative efforts that the EJI discusses elsewhere in their reports, public addresses, and web texts.

Throughout the rest of the Legacy Museum there are myriad artifacts, displays, and interactive technology that cover fragmentary portions of this race-conscious chronology that takes viewers from the early slave trade period to twenty-first-century carceral practices. For instance, a semi-enclosed amphitheater features numerous media that are used to enhance the experience of those who walk in, including multiple public screens that showcase the hate speech delivered by rhetors like George Wallace.

There is also an interactive screen with the caption "Warning: Graphic Content," which allows viewers to make their own personal decisions about whether they want to see pictures of lynchings by touching the screen, and an interactive map of the United States provides statistics on all of the counties that have had a lynching. Kentucky: 168, Arkansas: 492, Tennessee: 233, Mississippi: 654, Florida: 313, Georgia: 590, Michigan: 1.

Numerous objects are on display that serve as "forensic architecture" for Jim Crow remembrances, including stacks of jars full of dirt from lynching sites. An old NAACP flag that says "A man was lynched yesterday" reminds visitors of the activities of Walter White and other members of the NAACP who traveled to Washington, DC, in fruitless attempts to convince congressional leaders that that they needed to pass federal anti-lynching legislation.

Other artifacts from the Jim Crow era include signs reading "Whites only" and "negroes must move to the back of the bus." Art, too, plays a prominent role at the Legacy Museum, considering the force of a powerful sculpture by Titus Kaphar entitled *Doubt*, songs of resistance, and an area where visitors can document their own visitation in a camera booth.

Even though some of these museological spaces might give the visitor some temporary affective relief, there are other, more haunting areas that invite visitors to remember that it was not just scattered individuals but sometimes groups of hundreds or thousands who gathered together to witness mass lynching spectacles. This allows visitors to see that lynchings were not simply individuated acts that were carried out by members of the KKK but also collective social acts that could be witnessed in farming communities and small towns. Local stores at these places then sold morbid souvenirs after the burning and mutilation of a lynching victim.

The very arbitrariness of the arguments that were used to terrorize lynching victims are on full display at the Legacy Museum. Visitors who travel to Montgomery learn that Elizabeth Lawrence was lynched because she scolded some white children who threw rocks at her, and tourists find out that black men could lose their lives for allegedly violating informal social codes, such as knocking on the door of a white woman.[20]

In the same way that the metal panels and the positionality of commemorative plaques at the nearby National Memorial for Peace and Justice are intended to appeal to a variety of senses, the Legacy Museum's exhibits, oral recordings, and other artifacts provide the type of affective materials that allow visitors to feel as though they are traveling back in time to become witnesses to the spectacles and horrors of lynching events. "We want to create an institution that allows people to experience directly what this history means and what it does," Bryan Stevenson explained to reporter Erin Edgemon, and the Legacy Museum tries to fill in the historical and cultural gaps of epistemic knowledge that have been left by generations of silence.[21]

Stevenson's message is clear: we may have forgotten some of this, because those involved in the coproduction of institutional racism may have been more discreet about these racial injustices. Illicit lynchings led to "legal" lynchings, and the tactics that were used to ensure white domination involved more than de jure segregation.

Those who finish their tours of the Lynching Memorial and Legacy Museum are invited take in one overarching message: racial terrorism is no less nefarious when it appears in the guise of today's capital punishment, unfair sentencing, jury discrimination, or the mistreatment of African American individuals with disabilities than it was during the age of lynching.

Visitors can walk away simply having learned more about Jim Crow and the magnitude of lynchings, or they can join those who wish to interrogate the twenty-first-century racialized presumption that persons of color are guilty until proven innocent. The implicit argument here is that today's discriminatory practices have their own genealogies, which have taken many forms over the past several hundred years.

According to the EJI's epistemes, descendants of lynching victims, and neighbors of those who were victims, have to overcome the burden of proof that confronts terrorized subjects. This burden continues to lie with them rather than with the institutions that persecute them, and all this legal apparatus is hidden behind the "postracial" facade, the neoliberal framings of colorblindness.[22]

Invoking the abject and the macabre to make these types of public arguments about the need for major change involves the occasional use of multidirectional memories of the past. Here, in some of the last chronological and thematic stages of a typical tour of the Legacy Museum, the linkages that are made connect racial terrorist horrors with Holocaust allusions.[23]

(Re)membrances of the Great Migration and a Possible African American Holocaust

One could, of course, argue that a critical study of discourse/power/knowledge formations at the Legacy Museum might confirm that there is no comparison in scale, violence, or institutionalization between lynching memories and the World War II Holocaust. Possibly, some who are familiar with Holocaust histories would welcome the inclusion of studies of African slave trading, which might have contributed to the perpetration of other genocides. Learning about both the Holocaust and the African American holocaust might help those who adopt this multidirectional stance, allowing visitors to the museum to examine both topics without placing them in some competitive frame or genocidal hierarchy.

Do tourists who travel to the Legacy Museum reference these comparative genocidal usages of texts, bricks, photographs, gardens, waterfalls, iron bars, and other artifacts in the EJI's critiques of traditional civil rights memories, and if they do, should we view this as multidirectional or "competitive" remembrance?

This is not an easy question to answer, given what we believe to be a primary focus, in mainstream coverage of these Montgomery sites of memory, on the recovery of the lynching histories of those killed between 1870 and the 1950s. We are tempted to argue that what Michael Rothberg may have missed in his advocacy of multidirectional memories are the ways contentious sites of memory *might have both multidirectional and competitive features*, depending on the activist purposes of those who raise funds, build, and maintain these mass incarceration sites of memory. For example, learning about the millions who suffered because of centuries of "racial terrorism" may, or may not, catalyze interest in the study of what happened during the World War II Holocaust or the 1994 Rwandan genocide.

Regardless, there is little question that the EJI, within a very short time period, has altered the ways countless visitors and observers around the globe may be contextualizing the systematic nature of lynching in America's past. "Today," noted Sammy Feldblum after a visit to the Lynching Memorial and Legacy Museum, "deadly force has migrated into the legal system, where it still serves white supremacy, especially in the South," responding to the EJI's statement that "more than 80 percent of legal executions have occurred in states formerly of the Confederacy."[24] This type of argumentation provides a cartographic way of using histories and maps to compare historical lynchings with contemporary American executions.

Constitutive audiences and interpretative communities can be formed in many diverse ways, and at times it appears that some journalists do come close to acknowledging the existence of Stevenson's "postgenocide" American society. Writers, for example, have commented on how the Memorial to the Murdered Jews of Europe in Berlin, the Apartheid Museum in Johannesburg, and the Kigali Genocide Memorial in Rwanda have served as models for the building of the Lynching Memorial and the Legacy Museum in Montgomery—not to mention the National September 11 Memorial and Museum and the US Holocaust Memorial Museum. The very mention of these other sites prompted one writer to opine that their success provided an impetus for those who sought acknowledgment of what many call the "original sin" of the transatlantic slavery "genocide."[25]

Again, given the relative rarity of these types of investigatory or public references to genocidal claims—appearing only infrequently in the countless newspaper and magazine articles, journal essays, books, interviews, blogs, and documentaries on these Montgomery sites of memory that have appeared since 2015—we ourselves have to conclude that it may take time before *most future audiences* see these genocidal connections that are being advanced by EJI members and their supporters.[26]

This leads us at this point in this chapter to ask a key question: in spite of cultural hurdles, is the EJI signaling that it wants America to view the Great Migration to Chicago and elsewhere as a type of forgotten "genocide" or "black holocaust"?

While Bryan Stevenson admitted that the traditional civil rights narratives put out by others helped raise an "awareness about our history of slavery and terrorism, and segregation," that did not mean that people had an "appreciation" of the type of American history he was interested in seeing. Part of the work of the EJI, he explained, had to do with "reengaging" America so the nation could see that it was still "haunted" and "burdened" by this history of "racial injustice." At one key point in a 2017 interview, Stevenson made a rare, explicit reference that gestured toward a much larger genocide of indigenous peoples:

> We want there to be some acknowledgment that we're a post-genocide society, that when white settlers came to this continent, there were millions of native people here whom we've killed through famine and war and disease, and that we forced them off their land sometimes in cruel and barbaric ways. And instead of acknowledging that genocide we said, "No, those people are different, they're not really people, they're savages," and we used this narrative of racial difference

to justify this horrific behavior. That same narrative of racial difference was employed to justify centuries of slavery.[27]

This cofounder of the EJI noted that the Legacy Museum and the National Memorial for Peace and Justice in Montgomery could provide a different "lens" for studying these "reengaging" histories so that communities could be truly free.[28]

As we noted in the previous chapter, this raises the question of whether Stevenson is implying that true freedom, a precondition for reconciliation, requires the acknowledgment of an African American genocide, or is he referencing a Native American settler-colonial genocide? Or does the specific "narrative" that he wants to circulate involve what some genocide scholars call a "double genocide"?

In order to provide evidence and warrants for his claims, Stevenson talked to reporters about how the narrative of "racial difference" was formed long ago, and that these problems did not "end in 1865." As far as he was concerned, the "ghettos" that were formed after the relocation of black people in Boston, Cleveland, Chicago, Detroit, Los Angeles, and Oakland had everything to do with the legacy of racial terrorism and the Great Migration.[29]

More than a few seem to have been persuaded by this permutation of a multidirectional narrative. Jonathan Capehart, for example, writing for the *Washington Post*, remarked that after interviewing Stevenson he became convinced that his earlier intuition had been right, that those blacks who moved to Cleveland or Los Angeles "didn't go there as immigrants looking for new economic opportunities" but were there as "refugees and exiles from the terror in the American South."[30]

Note how this talk of refugees and exiles brings to mind cultural and ethnic diasporas in which expatriates try to make a living elsewhere as they suffer from the lingering influence of colonialization, imperial exploitation, postcolonial legacies, and so on.

The "lens" that the EJI, Stevenson, and the Legacy Museum coproduced was not simply reflecting some preexisting reality *but was creating a revised historical reality* as well. This was an alternative "context of civil rights," which did not just focus on the heroism of civil rights leaders during a relatively short reformist period that hid the "intense resistance to integration by white political leaders."[31] The type of engagement that the EJI was advocating, which called for a "more honest accounting," would include in the historical ledger the linkages that could be made between slave society, the places where "mass atrocities" were witnessed, and today's celebrations of Jefferson Davis's birthday.

Critical genealogists who are accustomed to reading about Friedrich Nietzsche's commentaries on the use and abuse of history, Walter Benjamin's constellations, or Michel Foucault's "cuts" can argue that it is no coincidence that the EJI finds ways of linking these genocidal slave horrors to today's culture wars and monumentalization arguments. The corrupting influence here, Bryan Stevenson averred, has everything to do with the way that Alabama publics could perform these celebrations without viewing them as offensive to people of color. As far as Stevenson was concerned, it did not appear that Alabama citizens who supported the maintenance of Confederate statuary were cognizant of the fact that these Confederate heroes' defense of slavery was wrong. As we noted earlier, Stevenson went so far as to argue that it would be "unconscionable for Adolf Hitler's birthday to be celebrated in Germany."[32] (see chapter 6).

Again, did any of these EJI linkages between lynching pasts and various holocausts resonate with American audiences?

The Legacy Museum highlights the magnitude of past horrors by noting not only historical presences but historical absences, and there are occasional clues that some visitors appreciate the radicalness of the EJI's vision. One message, which is conveyed in large, bold letters at the Lynching Memorial, lets visitors know that in spite of the archival documentation that has been collected, there are still anonymous victims of racial terror who should not be forgotten: "Thousands of African Americans are unknown victims of racial terror lynchings whose deaths cannot be documented, many whose names will never be known."

In the same way that the World War II Holocaust involved a double erasure—of lives as well as memories—so too has the circulation of Southern or American texts that divert attention from the true magnitude of racial terrorist horrors.

When Bryan Stevenson talks to the press about truth and reconciliation, historical silences, and the need to see the linkages between historical lynchings and contemporary death row politics, he rarely uses specific language that references the term "genocide," but this hasn't prevented others from treating the Lynching Memorial as a place that invites comparisons with other large-scale atrocities. Curtis Bunn, for example, began a journalistic narrative with this vignette: "When Bryan Stevenson visited South Africa, Rwanda and Germany over the course of a few years, he was struck by the compelling memorials of apartheid, genocide and the Holocaust."[33] Other commentaries hint at similar linkages, and the *Montgomery Advertiser* measured the pulse of visitors to the EJI's Lynching Memorial and Legacy Museum by asking them what they thought about these sites of memory.[34]

We, of course, as critical genealogists must note that the polysemic or polyvalent nature of these Montgomery sites has created situations in which visitors can use their experiences in ways that have little to do with either genocidal memories or Confederate remembrances. Marian Wright Edelman, the founder of the Children's Defense Fund, commented on how children shouldn't be dying from gun violence today, and that visitors to the Legacy Museum should not be "celebrating" this place without thinking about "even greater levels of harm" that come from unequal education and persistent violence.[35]

We conclude this chapter by arguing that it seems plausible that Bryan Stevenson and his Equal Justice Initiative built the Legacy Museum and the Lynching Memorial in Montgomery for very specific purposes, one of which may have been the desire to document an African American genocide—a genocide so widespread that it began during the transatlantic slave trading years and continued through the antebellum period, the heyday of lynching, peonage, the Great Migration, and today's mass incarceration practices.

Those who are familiar with reparations literature, postcolonial studies, indigeneity studies, critical race theorizing, and related studies might recognize the coherence of these types of radical narrations, but will accepting the premises of these arguments pose challenges to mainstream American audiences?

If critical genealogists pay attention to audience responses to Legacy Museum messages about the magnitude of these racial terrorist horrors, we believe they will find that some of these symbolic linkages have escaped the attention of many visitors to these hallowed Montgomery sites of memory. We are convinced that in spite of the Legacy Museum's visualities and texts on the horrors of mass incarceration, many visitors will want to fold the more radical EJI critiques back into the more popular, more recognizable, and more uplifting stories about great civil rights accomplishments. In other words, Ida B. Wells-Barnett may simply join Dr. Martin Luther King Jr. and Rosa Parks in the pantheon of traditional neoliberal civil rights monumentalization.

For example, visitors to the Lynching Memorial or the Legacy Museum can be deeply moved to learn about the nature, scope, and magnitude of American lynching without ever encountering a heated debate about today's mass incarceration practices. Ordinary citizens can become examples of what some academics call "strategic essentialists," social agents who are able to pick and choose which ideographs, which lines of argument, which parts of narratives they wish to accept or reject.

We have also argued that different audiences, based on the interpretative frames that they bring with them to Montgomery, can form multidirectional or competing memories as they visit the Legacy Museum. Nothing, for example, would prevent visitors from comparing the horrors of the Middle Passage or the traumas of the Great Migration with the Holocaust. But so far, we simply haven't seen those types of comparisons in the mainstream or alternative press.

Our critical textual analyses and our illustrative purposive sampling—taken from hundreds and hundreds of EJI materials, newspaper articles, and other commentaries on these two places—indicate that EJI supporters occasionally reference Native American genocides or the World War II Judeocide, but they do not advance arguments that might be interpreted as critiques of the uniqueness of the Shoah. The EJI brand of multidirectional argumentation that appears in the Legacy Museum and elsewhere underscores the horrors that led to the flight of millions during the Great Migration while avoiding any diminution of the importance of the World War II Holocaust.

Stevenson and the EJI, however, are not the only observers willing to argue that the traumas of racial pasts are transgenerational. Nicole Austin-Hillery, the executive director of the US program of Human Rights Watch, noted how studies of movements from slavery to sharecropping, from lynching to police brutality, from segregation to redlining and gentrification provide evidence of systemic biases that have followed personal biases.[36]

Only time will tell if future generations of Americans who visit the National Memorial for Truth and Justice or who write about the Legacy Museum will agree with Bryan Stevenson's and the EJI's more radical claims. After all, these social agents often go beyond describing racialized pasts as they demand major reforms.

In some of Stevenson's narratives of "postgenocide" America, he mentions how the public lynchings of the early decades of the twentieth century that were sometimes witnessed by tens of thousands have now gone "indoors" to courtrooms, where African Americans face unreliable verdicts and the "same kind of death sentencing and the same kind of abuse of color ... that existed outside the courtroom during the lynching era."[37]

Will other Americans who visit the Legacy Museum begin to revisit the question of why we incarcerate millions of people of color in disproportionate numbers? Will they dare to take this one step further, and treat this abuse as genocidal in nature?

CONCLUSION

The Future of "Race-Conscious" Memorialization in Twenty-First-Century America

MERCY. JUSTICE. REMEMBRANCE. REDEMPTION, ENDING "RACIAL TERROR." THESE are a few of the ideographic terms, some of the key discursive building blocks, that form the EJI's "New Reconstruction" campaigns and ideological formations. The previous chapters, using critical genealogical and participatory critical rhetoric (PCR) approaches, have enabled readers to see some of the promises and perils that are faced by those who try to use select representations of fraught lynching pasts to end America's "New Jim Crow" tactics.[1] For a variety of reasons, we have seen how Montgomery's National Memorial for Peace and Justice and the Legacy Museum have decided, for the most part, not to use those old sensationalist archival photographs of lynchings as they produce their own texts and visualities in an effort to change the way Americans conceptualize capital punishment, mass incarceration, the excessive use of life sentences without parole, and other forms of legal injustice.

On first impression, it might look as though the ideographic terms referenced above are relatively innocuous. Who, after all, can complain about the potential emancipatory function of these terms, especially in an American society where some sixty-eight million souls seem destined to spend part of their lives behind bars, individuals who will carry the burden of prison records?[2] Moreover, keep in mind the eternal wisdom behind the words of Maya Angelou that are etched in the very foundation of the Legacy Museum: "History, despite its wretched pain, cannot be unlived, but if faced with courage, need not be lived again."[3]

If critical genealogical scholars and readers dig a little deeper and study those fraught histories, and if they study the layers and layers of archival arguments that have been produced by people who have faced lynchings and depictions of lynchings in unflinching ways, they may change some of their first impressions as they realize that these hallowed Montgomery spaces and places are not just being used to set the lynching "record straight," but are also being used to produce one of those famous "first rough drafts of history" to aid the cause of those today who seek radical reform and restorative justice.

Although there have been other lynching museums in America, and although we have memorials to figures like Ida B. Wells-Barnett[4] and the activism of the NAACP, we need to give the EJI credit for attempting to create Southern sites of memory that might be able, in the long run, to mobilize millions of Americans who wish to become involved in mass incarceration reform. If they do succeed in going in this direction, and in radicalizing some discourse/power/knowledge formations, this could alter the rhetorical American landscapes of those who have been dismissive of reparations claims or talk of any African American holocaust.

Those who wish to provide nuanced critiques of the efforts of Bryan Stevenson, the EJI, and the Legacy Museum will need to be equipped with more than just first impressions. Some observers may not wish to grapple with difficult heritages, and they will be tempted to join those who recontextualize the EJI's efforts to fit within conventional stories of racial progress. That said, we are convinced that these readings "along the grain" of America's tales of exceptionalism and mythic racial progress after the 1960s civil rights movements miss the intentionalities, functionalities, and materialities of the National Memorial for Peace and Justice and the Legacy Museum.

Our interventionist acts in this book are intended to illustrate how Stevenson, the EJI, and their supporters who send in soil from half-forgotten lynching sites want us to read "against the grain" of habituated celebrations of civil rights successes.[5] These activists and their public allies don't want any of us to forget the enduring power of institutionalized white supremacy, which has had everything to do with forgotten lynching legacies.

The previous chapters of this book have shown how the EJI, as it tries to produce vernacular rhetorics that will resonate with diverse American communities, has to decide how it will handle delicate topics such as Confederate statue removal, the naming of particular lynchers, the representation of children at mass-spectacle lynchings, earlier statistical collections of reported lynchings, the use of graphic images, the documentation of an "African American holocaust" in a postgenocide age, the need for mercy for the guilty, reparations, and the end of capital punishment in America. The EJI wants to produce a radical *dispositif* that is capacious enough to include provocative critiques of America's racialized pasts, but that organization may want to walk gingerly around such topics as twenty-first-century white power and institutionalized white racism. This, we are convinced, is one of the reasons we don't see Bryan Stephenson appropriating the language of some critical sociologists who focus on investment in whiteness.

In the future, some of the epistemic features of the EJI's radical *dispositif* may have to be modified to include other stories of the lynching of Mexicans,[6] Chinese immigrants,[7] Jews like Leo Frank,[8] and even impoverished whites in the Midwest[9] and the South, who were configured as transgressive figures who had forfeited their lives.

Are these the types of radical symbolic messages that Americans, in this Trumpian era, want to hear? Are some US audiences at least willing to contemplate the possibility that they need to read or hear what the EJI has to say about lynching legacies and mass incarceration presents?[10]

As we write this conclusion, investigative journalists and scholars report that almost every week some local, regional, or national newspaper circulates a story about a particular county in some part of the United States that is asking the EJI to send them the coffin-like slab that represents their county to become part of a local lynching memorial. As with the European Holocaust's "stumbling stones," the participatory nature of these vernacular acts of personal and public consciousness raising provide visible indications that some Americans are hearing the EJI's messages about the need for atonement, mercy, acknowledgment, truth, and reconciliation.

In many states, discussions are taking place about historic lynchings that occurred in those states, and EJI representatives often appear at lynching memorial ceremonies. The EJI helps pay for markers for lynching victims, organizes seminars and conferences, and produces sophisticated websites filled with information about contemporary conditions in America's carceral system.

All of this extends the geopolitical reach of the EJI's messages as visitors, fund-raisers, and other interested parties become coparticipants in these complex rhetorical processes. Most people who leave comments in mainstream and alternative press outlets about these Montgomery sites of lynching memories seem to appreciate EJI's efforts, and many interviewees publicize their own involvement in EJI consciousness-raising efforts.

While many portions of this book have outlined those EJI efforts and connected these twenty-first-century activities to previous historical activism—the work of Ida B. Wells-Barnett, William White, or Thurgood Marshall, for instance—we have purposely focused on the crafting of elite and vernacular discourses about lynching that drifted along for many generations. Instead of trying to decide whether Bryan Stevenson needs to be placed in the pantheon of civil rights activism (he already is), we have devoted most of our attention to critical investigations of the crafting of the EJI's radical race-conscious epistemes.

In the twenty-first century, critical genealogists can now document renewed calls for the passage of federal anti-lynching legislation, and they can point to renascent interest in reviewing the evidence in the Emmett Till case.[11]

That said, where is there any scholarly, journalistic, legal, or public evidence that American citizens in the mainstream are demanding that their political representatives end capital punishment or reform discriminatory mass incarceration practices? Are these merely aspirational goals, and are critical rhetoricians expecting too much when they wonder why some of those who write paragraph after paragraph about the discovery of another lynching by the EJI do not take the next step and connect those lynching cultures to today's problematic American prison industrial complex? Is the notion of having a "New Reconstruction" only a critical race theory dream, with little chance of gaining realpolitik traction outside the halls of law schools?

To be fair, Bryan Stevenson is now often interviewed on matters of Southern prison reform, especially Alabama prisons. In April 2019, after the US Department of Justice issued a report condemning excessive violence, inmate deaths, and shortage of staff in state correctional systems, Alabama authorities indicated that they would try to fix their state's carceral problems.[12] When these authorities said that they wanted to immediately add five hundred more correctional officers, Stevenson replied that you cannot solve Alabama's carceral problems by building more prisons, without changing prison culture. "When you have a college football team who can't win a game," argued Stevenson, "you don't say, 'Let's build a new stadium, that'll fix our problems.'"[13]

In this conclusion, we take up the question of whether those who visit or write about the Legacy Museum or the National Memorial for Peace and Justice have made some of the same empirical or symbolic connections that we made as we reviewed the EJI's advocacy efforts.

It's one thing to visit the Lynching Memorial and perhaps dig up soil samples from lynching sites and send them to the Legacy Museum, and quite another to argue for a massive overhaul in how we think about the incarceration of African Americans, apologies for slave trading, or the need for African American reparations. How many American audiences are willing to give their warranted assent to the EJI's notions of "mercy," "truth," and "reconciliation," which allow for the possibility of the abolition of capital punishment, the end of the "adultification" of juvenile sentencing,[14] the reform of life without parole principles, and the mitigation of harsh criminal penalties for the guilty?

Here, we need to further develop an argument that we have been advancing throughout this book. The critical genealogical studies in our chapters have presented some of the reasons why many American communities are willing to acknowledge the problematics of antebellum, Reconstruction, post-Reconstruction, or even 1950s segregationist practices, but they are unwilling to see that these racialized pasts are at all related to capital punishment or the millions living in US prisons. Future researchers will be able to assess whether diverse American audiences will eventually become more receptive to the EJI's messages.

There is little doubt that the recent unanimous passage of federal anti-lynching legislation, which we discussed in the introduction of this book, was partly influenced by the public consciousness-raising efforts of Bryan Stevenson and the EJI, but one would be hard pressed to point out any consequential changes in mass incarceration practices, whether linked to EJI advocacy or not. Can this hesitancy be chalked up to a lack of knowledge about the depravity of the Middle Passage slave trade or the lynchings of some five thousand African Americans? Or is this a symptom of disagreements about the implicit statute of limitations for some atrocities?

We speculate that some people may avoid grappling with the EJI's claims about unfair detention practices because they view such claims as the politicization of lynching histories. They are willing to expend time and energy putting up markers along highways and on farmlands, or they may help fund the placement of markers in urban locations where individual blacks were lynched, or they may help collect historical information on "forgotten" lynchings. However, these same people seem to assiduously avoid any discussion of how these histories are related to today's prison practices. More than a few are willing to try to master *local* lynching pasts, and they are willing to try to get towns and states to put up commemorative markers for lynching victims, but that does not mean that they will join the ranks of those who want to take down Confederate statuary or provide mercy to the guilty. In April 2019, Nicole Goodkind, writing for *Newsweek*, described how the Texas legislature's heated debate about the state's Confederate monuments morphed into disputes about lynching statues and even the tearing down of Auschwitz.[15] Allegedly, one Democratic state representative, Jarvis Johnson, asked: "Because you guys want to continue to talk about history, should we erect a statue that demonstrated how slaves were disciplined? ... We want to teach, so should we erect a statue with slaves hanging from a tree? Should we erect a monument that demonstrates Indians being mutilated and run off their land?"[16]

Critical rhetoricians and other interdisciplinary scholars might argue that some of this reticence has to do with American reluctance to participate in what Dawn Marie McIntosh, Dreama Moon, and Thomas Nakayama call the interrogation of the "communicative power of whiteness."[17] Critical race scholars have been writing about various permutations of this "investment" in whiteness for many decades,[18] but these types of academic arguments may not resonate with those who don't see how racialized pasts have anything to do with their defense of capital punishment, minimum mandatory sentencing, or life without parole for the guilty.

Even EJI radicals appear to be circumspect in how they frame some historical continuities. Note how EJI writers don't hesitate to outline some of the contours of historical white supremacy—and expand the circumference of the circle of white historical figures involved in mass-spectacle lynchings—but, when it comes to characterizations of twenty-first-century white racism, those same writers narrow their focus to the activities of those on the "fringes" of American society such as white nationalists, the far right, the alternative right, and so on.[19]

As we noted earlier, strategic choices need be made when it comes to naming names during heated exchanges in the monument war or the culture war.

Journalists and laypersons can appreciate Stevenson's work ethic, but they may not be able to take the next step and link those lynching legacies to twenty-first-century problems with America's prison systems. For example, a few investigative journalists who have written about the EJI, the Legacy Museum, and/or the National Memorial for Peace and Justice are willing to also write about the problematics of wrongful convictions, but these are rare exceptions. There is little indication that decision-makers, journalists, or members of the public are willing to accept the argument that contemporary mass incarceration issues can be *causally linked* to a "new Jim Crow"[20] or twenty-first-century white supremacist thinking.

It is tempting to believe that decision-makers, investigative journalists, academics, and laypersons can learn from haunting lynching histories and work toward the goal of finding some essentialist or foundational "history," "truth," "justice," and "reconciliation." Todd Strange, the mayor of Montgomery, during the week that saw the opening of the Legacy Museum, reminisced about the proud historical tradition of civil rights in this city, including the 1955 "birth" of the movement "with the Montgomery Bus boycott." In an article in the *Montgomery Advertiser*, Mayor Strange went on to explain that the city was filled with monuments, memorials, and museums that documented its "status as a world leader in efforts to uplift the downtrodden."[21] He elaborated by mentioning how visitors can take the Rosa Parks historical bus ride, follow the route taken by the Freedom Riders, tour the parsonage of Martin Luther King Jr., and sign their names on the Civil Rights Memorial's Wall of Tolerance.[22] Conspicuously absent from Mayor Strange's commentary in April 2018 was any detailed discussion of the competing Confederate ideologies and memorializations that also dotted Montgomery's landscapes and memoryscapes.

EJI Efforts and the Polysemy of Mercy, Justice, Reconciliation, and other EJI Terminology

Many members of the EJI are aware of these memorial contests in the monument wars, and although some of these social agents write as if the discovery of some revelatory anti-lynching "history" will lead to inevitable social reforms, they are also aware of the legal, political, and cultural hurdles that stand in their way. These activists may be fully aware of the competitive histories and public memories that were produced by those who twisted the words of the post–Civil War amendments, who worried about the protection of white women during the Reconstruction years, or who focused on the alleged "states' rights" of those who refused to support the passage of federal anti-lynching legislation.

Some of the early portions of this book illustrated how lynching histories, photographs, and presentist prison statistics can be used, abused, and twisted in ways that fit all sorts of competing political, social, economic, and legal agendas. Lynching histories could be used to study "Judge Lynch" in ways that try to rationalize populist lynchings as if they were a part of the Western tradition of maintaining frontier law and order.[23] This may make it appear as though many American lynchers and their supporters were merely using extralegal force when local authorities failed to carry out their policing duties.

As we noted in the introduction and chapters 2–4, the pictures that were taken by entrepreneurial photographers to sell to lynchers as mementos would be appropriated by members of the NAACP and other organizations for deployment in anti-lynching campaigns. As W. Fitzhugh Brundage wrote in 2005:

> The "polyvocality" of many lynching images was seldom intentional. Professional photographers who captured the images of charred bodies of lynching victims or the gathered mob staring into a camera lens

were motivated presumably by profit; the consumers who purchased such images did so with the conviction that the keepsake preserved the memory of stalwart defenders of community and hearth. But the same images acquired different meanings in the hands of antilynching activists. . . . [P]hotographs of lynchings over time eroded, rather than bolstered, the legitimacy of mob violence.[24]

We would build on Brundage's insights and argue that some of the exact same data or narratives that Bryan Stevenson and the EJI have used to argue for the elimination of capital punishment—mythic tales of juvenile "superpredators"—can be recontextualized by those *who want more, not less, strict enforcement of mass incarceration structures.*

The EJI may not want to use the NAACP's old photographs, but they do want to produce their own abstract or concrete visual mediums to get across their own select reformist messages.

As we note in more detail below, there are no shortages of those who still want their legislators to get tough on crime and cut down on the aftereffects of the "War on Drugs."

By extending the work of Friedrich Nietzsche, Walter Benjamin, Michel Foucault, Ann Stoler, and others who have noted how myriad social agents have produced rhetorical histories or genealogies in stratifying and destratifying ways, we have invited readers of this book to see many of the presences and absences that are left out in the EJI's "history" that is being produced in these memory wars over lynching and mass incarceration.

Many of the presences that the EJI alludes to depend on the retrieval of select affective archival materials that are linked to transgenerational feelings of anger, outrage, frustration—and, occasionally, hope. If, as Bryan Stevenson's supporters argue, acknowledging some violent lynching "truth" precedes "true" reconciliation, then we need to contextualize how these abstract concepts are being applied in concrete, pragmatic, rhetorical situations. Only then can scholars and readers see their Foucauldian truth effects.

Our focus in this book has been on the rhetorical force of what the EJI and the Legacy Museum is trying to do—in realpolitik ways—with select race-conscious framings of these histories and memories. At this point in time, we wonder whether the EJI's Legacy Museum is going to have the same impact that the US Holocaust Memorial Museum has had on public consciousness raising about the Judeocide. One of the key issues that we have raised is the type of consciousness raising that may be witnessed.

We hope that these Montgomery sites of memory do become catalytic, but all of that future influence may depend on a number of situational factors, including the willingness of American audiences to see talk of truth and reconciliation, and reparations for lynching wrongs, as more than just attempts to establish white guilt or multicultural political correctness. We worry that polite silence—and not just adverse reactions—may greet those who outline and explain in detail the EJI's messages.

Ironically, the more that EJI members move away from the production of strategically ambiguous texts and visualities on America's lynching pasts, and the more clarity they provide regarding their twenty-first-century carceral goals, the more they risk alienating the average American visitor, who will likely contextualize all of this as just more identity politics.

What should critics and readers have to say about the differential ways that American audiences are responding to the EJI's consciousness-raising efforts regarding lynching pasts and mass incarceration presents?

As Michael McGee and other members of the critical rhetoric community have pointed out, when empowered societies concretize and operationalize some ideographic terms—like "mercy," "reconciliation," and so on—they may appropriate and deploy meanings of those abstract concepts in hegemonic ways. Many who read Bryan Stevenson's *Just Mercy*, for example, get to see some of the personal frustrations that led to his battles over everything from the taking down of Confederate memorials to the belated recognition of the trials and tribulations of black soldiers returning home from World War I and World War II.[25] That does not mean, however, that vernacular, public interpretations of "racial terrorism" are going to be deployed by empowered white audiences in ways that are going to lead to drastic carceral changes.

As we noted in chapter 8, American audiences can compartmentalize their viewing, and they can become strategic essentialists who selectively endorse what they view as salient US histories.

Many who visit the EJI's sites in Montgomery may want to believe that most caring Americans belong to the same interpretive communities that they do, whose members would see the same things that they see when they walk through the Lynching Memorial; these visitors may want to believe that everyone else who visits will realize that terms such as "mercy" and "acknowledgment" need to be interpreted in radical, race-conscious ways. But we are not as optimistic.

Not everyone is going to frame those evocative yet polysemic and polyvalent terms in the same way, and this is especially the case with traumatic lynching histories and memories. How many of those who read about these Montgomery spaces and places are going to broaden the circle of moral culpability beyond the KKK's agency in mass lynchings; how many will take seriously the idea that lynching legacies can be empirically linked to today's discriminatory prison practices? How many are going to see that Ida B. Wells-Barnett's discussion of lynching and black entrepreneurs has everything to do with today's intersectional dimensions of capital punishment—involving labor relations, gendered relationships, ethnic relationships, and even some scientific or legal knowledge formations?

How many are going to see how the EJI, in the Legacy Museum, could use the flag that once hung outside of the NAACP's headquarters in New York in 1936 ("A Man Was Lynched Yesterday") as a potent signifier in a new semiotic system of meaning that asks visitors to do more than simply reflect on the number of aggregated lynching statistics?[26] Are twenty-first-century mainstream audiences going to buy into the idea of needing a "New Reconstruction"?

After reviewing many artifacts, we are convinced that investigative journalists and lay audiences understand the importance of recovering "forgotten" lynching histories, but they are sure about what to do with some of the EJI's more consequentialist arguments?

Readers of Stevenson's *Just Mercy*—an incredibly moving story of the challenges facing lawyers who sacrifice much to help the indigent—will learn a great deal about the enduring power of white supremacy rhetorics in the South, the "adultification" of juvenile sentencing, capital punishment, imprisonment without parole, unfair jury selection processes, mass incarceration, and so on. Some of these same topics appear on EJI block sites and publications, but their display does not automatically mean that they will be able to persuade most Americans.

A 2019 article by Zak Cheney-Rice in *New York Magazine* gets at some of the difficulties that Stevenson and the EJI have had to face in both Alabama and the rest of the country, addressing the secular and sacred rhetorical strategies that we reference in earlier chapters:

Faith allows [Stevenson] to imagine an Alabama that does not exist. It keeps at bay the indifference of the cosmos and fuels his conviction in Dr. Martin Luther King Jr.'s maxim that the arc of the moral universe bends toward justice. Faith, Stevenson says, is why he's here: "It wouldn't make sense for me to be in Alabama if I didn't believe." Indeed, his adoptive home state is both an outlier and exemplar of the excesses of mass imprisonment and capital punishment. Like much of America, Alabama imprisons and executes black people at wildly disproportionate rates. Unlike most of the country, it executed prisoners overall at higher rates per capita than all but five other states between 1976 and 2015. Sixteen- and 17-year-olds are tried as adults automatically for some crimes here, including burglary. Stevenson's efforts to transform the status quo have met roadblocks at every turn.[27]

Some of the latest roadblocks include the tightening of restrictions on the communication of inmates, who are having an increasingly difficult time staying in touch with their families while in Alabama's prisons.

Those who have read *Just Mercy* may recognize that Bryan Stevenson is not simply filling his readable book with detailed, legalist studies of some of the major cases that he argued in front of the US Supreme Court. Instead, he adopts a conversational style that looks much like of some of the narrativizing that was recommended by the critical race theorists of the 1980s and 1990s. *Just Mercy* captivates readers with references to biblical parables about the "stonecatchers" who shield victims from those who throw stones at the disempowered or the accused. This is a powerful, rhetorical way of inviting readers to emulate the stonecatchers, to identify with Stevenson and the goals of the EJI.[28]

Those who agree with the ideological premises and the political worldview of the EJI will have no trouble finding reasons to join those who want to see "mercy" interpreted in radical ways. They may, in the future, form alliances with those who wish to conduct judicial reviews for people sentenced to life without parole or capital punishment. These dissenters may join those who argue that the provision of "justice" requires avoiding all-white juries in locales where a substantial percentage or a majority of the population are people of color. Some may even agree about the need to abolish capital punishment, and they may view the photographs and the captions displayed at the Legacy Museum through an ideological lens that enables them to appreciate the need to keep in mind the differences between punishment and *excessive* punishment.

We are convinced, however, that those who interpret these EJI ideographs in such radical ways are in the minority, and not in a position to efficaciously speak truth to power and drastically alter the state or federal laws that shape carceral governmentalities.

Granted, a review of some mediated texts does show that Bryan Stevenson and the EJI are not alone. In previous chapters, we noted how some of their work resonates with many of the arguments made by historical figures like Ida B. Wells-Barnett, and with members of the critical race theory movement. Other commentators might note how other arguments presented by Stevenson and the EJI appear to draw from secular and sacred canonical texts that have a great deal in common with Martin Luther King Jr.'s notion of the "beloved community."[29]

In some mass-mediated situations, Stevenson has been able to go beyond simply commenting on the need to recover lynching legacies and has commented further on the problems of today's prison industrial complex. In myriad ways, his lectures, fund-raising, legal work, and monumentalizing efforts in Montgomery provide illustrative models of civic engagement that we have argued are also examples of critical participatory rhetoric.

No wonder that in December 2019, an HBO documentary entitled "True Justice: Bryan Stevenson's Fight for Equality" aired for free; the EJI's website informed visitors that the documentary was told primarily through Stevenson's own words, with a narrative arc that went back to the infamous *Dred Scott* decision and then followed Stevenson's thirty years working with America's criminal justice system.[30] The website further mentioned that the documentary tracked the "intertwined histories of slavery, lynching, segregation, and mass incarceration."[31]

Studying Truth Effects and the Persuasive Power of EJI Rhetorics

No doubt Bryan Stevenson and his supporters have been able to accomplish what some members of the critical race theory community—hampered by "publish or perish" academic constraints—could not. Stevenson has found a way of moving talk of lynching histories and mass incarceration problematics beyond the ivory tower so that journalists, donors, and lay audiences can appreciate his advocacy of those who are "broken" or in need of "freedom." Note, for example, the presentist arguments that Stevenson managed to air during a *60 Minutes* episode with Oprah Winfrey as they toured parts of the National Memorial for Peace and Justice. As Winfrey notes, "Stevenson wants people to understand that lynchings were not just brutal footnotes in history," that in fact "they reflected a belief in racial differences that reinforced segregation in the 1950s and 1960s, and . . . resulted in a pattern of unequal justice today."[32] This is followed by a brief sample of mass-mediated argumentation about carceral problematics, which was presented to millions of *60 Minutes* viewers:

> BRYAN STEVENSON: And now we live in a landscape where you see young black boys and men being rounded up. One in three black male babies born in this country is expected to go to jail or prison.
>
> OPRAH WINFREY: You actually think that slavery and lynchings led to African Americans being disproportionately represented in the criminal justice system?

STEVENSON: Yes, I do. And I think, actually, it's not a hard thing to understand, you know, I look at–

WINFREY: I think it is a hard thing to understand for people who think people get locked up, people are locked up because they commit crimes.

STEVENSON: About 13 percent of the people illegally in possession of drugs in this country are black. That's about our proportion of the population. You know what percentage are arrested? That's about 35 percent. That is an echo of this consciousness that doesn't value the lives of these folks.[33]

As members of the EJI are fond of arguing, indifference, historical ignorance, structural problems, and the desire to maintain symbols of white supremacy all contribute to the coproduction of dysfunctional state and federal prison systems.

It would be easy to conclude that all of this is a matter of not knowing one's lynching "history" or not appreciating the need to show "mercy" or empathy, but what are we to make of polls and other information that put on display the sedimented formation of other knowledge productions? For example, in June 2018 a Pew Research Center poll showed that 54 percent of Americans still favored the death penalty for people who were convicted of murder.[34] Imagine how some of those polled, or those who share their worldview, would react to Stevenson's argument about the need to *provide mercy to many of the guilty*.

Stevenson's *Just Mercy* presents convincing arguments about why even some of the guilty deserve societal mercy, but this type of reasoning may not resonate with those who have been raised believing in the transcendent importance of retributive justice.

Effective Racialized Histories and Contested Mass Incarceration Pasts

The EJI has made some intriguing arguments about the racist, historical origins of "get tough on crime" policies, but we argue that it would be a mistake to chalk this up to the lingering influences of uncontested anti-lynching or mass incarceration rhetorics.

There are other potential causalities, and many other narrative frames, that could be used to explain some of the origins of those "get tough" policies.

Note, for example, the fascinating claims made by James Forman in his 2018 Pulitzer Prize–winning book, *Locking Up Our Own: Crime and Punishment in Black America*.[35] Forman provides an intriguing read of the politics behind the discursive production of the "war on crime," which involved substantial cohorts of *empowered black mayors, judges, and police officers* who worked in and around Washington, DC, between the 1970s and the first decades of the twenty-first century. Forman's study of the labor of individuals like former Washington mayor Marion Barry and former federal prosecutor Eric Holder shows that more than a few historical figures worried about the "lawlessness" of those involved with drugs who undermined the efforts of key leaders of civil rights movements that had flourished in prior years. In the process of fighting rising murder rates and perceptions about poor, black, drug-infested neighborhoods, rhetors like Barry and Holder contributed to the coproduction of "get tough" policies that led to situations where, ironically, black leaders were "locking up our own."

Forman's alternative historical reading can be used to interrogate many different types of lynching and civil rights histories, including EJI historicizing. This all underscores the point that the epistemes that are produced by the Legacy Museum—that focus on the lingering effects of lynching horrors and "racial terrorism"—provide readers with only one of many ways of reading partially forgotten lynching histories or framing mass incarceration practices.

This is why, in this book, instead of simply providing a descriptive explanation of the memorialization efforts of the EJI, and rather than joining the bandwagon of those who view Bryan Stevenson as "America's Mandela," we have traced the genealogical origins of many of the claims, evidence, and warrants that the EJI—and some of their detractors—have used in the coproduction of their persuasive, and yet selective, readings of the lynching and mass incarceration archives.

Assessing the Promise and Perils of the EJI's Race-Conscious Rhetorics

For those who treat Bryan Stevenson as a symbolic icon, it makes complete sense that many critical race scholars, laypersons interested in mastering lynching pasts, and criminologists interested in ending America's infatuation with capital punishment would desire to make a pilgrimage to the Lynching Memorial or the Legacy Museum in Montgomery, Alabama. They, along with sympathetic investigative journalists and students tracking down the names of lynching victims in their own home counties, are among the twenty-first century's warriors for social justice. Whether they realize it or not, their words and deeds make them a part of a very dense, and evolving, *dispositif* that has been coproduced over the years by individuals like the Frederick Douglass, Ida B. Wells-Barnett, W. E. B. Du Bois, and Walter White. Groups such as the Association of Southern Women for the Prevention of Lynching, the NAACP, the American Communists who helped the Scottsboro Boys, and the promoters of the traveling *Without Sanctuary* exhibit were all involved in circulating texts and visualities that served as antecedent genres for the race-conscious campaigns of the EJI.

These groups all shared a collective interest in trying to put an end to horrific lynchings and their effects, and the EJI continues this quest. In 2017, Lisa Kerr, in an essay on how to "end mass incarceration," characterized Bryan Stevenson as "the leading U.S. voice on the need for greater mercy and fairness in criminal justice."[36]

Perhaps, over the long term, Stevenson's voice will be viewed as prophetic, and more Americans will learn to appreciate the EJI's race-conscious messaging. In the future, perhaps more will appreciate that Stevenson and the EJI spent decades working with many needy defendants who were on death row or who faced all sorts of Kafkaesque legal hurdles. Stevenson's legal work at the EJI, his publication of *Just Mercy*, and the fund-raising that went into the building of structures like the Legacy Museum need to be viewed in this context. The same goes for the recent filmic interest in Stevenson's life story.[37]

In the short term, people who write essays about Montgomery's Lynching Memorial or Legacy Museum may have to be satisfied with commenting on the growing numbers of visitors who travel to those sites of memory as they reminisce about the historical origins of "racial terrorism." In the long term, it will be a much more difficult task to convince empowered American communities to take down their Confederate statuary or acknowledge that their defense of capital punishment has anything to do with the lynching of individuals like Henry Smith, J. Thomas Shipp, Laura Nelson, or Mary Turner.[38]

Perhaps it will take many more unlikely stonecatchers to arrive on America's carceral stage before the EJI's dreams come to fruition, and become reparatory.

NOTES

INTRODUCTION

1. Mihir Zaveri, "Senate Unanimously Passes Bill Making Lynching a Federal Crime," *New York Times*, December 20, 2018, https://www.nytimes.com/2018/12/20/us/lynching-federal-hate-crime.html. Years earlier, members of the Senate had issued an apology for their belated attempt at what we would call a form of restorative justice. See Sheryl Gay Stolberg, "Senate Issues Apology over Failure on Lynching Law," *New York Times*, June 14, 2005, https://www.nytimes.com/2005/06/14/politics/senate-issues-apology-over-failure-on-lynching-law.html; and Avis Thomas-Lester, "A Senate Apology for History on Lynching," *Washington Post*, June 14, 2005, https://www.washingtonpost.com/archive/politics/2005/06/14/a-senate-apology-for-history-on-lynching/324dade8-ec0e-46d9-9674-c81c247eb214/. As we write, though, the bill (or a latter-day version of it) is yet to be law. While the Justice for Victims of Lynching Act passed the Senate, the 115th Congress expired before the House could vote on the bill (January 3, 2019). The 116th Congress, though, introduced a revised version of the bill called the Emmett Till Antilynching Act for the Senate's consideration. See https://www.congress.gov/bill/116th-congress/senate-bill/488/text; and https://www.congress.gov/bill/116th-congress/house-bill/35.

2. Eli Watkins and Ted Barrett, "Senate Passes Anti-Lynching Bill in Renewed Effort to Make It a Federal Hate Crime," CNN, February 14, 2019, https://www.cnn.com/2019/02/14/politics/senate-anti-lynching-harris-booker/index.html.

3. Tal Kolan, "Kamala Harris' Anti-Lynching Bill Gets Second Chance at Becoming Law," *San Francisco Chronicle*, February 14, 2019, https://www.sfchronicle.com/politics/article/Kamala-Harris-anti-lynching-bill-gets-second-13617352.php.

4. Kolan, "Kamala Harris' Anti-Lynching Bill," para. 4.

5. Donald Trump, quoted in Jordan McDonald, "Trump Talks Criminal Justice Reform at Historically Black College Days after Comparing Impeachment Fight to a 'Lynching,'" CNBC, October 25, 2019, para. 16, https://www.cnbc.com/2019/10/25/trump-talks-criminal-justice-days-after-calling-impeachment-lynching.html.

6. Kamala Harris, quoted in McDonald, "Trump Talks Criminal Justice Reform," para. 21.

7. Cory Booker, quoted in McDonald, "Trump Talks Criminal Justice Reform," para. 19.

8. Marlene Park, "Lynching and Antilynching: Art and Politics in the 1930s," *Prospects: An Annual of American Cultural Studies* 18 (1993): 311–65.

9. The EJI has been working on collecting private funds for the building of the Legacy Museum and the National Memorial for Peace and Justice at the same time that they have been working to update historical lynching statistics. See Equal Justice Initiative, *Lynching*

in America: Confronting the Legacy of Racial Terror, 3rd ed. (Montgomery, AL: Equal Justice Initiative, 2017).

10. For more on these rhetorical cultures and their relationships to legal negotiations, see Marouf Hasian Jr., Celeste Michelle Condit, and John Louis Lucaites, "The Rhetorical Boundaries of 'The Law': A Consideration of the Rhetorical Culture of Legal Practice and the Case of the 'Separate but Equal' Doctrine," *Quarterly Journal of Speech* 82, no. 4 (1996): 323–42.

11. See, for example, Mary Louise Frampton, Ian F. Haney López, and Jonathan Simon, eds., *After the War on Crime: Race, Democracy, and a New Reconstruction* (New York: New York University Press, 2008); and Ian F. Haney-López, "Post-Racial Racism: Racial Stratification and Mass Incarceration in the Age of Obama," *California Law Review* 98 (2010): 1023–73.

12. Kirk Fuoss, "Lynching Performances, Theatres of Violence," *Text and Performance Quarterly* 19, no. 1 (1999): 4. See also Harvey Young, "The Black Body as Souvenir in American Lynching," *Theatre Journal* 57, no. 4 (2005): 639–57.

13. We are just beginning to see some of the earliest academic critiques of Montgomery's National Memorial for Peace and Justice and the Legacy Museum; see Lisa Kerr, "How to End Mass Imprisonment: The Legal and Cultural Strategies of Bryan Stevenson," *University of Toronto Law Journal* 67 (Winter 2017): 104–23; and José Medina, "Racial Violence, Emotional Friction, and Epistemic Activism," *Angelaki: Journal of the Theoretical Humanities* 24, no. 4 (2019): 22–37. Passing mention of these Montgomery sites of memory appears in Mari J. Matsuda, "Dissent in a Crowded Theater," *Southern Methodist University Law Review* 72, no. 3 (2019): 431–56. Although some journalists argue that the EJI built the "first" lynching memorial, that is not the case. See, for example, Dora Apel, "Memorialization and Its Discontents: America's First Lynching Memorial," *Mississippi Quarterly* 61, nos. 1–2 (Winter–Spring 2008): 217–35; and "Scholar: Duluth's Lynching Memorial Unique in U.S.," *Duluth News Tribune*, June 10, 2013, https://www.duluthnewstribune.com/news/2336527-scholar-duluths-lynching-memorial-unique-us.

14. Louis P. Masur, "Why It Took a Century to Pass an Anti-Lynching Law," *Washington Post*, December 28, 2018, https://www.washingtonpost.com/outlook/2018/12/28/why-it-took-century-pass-an-anti-lynching-law/?utm_term=.c796c815d8d5.

15. Masur, "Why It Took a Century."

16. Kenneth E. Foote, *Shadowed Ground: America's Landscapes of Violence and Tragedy* (Austin: University of Texas Press, 1997). See also Jonathan Markovitz, *Legacies of Lynching: Racial Violence and Memory* (Minneapolis: University of Minnesota Press, 2004); Sherrilyn A. Ifill, *On the Courthouse Lawn: Confronting the Legacy of Lynching in the Twenty-First Century* (Boston: Beacon Press, 2007); and Raj Andrew Ghoshal, "Transforming Collective Memory: Mnemonic Opportunity Structures and the Outcomes of Racial Violence Memory Movements," *Theory and Society* 42, no. 4 (July 2013): 329–50.

17. Brad Harper, "'Raw Emotions': Groups Grapple with Race after Visiting EJI Sites," *Montgomery Advertiser*, November 27, 2019, https://www.montgomeryadvertiser.com/story/news/2019/11/27/visiting-equal-justice-initiative-lynching-memorial-eji-groups-grapple-raw-emotions/4114344002/.

18. Stewart E. Tolnay and E. M. Beck, "'Racialized Terrorism' in the American South: Do Completed Lynchings Tell an Accurate Story?," *Social Science History* 42, no. 4 (Winter 2018): 677–701.

19. Tolnay and Beck, "Racialized Terrorism," 677–78.

20. Tiya Miles, "Review: National Museum of African American History and Culture," *Public History* 39, no. 2 (May 2017): 82–86.

21. Kingston W. Heath, "Toward a Humanistic Approach to Historical Preservation," *Journal of American Folklore* 132, no. 526 (Fall 2019): 390–411; and Corinne A. Kratz, "Where Did You Cry? Crafting Categories, Narratives, and Affect through Exhibit Design," *Kronos* 44, no. 1 (January 2018): 229–52.

22. Jane McFadden, "Equal Justice Initiative Legacy Museum: 'From Enslavement to Mass Incarceration,'" *Journal of American History* 106, no. 3 (December 2019): 708.

23. Harper, "'Raw Emotions': Groups Grapple with Race," para. 4.

24. For more on the Henry Smith lynching, see Orlando Patterson, *Rituals of Blood: Consequences of Slavery in Two American Centuries* (New York: Basic Civitas, 1998), 193.

25. Neta Alexander, "A Haunting Legacy of Racial Terror: The Thousands of Lynchings That Changed America," *Ha'aretz*, November 3, 2017, https://www.haaretz.com/us-news/.premium.MAGAZINE-how-racial-terror-permanently-altered-americas-demographics-1.5462682.

26. Patterson, *Rituals of Blood*, 193.

27. See Ed Pilkington, "The Sadism of White Men: Why America Must Atone for Its Lynchings," *The Guardian*, April 26, 2018, https://www.theguardian.com/world/2018/apr/26/lynchings-sadism-white-men-why-america-must-atone. See also Jamiles Lartey and Sam Morris, "How White Americans Used Lynchings to Terrorize and Control Black People," *The Guardian*, April 26, 2018, https://www.theguardian.com/us-news/2018/apr/26/lynchings-memorial-us-south-montgomery-alabama.

28. Marita Sturken, "Reenactment, Fantasy, and the Paranoia of History: Oliver Stone's Docudramas," *History and Theory* 46, no. 4 (December 1997): 64–79.

29. Equal Justice Initiative, *Lynching in America: Confronting the Legacy of Racial Terror*, 2nd ed. (Montgomery, AL: Equal Justice Initiative, 2015).

30. Pilkington, "The Sadism of White Men."

31. Meilan Solly, "Brooklyn Museum's 'Legacy of Lynching' Exhibition Confronts Racial Terror," *Smithsonian Magazine*, August 7, 2017, https://www.smithsonianmag.com/smart-news/brooklyn-museums-legacy-lynching-exhibition-confronts-racial-terror-180964288/.

32. For some excellent examples of journalistic interest in the work of Bryan Stevenson, the EJI, and the Legacy Museum, see Curtis Bunn, "Death Row Lawyer Bryan Stevenson Plans a Lynching Memorial in Alabama," *The Undefeated*, April 11, 2017, https://theundefeated.com/features/death-row-lawyer-bryan-stevenson-plans-a-lynching-memorial-in-alabama/; Nia-Malika Henderson, "This New Lynching Memorial Rewrites American History," CNN Travel, April 26, 2018, https://www.cnn.com/travel/article/lynching-memorial-montgomery-alabama/index.html; Philip Kennicott, "A Powerful Memorial in Montgomery Remembers the Victims of Lynching," *Washington Post*, April 24, 2018, https://www.washingtonpost.com/entertainment/museums/a-powerful-memorial-in-montgomery-remembers-the-victims-of-lynching/2018/04/24/3620e78a-471a-11e8-827e-190efaf1fee_story.html; and P. R. Lockhart, "A New Lynching Memorial Highlights America's Grim Legacy of

Racial Terrorism," *Vox*, April 26, 2018, https://www.vox.com/identities/2018/4/26/17286236/lynching-victims-memorial-alabama-equal-justice-initiative.

33. McFadden, "Equal Justice Initiative Legacy Museum," 706.

34. Arvind Dilawar, "A New Way to Memorialize Racial Violence," *The Nation*, November 14, 2019, para. 3, https://www.thenation.com/article/race-riot-chicago/.

35. For an example of Bryan Stevenson's rhetoric on liberation, see Alice Speri, "'I Don't Think We're Free in America': An Interview with Bryan Stevenson," *The Intercept*, January 2, 2017, https://theintercept.com/2017/01/02/i-dont-think-were-free-in-america-an-interview-with-bryan-stevenson/.

36. Jacqueline Jones Royster, "To Call a Thing by Its True Nature: The Rhetoric of Ida B. Wells," in *Reclaiming Rhetorica: Women in the Rhetorical Tradition*, ed. Andrea A. Lunsford (Pittsburgh: University of Pittsburgh Press, 1995), 167–84.

37. Jacqueline Jones Royster, preface to *Southern Horrors and Other Writings: The Anti-Lynching Campaign of Ida B. Wells, 1892–1900*, by Ida B. Wells, ed. Jacqueline Jones Royster, 2nd ed. (Boston: Bedford/St. Martins, 2016), ix.

38. Ersula Ore, *Lynching: Violence, Rhetoric, and American Identity* (Jackson: University Press of Mississippi, 2019), xv, 21.

39. Ore, *Lynching*, 102.

40. Ashraf H. A. Rushdy, *American Lynching* (New Haven, CT: Yale University Press, 2012).

41. Rushdy, *American Lynching*, xi.

42. A. Susan Owen and Peter Ehrenhaus, "The Moore's Ford Lynching Reenactment: Affective Memory and Racial Trauma," *Text and Performance Quarterly* 34, no. 1 (2014): 72–90; and Megan Eatman, "Loss and Lived Memory at the Moore's Ford Lynching Reenactment," *Advances in the History of Rhetoric* 20, no. 2 (2017): 153–66.

43. Kimberly A. Powell, "The Association of Southern Women for the Prevention of Lynching: Strategies of a Movement in the Comic Frame," *Communication Quarterly* 43, no. 1 (1995): 86–99.

44. Martha Solomon Watson, "Mary Church Terrell vs. Thomas Nelson Page: Gender, Race, and Class in Anti-Lynching Rhetoric," *Rhetoric and Public Affairs* 12, no. 1 (Spring 2009): 65–89.

45. Rushdy, *American Lynching*.

46. Ashraf H. A. Rushdy, *The End of American Lynching* (New Brunswick, NJ: Rutgers University Press, 2012), 16.

47. Our own poststructural and postcolonial critiques in this book have been influenced by some of the arguments that circulated long before the advent of the EJI or the Legacy Museum. Writers such as Hannah Arendt, Frantz Fanon, Aimé Césaire, and W. E. B. Du Bois were noticing the linkages that could be made between colonial or imperial horrors and the World War II Holocaust before Bryan Stevenson's commentaries. For some helpful critiques of some of those works, see Roberta Pergher et al., "The Holocaust: A Colonial Genocide? A Scholars' Forum," *Dapim: Studies on the Holocaust* 27, no. 1 (2013): 40–73. However, what is unique about the argumentation here is that the words and images produced by the EJI are occasionally used to emphasize the systematic nature of centuries of slavery abuses and

lynching traumas that can be compared with either international terrorism or the World War II Holocaust.

48. Christine Harold and Kevin Michael DeLuca, "Behold the Corpse: Violent Images and the Case of Emmett Till," *Rhetoric and Public Affairs* 8, no. 2 (Summer 2005): 263–86. These types of topics also resonate with investigative journalists. See, for example, Siddhartha Mitter, "After 'Open Casket': What Emmett Till Teaches Us Today," *Village Voice*, March 12, 2018, https://www.villagevoice.com/2018/03/12/after-open-casket-what-emmett-till-teaches-us-today/.

49. Davis W. Houck and Matthew A. Grindy, *Emmett Till and the Mississippi Press* (Jackson: University Press of Mississippi, 2008).

50. Houck and Grindy, *Emmett Till*, 10.

51. A. Susan Owen and Peter Ehrenhaus, "Looking at Lynching: Spectacle, Resistance and Contemporary Transformations," *Quarterly Journal of Speech* 97, no. 1 (February 2011): 100–113.

52. Jessy J. Ohl and Jennifer E. Potter, "United We Lynch: Post-Racism and the (Re) Membering of Racial Violence in *Without Sanctuary: Lynching Photography in America*," *Southern Communication Journal* 78, no. 3 (2013): 185–201.

53. Amy Helene Kirschke, *Art in Crisis: W .E. B. Du Bois and the Struggle for African American Identity and Memory* (Bloomington: Indiana University Press, 2007).

54. Markovitz, *Legacies of Lynching*.

55. Amy Louise Wood, *Lynching and Spectacle: Witnessing Racial Violence in America, 1890–1940* (Chapel Hill: University of North Carolina Press, 2009).

56. Owen and Ehrenhaus, "Looking at Lynching," 100. For examples of the type of interdisciplinary work that Owen and Ehrenhaus seem to be referencing, see Julie Buckner Armstrong, *Mary Turner and the Memory of Lynching* (Athens: University of Georgia Press, 2011); Stewart E. Tolnay and E. M. Beck, *A Festival of Violence: An Analysis of Southern Lynchings, 1882–1930* (Urbana: University of Illinois Press, 1995); W. Fitzhugh Brundage, ed., *Under Sentence of Death: Lynching in the South* (Chapel Hill: University of North Carolina Press, 1997); Arthur Raper, *The Tragedy of Lynching* (Chapel Hill: University of North Carolina Press, 1933); Anne P. Rice, ed., *Witnessing Lynching: American Writers Respond* (New Brunswick, NJ: Rutgers University Press, 2003); and Christopher Waldrep, *A History in Documents: Lynching in America* (New York: New York University Press, 2006).

57. Rhoda E. Howard-Hassmann and Anthony P. Lombardo, "Framing Reparations Claims: Differences between the African Movements and Jewish Social Movements for Reparations," *African Studies Review* 50, no. 1 (April 2007): 27.

58. Jacqueline Bacon, "Reading the Reparations Debate," *Quarterly Journal of Speech* 89, no. 3 (August 2003): 171.

59. We are glad to see a growing number of interdisciplinary scholars who have joined the ranks of those like Foucault and Stoler who read both along and across the grain. For an overview of the heuristic value of reading both along the grain, to get a textured sense of dominant ideologies, as well as against the grain, to see competing dissident ideologies, especially in colonial and imperial contexts, see Ann Laura Stoler, *Along the Archival Grain: Epistemic Anxieties and Colonial Common Sense* (Princeton, NJ: Princeton University Press, 2010). For more specific applications of critical genealogical work in studies of many of our

heterogeneous archives on lynching, the Reconstruction years, the Jim Crow years, and even twentieth-century civil rights progressivism, see Walter Benn Michaels, "Race into Culture: A Critical Genealogy of Cultural Identity," *Critical Inquiry* 18, no. 4 (Summer 1992): 655–85; and José Medina, "Toward a Foucaultian Epistemology of Resistance: Counter-Memory, Epistemic Friction, and Guerrilla Pluralism," *Foucault Studies*, no. 12 (October 2011): 9–35.

60. For more on considerations of *dispositifs* in the work of theorists like Foucault, see Stephen Legg, "Assemblage/Apparatus: Using Deleuze and Foucault," *Area* 43, no. 2 (June 2011): 128–33.

61. For some helpful examples of critical genealogies of racial formations in some colonial contexts, see Ann Laura Stoler, *Race and the Education of Desire: Foucault's History of Sexuality and the Colonial Order of Things* (Durham, NC: Duke University Press, 1995).

62. For a discussion of the differences that exist between critical discussions of "perspectives" and traditional ways of focusing on "method," see Raymie E. McKerrow, "Critical Rhetoric: Theory and Praxis," *Communication Monographs* 56, no. 2 (1989): 91–111.

63. For more on how to combine these critical rhetorical and qualitative ways of carrying out investigations of places and spaces, see Danielle Endres et al., "*In Situ* Rhetoric: Intersections between Qualitative Inquiry, Fieldwork, and Rhetoric," *Culture Studies/Critical Methodologies* 16, no. 6 (2016): 511–24.

64. Walter Benjamin, *Illuminations: Essays and Reflections*, ed. Hannah Arendt (New York: Schocken Books, 1969), 235.

65. Robyn Wiegman, "The Anatomy of Lynching," *Journal of the History of Sexuality* 3, no. 3 (January 1993): 445–67.

66. For a discussion on how these arguments about multidirectional memory formation are related to hegemonic and nonhegemonic ways of thinking about public rhetoric, see Michael Rothberg, "Between Auschwitz and Algeria: Multidirectional Memory and the Counterpublic Witness," *Critical Inquiry* 33, no. 1 (August 2006): 158–84.

67. See Jacques Derrida, "Archive Fever: A Freudian Impression," trans. Eric Prenowitz, *Diacritics* 25, no. 2 (Summer 1995): 9–63.

68. Friedrich Nietzsche, *Untimely Meditations*, ed. Daniel Breazeale, trans. R. J. Hollingdale (1873; Cambridge: Cambridge University Press, 2012).

69. Michael Rothberg, "From Gaza to Warsaw: Mapping Multidirectional Memory," *Criticism* 53, no. 4 (Fall 2011): 525.

70. Melissa Steyn, "The Ignorance Contract: Recollections of Apartheid Childhoods and the Construction of Epistemologies of Ignorance," *Identities: Global Studies in Culture and Power* 19, no. 1 (January 2012): 8–25.

71. Steyn, "The Ignorance Contract," 8–9.

72. For more on those who respond positively to Trump's tweeting and other provocations, see Justin Ward, "Day of the Trope: White Nationalist Memes Thrive on Reddit's r/The_Donald," Southern Poverty Law Center, April 19, 2018, https://www.splcenter.org/hatewatch/2018/04/19/day-trope-white-nationalist-memes-thrive-reddits-rthedonald.

73. Jonathan Capehart, "How the Terror of Lynchings in the Past Haunts Us Today and Our Future," *Washington Post*, June 27, 2017, para. 17, https://www.washingtonpost.com/blogs/post-partisan/wp/2017/06/27/how-the-terror-of-lynchings-in-the-past-haunt-us-today-and-our-future/?noredirect=on&utm_term=.1058766f5c24.

74. Bryan Stevenson, *Just Mercy: A Story of Justice and Redemption* (New York: Spiegel and Grau, 2014), 18.

75. Sammy Feldblum, "In Montgomery, a Harrowing, Beautiful Reckoning with Racial Terror," *Scalawag*, May 8, 2018, para. 11, https://www.scalawagmagazine.org/2018/05/in-montgomery-a-harrowing-beautiful-reckoning/.

CHAPTER 1

1. For one of the best overviews of the politics of the Reconstruction years, see Eric Foner, *Reconstruction: America's Unfinished Revolution, 1863–1877* (New York: HarperCollins, 1988). For excellent analyses of some of the historiographic wars that have taken place for more than a century over Reconstruction activities and their meanings, see Bernard A. Weisberger, "The Dark and Bloody Ground of Reconstruction Historiography," *Journal of Southern History* 25, no. 4 (November 1959): 427–47; Randall Kennedy, "Reconstruction and the Politics of Scholarship," *Yale Law Journal* 98, no. 3 (January 1989): 521–39; and Justin Behrend, "Expanding the Boundaries of Reconstruction," *Reviews in American History* 46, no. 1 (March 2018): 79–85.

2. Eric Foner, quoted in Brook Thomas, "The Unfinished Task of Grounding Reconstruction's Promise," *Journal of the Civil War Era* 7, no. 1 (March 2017): 16.

3. Ron Eyerman, *Cultural Trauma: Slavery and the Formation of African American Identity* (Cambridge: Cambridge University Press, 2001), 17; and Anne Rice, "How We Remember Lynching," *Nka: Journal of Contemporary African Art*, no. 20 (Fall 2006): 43.

4. Michael Pfeifer, quoted in Lorraine Boissoneault, "The Deadliest Massacre in Reconstruction-Era Louisiana Happened 150 Years Ago," *Smithsonian Magazine*, September 28, 2018, para. 17, https://www.smithsonianmag.com/history/story-deadliest-massacre-reconstruction-era-louisiana-180970420/.

5. Boissoneault, "The Deadliest Massacre," paras. 8–10.

6. Equal Justice Initiative, *Lynching in America*, 3rd ed., 10.

7. For background materials on the KKK, see David M. Chalmers, *Hooded Americanism: The First Century of the Ku Klux Klan, 1865–1965* (New York: Doubleday, 1965); Kathleen M. Blee, *Women of the Klan: Racism and Gender in the 1920s* (Berkeley: University of California Press, 1991); and Allen Trelease, *White Terror: The Ku Klux Klan Conspiracy and Southern Reconstruction* (Baton Rouge: Louisiana State University Press, 1995).

8. This chronicling of KKK violence, in turn, helped legitimate the use of federal troops during the Reconstruction years.

9. Vanessa Gregory, "A Lynching's Long Shadow," *New York Times Magazine*, April 25, 2018, para. 9, https://www.nytimes.com/2018/04/25/magazine/a-lynchings-long-shadow.html.

10. Bryan Stevenson, quoted in Jenn M. Jackson, "Lynching in the United States, Explained," *Teen Vogue*, October 2, 2017, para. 7, https://www.teenvogue.com/story/lynching-in-the-united-states-explained.

11. Katie Couric, "The Blood of Lynching Victims Is in This Soil," *National Geographic*, April 2018, https://www.nationalgeographic.com/magazine/2018/04/race-lynching-museum-katie-couric-alabama/.

12. As mentioned in the introduction, a *dispositif* is a major assemblage that brings together many ideological fragments in some empowered state apparatus. For more on the topic, see Matti Peltonen, "From Discourse to *Dispositif*: Michel Foucault's Two Histories," *Historical Reflections / Réflexions Historiques* 30, no. 2 (Summer 2004): 205–19.

13. James C. Scott, *Weapons of the Weak* (New Haven, CT: Yale University Press, 1985).

14. Ann Laura Stoler, "On Archiving as Dissensus," *Comparative Studies of South Asia, Africa, and the Middle East* 38, no. 1 (May 2018): 43–56.

15. For just one example of the types of laws that need to be read along the grain, see the oppressive nature of peonage laws that are critiqued in Pete Daniel, *The Shadow of Slavery: Peonage in the South, 1901–1969* (Urbana: University of Illinois Press, 1972).

16. For a helpful overview of the contentious nature of lynching labels, see Christopher Waldrep, "War of Words: The Controversy over the Definition of Lynching, 1899–1940," *Journal of Southern History* 66, no. 1 (February 2000): 75–100, https://doi.org/10.2307/2587438.

17. Wiegman, "The Anatomy of Lynching," 445.

18. Carole Emberton, *Beyond Redemption: Race, Violence, and the American South after the Civil War* (Chicago: University of Chicago Press, 2013), 4. See also Grace Elizabeth Hale, *Making Whiteness: The Culture of Segregation in the South, 1890–1940* (New York: Pantheon Books, 1998).

19. Stephen V. Ash, *A Massacre in Memphis: The Race Riot That Shook the Nation* (New York: Hill and Wang, 2013), 71.

20. Martha Hodes, "The Sexualization of Reconstruction Politics," *Journal of the History of Sexuality* 3, no. 3 (January 1993): 403.

21. Ore, *Lynching*, 51.

22. Ore, *Lynching*, 51.

23. Ore, *Lynching*, 28–39.

24. Ore, *Lynching*, 39–52.

25. George C. Rable, "The South and the Politics of Antilynching Legislation, 1920–1940," *Journal of Southern History* 51, no. 2 (May 1985): 202, https://doi.org/10.2307/2208825.

26. US Congress, *Report of the Joint Select Committee to Inquire into the Condition of Affairs in the Late Insurrectionary States*, 13 vols. (Washington, DC: Government Printing Office, 1872), 1:270.

27. Foner, *Reconstruction*, 425.

28. Hodes, "The Sexualization of Reconstruction Politics," 403.

29. Hodes, "The Sexualization of Reconstruction Politics," 407.

30. Hodes, "The Sexualization of Reconstruction Politics," 407–8.

31. Hodes, "The Sexualization of Reconstruction Politics," 408.

32. Hodes, "The Sexualization of Reconstruction Politics," 408.

33. US Congress, *Report of the Joint Select Committee*, 13:7, 14–15.

34. Verna Gates, "Protestors in Selma, Ala Will Try to Stop Klan Founder's Monument," Reuters, September 14, 2012, https://www.reuters.com/article/us-usa-alabama-statue/protestors-in-selma-ala-will-try-to-stop-klan-founders-monument-idUSBRE88C1LA20120913.

35. Hodes, "The Sexualization of Reconstruction Politics," 410.

36. Hodes, "The Sexualization of Reconstruction Politics," 410.

37. Joseph Rainey, "Congressional Debates," *Congressional Record*, 43rd Congress, 1st session, December 19, 1873, 344, quoted in Hodes, "The Sexualization of Reconstruction Politics," 404.

38. Equal Justice Initiative, *Lynching in America*, 3rd ed., 11.

39. Jeanhee Kim and Leslie Hart, "On Justice, and Mercy: Bryan Stevenson Delves into the Causes and Ills of Mass Incarceration and Racial Injustice, But Sees Hope in America's Future," *New York University Law News*, October 27, 2014, https://www.law.nyu.edu/news/ideas/Bryan-Stevenson-Q-and-A-Just-Mercy.

40. For a critical race theorist's critique of this colorblind or neoliberal way of framing legalist twentieth-century civil rights reform, see Richard Delgado, "A Comment on Rosenberg's New Edition of *The Hollow Hope*," *Northwestern University Law Review Colloquy* 103 (2008): 147–52.

41. Rable, "The South and the Politics of Antilynching Legislation," 202.

42. Lee D. Baker, *From Negro to Savage: Anthropology and the Construction of Race, 1896–1954* (Berkeley: University of California Press, 1998), 19.

43. Michael Cohen, "'The Ku Klux Government': Vigilantism, Lynching, and the Repression of the IWW," *Journal for the Study of Radicalism* 1, no. 1 (Spring 2007): 31–56.

44. James Elbert Cutler, *Lynch-Law: An Investigation into the History of Lynching in the United States* (1905; Montclair, NJ: Negro Universities Press, 1969), 207.

45. Cutler, *Lynch-Law*, 223–24.

46. J. T. Winston, from Bryan, Texas, letter, May 26, 1916, quoted in *The Nation*, June 22, 1916, 671.

47. James K. Vardaman, quoted in William F. Holmes, *The White Chief: James Kimble Vardaman* (Baton Rouge: Louisiana State University Press, 1970), 109.

48. W. E. B. Du Bois, *Writings by W. E. B. Du Bois in Periodicals Edited by Others*, edited by Herbert Aptheker, 2 vols. (Millwood, NY: Kraus-Thomson, 1983), 1:193.

49. "Prison Abuses in Mississippi: Under the Lease System Convicts Are Treated with Brutal Cruelty," *Chicago Tribune*, July 11, 1887, quoted in Bryan Stevenson, "A Presumption of Guilt," *New York Review of Books*, July 13, 2017, paras. 8–9, https://www.nybooks.com/articles/2017/07/13/presumption-of-guilt/.

50. Stevenson, "A Presumption of Guilt," para. 10.

51. William Worger, "Convict Labour, Industrialists and the State in the US South and South Africa, 1870–1930," *Journal of Southern African Studies* 30, no. 1 (2004): 76, https://doi.org/10.1080/0305707042000223942.

52. Worger, "Convict Labour," 73–77.

53. McFadden, "Equal Justice Initiative Legacy Museum," 707.

54. Worger, "Convict Labour," 73.

55. For a helpful discussion of the role that eugenics played in Southern racial politics, see Edward J. Larson, *Sex, Race, and Science: Eugenics in the Deep South* (Baltimore: Johns Hopkins University Press, 1995). Elsewhere, one of us has touched on the eugenic features of some of this societal and institutional racism that impacted American discussions of political, civil, and social rights; see Marouf A. Hasian Jr., *The Rhetoric of Eugenics in Anglo-American Thought* (Athens: University of Georgia Press, 1996).

56. Edward L. Ayers, *The Promise of the New South: Life after Reconstruction* (New York: Oxford University Press, 1992), 149.

57. Ayers, *The Promise of the New South*, 145.

58. See Benjamin R. Justesen, "George Henry White and the Anti-Lynching Bill of 1900," George Henry White: American Phoenix, September 18, 2016, https://www.georgehenrywhite.com/single-post/2016/09/17/George-Henry-White-and-the-Anti-Lynching-Bill-of-1900.

59. Kevin M. Levin, "The Pernicious Myth of the 'Loyal Slave' Lives On in Confederate Memorials," *Smithsonian Magazine*, August 17, 2017, para. 4, https://www.smithsonianmag.com/history/pernicious-myth-loyal-slave-lives-confederate-memorials-180964546/.

60. For one of Page's popular novels, see *In Ole Virginia* (New York: Charles Scribner's Sons, 1896). For his commentaries on lynching, see "The Lynching of Negroes: Its Cause and Its Prevention," *North American Review* 178, no. 566 (January 1904): 33–48. For a rhetorical critique of Page's rhetoric, see Watson, "Mary Church Terrell vs. Thomas Nelson Page."

61. See Trinyan Mariano, "The Law of Torts and the Logic of Lynching in Charles Chesnutt's *The Marrow of Tradition*," *Publications of the Modern Language Association* 128, no. 3 (May 2013): 559–74.

62. Levin, "The Pernicious Myth," para. 5.

63. Levin, "The Pernicious Myth," para. 11.

64. Karen L. Cox, "The Whole Point of Confederate Monuments Is to Celebrate White Supremacy," *Washington Post*, August 16, 2017, https://www.washingtonpost.com/news/posteverything/wp/2017/08/16/the-whole-point-of-confederate-monuments-is-to-celebrate-white-supremacy/.

65. See Henry E. Barber, "The Association of Southern Women for the Prevention of Lynching, 1930–1942," *Phylon* 34, no. 4 (1973): 378–89, https://www.jstor.org/stable/274253; and Rachel McBride Lindsey, "'This Barbarous Practice': Southern Churchwomen and Race in the Association of Southern Women for the Prevention of Lynching, 1930–1942," *Journal of Southern Religion* 16 (2014), http://jsreligion.org/issues/vol16/lindsey.html.

66. For many years, a sociologist by the name of Monroe Nathan Work collected statistics on lynching for Alabama's Tuskegee Institute. Several websites now honor his memory, forming their own interactive maps and lynching archives. See, for example, "Monroe and Florence Work Today," PlainTalkHistory, http://www.monroeworktoday.org/index.html?u=2&#; Laura Bliss, "A Comprehensive Map of American Lynchings," CityLab, January 17, 2017, https://www.citylab.com/equity/2017/01/a-comprehensive-map-of-american-lynchings/513293/?utm_source=SFTwitter; and Mark Berman, "Even More Black People Were Lynched in the U.S. Than Previously Thought, Study Finds," *Washington Post*, February 11, 2015, https://www.washingtonpost.com/news/post-nation/wp/2015/02/10/even-more-black-people-were-lynched-in-the-u-s-than-previously-thought-study-finds/.

67. See Robert L. Zangrando, *The NAACP Crusade against Lynching, 1909–1950* (Philadelphia: Temple University Press, 1980).

68. For more on "vernacular histories" of lynchings that resemble some of the ways that critical rhetoricians view these events, see Kidada E. Williams, *They Left Great Marks on Me: African American Testimonies of Racial Violence from Emancipation to World War I* (New York: New York University Press, 2012).

69. Michael J. Pfeifer, "At the Hands of Parties Unknown? The State of the Field of Lynching Scholarship," *Journal of American History* 101, no. 3 (December 2014): 844, https://doi.org/10.1093/jahist/jau640.

70. Pfeifer, "At the Hands of Parties Unknown?," 844. For key studies that have examined lynchings that were committed during and just after Reconstruction, see Emberton, *Beyond Redemption*; and Michael J. Pfeifer, *The Roots of Rough Justice: Origins of American Lynching* (Urbana: University of Illinois Press, 2011). For those who want to go even further back in history for colonial and antebellum discussions of lynching violence, see Manfred Berg, *Popular Justice: A History of Lynching in America* (Lanham, MD: Rowman and Littlefield, 2011).

71. Equal Justice Initiative, *Lynching in America*, 3rd ed.

CHAPTER 2

1. See Kratz, "Where Did You Cry?," 229–52.

2. Neill Matheson, "History and Survival: Charles Chesnutt and the Time of Conjure," *American Literary Realism* 43, no. 1 (Fall 2010): 1–22.

3. Rice, "How We Remember Lynching," 43.

4. On the celebration of the work of those who were willing to deploy parrhesia and speak truth to power, see Michel Foucault, *Fearless Speech*, ed. Joseph Pearson (Los Angeles: Semiotext(e), 2001).

5. "The Great Migration," Equal Justice Initiative, January 7, 2013, para. 1, https://eji.org/news/history-racial-injustice-great-migration/.

6. See, for example, Antonia I. Castañeda, "Women of Color and the Rewriting of Western History: The Discourse, Politics, and Decolonization of History," *Pacific Historical Review* 61, no. 4 (November 1992): 501–33.

7. For an excellent explanation of what it means to read across the grain of dominant public memories, see Barbie Zelizer, "Reading the Past against the Grain: The Shape of Memory Studies," *Critical Studies in Mass Communication* 12, no. 2 (June 1995): 214–39.

8. Jacobus tenBroek, *Equal under Law* (Springfield, OH: Collier Books, 1969), 180.

9. Ida B. Wells-Barnett, *Lynch Law in Georgia* (Chicago: Chicago Colored Citizens, 1899), 9.

10. Wells-Barnett, *Lynch Law in Georgia*, 8.

11. Ida B. Wells, *Southern Horrors and Other Writings: The Anti-Lynching Campaign of Ida B. Wells, 1892–1900*, ed. Jacqueline Jones Royster (New York: Bedford/St. Martin's, 1996), 9; and Matsuda, "Dissent in a Crowded Theater," 449. The elite and public archives on Wells-Barnett's contributions to anti-lynching are massive and are still growing, as her militancy resonates with twenty-first-century social agents. See, for example, Ida B. Wells, *Crusade for Justice: The Autobiography of Ida B. Wells*, ed. Alfreda M. Duster (Chicago: University of Chicago Press, 1970); Ida B. Wells, *The Memphis Diary of Ida B. Wells: An Intimate Portrait of the Activist as a Young Woman*, ed. Miriam Decosta-Willis (Boston: Beacon Press, 1995); Linda O. McMurry, *To Keep the Waters Troubled: The Life of Ida B. Wells* (New York: Oxford University Press, 1998); Patricia Ann Schechter, *Ida B. Wells-Barnett and American Reform, 1880–1930* (Chapel Hill: University of North Carolina Press, 2001); Paula J. Giddings, *Ida: A*

Sword among Lions; Ida B. Wells and the Campaign against Lynching (New York: Amistad, 2008); and Mia Bay, *To Tell the Truth Freely: The Life of Ida B. Wells* (New York: Hill and Wang, 2009).

12. Ore, *Lynching*, 20.

13. On some of the intersectional features of the Progressive Era, see Noralee Frankel and Nancy S. Dye, eds., *Gender, Class, Race, and Reform in the Progressive Era* (Lexington: University Press of Kentucky, 2001); and Christine Emba, "Intersectionality," *Washington Post*, September 21, 2015, https://www.washingtonpost.com/news/in-theory/wp/2015/09/21/intersectionality-a-primer/?utm_term=.244a613fb80f.

14. See Michael Mezzano, "The Progressive Origins of Eugenics Critics: Raymond Pearl, Herbert S. Jennings, and the Defense of Scientific Inquiry," *Journal of the Gilded Age and the Progressive Era* 4, no. 1 (January 2005): 83–97.

15. See Christine B. Hickman, "The Devil and the One Drop Rule: Racial Categories, African Americans, and the U.S. Census," *Michigan Law Review* 95, no. 5 (March 1997): 1161–265.

16. Leigh Raiford, "Ida B. Wells and the Shadow Archive," in *Pictures and Progress: Early Photography and the Making of African American Identity*, ed. Maurice O. Wallace and Shawn Michelle Smith (Durham, NC: Duke University Press, 2012), 309–15.

17. Marouf Hasian Jr., "Judicial Rhetoric in a Fragmentary World: 'Character' and Storytelling in the Leo Frank Case," *Communication Monographs* 64, no. 3 (1997): 250–69.

18. David Squires, "Outlawry: Ida B. Wells and Lynch Law," *American Quarterly* 67, no. 1 (March 2015): 154.

19. These archives are being constantly updated. See, for example, Charles Seguin and David Rigby, "National Crimes: A New National Data Set of Lynchings in the United States, 1883 to 1941," *Socius: Sociological Research for a Dynamic World* 5 (January 2019): 1–9, https://doi.org/10.1177/2378023119841780.

20. See Bryan Wagner, *Disturbing the Peace: Black Culture and the Police Power after Slavery* (Cambridge, MA: Harvard University Press, 2009).

21. See Ladelle McWhorter, *Racism and Sexual Oppression in Anglo-America: A Genealogy* (Bloomington: Indiana University Press, 2009).

22. Royster, "To Call a Thing by Its True Nature."

23. Jamil Smith, "On a Hill in Alabama, the Lynched Haunt Us," *Rolling Stone*, May 6, 2018, para. 3, https://www.rollingstone.com/politics/politics-features/on-a-hill-in-alabama-the-lynched-haunt-us-629262/.

24. Lori Amber Roessner, "Constructing Monuments to the Memory of Ida B. Wells-Barnett: Institutionalization of Reputation, Memory Distortion, and Cultural Amnesia," in *Political Pioneer of the Press: Ida B. Wells-Barnett and Her Transnational Crusade for Social Justice*, ed. Lori Amber Roessner and Jodi L. Rightler-McDaniels (Lanham, MD: Lexington Books, 2018), 107.

25. For Michael Rothberg's take on competitive and multidirectional memories in segregationist contexts, see "Against Zero-Sum Logic: A Response to Walter Benn Michaels," *American Literary History* 18, no. 2 (Summer 2006): 303–11.

26. *Plessy v. Ferguson* 163 (U.S. 537 1896).

27. Justice Henry Billings Brown, majority opinion, *Plessy v. Ferguson*.

28. For a discussion of the dominant sociological views of the times as well as an insightful analysis of some of the power dynamics that revolved around the *Plessy* case, see Mark Golub, "Plessy as 'Passing': Judicial Responses to Ambiguously Raced Bodies in *Plessy v. Ferguson*," *Law and Society Review* 39, no. 3 (September 2005): 563–600.

29. Justice John Marshall Harlan, dissenting opinion, *Plessy v. Ferguson*. Ellipses are sometimes used by those who wish to bracket out what Justice Harlan had to say about some foreigners who sought citizenship, so that writers could focus on the prophetic nature of his commentary.

30. See Gabriel Jackson Chin, "The *Plessy* Myth: Justice Harlan and the Chinese Cases," *Iowa Law Review* 82 (1996): 151–82.

31. See Paul A. Kramer, *The Blood of Government: Race, Empire, the United States, and the Philippines* (Chapel Hill: University of North Carolina Press, 2006).

32. See Sebastián Gil-Riaño, "Relocating Anti-Racist Science: The 1950 UNESCO Statement on Race and Economic Development in the Global South," *British Journal for the History of Science* 51, no. 2 (June 2018): 281–303.

33. Michel Foucault, "Nietzsche, Genealogy, History," in *The Essential Foucault: Selections from the Essential Works of Foucault, 1954–1984*, ed. Paul Rabinow and Nikolas Rose, 350–69 (New York: New Press, 2003).

34. Mark Elliott, "Race, Color Blindness, and the Democratic Public: Albion W. Tourgée's Radical Principles in *Plessy v. Ferguson*," *Journal of Southern History* 67, no. 2 (May 2001): 287–330.

35. From an incisive essay critiquing this case by a member of the critical race theory movement, see Cheryl I. Harris, "Whiteness as Property," *Harvard Law Review* 106, no. 8 (June 1993): 1707–91. See also Roberto Avant-Mier and Marouf Hasian Jr., "In Search of the Power of Whiteness: A Genealogical Exploration of Negotiated Racial Identities in America's Ethnic Past," *Communication Quarterly* 50, nos. 3–4 (2002): 391–409, https://doi.org/10.1080/01463370209385674.

36. Hubert H. Bancroft, *Popular Tribunals* (San Francisco: History Company, 1887), vii. For a critique of Bancroft's works on lynching, see Berg, *Popular Justice*.

37. Bancroft, *Popular Tribunals*, 8–9.

38. Berg, *Popular Justice*; Squires, "Outlawry," 149.

39. Ray Stannard Baker, *Following the Color Line: An Account of Negro Citizenship in the American Democracy* (New York: Doubleday, Page and Company, 1908), 205.

40. For a critique of some of these African American post-Reconstruction and Progressive rhetorics, see Celeste Michelle Condit and John Louis Lucaites, *Crafting Equality: America's Anglo-African Word* (Chicago: University of Chicago Press, 1993).

41. Christopher Waldrep, *The Many Faces of Judge Lynch: Extralegal Violence and Punishment in America* (New York: Palgrave Macmillan, 2002).

42. Squires, "Outlawry," 153.

43. Shirley Wilson Logan, "Ida B. Wells: Lynch Law in All of Its Phases (13 February 1893)," *Voices of Democracy: The U.S. Oratory Project* 2 (Fall 2007): 50–65, http://voicesofdemocracy.umd.edu/wells-lynch-law-speech-text/.

44. For a critique of Wells-Barnett's commentaries on Winchester rifles, see Simone W. Davis, "The 'Weak Race' and the Winchester: Political Voices in the Pamphlets of Ida B.

Wells-Barnett," *Legacy* 12, no. 2 (1995): 77–97. For excellent discussions of Wells-Barnett's view on "terrorism," see Jeffory A. Clymer, *America's Culture of Terrorism: Violence, Capitalism, and the Written Word* (Chapel Hill: University of North Carolina Press, 2003); and Squires, "Outlawry."

45. Tommy J. Curry, "The Fortune of Wells: Ida B. Wells-Barnett's Use of T. Thomas Fortune's Philosophy of Social Agitation as a Prolegomenon to Militant Social Rights Activism," *Transactions of the Charles S. Peirce Society* 48, no. 4 (Fall 2012): 456–82.

46. Squires, "Outlawry," 142.

47. For a key analysis of Wells-Barnett's overseas activism, see Teresa Zackodnik, "Ida B. Wells and 'American Atrocities' in Britain," *Women's Studies International Forum* 28, no. 4 (July–August 2005): 259.

48. Raiford, "Ida B. Wells and the Shadow Archive," 307.

49. See Wells, *Crusade for Justice*, 47–51; and "The People's Grocery Lynchings (Thomas Moss, Will Stewart, Calvin McDowell)," Lynching Sites Project, Memphis, n.d., https://lynchingsitesmem.org/lynching/peoples-grocery-lynchings-thomas-moss-will-stewart-calvin-mcdowell.

50. Logan, "Ida B. Wells: Lynch Law in All of Its Phases," 51.

51. Ida B. Wells-Barnett, *On Lynchings* (New York: Arno Press, 1969), 45.

52. Squires, "Outlawry," 152.

53. Squires, "Outlawry," 152.

54. Wells, *Crusade for Justice*, 52.

55. Giddings, *Ida: A Sword among Lions*, 214.

56. Wells-Barnett, *On Lynchings*, 29.

57. Wells-Barnett, *On Lynchings*, 30.

58. Wells-Barnett, *On Lynchings*, 30.

59. Squires, "Outlawry," 151.

60. Wells-Barnett, *On Lynchings*, 60.

61. Peter Ehrenhaus and A. Susan Owen, "Race Lynching and Christian Evangelicalism: Performances of Faith," *Text and Performance Quarterly* 24, nos. 3–4 (2004): 276–301, https://doi.org/10.1080/1046293042000312779.

62. Wells-Barnett, *On Lynchings*, 44.

63. Raiford, "Ida B. Wells and the Shadow Archive," 299.

64. Squires, "Outlawry," 155.

65. For more theoretical discussions of the concept of "image events," see John W. Delicath and Kevin Michael DeLuca, "Image Events, the Public Sphere, and Argumentative Practice: The Case of Radical Environmental Groups," *Argumentation* 17, no. 3 (September 2003): 315–33.

66. Shawn Michelle Smith, *Photography on the Color Line: W. E. B. Du Bois, Race, and Visual Culture* (Durham, NC: Duke University Press, 2004).

67. The photograph of Ray Porter's lynching in Clanton, Alabama, in 1891 from which a postcard was made was taken by W. R. Martin and reproduced in Ida B. Wells-Barrett in *The Red Record: Tabulated Statistics and Alleged Causes of Lynching in the United States* (New York: Open Road, 1895). See also Leigh Raiford, *Imprisoned in a Luminous Glare:*

Photography and the African American Freedom Struggle (Chapel Hill: University of North Carolina Press, 2011).

68. Raiford, "Ida B. Wells and the Shadow Archive," 306.

69. Frederick Douglass, preface to *The Red Record: Tabulated Statistics and Alleged Causes of Lynching in the United States*, by Ida B. Wells-Barnett (New York: Open Road, 1895).

70. See Patrick Brantlinger, *Dark Vanishings: Discourse on the Extinction of Primitive Races, 1800–1930* (Ithaca, NY: Cornell University Press, 2003).

71. Ida B. Wells-Barnett, "Lynch Law in the U.S.," *Birmingham Daily Post*, May 14, 1894, quoted in Curry, "The Fortune of Wells," 482.

72. Dorothy Sterling, *Black Foremothers: Three Lives* (New York: Feminist Press, 1988), 95.

73. Sterling, *Black Foremothers*, 95.

74. Wells-Barnett, *The Red Record*.

75. "British Anti-Lynchers," *New York Times*, August 2, 1894, 4.

76. "British Anti-Lynchers," *New York Times*.

77. Eleanor Tayleur, "The Negro Woman: Social and Moral Decadence," *Outlook* 75 (January 10, 1904): 266–71.

78. Tayleur, "The Negro Woman."

79. Tayleur, "The Negro Woman," 183.

80. Baker, *Following the Color Line*, 215; and Squires, "Outlawry," 161n40.

81. Baker, *Following the Color Line*, 185.

82. Squires, "Outlawry," 143.

83. Squires, "Outlawry," 142.

84. Squires, "Outlawry."

85. Wells-Barnett, *On Lynchings*, 26.

86. Wells-Barnett, *On Lynchings*, 680.

87. Lawrie Balfour, "Ida B. Wells and 'Color Line Justice': Rethinking Reparations in Feminist Terms," *Perspectives on Politics* 13, no. 3 (September 2015): 680–96, https://doi.org/10.1017/S1537592715001243.

88. Ida B. Wells-Barnett, *Mob Rule in New Orleans: Robert Charles and His Fight to Death, the Story of His Life, Burning Human Beings Alive, Other Lynching Statistics* (n.p.: n.p., 1900): 154.

89. It could be argued that the EJI's efforts were preserving, reproducing, and recirculating more of the radical argumentative threads that were woven into the countermemory tapestries that had been produced by earlier generations of African American activists. For example, Frederick Douglass, one of Wells-Barnett's supporters, shocked his listeners in 1886 and 1887 when he refused to argue that the Civil War had brought totalizing, massive help to all persons of color. He treated the passage of the Emancipation Proclamation as an event that had helped blacks, but he maintained that African Americans were not truly free.

90. Curry, "The Fortune of Wells," 456.

91. Here, Squires is alluding to the biopolitical and thanatopolitical ideas of Giorgio Agamben: it is the "sovereign" who gets to decide who will be "Homo Sacer," a person who can

be killed with impunity and who will have to answer to the "rule of law." Giorgio Agamben, *Homo Sacer: Sovereign Power and Bare Life*, trans. Daniel Heller-Roazen (Stanford, CA: Stanford University Press, 1998). As political philosophers and others are fond of reminding us, Carl Schmitt, a German legal thinker, once argued that the "Sovereign" was the one who "decides on the exception." Carl Schmitt, *Political Theology: Four Chapters on the Concept of Sovereignty*, trans. George Schwab (Cambridge, MA: MIT Press, 1985), 5.

92. Roessner, "Constructing Monuments," 121.

93. DeNeen L. Brown, "'Fearless' Ida B. Wells Honored by New Lynching Museum for Fighting Racial Terrorism," *Washington Post*, April 27, 2018, https://www.washingtonpost.com/news/retropolis/wp/2018/04/26/fearless-ida-b-wells-honored-by-new-lynching-memorial-for-fighting-racial-terror/. See also "Honors, at Last, for Ida B. Wells, 'a Sword among Lions,'" *New York Times*, July 31, 2018, https://www.nytimes.com/2018/07/31/opinion/honors-at-last-for-ida-b-wells-a-sword-among-lions.html.

94. Patricia J. Williams, "Ida B. Wells-Barnett Deserves a Bigger Statue," *The Nation*, May 2, 2018, https://www.thenation.com/article/archive/ida-b-wells-barnett-deserves-a-bigger-statue/.

95. Williams, "Ida B. Wells-Barnett Deserves a Bigger Statue," para. 6.

CHAPTER 3

1. See, for example, Equal Justice Initiative, *Lynching in America*, 3rd ed., report summary.
2. Waldrep, "War of Words."
3. Rushdy, *The End of American Lynching*. For helpful readings that explain some of these ASWPL motivations, see Jessie Daniel Ames, "Editorial Treatment of Lynchings," *Public Opinion Quarterly* 2, no. 1 (January 1938): 77–84, https://doi.org/10.1086/265154; and Jacqueline Dowd Hall, *Revolt against Chivalry: Jessie Daniel Ames and the Women's Campaign against Lynching* (1974; New York: Columbia University Press, 1993).
4. For discussion of the clusters of anti-lynching arguments that were produced by members of the NAACP, see Walter White, "The Costigan-Wagner Bill," *The Crisis* 42, no. 1 (January 1935): 10–11, 29; George S. Schuyler, "Scripture for Lynchers," *The Crisis* 42, no. 1 (January 1935): 12; August Meier and John H. Bracey Jr., "The NAACP as a Reform Movement, 1909–1965: 'To Reach the Conscience of America,'" *Journal of Southern History* 59, no. 1 (February 1993): 3–30, https://doi.org/10.2307/2210346; and Robin Bernice Balthrope, "Lawlessness and the New Deal: Congress and Anti-Lynching Legislation, 1934–1938" (PhD diss., Ohio State University, 1995).
5. Park, "Lynching and Antilynching," 338. See also Philip Dray, *At the Hands of Parties Unknown: The Lynching of Black America* (New York: Crown, 2006).
6. Waldrep, "War of Words," 75.
7. Tolnay and Beck, "Racialized Terrorism," 682.
8. The archives at Tuskegee Institute in 1979 indicated that some 3,445 blacks and 1,297 whites had been lynched. This figure also appears in Zangrando, *The NAACP Crusade*, 4–7. Compare this with other statistics that mention the chronicling of between four and five thousand lynchings.

9. Nina Silber, "How the New Monument to Lynching Unravels a Historical Lie," *Washington Post*, May 2, 2018, para. 1, https://www.washingtonpost.com/news/made-by-history/wp/2018/05/02/how-the-new-monument-to-lynching-unravels-a-historical-lie.

10. Silber, "How the New Monument," para. 3.

11. Silber, "How the New Monument," para. 5.

12. Waldrep, "War of Words," 76.

13. Claudine L. Ferrell, *Nightmare and Dream: Antilynching in Congress, 1917–1922* (New York: Garland, 1986).

14. Waldrep, "War of Words," 76.

15. Cutler, *Lynch-Law*, 276.

16. Cutler, *Lynch-Law*, 276.

17. Walter White, *Rope and Faggot: A Biography of Judge Lynch* (1929; New York: Arno Press, 1969). See also Walter White, *The Fire in the Flint* (New York: Alfred A. Knopf, 1924); and Walter White, *A Man Called White: An Autobiography of Walter White* (1948; Athens: University of Georgia Press, 1995).

18. For more on the Alabama 1901 constitutional debates, see Wanda Madison Minor, "The Rhetorical Construction of White Supremacy in Alabama's 1901 Constitution: A Critical-Historical Study" (PhD diss., University of Alabama, 2008); and Waldrep, "War of Words," 77.

19. Waldrep, "War of Words," 78. For background material on Monroe Work's statistical efforts on behalf of the anti-lynching cause, see Linda O. McMurry, *Recorder of the Black Experience: A Biography of Monroe Nathan Work* (Baton Rouge: Louisiana State University Press, 1985), 118–27; and Mark Tucker, "'You Can't Argue with Facts': Monroe Nathan Work as Information Officer, Editor, and Bibliographer," *Libraries and Culture* 26, no. 1 (Winter 1991): 151–68.

20. For several examples of the recording of the Johnson deaths, see NAACP, *Tenth Annual Report of the National Association for the Advancement of Colored People, for the Year 1919* (New York: National Association for the Advancement of Colored People, 1920); and Committee on the Judiciary Staff, Hearings before a Subcommittee of the Committee on the Judiciary, U.S. Senate, 69th Congress, 1st Session, "To Prevent and Punish the Crime of Lynching" (Washington, DC: Government Printing Office, 1926).

21. Waldrep, "War of Words, 79. See, for example, *United States v. Cruikshank*, 92 U.S. 542 (1876); and *United States v. Harris*, 106 U.S. 629 (1883).

22. See, for example, Albert E. Pillsbury, "A Brief Inquiry into a Federal Remedy for Lynching," *Harvard Law Review* 15, no. 9 (May 1902): 707–13.

23. NAACP, *Thirty Years of Lynching in the United States, 1889–1918* (New York: National Association for the Advancement of Colored People, 1919).

24. NAACP, *Thirty Years of Lynching*; and Park, "Lynching and Antilynching," 311.

25. Watson, "Mary Church Terrell vs. Thomas Nelson Page," 66.

26. Ore, *Lynching*, 20.

27. Joshua Rothman, "When Bigotry Paraded through the Streets," *Atlantic*, December 4, 2016, https://www.theatlantic.com/politics/archive/2016/12/second-klan/509468/.

28. Rothman, "When Bigotry Paraded," para. 11.

29. Rothman, "When Bigotry Paraded."

30. Rothman, "When Bigotry Paraded," paras. 4–5.

31. William F. Pinar, "The N.A.A.C.P. and the Struggle for Antilynching Federal Legislation, 1917–1950," *Counterpoints* 163 (2001): 689.

32. Pinar, "The N.A.A.C.P.," 692.

33. Winfield Collins, quoted in Ferrell, *Nightmare and Dream*, 86; and Pinar, "The N.A.A.C.P.," 691.

34. James Harmon Chadbourn, *Lynching and the Law* (Chapel Hill: University of North Carolina Press, 1933), 5.

35. Arthur I. Waskow, *From Race Riot to Sit-In, 1919 and the 1960s: A Study in the Connections Between Conflict and Violence* (Garden City, NY: Anchor Books, 1967).

36. Rable, "The South and the Politics of Antilynching Legislation," 203.

37. Waldrep, "War of Words," 80.

38. For more on the Dyer Anti-Lynching Bill, see Zangrando, *The NAACP Crusade*, 64; and Ferrell, *Nightmare and Dream*.

39. Rable, "The South and the Politics of Antilynching Legislation," 203.

40. Waldrep, "War of Words," 80.

41. See Adam Winkler, "'Corporations Are People' Is Built on an Incredible 19th-Century Lie," *Atlantic*, March 5, 2018, https://www.theatlantic.com/business/archive/2018/03/corporations-people-adam-winkler/554852/.

42. Rable, "The South and the Politics of Antilynching Legislation," 204.

43. Rable, "The South and the Politics of Antilynching Legislation," 205.

44. Rable, "The South and the Politics of Antilynching Legislation," 205.

45. James Weldon Johnson, *Along This Way: The Autobiography of James Weldon Johnson* (New York: Viking Press, 1933), 373.

46. This phrase borrows from Ernest G. Bormann, "Fetching Good out of Evil: A Rhetorical Use of Calamity," *Quarterly Journal of Speech* 63, no. 2 (1977): 130–39.

47. White, *A Man Called White*.

48. White, *A Man Called White*, 40.

49. White, *A Man Called White*, 41.

50. Waldrep, "War of Words," 80.

51. Waldrep, "War of Words," 80.

52. Waldrep, "War of Words," 81.

53. Waldrep, "War of Words," 81.

54. Waldrep, "War of Words," 81.

55. Waldrep, "War of Words," 82.

56. Jessie Daniel Ames, *The Changing Character of Lynching, 1931–1941* (1942; New York: Abraham's Magazine Service Press, 1973), 23–32.

57. See Barber, "The Association of Southern Women."

58. Powell, "The Association of Southern Women."

59. Tessa Brown, "Constellating White Women's Cultural Rhetorics: The Association of Southern Women for the Prevention of Lynching and Its Contemporary Scholars," *Peitho Journal* 20, no. 2 (2018): 245.

60. Jessie Daniel Ames, quoted in Waldrep, "War of Words," 82.

61. "Lynchers in Congress," *Reflector* (Charlottesville, VA), no. 47, June 30, 1934, 1, http://www2.vcdh.virginia.edu/afam/reflector/6.30.34.law.html.

62. "Lynchers in Congress," *Reflector*, 1.

63. Raper, *The Tragedy of Lynching*, 47.

64. Raper, *The Tragedy of Lynching*, 38.

65. "NAACP History: Costigan Wagner Bill," NAACP, 2018, https://www.naacp.org/naacp-history-costigan-wagner-act/.

66. Walter White, quoted in Park, "Lynching and Antilynching," 326.

67. Walter White, quoted in Park, "Lynching and Antilynching," 326.

68. Park, "Lynching and Antilynching," 329.

69. Park, "Lynching and Antilynching," 330.

70. Winston Burdett, quoted in Park, "Lynching and Antilynching," 329.

71. "NAACP History: Costigan Wagner Bill," para. 2.

72. RhapsodyinBooks, "January 5, 1934: The Costigan-Wagner Anti-Lynching Bill Is Proposed to the Senate," Legal Legacy, January 5, 2017, para. 3, https://legallegacy.wordpress.com/2017/01/05/january-5-1934-the-costigan-wagner-anti-lynching-bill-is-proposed-to-the-senate/.

73. Thurgood Marshall, quoted in RhapsodyinBooks, "January 5, 1934," para. 4.

74. Pinar, "The N.A.A.C.P.," 730.

75. Pinar, "The N.A.A.C.P.," 730.

76. Rable, "The South and the Politics of Antilynching Legislation," 210.

77. RhapsodyinBooks, "January 5, 1934," para. 4.

78. Rable, "The South and the Politics of Antilynching Legislation," 208.

79. Rable, "The South and the Politics of Antilynching Legislation," 210.

80. Silber, "How the New Monument," para. 8.

81. Silber, "How the New Monument," para. 8.

82. Rable, "The South and the Politics of Antilynching Legislation," 210–11.

83. Silber, "How the New Monument," para. 9.

84. Silber, "How the New Monument," para. 6.

85. Walter White, quoted in Silber, "How the New Monument," para. 13.

86. For more on *Lynch Justice at Work*, see James S. Allen, *Organizing in the Depression South: A Communist's Memoir* (Minneapolis: MEP Publications, 2001).

87. Beth Tompkins Bates, "A New Crowd Challenges the Agenda of the Old Guard in the NAACP, 1943–1941," *American Historical Review* 102, no. 2 (April 1997): 343. On Randolph's radicalism, see Paul Pfeffer, *A. Philip Randolph, Pioneer of the Civil Rights Movement* (Baton Rouge: Louisiana State University Press, 1990).

88. Albert Blaustein and Robert L. Zangrando, *Civil Rights and African Americans: A Documentary History* (Evanston, IL: Northwestern University Press, 1991), 346–50.

89. W. E. B. Du Bois, quoted in Rebecca N. Hill, *Men, Mobs, and Law: Anti-Lynching and Labor Defense in U.S. Radical History* (Durham, NC: Duke University Press, 2008), 128.

90. Pinar, "The N.A.A.C.P.," 715–16.

91. Wells, *Crusade for Justice*.

92. Wells, *Crusade for Justice*, 420.

93. Pinar, "The N.A.A.C.P.," 717.

94. Wells, *Crusade for Justice*, 403.

95. See Zangrando, *The NAACP Crusade*.

96. Background information on the ILD can be found in Charles H. Martin, "The International Labor Defense and Black America," *Labor History* 26, no. 2 (1985): 165–94, https://doi.org/10.1080/00236568508584794.

97. Bates, "A New Crowd Challenges the Agenda," 343.

98. Mark Naison, *Communists in Harlem during the Depression* (Urbana: University of Illinois Press, 1985), 62.

99. Park, "Lynching and Anti-Lynching," 322.

100. For overviews of the Scottsboro cases, see Dan T. Carter, *Scottsboro: A Tragedy of the American South* (Baton Rouge: Louisiana State University Press, 1969); Hugh T. Murray Jr., "The NAACP versus the Communist Party: The Scottsboro Rape Cases, 1931–1932," *Phylon* 28, no. 3 (1967): 267–87, https://doi.org/10.2307/273666; and Robin D. G. Kelley, "Memory and Politics," *The Nation*, October 3, 1994, 353. Eventually the US Supreme Court heard some of the arguments in the Scottsboro cases, and in 1932 they reversed the death sentences and granted the defendants a new trial. See *Powell v. Alabama*, 287 U.S. 45 (1932).

101. Harry Haywood, "The Scottsboro Decision: Victory of Revolutionary Struggle over Reformist Betrayal," *The Communist* 11 (December 1932): 1065–75, cited in Park, "Lynching and Anti-Lynching," 358.

102. Rable, "The South and the Politics of Antilynching Legislation," 213.

103. See Virginius Dabney, "Dixie Rejects Lynching," *The Nation*, November 27, 1937, 579–80.

104. Rable, "The South and the Politics of Antilynching Legislation," 213.

105. Chadbourn, *Lynching and the Law*.

106. Waldrep, "War of Words," 76. See Josephus Daniels, *Editor in Politics* (Chapel Hill: University of North Carolina Press, 1941), 401, 494.

107. Zangrando, *The NAACP Crusade*, 18.

108. Hillary Crosley Coker, "*NYT* Omits Exactly Who Lynched 4,000 Blacks in the South," Jezebel, February 11, 2015, https://jezebel.com/nyt-omits-exactly-who-lynched-40-000-blacks-in-the-sout-1685189739.

109. Kamala D. Harris, "Senators Harris and Booker Lead Historic Passage of Federal Anti-Lynching Legislation," Harris.senate.gov, December 19, 2018, para. 2, https://www.harris.senate.gov/news/press-releases/senators-harris-and-booker-lead-historic-passage-of-federal-anti-lynching-legislation.

110. Harris, "Senators Harris and Booker," para. 3.

CHAPTER 4

1. See NAACP, *Burning at the Stake in the United States, 1889–1918* (New York: National Association for the Advancement of Colored People, 1919); Zangrando, *The NAACP Crusade*; Genna Rae McNeil, *Groundwork: Charles Hamilton Houston and the Struggle for Civil Rights* (Philadelphia: University of Pennsylvania Press, 1983); and Julius E. Thompson, "Charles Hamilton Houston and the Struggle against Lynching in the United States,

1930–1939," in *Charles H. Houston: An Interdisciplinary Study of Civil Rights Leadership*, ed. James L. Conyers Jr. (Lanham, MD: Lexington Books, 2012), 195.

2. "Remembering Elbert Williams, NAACP Activist Lynched in 1940," Equal Justice Initiative, June 22, 2016, https://eji.org/news/eji-joint-remembrance-lynching-elbert-williams. See also Emily Littleton, "The Ultimate Sacrifice for a Hopeful Future," *Jackson Sun*, June 20, 2016, https://www.jacksonsun.com/story/news/local/2016/06/20/ultimate-sacrifice-hopeful-future/86148916/.

3. Littleton, "The Ultimate Sacrifice," para. 2.

4. Rable, "The South and the Politics of Antilynching Legislation," 201.

5. Michel Foucault, *The Order of Things: An Archaeology of the Human Sciences* (New York: Vintage Books, 1973), xix.

6. Park, "Lynching and Antilynching," 311.

7. Park, "Lynching and Antilynching," 311.

8. Mary L. Dudziak, "Desegregation as a Cold War Imperative," *Stanford Law Review* 41, no. 1 (November 1988): 61–120.

9. Park, "Lynching and Antilynching," 311.

10. Bates, "A New Crowd Challenges the Agenda."

11. Roy Wilkins, quoted in Bates, "A New Crowd Challenges the Agenda," 340.

12. W. E. Burghardt Du Bois, "The Talented Tenth," in *The Negro Problem*, ed. Booker T. Washington (New York: Arno Press, 1969), 31–75.

13. Bates, "A New Crowd Challenges the Agenda," 340. Excellent overviews of the NAACP's involvement with court activism can be found in Richard Kluger, *Simple Justice: The History of* Brown v. Board of Education *and Black America's Struggle for Equality* (New York: Alfred A. Knopf, 1975); and Mark V. Tushnet, *The NAACP's Legal Strategy against Segregated Education, 1925–1950* (Chapel Hill: University of North Carolina Press, 1987).

14. For materials on some of these shifts in strategizing, see Kluger, *Simple Justice*.

15. Bates, "A New Crowd Challenges the Agenda," 341. For more on the calls for more militancy, see Robert Korstad and Nelson Lichtenstein, "Opportunities Found and Lost: Labor, Radicals, and the Early Civil Rights Movement," *Journal of American History* 75, no. 3 (December 1988): 786–811, https://doi.org/10.2307/1901530; and Robin D. G. Kelley, *Hammer and Hoe: Alabama Communists during the Great Depression* (Chapel Hill: University of North Carolina Press, 1990).

16. L. C. Dunn, "Statement on the Nature of Race and Race Differences," UNESCO, June 1951, http://www.honestthinking.org/en/unesco/UNESCO.1951.Statement_on_Race.htm.

17. Meier and Bracey, "The NAACP as a Reform Movement," 20.

18. Meier and Bracey, "The NAACP as a Reform Movement," 24.

19. Meier and Bracey, "The NAACP as a Reform Movement," 24.

20. See, for example, Kruger, *Simple Justice*; and Dudziak, "Desegregation as a Cold War Imperative."

21. Meier and Bracey, "The NAACP as a Reform Movement," 21.

22. For excellent overviews of some of the various meanings of the Emmett Till murder case, see Stephen Whitfield, *A Death in the Delta: The Story of Emmett Till* (New York: Free Press, 1988); and Jacqueline Goldsby, "The High Tech and Low Tech of It: The Meaning

of Lynching and the Death of Emmett Till," *Yale Journal of Criticism* 9, no. 2 (Fall 1996): 245–82.

23. Pinar, "The N.A.A.C.P."

24. Zangrando, *The NAACP Crusade*.

25. "Executive Order 8802: Prohibition of Discrimination in the Defense Industry (1941)," Our Documents.gov, https://www.ourdocuments.gov/doc.php?flash=false&doc=72.

26. Pinar, "The N.A.A.C.P.," 741.

27. Condit and Lucaites, *Crafting Equality*.

28. Dominic J. Capeci Jr., *The Lynching of Cleo Wright* (Lexington: University Press of Kentucky, 1998).

29. Capeci, *The Lynching of Cleo Wright*, 1.

30. Pinar, "N.A.A.C.P.," 744.

31. Pinar, "N.A.A.C.P.," 746.

32. Lillian Smith, *Killers of the Dream* (1949; New York: W. W. Norton, 1963).

33. W. Fitzhugh Brundage, *Lynching in the New South: Georgia and Virginia, 1880–1930* (Urbana: University of Illinois Press, 1993), 245.

34. Pinar, "The N.A.A.C.P.," 689.

35. *Smith v. Allright*, 321 U.S. 649 (1944).

36. Meier and Bracey, "The NAACP as a Reform Movement," 4.

37. See Dave Tell, *Remembering Emmett Till* (Chicago: University of Chicago Press, 2019).

38. Dennis Parker, "More Than 60 Years after His Brutal Murder, Emmett Till Deserves Justice," Common Dreams, August 29, 2018, https://www.commondreams.org/views/2018/08/29/more-60-years-after-his-brutal-murder-emmett-till-deserves-justice.

39. Petula Dvorak, "Funeral for Emmett Till, Lynched in 1955, Unfolds Every Day in the Nation's Capital," *Washington Post*, July 13, 2018, para. 1, https://www.washingtonpost.com/local/lynched-in-1955-emmett-tills-funeral-unfolds-every-day-in-the-nations-capital/2018/07/12/78b6886a-8604-11e8-8f6c-46cb43e3f306_story.html.

40. Dvorak, "Funeral for Emmett Till," paras. 1–4.

41. Kristine Phillips, Wesley Lowery, and Devlin Barrett, "New Details in Book about Emmett Till's Death Prompted Officials to Reopen Investigation," *Washington Post*, July 13, 2018, para. 4, https://www.washingtonpost.com/news/retropolis/wp/2018/07/12/emmett-tills-case-has-been-reopened-his-brutal-death-in-1955-put-a-spotlight-on-racial-violence/.

42. Phillips, Lowery, and Barrett, "New Details in Book," para. 12.

43. See Wesley Lowery, "Emmett Till's Death, and History, Is Fading in This Mississippi Town," *Washington Post*, September 7, 2015, https://www.washingtonpost.com/national/emmett-tills-death-and-history-is-fading-in-this-mississippi-town/2015/09/07/e04444c6-500c-11e5-933e-7d06c647a395_story.html?utm_term=.bod6dofb7d7e.

44. Phillips, Lowery, and Barrett, "New Details in Book," paras. 25–27.

45. Carolyn Bryant, quoted in Phillips, Lowery, and Barrett, "New Details in Book," para. 4.

46. David L. Eng and David Kazanjian, eds., *Loss: The Politics of Mourning* (Berkeley: University of California Press, 2003), 1.

47. Pinar, "The N.A.A.C.P.," 729.
48. "South Goes Whole Year without Single Lynching," *New York Times*, May 10, 1940, 15.
49. "South Goes Whole Year," *New York Times*.
50. For more on the psychological and social aspects of Ames's activism, see Hall, *Revolt against Chivalry*.
51. W. E. B. Du Bois, *The Souls of Black Folk*, in *The Oxford W. E. B. Du Bois Reader*, ed. Eric J. Sundquist (1903; New York: Oxford University Press, 1996), 97–240.
52. W. E. B. Du Bois, "The Negro and the Warsaw Ghetto," *Jewish Life* 6, no. 7 (1952): 14–15.
53. Michael Rothberg, "W. E. B. Du Bois in Warsaw: Holocaust Memory and the Color Line, 1949–1952," *Yale Journal of Criticism* 14, no. 1 (March 2001): 171.
54. John Durham Peters, *Speaking into the Air: A History of the Idea of Communication* (Chicago: University of Chicago Press, 1999), 3.
55. Ferrell, *Nightmare and Dream*, 1.
56. Pfeifer, "At the Hands of Parties Unknown?," 832.
57. See Barbara Holden-Smith, "Lynching, Federalism, and the Intersection of Race and Gender in the Progressive Era," *Yale Journal of Law and Feminism* 8, no. 1 (1996): 31–78.
58. Richard Delgado, "The Law of the Noose: A History of Latino Lynching," *Harvard Civil Rights–Civil Liberties Law Review* 44, no. 2 (Summer 2009): 297–312, 297n5.
59. Delgado, "The Law of the Noose," 297n5.
60. Anthony V. Alfieri, "Lynching Ethics: Toward a Theory of Racialized Defenses," *Michigan Law Review* 95, no. 5 (February 1997): 1066.
61. Jeannine Bell, "The Hangman's Noose and the Lynch Mob: Hate Speech and the Jena Six," *Harvard Civil Rights–Civil Liberties Law Review* 44, no. 2 (Summer 2009): 329.
62. Bell, "The Hangman's Noose and the Lynch Mob," 329–30.
63. Matsuda, "Dissent in a Crowded Theater."
64. James Allen, Hilton Als, John Lewis, and Leon F. Litwack, *Without Sanctuary: Lynching Photography in America* (Santa Fe: Twin Palms Publishers, 2000).
65. Allen et al., *Without Sanctuary*.
66. Allen et al., *Without Sanctuary*.
67. Allen et al., *Without Sanctuary*.
68. Ehrenhaus and Owen, "Race Lynching and Christian Evangelicalism."
69. Ehrenhaus and Owen, "Race Lynching and Christian Evangelicalism."
70. Berg, *Popular Justice*.
71. Terry Gross, "As New Lynching Memorial Opens, A Look Back on America's History of Racial Terrorism," National Public Radio, May 4, 2018, https://www.npr.org/2018/05/04/608477810/as-new-lynching-memorial-opens-a-look-back-on-americas-history-of-racial-terrori.
72. Gregory, "A Lynching's Long Shadow."
73. Gaen Murphree, "Lynching in America: A Grim History," letter to the editor, *New York Times*, February 19, 2015, https://www.nytimes.com/2015/02/19/opinion/lynching-in-america-a-grim-history.html.
74. Harold and DeLuca, "Behold the Corpse."
75. Ore, *Lynching*, 97.

76. For a critique of this specific postcard, see Michele Faith Wallace, "The Good Lynching and 'The Birth of a Nation': Discourses and Aesthetics of Jim Crow," *Cinema Journal* 43, no. 1 (Autumn 2003): 85–104.

77. Roland Barthes, *Camera Lucida: Reflections on Photography* (New York: Macmillan, 1981).

78. Gross, "As New Lynching Memorial Opens."

79. For a detailed critique of Joe Myers's message, see Smith, *Photography on the Color Line*, 122–25. Smith contends that by "sending the postcard, Joe perhaps demonstrates to his mother how he participates in upholding the mythology of pure white motherhood that fueled so many lynchings; he 'protects' white womanhood, he 'defends' his mother."

80. Gross, "As New Lynching Memorial Opens."

81. Gross, "As New Lynching Memorial Opens."

82. Gross, "As New Lynching Memorial Opens."

83. Gregory, "A Lynching's Long Shadow," para. 16.

84. Brent Staples, "The Perils of Growing Comfortable with Evil," *New York Times*, April 9, 2000, https://www.nytimes.com/2000/04/09/opinion/editorial-observer-the-perils-of-growing-comfortable-with-evil.html. See also Susan Sontag, *On Photography* (1977; New York: Macmillan, 2001).

85. Staples, "The Perils of Growing Comfortable," para. 9.

86. Markovitz, *Legacies of Lynching*; see also Kirschke, *Art in Crisis*; and Wood, *Lynching and Spectacle*.

87. Jim Auchmutey, "Lynching Exhibit Confronts South's Ugly Past," *Atlanta Journal-Constitution*, April 28, 2002.

88. Auchmutey, "Lynching Exhibit Confronts South's Ugly Past."

89. Auchmutey, "Lynching Exhibit Confronts South's Ugly Past."

90. Owen and Ehrenhaus, "Looking at Lynching."

91. Quoted in Brian Lyman, "'Without Sanctuary' and How We Remember Lynching," *Montgomery Advertiser*, April 25, 2018, paras. 34–35, https://www.montgomeryadvertiser.com/story/news/2018/04/25/without-sanctuary-and-how-we-remember-lynching/499641002/.

92. Quoted in Lyman, "Without Sanctuary," paras. 34–35.

93. For more on the rhetorical act of witnessing, see Bradford Vivian, *Commonplace Witnessing: Rhetorical Invention, Historical Remembrance, and Public Culture* (New York: Oxford University Press, 2017).

94. The website is available at https://withoutsanctuary.org/.

95. Rice, "How We Remember Lynching."

96. Gregory, "A Lynching's Long Shadow," para. 16.

97. Sheryl Gay Stolberg, "The Senate Apologizes, Mostly," *New York Times*, June 19, 2005, https://www.nytimes.com/2005/06/19/weekinreview/the-senate-apologizes-mostly.html.

98. Ohl and Potter, "United We Lynch," 185.

99. Ohl and Potter, "United We Lynch," 192.

100. Harold and DeLuca, "Behold the Corpse."

101. Lyman, "Without Sanctuary."

102. Lyman, "Without Sanctuary."

103. Ehrenhaus and Owen, "Race Lynching and Christian Evangelicalism," 294.

104. Ehrenhaus and Owen, "Race Lynching and Christian Evangelicalism," 294.

105. bell hooks, "The Oppositional Gaze: Black Female Spectators," in *Feminist Film Theory: A Reader*, ed. Sue Thornham (New York: New York University Press, 1999), 319.

106. James Weldon Johnson, "The Practice of Lynching: A Picture, the Problem, and What Shall Be Done about It," *Century Magazine* (November 1927), 65–70.

CHAPTER 5

1. For a fine overview of some of Stevenson's legal theorizing, see Bryan Stevenson, "Crime, Punishment, and Executions in the Twenty-First Century," *Proceedings of the American Philosophical Society* 147, no. 1 (March 2003): 24–29. For a related but different take on issues of capital punishment, see Kenneth Williams, *Most Deserving of Death? An Analysis of the Supreme Court's Death Penalty Jurisprudence* (New York: Routledge, 2012).

2. Stevenson, "A Presumption of Guilt," para. 5. See also James McWilliams, "Bryan Stevenson on What Well-Meaning White People Need to Know about Race," *Pacific Standard*, February 6, 2018, updated February 18, 2019, https://psmag.com/magazine/bryan-stevenson-ps-interview.

3. McWilliams, "Bryan Stevenson," para. 1.

4. Tolnay and Beck, *A Festival of Violence*.

5. For a list of individuals and organizations that Bryan Stevenson credits for helping keep statistics on aggregate numbers of lynchings, see Stevenson, "A Presumption of Guilt."

6. Rice, "How We Remember Lynching," 41.

7. Bryan Stevenson, quoted in Tim Adams, "Interview, Bryan Stevenson: 'America's Mandela,'" *The Guardian*, February 1, 2015, para. 7, https://www.theguardian.com/us-news/2015/feb/01/bryan-stevenson-americas-mandela.

8. For an excellent journalistic explanation of the relationship between lynching histories and the EJI's interest in capital punishment reform, see Liliana Segura, "The Stepchild of Lynching: Alabama's Lynching Memorial and the Legacy of Racial Terror in the South," *The Intercept*, June 17, 2018, https://theintercept.com/2018/06/17/lynching-museum-alabama-death-penalty/.

9. Adams, "Interview, Bryan Stevenson."

10. Bryan Stevenson, "We Need to Talk about an Injustice," TED Talks, March 5, 2012, https://www.ted.com/talks/bryan_stevenson_we_need_to_talk_about_an_injustice?language=en.

11. See, for example, Christine Ajudua, "How Alabama's New Memorial to Victims of Lynching Could Change America," *AFAR*, July 31, 2018, para. 3, https://www.afar.com/magazine/how-alabamas-new-memorial-to-victims-of-lynching-could-change-america.

12. Adams, "Interview, Bryan Stevenson," para. 3.

13. For Bright's own critique of America's death penalty, see Stephen B. Bright, "Discrimination, Death and Denial: The Tolerance of Racial Discrimination in Infliction of the Death Penalty," *Santa Clara Law Review* 35, no. 2 (1995): 433–84. See also Stephen B. Bright, "Imposition of the Death Penalty upon the Poor, Racial Minorities, the Intellectually Disabled, and the Mentally Ill," paper presented at the Program of the High Commissioner for Human Rights of the United Nations, New York, April 24, 2014, http://www.law.nyu.edu/sites/default/files/upload_documents/Bright-Death-Penalty-UN-April-2014.pdf.

14. Stevenson, "A Presumption of Guilt."
15. Stevenson, "A Presumption of Guilt," para. 6.
16. Jennifer Rae Taylor, quoted in Stevenson, "A Presumption of Guilt."
17. Stevenson, "A Presumption of Guilt," para. 7.
18. Stevenson, "A Presumption of Guilt," para. 10.
19. Stevenson, "A Presumption of Guilt," para. 13.
20. Stevenson, "A Presumption of Guilt," paras. 13–14.
21. Stevenson, "A Presumption of Guilt," paras. 14–15.
22. Stevenson, "A Presumption of Guilt," para. 16.
23. For a helpful discussion of transgenerational transmission of traumatic memories, see Marianne Hirsch, *The Generation of Postmemory: Writing and Visual Culture after the Holocaust* (New York: Columbia University Press, 2012).
24. Stevenson, "A Presumption of Guilt," para. 18.
25. Kevin Conley, "Bryan Stevenson Is Working to Transform How Society's Most Vulnerable Access Legal Aid," *Town and Country*, May 2, 2016, https://www.townandcountrymag.com/society/politics/a5602/bryan-stevenson-equal-justice-initiative/.
26. Stevenson, "A Presumption of Guilt," para. 17.
27. Segura, "The Stepchild of Lynching," para. 6.
28. Segura, "The Stepchild of Lynching," paras. 6–14.
29. Segura, "The Stepchild of Lynching," para. 9.
30. Raper, *The Tragedy of Lynching*.
31. Segura, "The Stepchild of Lynching," para. 11.
32. Segura, "The Stepchild of Lynching," para. 14. Kenneth Williams's execution has become a lynchpin for cries against the death penalty, given the violent, torturous nature of his death. One of eight men whom Arkansas rushed to execute before the state's supply of the sedative midazolam, used in the lethal injection, expired, Williams suffered a torturous death. According to the EJI's description, Williams "lurched violently against the leather straps that bound him to the gurney 20 times." Witnesses reported that Williams then went through "[h]eavy breathing—a striving for air—for the next three minutes." "Arkansas Executions Underscore Threshold Question, Do We Deserve to Kill?," Equal Justice Initiative, May 5, 2017, https://eji.org/news/arkansas-executions-underscore-threshold-question-do-we-deserve-to-kill/.
33. For more on the significance of the Willie Francis death, see Deborah W. Denno, "When Willie Francis Died: The 'Disturbing' Story behind One of the Eighth Amendment's Most Enduring Standards of Risk," in *Death Penalty Stories*, ed. John H. Blume and Jordan M. Steiker (Eagan, MN: Foundation Press, 2009), 46.
34. Segura, "The Stepchild of Lynching," para. 16. As Sherrilyn Ifill noted in her acclaimed book *On the Courthouse Lawn: Confronting the Legacy of Lynching in the Twenty-First Century*, the mainstream American press helped create a "consensus story" that somehow the lynchers must have been "outsiders" who "could not be recognized." This type of mantra could be used to help shield the thousands who attended the lynchings, as well as those who organized and carried them out. We argue that, now, the mainstream press could help the EJI provide counternarrative critiques of this old "consensus" story.
35. Segura, "The Stepchild of Lynching," para. 18.

36. Stevenson, *Just Mercy*, 14–15.
37. Adams, "Interview, Bryan Stevenson," para. 6.
38. Stevenson, *Just Mercy*, 250.
39. Stevenson, *Just Mercy*, 157.
40. Stevenson, *Just Mercy*, 157–58.
41. Stevenson, *Just Mercy*, 158.
42. Stevenson, *Just Mercy*, 159.
43. Stevenson, *Just Mercy*, 159.
44. Stevenson, *Just Mercy*, 243.
45. Pete Earley, *Circumstantial Evidence: Death, Life, and Justice in a Southern Town* (New York: Random House, 1995).
46. David J. Leonard, "White Anti-Racists Must Be 'Stone Catchers' for Oppressed People," *The Root*, November 15, 2016, https://www.theroot.com/white-anti-racists-must-be-stone-catchers-for-oppress-1790857731.
47. Bryan Stevenson, quoted in "Bryan Stevenson Talks to Oprah about Why We Need to Abolish the Death Penalty," Equal Justice Initiative, November 28, 2015, para. 4, https://eji.org/news/bryan-stevenson-tells-oprah-winfrey-why-we-should-abolish-death-penalty.
48. "Bryan Stevenson Talks to Oprah," para. 5.
49. Robert Siegel, "After Arkansas Executions, Lawyer Criticizes Use of Capital Punishment," National Public Radio, May 1, 2017, para. 1, https://www.npr.org/2017/05/01/526436000/after-arkansas-executions-lawyer-criticizes-use-of-capital-punishment.
50. Siegel, "After Arkansas Executions," para. 4.
51. Siegel, "After Arkansas Executions," paras. 6–11.
52. Brigid Delaney, "Bryan Stevenson: If It's Not Right to Rape a Rapist, How Can It Be OK to Kill a Killer?," *The Guardian*, February 17, 2015, https://www.theguardian.com/world/2015/feb/17/bryan-stevenson-if-its-not-right-to-a-rapist-how-can-it-be-ok-to-kill-a-killer.
53. Delaney, "Bryan Stevenson: If It's Not Right to Rape a Rapist," para. 4.
54. For other comparisons of these abolition practices, see Bharat Malkani, *Slavery and the Death Penalty: A Study in Abolition* (Milton Park, Oxon, England: Routledge, 2018).
55. Jeffrey Toobin, "The Legacy of Lynching, on Death Row," *New Yorker*, August 22, 2016, https://www.newyorker.com/magazine/2016/08/22/bryan-stevenson-and-the-legacy-of-lynching.
56. Adams, "Interview, Bryan Stevenson," para. 9.
57. Justice Harry Blackmun, dissenting opinion, *Collins v. Collins*, 510 U.S. 1141, 1145 (1994).

CHAPTER 6

1. "Alabama Lawmakers Protect Confederate Memorials," Equal Justice Initiative, May 29, 2017, paras. 1–2, https://eji.org/news/alabama-lawmakers-protect-confederate-memorials.
2. "Alabama Lawmakers Protect Confederate Memorials," para. 3.
3. "Alabama Lawmakers Protect Confederate Memorials," para. 3.
4. A. Dirk Moses, "'White Genocide' and the Ethics of Public Analysis," *Journal of Genocide Research* 21, no. 2 (2019): 201–13.

5. "Alabama Lawmakers Protect Confederate Memorials," para. 3.

6. For a helpful overview of many of these controversies, see Jess R. Phelps and Jessica Owley, "Etched in Stone: Historic Preservation Law and Confederate Monuments," *Florida Law Review* 71 (2019): 627–87.

7. Kirk Savage, *Monument Wars: Washington, D.C., the National Mall, and the Transformation of the Memorial Landscape* (Berkeley: University of California Press, 2009). We sympathize with Savage's critiques of the creeping urbanization on the National Mall, and we are intrigued by his call for temporary moratoriums on the building of some structures. At the same time, we extend Savage's notion of "monument wars" to include controversies over many other memoryscapes that are happening across the country.

8. "Weekend Read: Confederate Monuments Are Going Down, Lynching Memorials Are Going Up," Southern Poverty Law Center, April 27, 2018, https://www.splcenter.org/news/2018/04/27/weekend-read-confederate-monuments-are-going-down-lynching-memorials-are-going.

9. Emanuella Grinberg, "New Confederate Monuments Are Going Up and These Are the People behind Them," CNN, August 24, 2017, https://www.cnn.com/2017/08/18/us/new-confederate-monuments/index.html. See also Nicole M. Elias and Sean McCandless, "Administrative Decision-Making amid Competing Public Sector Values: Confederate Statue Removal in Baltimore, Maryland," *Journal of Public Affairs Education* 25, no. 3 (2019): 412–22.

10. W. Fitzhugh Brundage, "Exclusion, Inclusion, and the Politics of Confederate Commemoration in the American South," *Politics, Groups, and Identities* 6, no. 2 (2018): 324–30, https://doi.org/10.1080/21565503.2018.1454332.

11. Patrik Jonsson, "The Future of America's Past: Should We 'Explain' Confederate Statues?," *Christian Science Monitor*, August 22, 2019, para. 6–7, https://www.csmonitor.com/USA/Society/2019/0822/The-future-of-America-s-past-Should-we-explain-Confederate-statues.

12. William Ferris, quoted in Jonsson, "The Future of America's Past," para. 9.

13. Ezra Klein, "Bryan Stevenson Explains How It Feels to Grow Up Black amid Confederate Monuments," *Vox*, May 24, 2017, https://www.vox.com/2017/5/24/15675606/bryan-stevenson-confederacy-monuments-slavery-ezra-klein.

14. Campbell Robertson, "A Lynching Memorial Is Opening: The Country Has Never Seen Anything Like It," *New York Times*, April 25, 2018, https://www.nytimes.com/2018/04/25/us/lynching-memorial-alabama.html.

15. Others before us have also noted some of these symbolic linkages. See, for example, Rebecca Solnit, "The Monument Wars," *Harper's Magazine*, January 2017, https://harpers.org/archive/2017/01/the-monument-wars/.

16. Chris Flood, "Montgomery: Still the Heart of Confederacy," *Cape Gazette* (Lewes, DE), May 4, 2018, https://www.capegazette.com/article/montgomery-still-heart-confederacy/156142.

17. Jalane Schmidt, quoted in Jonsson, "The Future of America's Past," para. 36.

18. Leada Gore, "Which State Has the Most Confederate Monuments? And No, It's Not Alabama," AL.com, August 17, 2018, updated March 6, 2019, https://www.al.com/news/index.ssf/2018/08/which_state_has_the_most_confe.html.

19. John Archibald, "Alabama Capitol Statue Honors Doctor Who Experimented on Slaves," AL.com, October 19, 2016, updated March 6, 2019, https://www.al.com/opinion/index.ssf/2016/10/is_that_a_statue_of_a_saint_or.html; and Diana E. Axelsen, "Women as Victims of Medical Experimentation: J. Marion Sims' Surgery on Slave Women, 1845–1850," *Sage* 2, no. 2 (Fall 1985): 10–13.

20. "The Confederate Flag's Tumultuous 155-Year History," AL.com, October 24, 2018, updated July 25, 2019, https://www.al.com/expo/news/erry-2018/10/3aeb6df8ab5121/the-confederate-flags-tumultuo.html.

21. Mark Berman, "Alabama Governor Has Confederate Flag Removed from State Capitol Grounds," *Washington Post*, June 24, 2015, https://www.washingtonpost.com/news/post-nation/wp/2015/06/24/alabama-governor-has-confederate-flag-removed-from-state-capitol-grounds/?utm_term=.593fb8c88214.

22. Klein, "Bryan Stevenson Explains How It Feels."

23. Klein, "Bryan Stevenson Explains How It Feels."

24. Nietzsche, *Untimely Meditations*, 75.

25. See Danielle Endres and Samantha Senda-Cook, "Location Matters: The Rhetoric of Place in Protest," *Quarterly Journal of Speech* 97, no. 3 (2011): 257–82, https://doi.org/10.1080/00335630.2011.585167.

26. Endres and Senda-Cook, "Location Matters."

27. Endres and Senda-Cook, "Location Matters."

28. Stevenson, *Just Mercy*.

29. Stevenson, *Just Mercy*.

30. Stevenson, *Just Mercy*, 193; and Kat Eschner, "Some States Celebrate MLK Day and Robert E. Lee's Birthday on the Same Day," *Smithsonian Magazine*, January 16, 2017, https://www.smithsonianmag.com/smart-news/some-states-celebrate-mlk-day-and-robert-e-lees-birthday-same-day-180961772/.

31. Rick Hampson, "Confederate Memorials Turn Up Faster Than They Can Be Removed a Year after Charlottesville," *USA Today*, August 6, 2018, updated August 7, 2018, https://www.usatoday.com/story/news/nation/2018/08/06/confederate-memorials-list-longer-usa-public-remove/891739002/.

32. Valerie Strauss, "FYI, Alabama's Constitution Still Calls for 'Separate Schools for White and Colored Children,'" *Washington Post*, March 10, 2017, https://www.washingtonpost.com/news/answer-sheet/wp/2017/03/10/fyi-alabamas-constitution-still-calls-for-separate-schools-for-white-and-colored-children/.

33. Strauss, "FYI, Alabama's Constitution Still Calls."

34. Michael Harriot, "Court Rules Alabama Town's School Segregation Too Racist . . . Even for Alabama," *The Root*, February 13, 2018, https://www.theroot.com/court-rules-alabama-towns-school-segregation-too-racist-1822976807.

35. Molly Olmstead, "How Did an Alabama County Just Open Its First Integrated School? Nearly 65 Years after the *Brown v. Board* Ruling," *Slate*, August 15, 2018, para. 6, https://slate.com/news-and-politics/2018/08/alabama-county-opens-first-integrated-school-in-2018-heres-why-it-took-so-long.html.

36. Endres and Senda-Cook, "Location Matters."

37. "Hatewatch," Southern Poverty Law Center, June 9, 2016, https://www.splcenter.org/hatewatch/2016/06/09?keyword=&page=2.

38. James E. Young, "The Counter-Monument: Memory against Itself in Germany Today," *Critical Inquiry* 18, no. 2 (Winter 1992): 267–96, https://doi.org/10.1086/448632.

39. Michael Rothberg, *Multidirectional Memory: Remembering the Holocaust in the Age of Decolonization* (Stanford, CA: Stanford University Press, 2009).

40. V. William Balthrop, "Culture, Myth, and Ideology as Public Argument: An Interpretation of the Ascent and Demise of 'Southern Culture,'" *Communication Monographs* 51, no. 4 (1984): 339–52, https://doi.org/10.1080/03637758409390206.

41. Joe Heim, "Recounting a Day of Rage, Hate, Violence and Death," *Washington Post*, August 14, 2017, https://www.washingtonpost.com/graphics/2017/local/charlottesville-timeline/?utm_term=.d2bae8b563e2.

42. Heim, "Recounting a Day of Rage."

43. Heim, "Recounting a Day of Rage."

44. James Chase Sanchez, "Trump, the KKK, and the Versatility of White Supremacy Rhetoric," *Journal of Contemporary Rhetoric* 8, nos. 1–2 (2018): 46.

45. Sanchez, "Trump, the KKK, and the Versatility of White Supremacy Rhetoric."

46. Gary LaFree, "Is Antifa a Terrorist Group?," *Society* 55, no. 3 (June 2018): 248–52.

47. See Samuel Perry, "President Trump and Charlottesville: Uncivil Mourning and White Supremacy," *Journal of Contemporary Rhetoric* 8, nos. 1–2 (2018): 57–71.

48. For helpful critiques of the August 2017 Charlottesville events, see Hawes Spencer, *Summer of Hate: Charlottesville, USA* (Charlottesville: University of Virginia Press, 2018); Louis P. Nelson and Claudrena N. Harold, eds., *Charlottesville 2017: The Legacy of Race and Inequity* (Charlottesville: University of Virginia Press, 2018); and Joshua Arthurs, "The Anatomy of Controversy, from Charlottesville to Rome," *Modern Italy* 24, no. 2 (May 2019): 123–38.

49. Liam Stack, "Charlottesville Confederate Statues Are Protected by State Law, Judge Rules," *New York Times*, May 1, 2019, https://www.nytimes.com/2019/05/01/us/charlottesville-confederate-statues.html.

50. Mitch Landrieu, "Mitch Landrieu's Speech on the Removal of Confederate Monuments in New Orleans," *New York Times*, May 23, 2017, https://www.nytimes.com/2017/05/23/opinion/mitch-landrieus-speech-transcript.html.

51. Donald Trump, quoted in Julia Zorthian, "President Trump Says It's 'Sad' to See U.S. Culture 'Ripped Apart' by Removing Confederate Statues," *Time*, August 17, 2017, paras. 1–2, https://time.com/4904510/donald-trump-twitter-confederate-statues/.

52. Zorthian, "President Trump Says It's 'Sad.'"

53. German Lopez, "Mississippi Lawmaker: Leaders Taking Down Confederate Monuments 'Should Be LYNCHED,'" *Vox*, May 22, 2017, https://www.vox.com/identities/2017/5/22/15675604/confederate-monuments-karl-oliver.

54. Hampson, "Confederate Memorials Turn Up Faster Than They Can Be Removed."

55. Hampson, "Confederate Memorials Turn Up Faster Than They Can Be Removed."

56. Balthrop, "Culture, Myth, and Ideology as Public Argument."

57. Balthrop, "Culture, Myth, and Ideology as Public Argument."

58. Tyler Stiem, "Statue Wars: What Should We Do with Troublesome Monuments?," *The Guardian*, September 26, 2018, https://www.theguardian.com/cities/2018/sep/26/statue-wars-what-should-we-do-with-troublesome-monuments.

59. Charles Arthur Willard, *Argumentation and the Social Grounds of Knowledge* (Tuscaloosa: University of Alabama Press, 1983), 267.

60. Scott P. Marler, "Removing the Confederate Monuments in New Orleans Was Only a First Step toward Righting the Wrongs of History," *The Nation*, June 14, 2017, https://www.thenation.com/article/archive/removing-the-confederate-monuments-in-new-orleans-was-only-a-first-step-toward-righting-the-wrongs-of-history/.

61. See, for example, Margot Patterson, "The Fleeting Satisfaction of Pulling Down Confederate Monuments," *America: The Jesuit Review*, September 18, 2017, https://www.americamagazine.org/politics-society/2017/09/18/fleeting-satisfaction-pulling-down-confederate-monuments.

62. Patterson, "The Fleeting Satisfaction," paras. 6–7.

63. Marler, "Removing the Confederate Monuments."

64. Vered Vinitzky-Seroussi and Chana Teeger, "Unpacking the Unspoken: Silence in Collective Memory and Forgetting," *Social Forces* 88, no. 3 (March 2010): 1103–22.

65. Marler, "Removing the Confederate Monuments."

66. Klein, "Bryan Stevenson Explains How It Feels," para. 21.

67. Klein, "Bryan Stevenson Explains How It Feels," para. 21.

68. Susan Neiman, *Learning from the Germans: Race and the Memory of Evil* (New York: Farrar, Straus and Giroux, 2019). For more on the stumbling stones, see Sam Mercadante, "Memory and Provocation: Munich's Memorial Stumbling Stones," Wiener Holocaust Library Blog, October 24, 2018, https://www.wienerlibrary.co.uk/Blog?item=350&returnoffset=20.

69. Nieman, *Learning from the Germans*.

70. Klein, "Bryan Stevenson Explains How It Feels," para. 22.

71. Kay Ivey (@kayiveyforgov), "We can't change or erase our history," Twitter, April 17, 2018, 9:00 p.m., https://twitter.com/kayiveyforgov/status/986243034311528449?lang=en; and Avery Anapol, "Alabama Governor Defends Confederate Monuments: We Don't Need 'Out-of-State Liberals' Telling Us What to Do," *The Hill*, April 17, 2018, https://thehill.com/homenews/state-watch/383616-alabama-governor-defends-confederate-monuments-we-dont-need-out-of-state.

72. Anapol, "Alabama Governor Defends Confederate Monuments," para. 8.

73. "NAACP Blasts Alabama Gov. Kay Ivey over Confederate Monument Ad," Al.com, April 19, 2018, updated March 7, 2019, https://www.al.com/news/2018/04/naacp_blasts_alabama_gov_kay_i.html.

74. Bob Wieland, quoted in Sam Levin, "Lynching Memorial Leaves Some Quietly Seething: 'Let Sleeping Dogs Lie,'" *The Guardian*, April 28, 2018, para. 8, https://www.theguardian.com/us-news/2018/apr/28/lynching-memorial-backlash-montgomery-alabama.

75. Levin, "Lynching Memorial Leaves Some Quietly Seething," para. 8.

76. Levin, "Lynching Memorial Leaves Some Quietly Seething," para. 9.

77. Levin, "Lynching Memorial Leaves Some Quietly Seething," para. 10.

78. Tommy Rhodes, quoted in Levin, "Lynching Memorial Leaves Some Quietly Seething," para. 10.

79. Randall Hughey, quoted in Levin, "Lynching Memorial Leaves Some Quietly Seething," paras. 11–12.

80. Jim Massey, quoted in Levin, "Lynching Memorial Leaves Some Quietly Seething," para. 15.

81. Jessica Reed, Jamiles Lartey, Ed Pilkington, Sam Levin, John Mulholland, and Tom Silverstone, "America's First Memorial to Victims of Lynching Opens in Alabama: Live Updates," *The Guardian*, April 26, 2018, updated November 15, 2019, https://www.the guardian.com/us-news/live/2018/apr/26/americas-first-memorial-to-lynching-victims-opens-in-alabama-live-updates?page=with:block-5ae252bae4b05b151652aa76#block-5ae252bae4b05b151652aa76.

82. Brian Major, quoted in Beth J. Harpaz, "Lynching Memorial May Be Game-Changer for Montgomery Tourism," Associated Press, May 17, 2018, para. 6, https://apnews.com/1603c370733140bba371032a60a5e858/Lynching-memorial-may-be-game-changer-for-Montgomery-tourism/.

83. Harpaz, "Lynching Memorial May Be Game-Changer," para. 6.

84. Harpaz, "Lynching Memorial May Be Game-Changer," para. 6.

85. Margaret Renkl, "A Museum That Makes White Liberals See the Horror of White Supremacy," *New York Times*, June 25, 2018, https://www.nytimes.com/2018/06/25/opinion/legacy-museum-white-supremacy-lynchings.html.

86. Stiem, "Statue Wars."

87. Nicholas Mirzoeff, "The Right to Look," *Critical Inquiry* 37, no. 3 (Spring 2011): 473–96, https://doi.org/10.1086/659354.

88. Beth Hinderliter, William Kaizen, Vered Maimon, Jaleh Mansoor, and Seth McCormick, eds., *Communities of Sense: Rethinking Aesthetics and Politics* (Durham, NC: Duke University Press, 2009).

89. Doria Johnson, quoted in Jeffrey Collins, "Lynching Memorial Rises Near Revered Confederate Sites," Associated Press, October 21, 2016, para. 8, https://www.apnews.com/215b3508fdf9410382a5e76d6793f6f1.

90. Robert Hayes, quoted in Collins, "Lynching Memorial Rises," para. 22.

91. Robert Hayes, quoted in Collins, "Lynching Memorial Rises," para. 22.

92. Robert Hayes, quoted in Collins, "Lynching Memorial Rises," para. 22.

CHAPTER 7

1. Jean Song, "Alabama Lynching Memorial Aims to Confront Ramifications of Slavery," CBS News, August 16, 2016, para. 2, https://www.cbsnews.com/news/alabama-lynching-memorial-slavery-history-museum-equal-justice-initiative/.

2. The Equal Justice Initiative was formed in 1993 by African American public interest lawyers.

3. In order to publicize the opening of the National Memorial for Peace and Justice, the EJI orchestrated conferences, panel presentations, and visits from well-known politicians, civic leaders, musicians, and others who helped with the inaugural ceremony.

4. Bryan Stevenson, quoted in Patrick Sisson, "New Memorial for Lynching Victims Reaches for Truth and Reconciliation," *Curbed*, April 24, 2018, para. 27, https://www.curbed.com/2018/4/24/17275094/montgomery-slavery-lynching-museum-eji.

5. Ernie Suggs and Rosalind Bentley, "New Memorial in Montgomery Recalls Killings of 5,000," *Atlanta Journal-Constitution*, May 6, 2018, https://www.ajc.com/news/local/mary-turner-lynching-savage-horrific-but-not-uncommon/W81Pe1p5i6tqsftJ8otKyO/.

6. Suggs and Bentley, "New Memorial in Montgomery," para. 13.

7. Michael Middleton, Aaron Hess, Danielle Endres, and Samantha Senda-Cook, *Participatory Critical Rhetoric: Theoretical and Methodological Foundations for Studying Rhetoric in Situ* (Lanham, MD: Lexington Books, 2015).

8. For examples of rhetorical analysis that takes into account some of the influences of postmodern thinking on memorialization practices, see Carole Blair, Marsha S. Jeppeson, and Enrico Pucci Jr., "Public Memorializing in Postmodernity: The Vietnam Veterans Memorial as Prototype," *Quarterly Journal of Speech* 77, no. 3 (1991): 263–88; and Carole Blair and Neil Michel, "Reproducing Civil Rights Tactics: The Rhetorical Performances of the Civil Rights Memorial," *Rhetoric Society Quarterly* 30, no. 2 (Spring 2000): 31–55.

9. Michael Warner, "Publics and Counterpublics," *Public Culture* 14, no. 1 (Winter 2002): 49–90.

10. See Cristin Ellis, *Antebellum Posthuman: Race and Materiality in the Mid-Nineteenth Century* (New York: Fordham University Press, 2018).

11. John Lennon and Malcolm Foley, *Dark Tourism: The Attraction of Death and Disaster* (San Francisco: Cengage Learning EMEA, 2000).

12. For more on pilgrimages, see Marouf Hasian Jr., "Remembering and Forgetting the 'Final Solution': A Rhetorical Pilgrimage through the US Holocaust Memorial Museum," *Critical Studies in Media Communication* 21, no. 1 (2004): 64–92.

13. For other lynching studies applying Pierre Nora's work on these sites of memory, see Leigh Raiford, "Photography and the Practices of Critical Black Memory," *History and Theory* 48, no. 4 (December 2009): 112–29.

14. Equal Justice Initiative, *The National Memorial for Peace and Justice* (Montgomery, AL: Equal Justice Initiative, 2018).

15. Erica Ayisi, "Lynching Memorial: Ghanaian Artist Hopes Sculpture Captures Shared Pain between African Americans and the Motherland," *The Root*, May 7, 2018, para. 28, https://www.theroot.com/lynching-memorial-ghanian-artist-hopes-sculpture-captu-1825817044.

16. "Masud Olufani Responds to Montgomery's National Memorial for Peace and Justice," *Burnaway: The Voice of Art in the South*, May 22, 2018, para. 3, https://burnaway.org/feature/masud-olufani-montgomerys-national-memorial-peace-justice/.

17. Kennicott, "A Powerful Memorial in Montgomery," para. 2.

18. Brundage, *Lynching in the New South*.

19. Young, "The Black Body as Souvenir," 640.

20. Nia-Malika Henderson, "This New Lynching Memorial Rewrites American History," CNN Travel, April 26, 2018, paras. 20–21, https://www.cnn.com/travel/article/lynching-memorial-montgomery-alabama/index.html.

21. Kimber Williams, "Journey toward Justice: Confronting America's Legacy of Slavery and Lynching Prepares Students to Lead Communities on the Road to Racial

Reconciliation," Emory News Center, Emory University, December 14, 2018, para. 55, https://news.emory.edu/features/2018/12/journey-toward-justice/index.html.

22. Jesse Wegman, "At This Memorial, the Monuments Bleed," *New York Times*, April 25, 2018, para. 15, https://www.nytimes.com/2018/04/25/opinion/alabama-lynching-memorial.html.

23. Sisson, "New Memorial for Lynching Victims."

24. Kennicott, "A Powerful Memorial in Montgomery," para. 6.

25. Ari Y. Kelman, "At the National Memorial for Peace and Justice in Alabama, a Lesson in Memory and Responsibility," *Tablet*, May 1, 2018, para. 1, https://www.tabletmag.com/scroll/260961/at-the-national-memorial-for-peace-and-justice-in-alabama-a-lesson-in-memory-and-responsibility.

26. Bradford Vivian, "Witnessing Time: Rhetorical Form, Public Culture, and Popular Historical Education," *Rhetoric Society Quarterly* 44, no. 3 (2014): 204–19.

27. Friedrich Nietzsche, *The Anti-Christ* (1895; New York: SoHo Books, 2013).

28. Andrew J. Yawn, "Path of Reconciliation: A Walk through the Nation's First Lynching Memorial," *Montgomery Advertiser*, April 23, 2018, para. 5, https://www.montgomeryadvertiser.com/story/news/2018/04/23/reconciliation-walk-through-nations-first-lynching-memorial-eji-peace-justice-memorial-montgomery/544474002/.

29. Robertson, "A Lynching Memorial Is Opening," para. 4.

30. Jonathan Capehart, "The Lynching Memorial Ends Our National Silence on Racial Terrorism," *Washington Post*, April 26, 2018, para. 19, https://www.washingtonpost.com/blogs/post-partisan/wp/2018/04/26/the-lynching-memorial-ends-our-national-silence-on-racial-terrorism/. Italics added to emphasize the difference in this reading from our own. While Capehart assumes that the visitor is the one in a position of judgment as "the inverse" of the lynched, the visitor, to us, becomes the victim and the one who is subject to judgment from the monuments-made-spectators. This, we feel, is the memorial's way, at least in part, of performing "justice."

31. Williams, "Journey toward Justice," para. 58.

32. Williams, "Journey toward Justice," para. 56.

33. Capehart, "The Lynching Memorial Ends Our National Silence," para. 20.

34. Tia Mitchell, "DeKalb County to Acknowledge Lynchings through Historical Marker," *Atlanta Journal-Constitution*, January 22, 2019, para. 1, https://www.ajc.com/news/local-govt—politics/dekalb-county-acknowledge-lynchings-through-historical-marker/I9YG2Jno8Jhqu41aEdSorO/.

35. Gilles Deleuze and Félix Guattari, *A Thousand Plateaus: Capitalism and Schizophrenia*, trans. Brian Massumi (Minneapolis: University of Minnesota Press, 1987).

36. Yawn, "Path of Reconciliation," para. 19.

37. Kennicott, "A Powerful Memorial in Montgomery," para. 10.

38. For more on the rhetoricity of place, see Endres and Senda-Cook, "Location Matters."

39. Mike Cason, "Memorial to Lynching Victims Could Be Coming to Birmingham's Linn Park," AL.com, November 29, 2018, updated November 30, 2018, para. 10, https://www.al.com/news/2018/11/jefferson-county-group-aims-to-memorialize-victims-of-lynching.html.

40. "Duluth Lynchings," Minnesota Historical Society, n.d., https://www.mnhs.org/duluthlynchings/lynchings.php.

41. Monica Davey, "Letter from Duluth: It Did Happen Here; The Lynching That a City Forgot," *New York Times*, December 4, 2003, https://www.nytimes.com/2003/12/04/us/letter-from-duluth-it-did-happen-here-the-lynching-that-a-city-forgot.html.

42. Warren Read, *The Lyncher in Me: A Search for Redemption in the Face of History* (Saint Paul: Minnesota Historical Society Press, 2008).

43. Read, *The Lyncher in Me*.

44. Brady Slater, "Bus to Montgomery: Duluth Contingent Set for Historic Trip to Lynching Memorial," *Duluth News Tribune*, April 23, 2018, para. 4, https://www.duluthnewstribune.com/news/education/4435837-bus-montgomery-duluth-contingent-set-historic-trip-lynching-memorial. See also Tom Weber, "Duluth to Montgomery: Lynching Memorial 'Overwhelming,'" Minnesota Public Radio News, May 21, 2018, https://www.mprnews.org/story/2018/05/08/lynching_memorial_museum_montgomery_alabama_duluth_minnesota_eji_equal_justice_initiative.

45. Brady Slater, "'Overwhelming in a Good Way': Duluth Delegation Visits Lynching Memorial," *Duluth News Tribune*, April 28, 2018, para. 18, https://www.duluthnewstribune.com/news/education/4437548-overwhelming-good-way-duluth-delegation-visits-lynching-memorial.

46. P. R. Lockhart, "After More Than 200 Attempts, the Senate Has Finally Passed Anti-Lynching Legislation," *Vox*, December 21, 2018, para. 30, https://www.vox.com/identities/2018/12/21/18151805/senate-lynching-legislation-hate-crimes-booker-harris-scott.

47. Lockhart, "After More Than 200 Attempts."

48. See, e.g., Blair and Michel, "Reproducing Civil Rights Tactics."

49. Stoler, *Along the Archival Grain*.

50. Middleton et al., *Participatory Critical Rhetoric*.

51. Blair et al., "Public Memorializing in Postmodernity."

52. Terry Gross, "Comic Roy Wood Jr. Taps into America's Psyche on 'The Daily Show,'" National Public Radio, January 25, 2019, https://www.npr.org/2019/01/25/688680573/comic-roy-wood-jr-taps-into-americas-psyche-on-the-daily-show.

53. Brent Staples, "Traveling While Black: The Green Book's Black History; Lessons from the Jim Crow–Era Travel Guide for African-American Elites," *New York Times*, January 25, 2019, https://www.nytimes.com/2019/01/25/opinion/green-book-black-travel.html?action=click&module=Opinion&pgtype=Homepage.

54. For more on the cultural and rhetorical roles of forgetting in public memory, see Bradford Vivian's eloquent book, *Public Forgetting: The Rhetoric and Politics of Beginning Again* (University Park: Pennsylvania State University Press, 2010).

55. Dana King, "Guided by Justice," Dana King Art, January 29, 2019, para. 1, https://danakingart.com/#/guided-by-justice/.

56. Kerr Houston, "Recasting the Past: Hank Willis Thomas in South Africa," BmoreArt, July 10, 2014, para. 10, http://www.bmoreart.com/2014/07/recasting-the-past-hank-willis-thomas-in-south-africa.html.

57. Robertson, "A Lynching Memorial Is Opening."

58. Some of these counterpoints have to do with the continuous task of putting up markers at once-forgotten lynching sites in some of those 805 counties. See Brad Harper, "One Year Later, EJI Plans New Sites after Launching Memorial to Lynching Victims," *Montgomery Advertiser*, April 26, 2019, updated November 6, 2019, https://www.montgomeryadvertiser.com/story/news/2019/04/26/eji-plans-new-sites-year-after-launching-memorial-lynching-victims/3542053002/.

59. Kendall R. Phillips, ed., *Framing Public Memory* (Tuscaloosa: University of Alabama Press, 2004).

60. Judith Butler, *Precarious Life: The Powers of Mourning and Violence* (New York: Verso, 2006).

CHAPTER 8

1. Kennicott, "A Powerful Memorial in Montgomery."

2. Paul Kersey, "New Lynching Memorial Celebrates White Guilt," *Unz Review*, May 7, 2018, para. 2, https://www.unz.com/article/new-lynching-memorial-celebrates-white-guilt/.

3. Kersey, "New Lynching Memorial Celebrates White Guilt," para. 10.

4. "The Biggest Lie in the White Supremacist Propaganda Playbook: Unraveling the Truth about 'Black-on-White Crime,'" Southern Poverty Law Center, June 14, 2018, https://www.splcenter.org/20180614/biggest-lie-white-supremacist-propaganda-playbook-unraveling-truth-about-%E2%80%98black-white-crime.

5. Levin, "Lynching Memorial Leaves Some Quietly Seething," para. 4.

6. Levin, "Lynching Memorial Leaves Some Quietly Seething."

7. In "Nietzsche, Genealogy, History," Foucault writes: "[H]istory becomes 'effective' to the degree that it introduces discontinuity into our very being—as it divides our emotions, dramatizes our instincts, multiplies our body and sets it against itself. 'Effective' history deprives the self of the reassuring stability of life and nature, and will not permit itself to be transported by a voiceless obstinacy toward a millennial ending. . . . This is because knowledge is not made for understanding; it is made for cutting." Foucault, "Nietzsche, Genealogy, History," 360.

8. On the constant archival cycles of building and ruination, see Ann Laura Stoler, ed., *Imperial Debris: On Ruins and Ruination* (Durham, NC: Duke University Press, 2013).

9. Young, "The Counter-Monument."

10. Peters, *Speaking into the Air*, 3.

11. For earlier references to this "African American Holocaust," see Robert Eaglestone, "'You Would Not Add to My Suffering if You Knew What I Have Seen': Holocaust Testimony and Contemporary African Trauma Literature," *Studies in the Novel* 40, nos. 1–2 (Summer 2008): 72–85.

12. Space limitations prevent us from going into the international dimensions of questions regarding slave trade reparations, but at the present time many former subjects of colonial empires are also seeking reparations for colonial and imperial slave trade abuses. For a short discussion of some of these global issues, see Kris Manjapra, "When Will Britain Face Up to Its Crimes against Humanity?," *The Guardian*, March 29, 2018, https://www.theguardian.com/news/2018/mar/29/slavery-abolition-compensation-when-will-britain-face-up-to-its-crimes-against-humanity.

13. Pilkington, "The Sadism of White Men."

14. For more on the importance of place for social critiques, see Endres and Senda-Cook, "Location Matters."

15. Eyal Weizman, *Forensic Architecture: Violence at the Threshold of Detectability* (New York: Zone Books, 2017).

16. Allyson Hobbs and Nell Freudenberger, "A Visit to Montgomery's Legacy Museum," *New Yorker*, July 17, 2018, para. 5, https://www.newyorker.com/culture/personal-history/a-visit-to-montgomerys-legacy-museum.

17. For an overview of the use of eugenical and Social Darwinian arguments during the interwar years, see Hasian, *The Rhetoric of Eugenics*.

18. See, for example, Samantha Raphelson, "Lynching Memorial in Alabama Remembers the Victims of Unacknowledged Terror," National Public Radio, April 26, 2018, https://www.npr.org/2018/04/26/605736519/lynching-memorial-in-alabama-remembers-the-victims-of-unacknowledged-terror.

19. Equal Justice Initiative, *The Legacy Museum: From Enslavement to Mass Incarceration* (Montgomery, AL: Equal Justice Initiative, 2018), 2.

20. Mike Cason, "Memorial, Museum, Recount Terror of Lynching, Slavery's Legacies," AL.com, April 23, 2018, updated March 6, 2019, para. 13, https://www.al.com/news/index.ssf/2018/04/memorial_museum_tell_stories_0.html.

21. Erin Edgemon, "Construction Underway on Nation's First Lynching Memorial, Racial Justice Museum in Montgomery," AL.com, April 12, 2017, updated January 13, 2019, para. 2, https://www.al.com/news/montgomery/index.ssf/2017/04/construction_underway_on_racia.html.

22. For helpful critiques of some of this postracial thinking, see Darrel Enck-Wanzer, "Barack Obama, the Tea Party, and the Threat of Race: On Racial Neoliberalism and Born Again Racism," *Communication, Culture and Critique* 4, no. 1 (March 2011): 23–30, https://doi.org/10.1111/j.1753-9137.2010.01090.x; Kent A. Ono, "Postracism: A Theory of the 'Post-' as Political Strategy," *Journal of Communication Inquiry* 34, no. 3 (2010): 227–33; and Bradley Jones and Roopali Mukherjee, "From California to Michigan: Race, Rationality, and Neoliberal Governmentality," *Communication and Critical/Cultural Studies* 7, no. 4 (2010): 401–22, https://doi.org/10.1080/14791420.2010.523431.

23. Rothberg, *Multidirectional Memory*.

24. Feldblum, "In Montgomery, a Harrowing, Beautiful Reckoning," para. 10.

25. Kriston Capps, "Hanged, Burned, Shot, Drowned, Beaten," *Atlantic*, November 2017, https://www.theatlantic.com/magazine/archive/2017/11/a-national-monument-to-americas-known-victims-of-lynching/540663/.

26. Again, we note that such journalistic mentions of these other genocidal sites of memory can take place without any weighing or comparative evaluation of the uniqueness of either slave genocides or the World War II Holocaust.

27. Bryan Stevenson, quoted in Speri, "I Don't Think We're Free in America," para. 6.

28. Speri, "I Don't Think We're Free in America," paras. 6–7.

29. Speri, "I Don't Think We're Free in America," para. 7.

30. Capehart, "How the Terror of Lynchings," para. 13.

31. Speri, "I Don't Think We're Free in America," para. 8.

32. Speri, "I Don't Think We're Free in America," paras. 8–10.
33. Bunn, "Death Row Lawyer Bryan Stevenson," para. 1.
34. Yawn, "Path of Reconciliation."
35. Comments after Reed et al., "America's First Memorial to Victims of Lynching."
36. Andrew Yawn, "EJI Lynching Memorial: A Place of Healing in the Heart of Dixie," *Montgomery Advertiser*, April 27, 2018, updated January 20, 2019, para. 31, https://www.montgomeryadvertiser.com/story/news/local/lynchinglegacy/2018/04/27/how-ejis-lynching-memorial-heal-legacy-trauma-montgomery-peace-justice-equal-initiative/552798002/.
37. Capehart, "How the Terror of Lynchings," para. 16.

CONCLUSION

1. Michelle Alexander, *The New Jim Crow: Mass Incarceration in the Age of Colorblindness* (New York: New Press, 2010).
2. Stevenson, *Just Mercy*.
3. Maya Angelou, quoted in Todd Strange, "Mayor Strange: Memorial to Lynching Victims Looks to Nation's Past, and Its Future," *Montgomery Advertiser*, April 25, 2018, para. 5, https://www.montgomeryadvertiser.com/story/opinion/columnists/2018/04/25/mayor-strange-memorial-lynching-victims-looks-nations-past-and-its-future/550645002/.
4. For more on various commemorative efforts to remember Ida B. Wells-Barnett since 1970, see Roessner, "Constructing Monuments," 107–28.
5. For an example of someone else who suggests that we read against the grain of some lynching historical representations, see Kirsten M. Lew, "From Social Problems to Maternal Melodrama: The Lost Lynching Scene in John M. Stahl's *Imitation of Life*," *Film History* 30, no. 4 (Winter 2018): 107–26.
6. William D. Carrigan and Clive Webb, "When Americans Lynched Mexicans," *New York Times*, February 20, 2015, https://www.nytimes.com/2015/02/20/opinion/when-americans-lynched-mexicans.html.
7. See Beth Lew-Williams, *The Chinese Must Go: Violence, Exclusion, and the Making of the Alien in America* (Cambridge, MA: Harvard University Press, 2018).
8. Jeffrey Melnick, *Black-Jewish Relations on Trial: Leo Frank and Jim Conley in the New South* (Jackson: University Press of Mississippi, 2000).
9. Research is ongoing about whether a person's white status protected them from some lynchings. See David Rigby and Charles Seguin, "The Racial Position of European Immigrants 1883–1941: Evidence from Lynching in the Midwest," *Social Currents* 5, no. 5 (2018): 438–57.
10. For an argument that closely resembles the EJI's, see Megan Saad, "Mass Incarceration as a Contemporary Racial Project in North America and Its Stratification across Racialized and Gendered Lines," *Prandium* 1, no. 1 (Fall 2017): 1–11.
11. Jay Reeves, "Emmett Till Inquiry Continues; 6 Other 'Cold Cases' Closed," *Clarion-Ledger*, September 25, 2019, https://www.clarionledger.com/story/news/2019/09/25/emmett-till-inquiry-continues-6-other-cold-cases-closed/2438529001/.
12. Kim Chandler, "Fed's Report Condemning Alabama Prisons: State Vows Action," WBHM, April 8, 2019, paras. 1–2, https://wbhm.org/2019/feds-report-condemning-alabama-prisons-state-vows-action/.

13. Bryan Stevenson, quoted in Chandler, "Fed's Report Condemning Alabama Prisons," paras. 18–20. See also "Alabama Prison Conditions Remain Unchanged Weeks after Prison Murders," Equal Justice Initiative, April 1, 2019, https://eji.org/news/alabama-prison-conditions-unchanged-after-prison-murders/.

14. Erin Killeen, "The Increased Criminalization of African American Girls," *Georgetown Law*, April 17, 2019, https://www.law.georgetown.edu/poverty-journal/blog/the-increased-criminalization-of-african-american-girls/.

15. Nicole Goodkind, "Texas Confederate Monuments Debate Invokes Talk of Statues of Lynching, Tearing Down Auschwitz," *Newsweek*, April 10, 2019, https://www.newsweek.com/texas-confederate-monuments-lynching-auschwitz-1392438.

16. Jarvis Johnson, quoted in Goodkind, "Texas Confederate Monuments Debate," para. 3.

17. Dawn Marie D. McIntosh, Dreama G. Moon, and Thomas K. Nakayama, eds., *Interrogating the Communicative Power of Whiteness* (New York: Routledge, 2019).

18. For more on those possessory investments in whiteness, see Angela P. Harris, "Race and Essentialism in Feminist Legal Theory," *Stanford Law Review* 42, no. 3 (February 1990): 581–616; and George Lipsitz, "The Possessive Investment in Whiteness: Racialized Social Democracy and the 'White' Problem in American Studies," *American Quarterly* 47, no. 3 (September 1995): 369–87.

19. Bryan Stevenson discussed some of this culpability in an interview he gave before the opening of the Lynching Memorial; see Bunn, "Death Row Lawyer Bryan Stevenson."

20. There is evidence that members of America's executive branch have been aware of the arguments that are circulating regarding this "new Jim Crow." See Peniel E. Joseph, "Obama Is Chipping Away at the 'New Jim Crow,' but More Needs to Be Done," *The Guardian*, April 27, 2016, https://www.theguardian.com/commentisfree/2016/apr/27/barack-obama-new-jim-crow-progress-mass-incarceration.

21. Strange, "Mayor Strange: Memorial to Lynching Victims," para. 3.

22. Strange, "Mayor Strange: Memorial to Lynching Victims," para. 3.

23. See, for example, Cutler, *Lynch-Law*.

24. W. Fitzhugh Brundage, "Conclusion: Reflections on Lynching Scholarship," *American Nineteenth Century History* 6, no. 3 (September 2005): 408, https://doi.org/10.1080/14664650500381116.

25. Stevenson, *Just Mercy*.

26. For earlier usages of this flag in 2016, see Jenni Avins, "The NAACP's 'A Man Was Lynched Yesterday' Flag Has Been Reprised and Hangs in New York City," *Quartz*, July 10, 2016, https://qz.com/727602/the-naacps-a-man-was-lynched-yesterday-flag-has-been-reprised-and-hangs-in-new-york-city/.

27. Zak Cheney-Rice, "Bryan Stevenson on His 'Not Entirely Rational' Quest for Justice," *New York Magazine*, June 25, 2019, para. 9, http://nymag.com/intelligencer/2019/06/bryan-stevensons-not-entirely-rational-quest-for-justice.html.

28. For examples of how even prison inmates are aware of Stevenson's discussions of stonecatchers, see Fiona Koefoed-Jespersen, "Stone-Catcher," Prison Fellowship, September 18, 2019, https://prisonfellowship.org.uk/prisoner-story/stone-catcher/.

29. See David Paulsen, "Pilgrimage Connects Racism to America's Core, Focusing Executive Council's Work for Change," Episcopal News Service, October 21, 2019, https://

www.episcopalnewsservice.org/2019/10/21/pilgrimage-connects-racism-to-americas-core-focusing-executive-councils-work-for-change/.

30. "True Justice: About the Film," Equal Justice Initiative, n.d., paras. 1–3, https://eji.org/projects/true-justice/.

31. "True Justice: About the Film," Equal Justice Initiative, para. 3.

32. See the exchange between Oprah Winfrey and Bryan Stevenson, quoted in Toni Johnson, "Bryan Stevenson and the Memorial to Victims of Lynching," Art for Justice Fund, April 30, 2018, paras. 4–10, https://artforjusticefund.org/inside-the-memorial-to-victims-of-lynching/.

33. Johnson, "Bryan Stevenson and the Memorial," paras. 4–10.

34. J. Baxter Oliphant, "Public Support for the Death Penalty Ticks Up," Pew Research Center, June 11, 2018, http://www.pewresearch.org/fact-tank/2018/06/11/us-support-for-death-penalty-ticks-up-2018/.

35. James Forman Jr., *Locking Up Our Own: Crime and Punishment in Black America* (New York: Farrar, Straus and Giroux, 2017).

36. Kerr, "How to End Mass Imprisonment."

37. Donna M. Owens, "Inspiration behind 'Just Mercy' Hopes Film 'Motivates' Viewers 'to Get Involved' in Criminal Justice System," *Essence*, January 13, 2020, https://www.essence.com/entertainment/only-essence/bryan-stevenson-just-mercy/.

38. See Evelyn M. Simien, "Lynching Memorial Shows Women Were Victims, Too," *The Conversation*, April 24, 2018, https://theconversation.com/lynching-memorial-shows-women-were-victims-too-95029.

BIBLIOGRAPHY

BOOKS

Agamben, Giorgio. *Homo Sacer: Sovereign Power and Bare Life.* Translated by Daniel Heller-Roazen. Stanford, CA: Stanford University Press, 1998.

Alexander, Michelle. *The New Jim Crow: Mass Incarceration in the Age of Colorblindness.* New York: New Press, 2010.

Allen, James S. *Organizing in the Depression South: A Communist's Memoir.* Minneapolis: MEP Publications, 2001.

Allen, James, Hilton Als, John Lewis, and Leon F. Litwack. *Without Sanctuary: Lynching Photography in America.* Santa Fe: Twin Palms Publishers, 2000.

Ames, Jessie Daniel. *The Changing Character of Lynching, 1931-1941.* 1942. Reprint, New York: Abraham's Magazine Service Press, 1973.

Armstrong, Julie Buckner. *Mary Turner and the Memory of Lynching.* Athens: University of Georgia Press, 2011.

Ash, Stephen V. *A Massacre in Memphis: The Race Riot That Shook the Nation.* New York: Hill and Wang, 2013.

Ayers, Edward L. *The Promise of the New South: Life after Reconstruction.* New York: Oxford University Press, 1992.

Baker, Lee D. *From Negro to Savage: Anthropology and the Construction of Race, 1896-1954.* Berkeley: University of California Press, 1998.

Baker, Ray Stannard. *Following the Color Line: An Account of Negro Citizenship in the American Democracy.* New York: Doubleday, Page and Company, 1908.

Bancroft, Hubert H. *Popular Tribunals.* San Francisco: History Company, 1887.

Barthes, Roland. *Camera Lucida: Reflections on Photography.* New York: Macmillan, 1981.

Bay, Mia. *To Tell the Truth Freely: The Life of Ida B. Wells.* New York: Hill and Wang, 2009.

Bell, Derrick. *And We Are Not Saved: The Elusive Quest for Racial Justice.* New York: Basic Books, 1987.

Benjamin, Walter. *Illuminations: Essays and Reflections.* Edited by Hannah Arendt. New York: Schocken Books, 1969.

Berg, Manfred. *Popular Justice: A History of Lynching in America.* Lanham, MD: Rowman and Littlefield, 2011.

Blaustein, Albert, and Robert L. Zangrando. *Civil Rights and African Americans: A Documentary History.* Evanston, IL: Northwestern University Press, 1991.

Blee, Kathleen M. *Women of the Klan: Racism and Gender in the 1920s.* Berkeley: University of California Press, 1991.

Brantlinger, Patrick. *Dark Vanishings: Discourse on the Extinction of Primitive Races, 1800-1930.* Ithaca, NY: Cornell University Press, 2003.

Brundage, W. Fitzhugh. *Lynching in the New South: Georgia and Virginia, 1880–1930*. Urbana: University of Illinois Press, 1993.

Brundage, W. Fitzhugh, ed. *Under Sentence of Death: Lynching in the South*. Chapel Hill: University of North Carolina Press, 1997.

Butler, Judith. *Precarious Life: The Powers of Mourning and Violence*. New York: Verso, 2006.

Capeci, Dominic J., Jr. *The Lynching of Cleo Wright*. Lexington: University Press of Kentucky, 1998.

Carter, Dan T. *Scottsboro: A Tragedy of the American South*. Baton Rouge: Louisiana State University Press, 1969.

Chadbourn, James Harmon. *Lynching and the Law*. Chapel Hill: University of North Carolina Press, 1933.

Chalmers, David M. *Hooded Americanism: The First Century of the Ku Klux Klan, 1865–1965*. New York: Doubleday, 1965.

Clymer, Jeffory A. *America's Culture of Terrorism: Violence, Capitalism, and the Written Word*. Chapel Hill: University of North Carolina Press, 2003.

Condit, Celeste Michelle, and John Louis Lucaites. *Crafting Equality: America's Anglo-African Word*. Chicago: University of Chicago Press, 1993.

Cutler, James Elbert. *Lynch-Law: An Investigation into the History of Lynching in the United States*. 1905. Reprint, Montclair, NJ: Negro Universities Press, 1969.

Daniel, Pete. *The Shadow of Slavery: Peonage in the South, 1901–1969*. Urbana: University of Illinois Press, 1972.

Daniels, Josephus. *Editor in Politics*. Chapel Hill: University of North Carolina Press, 1941.

Deleuze, Gilles, and Félix Guattari. *A Thousand Plateaus: Capitalism and Schizophrenia*. Translated by Brian Massumi. Minneapolis: University of Minnesota Press, 1987.

Drake, St. Clair, and Horace R. Cayton. *Black Metropolis: A Study of Negro Life in the Northern City*. New York: Harcourt, Brace and Company, 1945.

Dray, Philip. *At the Hands of Parties Unknown: The Lynching of Black America*. New York: Crown, 2006.

Du Bois, W. E. B. *Writings by W. E. B. Du Bois in Periodicals Edited by Others*. Edited by Herbert Aptheker. 2 vols. Millwood, NY: Kraus-Thomson, 1982.

Earley, Pete. *Circumstantial Evidence: Death, Life, and Justice in a Southern Town*. New York: Random House, 1995.

Ellis, Cristin. *Antebellum Posthuman: Race and Materiality in the Mid-Nineteenth Century*. New York: Fordham University Press, 2018.

Emberton, Carole. *Beyond Redemption: Race, Violence, and the American South after the Civil War*. Chicago: University of Chicago Press, 2013.

Eng, David L., and David Kazanjian, eds. *Loss: The Politics of Mourning*. Berkeley: University of California Press, 2003.

Equal Justice Initiative. *The Legacy Museum: From Enslavement to Mass Incarceration*. Montgomery, AL: Equal Justice Initiative, 2018.

Equal Justice Initiative. *Lynching in America: Confronting the Legacy of Racial Terror*. 2nd ed. Montgomery, AL: Equal Justice Initiative, 2015.

Equal Justice Initiative. *Lynching in America: Confronting the Legacy of Racial Terror*. 3rd ed. Montgomery, AL: Equal Justice Initiative, 2017.

Equal Justice Initiative. *The National Memorial for Peace and Justice*. Montgomery, AL: Equal Justice Initiative, 2018.

Eyerman, Ron. *Cultural Trauma: Slavery and the Formation of African American Identity*. Cambridge: Cambridge University Press, 2001.

Ferrell, Claudine L. *Nightmare and Dream: Antilynching in Congress, 1917–1922*. New York: Garland, 1986.

Foner, Eric. *Reconstruction: America's Unfinished Revolution, 1863–1877*. New York: HarperCollins, 1988.

Foote, Kenneth E. *Shadowed Ground: America's Landscapes of Violence and Tragedy*. Austin: University of Texas Press, 1997.

Forman, James, Jr. *Locking Up Our Own: Crime and Punishment in Black America*. New York: Farrar, Straus and Giroux, 2017.

Foucault, Michel. *Discipline and Punish: The Birth of the Prison*. Translated by Alan Sheridan. New York: Vintage Books, 2012.

Foucault, Michel. *Fearless Speech*. Edited by Joseph Pearson. Los Angeles: Semiotext(e), 2001.

Foucault, Michel. *The History of Sexuality*. Vol. 1, *An Introduction*. Translated by Robert Hurley. New York: Vintage Books, 1990.

Foucault, Michel. *The Order of Things: An Archaeology of the Human Sciences*. New York: Vintage Books, 1973.

Frampton, Mary Louise, Ian F. Haney-López, and Jonathan Simon, eds. *After the War on Crime: Race, Democracy, and a New Reconstruction*. New York: New York University Press, 2008.

Frankel, Noralee, and Nancy S. Dye, eds. *Gender, Class, Race, and Reform in the Progressive Era*. Lexington: University Press of Kentucky, 2001.

Giddings, Paula J. *Ida: A Sword among Lions; Ida B. Wells and the Campaign against Lynching*. New York: Amistad, 2008.

Goffman, Erving. *Stigma: Notes on the Management of Spoiled Identity*. New York: Simon and Schuster, 2009.

Hale, Grace Elizabeth. *Making Whiteness: The Culture of Segregation in the South, 1890–1940*. New York: Pantheon Books, 1998.

Hall, Jacqueline Dowd. *Revolt against Chivalry: Jessie Daniel Ames and the Women's Campaign against Lynching*. 1974. Reprint, New York: Columbia University Press, 1993.

Hasian, Marouf A., Jr. *The Rhetoric of Eugenics in Anglo-American Thought*. Athens: University of Georgia Press, 1996.

Hill, Rebecca N. *Men, Mobs, and Law: Anti-Lynching and Labor Defense in U.S. Radical History*. Durham, NC: Duke University Press, 2008.

Hinderliter, Beth, William Kaizen, Vered Maimon, Jaleh Mansoor, and Seth McCormick, eds. *Communities of Sense: Rethinking Aesthetics and Politics*. Durham, NC: Duke University Press, 2009.

Hirsch, Marianne. *The Generation of Postmemory: Writing and Visual Culture after the Holocaust*. New York: Columbia University Press, 2012.

Holmes, William F. *The White Chief: James Kimble Vardaman*. Baton Rouge: Louisiana State University Press, 1970.

Houck, Davis W., and Matthew A. Grindy. *Emmett Till and the Mississippi Press*. Jackson: University Press of Mississippi, 2008.

Ifill, Sherrilyn A. *On the Courthouse Lawn: Confronting the Legacy of Lynching in the Twenty-First Century*. Boston: Beacon Press, 2007.

Johnson, James Weldon. *Along This Way: The Autobiography of James Weldon Johnson*. New York: Viking Press, 1933.

Kelley, Robin D. G. *Hammer and Hoe: Alabama Communists during the Great Depression*. Chapel Hill: University of North Carolina Press, 1990.

Kirschke, Amy Helene. *Art in Crisis: W. E. B. Du Bois and the Struggle for African American Identity and Memory*. Bloomington: Indiana University Press, 2007.

Kluger, Richard. *Simple Justice: The History of* Brown v. Board of Education *and Black America's Struggle for Equality*. New York: Alfred A. Knopf, 1975.

Kramer, Paul A. *The Blood of Government: Race, Empire, the United States, and the Philippines*. Chapel Hill: University of North Carolina Press, 2006.

Larson, Edward J. *Sex, Race, and Science: Eugenics in the Deep South*. Baltimore: Johns Hopkins University Press, 1995.

Lennon, John, and Malcolm Foley. *Dark Tourism: The Attraction of Death and Disaster*. San Francisco: Cengage Learning EMEA, 2000.

Lew-Williams, Beth. *The Chinese Must Go: Violence, Exclusion, and the Making of the Alien in America*. Cambridge, MA: Harvard University Press, 2018.

Malkani, Bharat. *Slavery and the Death Penalty: A Study in Abolition*. Milton Park, Oxon, England: Routledge, 2018.

Markovitz, Jonathan. *Legacies of Lynching: Racial Violence and Memory*. Minneapolis: University of Minnesota Press, 2004.

McIntosh, Dawn Marie D., Dreama G. Moon, and Thomas K. Nakayama, eds. *Interrogating the Communicative Power of Whiteness*. New York: Routledge, 2019.

McMurry, Linda O. *Recorder of the Black Experience: A Biography of Monroe Nathan Work*. Baton Rouge: Louisiana State University Press, 1985.

McMurry, Linda O. *To Keep the Waters Troubled: The Life of Ida B. Wells*. New York: Oxford University Press, 1998.

McNeil, Genna Rae. *Groundwork: Charles Hamilton Houston and the Struggle for Civil Rights*. Philadelphia: University of Pennsylvania Press, 1983.

McWhorter, Ladelle. *Racism and Sexual Oppression in Anglo-America: A Genealogy*. Bloomington: Indiana University Press, 2009.

Melnick, Jeffrey. *Black-Jewish Relations on Trial: Leo Frank and Jim Conley in the New South*. Jackson: University Press of Mississippi, 2000.

Middleton, Michael, Aaron Hess, Danielle Endres, and Samantha Senda-Cook. *Participatory Critical Rhetoric: Theoretical and Methodological Foundations for Studying Rhetoric in Situ*. Lanham, MD: Lexington Books, 2015.

Murakawa, Naomi. *The First Civil Right: How Liberals Built Prison America*. New York: Oxford University Press, 2014.

NAACP. *Burning at the Stake in the United States, 1889–1918*. New York: National Association for the Advancement of Colored People, 1919.

NAACP. *Tenth Annual Report of the National Association for the Advancement of Colored People, for the Year 1919*. New York: National Association for the Advancement of Colored People, 1920.

NAACP. *Thirty Years of Lynching in the United States, 1889–1918*. New York: National Association for the Advancement of Colored People, 1919.
Naison, Mark. *Communists in Harlem during the Depression*. Urbana: University of Illinois Press, 1985.
Neiman, Susan. *Learning from the Germans: Race and the Memory of Evil*. New York: Farrar, Straus and Giroux, 2019.
Nelson Louis P., and Claudrena N. Harold. *Charlottesville 2017: The Legacy of Race and Inequity*. Charlottesville: University of Virginia Press, 2018.
Nietzsche, Friedrich. *The Anti-Christ*. 1895. Reprint, New York: SoHo Books, 2013.
Nietzsche, Friedrich. *Untimely Meditations*. Edited by Daniel Breazeale. Translated by R. J. Hollingdale. 1873. Reprint, Cambridge: Cambridge University Press, 2012.
Ore, Ersula. *Lynching: Violence, Rhetoric, and American Identity*. Jackson: University Press of Mississippi, 2019.
Page, Thomas Nelson. *In Ole Virginia*. New York: Charles Scribner's Sons, 1896.
Patterson, Orlando. *Rituals of Blood: Consequences of Slavery in Two American Centuries*. New York: Basic Civitas, 1998.
Peters, John Durham. *Speaking into the Air: A History of the Idea of Communication*. Chicago: University of Chicago Press, 1999.
Pfeffer, Paul. *A. Philip Randolph, Pioneer of the Civil Rights Movement*. Baton Rouge: Louisiana State University Press, 1990.
Pfeifer, Michael J. *The Roots of Rough Justice: Origins of American Lynching*. Urbana: University of Illinois Press, 2011.
Phillips, Kendall R., ed. *Framing Public Memory*. Tuscaloosa: University of Alabama Press, 2004.
Rabaka, Reiland. *Forms of Fanonism: Frantz Fanon's Critical Theory and the Dialectics of Decolonization*. Lanham, MD: Lexington Books, 2011.
Raiford, Leigh. *Imprisoned in a Luminous Glare: Photography and the African American Freedom Struggle*. Chapel Hill: University of North Carolina Press, 2011.
Raper, Arthur. *The Tragedy of Lynching*. Chapel Hill: University of North Carolina Press, 1933.
Read, Warren. *The Lyncher in Me: A Search for Redemption in the Face of History*. Saint Paul: Minnesota Historical Society Press, 2008.
Rice, Anne P., ed. *Witnessing Lynching: American Writers Respond*. New Brunswick, NJ: Rutgers University Press, 2003.
Ross, B. Joyce. *J. E. Spingarn and the Rise of the NAACP, 1911–1939*. New York: Atheneum, 1972.
Rothberg, Michael. *Multidirectional Memory: Remembering the Holocaust in the Age of Decolonization*. Stanford, CA: Stanford University Press, 2009.
Rushdy, Ashraf H. A. *American Lynching*. New Haven: Yale University Press, 2012.
Rushdy, Ashraf H. A. *The End of American Lynching*. New Brunswick, NJ: Rutgers University Press, 2012.
Savage, Kirk. *Monument Wars: Washington, D.C., the National Mall, and the Transformation of the Memorial Landscape*. Berkeley: University of California Press, 2009.
Schechter, Patricia Ann. *Ida B. Wells-Barnett and American Reform, 1880–1930*. Chapel Hill: University of North Carolina Press, 2001.

Schmitt, Carl. *Political Theology: Four Chapters on the Concept of Sovereignty.* Translated by George Schwab. Cambridge, MA: MIT Press, 1985.
Scott, James C. *Weapons of the Weak.* New Haven, CT: Yale University Press, 1985.
Shay, Frank. *Judge Lynch: His First Hundred Years.* New York: Washburn, 1938.
Smith, Lillian. *Killers of the Dream.* 1949. Reprint, New York: W. W. Norton, 1963.
Smith, Shawn Michelle. *Photography on the Color Line: W. E. B. Du Bois, Race, and Visual Culture.* Durham, NC: Duke University Press, 2004.
Sodaro, Amy. *Exhibiting Atrocity: Memorial Museums and the Politics of Past Violence.* New Brunswick, NJ: Rutgers University Press, 2018.
Sontag, Susan. *On Photography.* 1977. Reprint, New York: Macmillan, 2001.
Spencer, Hawes. *Summer of Hate: Charlottesville, USA.* Charlottesville: University of Virginia Press, 2018.
Squires, Catherine R. *The Post-Racial Mystique: Media and Race in the Twenty-First Century.* New York: New York University Press, 2014.
Sterling, Dorothy. *Black Foremothers: Three Lives.* New York: Feminist Press, 1988.
Stevenson, Bryan. *Just Mercy: A Story of Justice and Redemption.* New York: Spiegel and Grau, 2014.
Stoler, Ann Laura. *Along the Archival Grain: Epistemic Anxieties and Colonial Common Sense.* Princeton, NJ: Princeton University Press, 2010.
Stoler, Ann Laura, ed. *Imperial Debris: On Ruins and Ruination.* Durham, NC: Duke University Press, 2013.
Stoler, Ann Laura. *Race and the Education of Desire: Foucault's History of Sexuality and the Colonial Order of Things.* Durham, NC: Duke University Press, 1995.
Tell, Dave. *Remembering Emmett Till.* Chicago: University of Chicago Press, 2019.
TenBroek, Jacobus. *Equal Under Law.* Springfield, OH: Collier Books, 1969.
Tolnay, Stewart E., and E. M. Beck. *A Festival of Violence: An Analysis of Southern Lynchings, 1882–1930.* Urbana: University of Illinois Press, 1995.
Trelease, Allen. *White Terror: The Ku Klux Klan Conspiracy and Southern Reconstruction.* Baton Rouge: Louisiana State University Press, 1995.
Tushnet, Mark V. *The NAACP's Legal Strategy against Segregated Education, 1925–1950.* Chapel Hill: University of North Carolina Press, 1987.
US Congress. *Report of the Joint Select Committee to Inquire into the Condition of Affairs in the Late Insurrectionary States.* 13 vols. Washington, DC: Government Printing Office, 1872.
Vivian, Bradford. *Commonplace Witnessing: Rhetorical Invention, Historical Remembrance, and Public Culture.* New York: Oxford University Press, 2017.
Vivian, Bradford. *Public Forgetting: The Rhetoric and Politics of Beginning Again.* University Park: Pennsylvania State University Press, 2010.
Wagner, Bryan. *Disturbing the Peace: Black Culture and the Police Power after Slavery.* Cambridge, MA: Harvard University Press, 2009.
Waldrep, Christopher. *A History in Documents: Lynching in America.* New York: New York University Press, 2006.
Waldrep, Christopher. *The Many Faces of Judge Lynch: Extralegal Violence and Punishment in America.* New York: Palgrave Macmillan, 2002.

Waskow, Arthur I. *From Race Riot to Sit-In, 1919 and the 1960s: A Study in the Connections Between Conflict and Violence.* Garden City, NY: Anchor Books, 1967.
Weizman, Eyal. *Forensic Architecture: Violence at the Threshold of Detectability.* New York: Zone Books, 2017.
Wells, Ida B. *Crusade for Justice: The Autobiography of Ida B. Wells.* Edited by Alfreda M. Duster. Chicago: University of Chicago Press, 1970.
Wells, Ida B. *The Memphis Diary of Ida B. Wells: An Intimate Portrait of the Activist as a Young Woman.* Edited by Miriam Decosta-Willis. Boston: Beacon Press, 1995.
Wells, Ida B. *Southern Horrors and Other Writings: The Anti-Lynching Campaign of Ida B. Wells, 1892–1900,* edited by Jacqueline Jones Royster. New York: Bedford/St. Martin's, 1996.
Wells-Barnett, Ida B. *Lynch Law in Georgia.* Chicago: Chicago Colored Citizens, 1899.
Wells-Barnett, Ida B. *Mob Rule in New Orleans: Robert Charles and His Fight to Death, the Story of His Life, Burning Human Beings Alive, Other Lynching Statistics.* N.p.: n.p., 1900.
Wells-Barnett, Ida B. *On Lynchings.* New York: Arno Press, 1969.
Wells-Barnett, Ida B. *The Red Record: Tabulated Statistics and Alleged Causes of Lynching in the United States.* New York: Open Road, 1895.
White, Walter. *The Fire in the Flint.* New York: Alfred A. Knopf, 1924.
White, Walter. *A Man Called White: An Autobiography of Walter White.* 1948. Reprint, Athens: University of Georgia Press, 1995.
White, Walter. *Rope and Faggot: A Biography of Judge Lynch.* 1929. Reprint, New York: Arno Press, 1969.
Whitfield, Stephen. *A Death in the Delta: The Story of Emmett Till.* New York: Free Press, 1988.
Willard, Charles Arthur. *Argumentation and the Social Grounds of Knowledge.* Tuscaloosa: University of Alabama Press, 1983.
Williams, Kenneth. *Most Deserving of Death? An Analysis of the Supreme Court's Death Penalty Jurisprudence.* New York: Routledge, 2012.
Williams, Kidada E. *They Left Great Marks on Me: African American Testimonies of Racial Violence from Emancipation to World War I.* New York: New York University Press, 2012.
Wood, Amy Louise. *Lynching and Spectacle: Witnessing Racial Violence in America, 1890–1940.* Chapel Hill: University of North Carolina Press, 2009.
Zangrando, Robert L. *The NAACP Crusade against Lynching, 1909–1950.* Philadelphia: Temple University Press, 1980.

BOOK CHAPTERS

Denno Deborah W. "When Willie Francis Died: The 'Disturbing' Story behind One of the Eighth Amendment's Most Enduring Standards of Risk." In *Death Penalty Stories,* edited by John H. Blume and Jordan M. Steiker, 17–94. Eagan, MN: Foundation Press, 2009.
Douglass, Frederick. Preface to *The Red Record: Tabulated Statistics and Alleged Causes of Lynching in the United States,* by Ida B. Wells-Barnett. New York: Open Road, 1895.
Du Bois, W. E. B. *The Souls of Black Folk.* In *The Oxford W. E. B. Du Bois Reader.* Edited by Eric J. Sundquist, 97–240. 1903. Reprint, New York: Oxford University Press, 1996.
Du Bois, W. E. Burghardt. "The Talented Tenth." In *The Negro Problem,* edited by Booker T. Washington, 31–75. New York: Arno Press, 1969.

Foucault, Michel. "Nietzsche, Genealogy, History." In *The Essential Foucault: Selections from the Essential Works of Foucault, 1954–1984*. Edited by Paul Rabinow and Nikolas Rose, 350–69. New York: New Press, 2003.

Ghanim, Honaida. "Thanatopolitics: The Case of the Colonial Occupation in Palestine." In *Thinking Palestine*, edited by Ronit Lentin, 65–81. London: Zed Books, 2008.

hooks, bell. "The Oppositional Gaze: Black Female Spectators." In *Feminist Film Theory: A Reader*, edited by Sue Thornham, 307–19. New York: New York University Press, 1999.

Raiford, Leigh. "Ida B. Wells and the Shadow Archive." In *Pictures and Progress: Early Photography and the Making of African American Identity*, edited by Maurice O. Wallace and Shawn Michelle Smith, 299–320. Durham, NC: Duke University Press, 2012.

Roessner, Lori Amber. "Constructing Monuments to the Memory of Ida B. Wells-Barnett: Institutionalization of Reputation, Memory Distortion, and Cultural Amnesia." In *Political Pioneer of the Press: Ida B. Wells-Barnett and Her Transnational Crusade for Social Justice*, edited by Lori Amber Roessner and Jodi L. Rightler-McDaniels, 107–27. Lanham, MD: Lexington Books, 2018.

Royster, Jacqueline Jones. Preface to *Southern Horrors and Other Writings: The Anti-Lynching Campaign of Ida B. Wells, 1892–1900*, by Ida B. Wells, edited by Jacqueline Jones Royster, 2nd ed., vii–ix. Boston: Bedford/St. Martins, 2016.

Royster, Jacqueline Jones. "To Call a Thing by Its True Nature: The Rhetoric of Ida B. Wells." In *Reclaiming Rhetorica: Women in the Rhetorical Tradition*, edited by Andrea A. Lunsford, 167–84. Pittsburgh: University of Pittsburgh Press, 1995.

Thompson, Julius E. "Charles Hamilton Houston and the Struggle against Lynching in the United States, 1930–1939." In *Charles H. Houston: An Interdisciplinary Study of Civil Rights Leadership*, edited by James L. Conyers Jr., 195–202. Lanham, MD: Lexington Books, 2012.

JOURNAL ARTICLES

Abramson, Daniel. "Maya Lin and the 1960s: Monuments, Time Lines, and Minimalism." *Critical Inquiry* 22, no. 4 (Summer 1996): 679–709.

Ames, Jessie Daniel. "Editorial Treatment of Lynchings." *Public Opinion Quarterly* 2, no. 1 (January 1938): 77–84. At https://doi.org/10.1086/265154.

Apel, Dora. "Memorialization and Its Discontents: America's First Lynching Memorial." *Mississippi Quarterly* 61, nos. 1–2 (Winter–Spring 2008): 217–35.

Arthurs, Joshua. "The Anatomy of Controversy, from Charlottesville to Rome." *Modern Italy* 24, no. 2 (May 2019): 123–38.

Avant-Mier, Roberto, and Marouf Hasian Jr. "In Search of the Power of Whiteness: A Genealogical Exploration of Negotiated Racial Identities in America's Ethnic Past." *Communication Quarterly* 50, nos. 3–4 (2002): 391–409. At https://doi.org/10.1080/01463370209385674.

Axelsen, Diana E. "Women as Victims of Medical Experimentation: J. Marion Sims' Surgery on Slave Women, 1845–1850." *Sage* 2, no. 2 (Fall 1985): 10–13.

Bacon, Jacqueline. "Reading the Reparations Debate." *Quarterly Journal of Speech* 89, no. 3 (August 2003): 171–95. At https://doi.org/10.1080/0033563032000125304.

Balfour, Lawrie. "Ida B. Wells and 'Color Line Justice': Rethinking Reparations in Feminist Terms." *Perspectives on Politics* 13, no. 3 (September 2015): 680–96. At https://doi.org/10.1017/S1537592715001243.

Balthrop, V. William. "Culture, Myth, and Ideology as Public Argument: An Interpretation of the Ascent and Demise of 'Southern Culture.'" *Communication Monographs* 51, no. 4 (1984): 339–52. At https://doi.org/10.1080/03637758409390206.

Barber, Henry E. "The Association of Southern Women for the Prevention of Lynching, 1930–1942." *Phylon* 34, no. 4 (1973): 378–89. At https://www.jstor.org/stable/274253.

Bates, Beth Tompkins. "A New Crowd Challenges the Agenda of the Old Guard in the NAACP, 1933–1941." *American Historical Review* 102, no. 2 (April 1997): 340–77.

Behrend, Justin. "Expanding the Boundaries of Reconstruction." *Reviews in American History* 46, no. 1 (March 2018): 79–85. At https://doi.org/10.1353/rah.2018.0012.

Blair, Carole, Marsha S. Jeppeson, and Enrico Pucci Jr. "Public Memorializing in Postmodernity: The Vietnam Veterans Memorial as Prototype." *Quarterly Journal of Speech* 77, no. 3 (1991): 263–88.

Blair, Carole, and Neil Michel. "Reproducing Civil Rights Tactics: The Rhetorical Performances of the Civil Rights Memorial." *Rhetoric Society Quarterly* 30, no. 2 (Spring 2000): 31–55.

Bormann, Ernest G. "Fetching Good out of Evil: A Rhetorical Use of Calamity." *Quarterly Journal of Speech* 63, no. 2 (1977): 130–39.

Brown, Tessa. "Constellating White Women's Cultural Rhetorics: The Association of Southern Women for the Prevention of Lynching and Its Contemporary Scholars." *Peitho Journal* 20, no. 2 (2018): 233–60.

Brundage, W. Fitzhugh. "Conclusion: Reflections on Lynching Scholarship." *American Nineteenth Century History* 6, no. 3 (September 2005): 401–14. At https://doi.org/10.1080/14664650500381116.

Brundage, W. Fitzhugh. "Exclusion, Inclusion, and the Politics of Confederate Commemoration in the American South." *Politics, Groups, and Identities* 6, no. 2 (2018): 324–30. At https://doi.org/10.1080/21565503.2018.1454332.

Castañeda, Antonia I. "Women of Color and the Rewriting of Western History: The Discourse, Politics, and Decolonization of History." *Pacific Historical Review* 61, no. 4 (November 1992): 501–33.

Ceccarelli, Leah. "Polysemy: Multiple Meanings in Rhetorical Criticism." *Quarterly Journal of Speech* 84, no. 4 (1998): 395–415.

Cisneros, J. David. "A Nation of Immigrants and a Nation of Laws: Race, Multiculturalism, and Neoliberal Exception in Barack Obama's Immigration Discourse." *Communication, Culture and Critique* 8, no. 3 (2015): 356–75. At https://doi.org/10.1111/cccr.12088.

Cohen, Michael. "'The Ku Klux Government': Vigilantism, Lynching, and the Repression of the IWW." *Journal for the Study of Radicalism* 1, no. 1 (Spring 2007): 31–56.

Curry, Tommy J. "The Fortune of Wells: Ida B. Wells-Barnett's Use of T. Thomas Fortune's Philosophy of Social Agitation as a Prolegomenon to Militant Social Rights Activism." *Transactions of the Charles S. Peirce Society* 48, no. 4 (Fall 2012): 456–82.

Davis, Simone W. "The 'Weak Race' and the Winchester: Political Voices in the Pamphlets of Ida B. Wells-Barnett." *Legacy* 12, no. 2 (1995): 77–97.

De La Garza, Antonio Tomas, and Kent A. Ono. "Retheorizing Adaptation: *Differential Adaptation* and Critical Intercultural Communication." *Journal of International and Intercultural Communication* 8, no. 4 (2015): 269–89. At https://doi.org/10.1080/17513057.2015.1087097.

Delicath, John W., and Kevin Michael DeLuca. "Image Events, the Public Sphere, and Argumentative Practice: The Case of Radical Environmental Groups." *Argumentation* 17, no. 3 (September 2003): 315–33.

Derrida, Jacques. "Archive Fever: A Freudian Impression." Translated by Eric Prenowitz. *Diacritics* 25, no. 2 (Summer 1995): 9–63.

Du Bois, W. E. B. "The Negro and the Warsaw Ghetto." *Jewish Life* 6, no. 7 (1952): 14–15.

Eaglestone, Robert. "'You Would Not Add to My Suffering if You Knew What I Have Seen': Holocaust Testimony and Contemporary African Trauma Literature." *Studies in the Novel* 40, nos. 1–2 (Summer 2008): 72–85.

Eatman, Megan. "Loss and Lived Memory at the Moore's Ford Lynching Reenactment." *Advances in the History of Rhetoric* 20, no. 2 (2017): 153–66. At https://doi.org/10.1080/15362426.2017.1325411.

Ehrenhaus, Peter, and A. Susan Owen. "Race Lynching and Christian Evangelicalism: Performances of Faith." *Text and Performance Quarterly* 24, nos. 3–4 (2004): 276–301. At https://doi.org/10.1080/1046293042000312779.

Elias Nicole M., and Sean McCandless. "Administrative Decision-Making amid Competing Public Sector Values: Confederate Statue Removal in Baltimore, Maryland." *Journal of Public Affairs Education* 25, no. 3 (2019): 412–22.

Elliott, Mark. "Race, Color Blindness, and the Democratic Public: Albion W. Tourgée's Radical Principles in *Plessy v. Ferguson*." *Journal of Southern History* 67, no. 2 (May 2001): 287–330.

Enck-Wanzer, Darrel. "Barack Obama, the Tea Party, and the Threat of Race: On Racial Neoliberalism and Born Again Racism." *Communication, Culture and Critique* 4, no. 1 (March 2011): 23–30. At https://doi.org/10.1111/j.1753-9137.2010.01090.x.

Endres, Danielle, Aaron Hess, Samantha Senda-Cook, and Michael Middleton. "*In Situ* Rhetoric: Intersections between Qualitative Inquiry, Fieldwork, and Rhetoric." *Culture Studies/Critical Methodologies* 16, no. 6 (2016): 511–24.

Endres, Danielle, and Samantha Senda-Cook. "Location Matters: The Rhetoric of Place in Protest." *Quarterly Journal of Speech* 97, no. 3 (2011): 257–82. At https://doi.org/10.1080/00335630.2011.585167.

Fuoss, Kirk. "Lynching Performances, Theatres of Violence." *Text and Performance Quarterly* 19, no. 1 (1999): 1–37. At https://doi.org/10.1080/10462939909366245.

Ghoshal, Raj Andrew. "Transforming Collective Memory: Mnemonic Opportunity Structures and the Outcomes of Racial Violence Memory Movements." *Theory and Society* 42, no. 4 (July 2013): 329–50.

Gil-Riaño, Sebastián. "Relocating Anti-Racist Science: The 1950 UNESCO Statement on Race and Economic Development in the Global South." *British Journal for the History of Science* 51, no. 2 (June 2018): 281–303.

Goldsby, Jacqueline. "The High Tech and Low Tech of It: The Meaning of Lynching and the Death of Emmett Till." *Yale Journal of Criticism* 9, no. 2 (Fall 1996): 245–82.

Harold, Christine, and Kevin Michael DeLuca. "Behold the Corpse: Violent Images and the Case of Emmett Till." *Rhetoric and Public Affairs* 8, no. 2 (Summer 2005): 263–86. At https://doi.org/10.1353/rap.2005.0075.

Hasian, Marouf, Jr. "Judicial Rhetoric in a Fragmentary World: 'Character' and Storytelling in the Leo Frank Case." *Communication Monographs* 64, no. 3 (1997): 250–69.

Hasian, Marouf, Jr. "Remembering and Forgetting the 'Final Solution': A Rhetorical Pilgrimage through the US Holocaust Memorial Museum." *Critical Studies in Media Communication* 21, no. 1 (2004): 64–92.

Hasian, Marouf, Jr., Celeste Michelle Condit, and John Louis Lucaites. "The Rhetorical Boundaries of 'The Law': A Consideration of the Rhetorical Culture of Legal Practice and the Case of the 'Separate but Equal' Doctrine." *Quarterly Journal of Speech* 82, no. 4 (1996): 323–42. At https://doi.org/10.1080/00335639609384161.

Hasian, Marouf, Jr., and Earl Croasmun. "Rhetoric's Revenge: The Prospect of a Critical Legal Rhetoric." *Philosophy and Rhetoric* 29, no. 4 (1996): 384–99.

Hasian, Marouf, Jr., and Fernando Delgado. "The Trials and Tribulations of Racialized Critical Rhetorical Theory: Understanding the Rhetorical Ambiguities of Proposition 187." *Communication Theory* 8, no. 3 (August 1998): 245–70. At https://doi.org/10.1111/j.1468-2885.1998.tb00221.x.

Haywood, Harry. "The Scottsboro Decision: Victory of Revolutionary Struggle over Reformist Betrayal." *The Communist* 11 (December 1932): 1065–75.

Heath, Kingston W. "Toward a Humanistic Approach to Historical Preservation." *Journal of American Folklore* 132, no. 526 (Fall 2019): 390–411.

Higashi, Julie. "The Politics of History in Memorial Museums." *Museum International* 71, nos. 1–2 (2019): 96–103.

Hodes, Martha. "The Sexualization of Reconstruction Politics." *Journal of the History of Sexuality* 3, no. 3 (January 1993): 402–17.

Howard-Hassmann, Rhoda E. "Reparations for the Slave Trade: Rhetoric, Law, History and Political Realities." *Canadian Journal of African Studies* 41, no. 3 (2007): 427–54.

Howard-Hassmann, Rhoda E., and Anthony P. Lombardo. "Framing Reparations Claims: Differences between the African Movements and Jewish Social Movements for Reparations." *African Studies Review* 50, no. 1 (April 2007): 27–48. At https://doi.org/10.1353/arw.2005.0107.

Jones, Bradley, and Roopali Mukherjee. "From California to Michigan: Race, Rationality, and Neoliberal Governmentality." *Communication and Critical/Cultural Studies* 7, no. 4 (2010): 401–22. At https://doi.org/10.1080/14791420.2010.523431.

Korstad, Robert, and Nelson Lichtenstein. "Opportunities Found and Lost: Labor, Radicals, and the Early Civil Rights Movement." *Journal of American History* 75, no. 3 (December 1988): 786–811. At https://doi.org/10.2307/1901530.

Kratz, Corinne A. "Where Did You Cry? Crafting Categories, Narratives, and Affect through Exhibit Design." *Kronos* 44, no. 1 (January 2018): 229–52.

LaFree, Gary. "Is Antifa a Terrorist Group?" *Society* 55, no. 3 (June 2018): 248–52.

Legg, Stephen. "Assemblage/Apparatus: Using Deleuze and Foucault." *Area* 43, no. 2 (June 2011): 128–33.

Lew, Kirsten M. "From Social Problems to Maternal Melodrama: The Lost Lynching Scene in John M. Stahl's *Imitation of Life*." *Film History* 30, no. 4 (Winter 2018): 107–26.

Lindsey, Rachel McBride. "'This Barbarous Practice': Southern Churchwomen and Race in the Association of Southern Women for the Prevention of Lynching, 1930–1942." *Journal of Southern Religion* 16 (2014). At http://jsreligion.org/issues/vol16/lindsey.html.

Lipsitz, George. "The Possessive Investment in Whiteness: Racialized Social Democracy and the 'White' Problem in American Studies." *American Quarterly* 47, no. 3 (September 1995): 369–87.

Logan, Shirley Wilson. "Ida B. Wells: Lynch Law in All of Its Phases (13 February 1893)." *Voices of Democracy: The U.S. Oratory Project* 2 (Fall 2007): 50–65. At http://voicesofdemocracy.umd.edu/wells-lynch-law-speech-text/.

Lucaites, John Louis. "Between Rhetoric and 'The Law': Power, Legitimacy, and Social Change." *Quarterly Journal of Speech* 76, no. 4 (1990): 435–49. At https://doi.org/10.1080/00335639009383935.

Mack, Kenneth W. "Law, Society, Identity, and the Making of the Jim Crow South: Travel and Segregation on Tennessee Railroads, 1875–1905." *Law and Social Inquiry* 24, no. 2 (Spring 1999): 377–409. At https://doi.org/10.1111/j.1747-4469.1999.tb00134.x.

Mariano, Trinyan. "The Law of Torts and the Logic of Lynching in Charles Chesnutt's *The Marrow of Tradition*." *Publications of the Modern Language Association* 128, no. 3 (May 2013): 559–74.

Martin, Charles H. "The International Labor Defense and Black America." *Labor History* 26, no. 2 (1985): 165–94. At https://doi.org/10.1080/00236568508584794.

Martinez, Aja Y. "Critical Race Theory: Its Origins, History, and Importance to the Discourses and Rhetorics of Race." *Frame* 27, no. 2 (2014): 109–27.

Matheson, Neill. "History and Survival: Charles Chesnutt and the Time of Conjure." *American Literary Realism* 43, no. 1 (Fall 2010): 1–22.

McFadden Jane. "Equal Justice Initiative Legacy Museum: 'From Enslavement to Mass Incarceration.'" *Journal of American History* 106, no. 3 (December 2019): 703–8.

McGee, Michael Calvin. "The 'Ideograph': A Link between Rhetoric and Ideology." *Quarterly Journal of Speech* 66, no. 1 (1980): 1–16.

McKerrow, Raymie E. "Critical Rhetoric: Theory and Praxis." *Communication Monographs* 56, no. 2 (1989): 91–111.

Medina, José. "Racial Violence, Emotional Friction, and Epistemic Activism." *Angelaki: Journal of the Theoretical Humanities* 24, no. 4 (2019): 22–37.

Medina, José. "Toward a Foucaultian Epistemology of Resistance: Counter-Memory, Epistemic Friction, and Guerrilla Pluralism." *Foucault Studies*, no. 12 (October 2011): 9–35. At https://doi.org/10.22439/fs.v0i12.3335.

Meier, August, and John H. Bracey Jr. "The NAACP as a Reform Movement, 1909–1965: 'To Reach the Conscience of America.'" *Journal of Southern History* 59, no. 1 (February 1993): 3–30. At https://doi.org/10.2307/2210346.

Mezzano, Michael. "The Progressive Origins of Eugenics Critics: Raymond Pearl, Herbert S. Jennings, and the Defense of Scientific Inquiry." *Journal of the Gilded Age and the Progressive Era* 4, no. 1 (January 2005): 83–97.

Michaels, Walter Benn. "Race into Culture: A Critical Genealogy of Cultural Identity." *Critical Inquiry* 18, no. 4 (Summer 1992): 655–85. At https://doi.org/10.1086/448651.

Miles, Tiya. "Review: National Museum of African American History and Culture." *Public History* 39, no. 2 (May 2017): 82–86.

Mirzoeff, Nicholas. "The Right to Look." *Critical Inquiry* 37, no. 3 (Spring 2011): 473–96. At https://doi.org/10.1086/659354.

Moses, A. Dirk. "'White Genocide' and the Ethics of Public Analysis." *Journal of Genocide Research* 21, no. 2 (2019): 201–13.

Murray, Hugh T., Jr. "The NAACP versus the Communist Party: The Scottsboro Rape Cases, 1931–1932." *Phylon* 28, no. 3 (1967): 267–87. At https://doi.org/10.2307/273666.

Nealy, Michelle J. "Black Men: Left Out and Locked Up." *Diverse: Issues in Higher Education* 24, no. 26 (February 2008): 20–22.

Neville-Shepard, Ryan. "Rand Paul at Howard University and the Rhetoric of the New Southern Strategy." *Western Journal of Communication* 82, no. 1 (January–February 2018): 20–39.

Ohl, Jessy J., and Jennifer E. Potter. "United We Lynch: Post-Racism and the (Re)Membering of Racial Violence in *Without Sanctuary: Lynching Photography in America*." *Southern Communication Journal* 78, no. 3 (2013): 185–201.

Ono, Kent A. "Postracism: A Theory of the 'Post-' as Political Strategy." *Journal of Communication Inquiry* 34, no. 3 (2010): 227–33.

Owen, A. Susan, and Peter Ehrenhaus. "Looking at Lynching: Spectacle, Resistance and Contemporary Transformations." *Quarterly Journal of Speech* 97, no. 1 (February 2011): 100–113. At https://doi.org/10.1080/00335630.2010.541276.

Owen, A. Susan, and Peter Ehrenhaus. "The Moore's Ford Lynching Reenactment: Affective Memory and Race Trauma." *Text and Performance Quarterly* 34, no. 1 (2014): 72–90. At https://doi.org/10.1080/10462937.2013.856461.

Page, Thomas Nelson. "The Lynching of Negroes: Its Cause and Its Prevention." *North American Review* 178, no. 566 (January 1904): 33–48.

Park, Marlene. "Lynching and Antilynching: Art and Politics in the 1930s." *Prospects: An Annual of American Cultural Studies* 18 (1993): 311–65.

Peltonen, Matti. "From Discourse to *Dispositif*: Michel Foucault's Two Histories." *Historical Reflections / Réflexions Historiques* 30, no. 2 (Summer 2004): 205–19.

Pergher, Roberta, Mark Roseman, Jürgen Zimmerer, Shelley Baranowski, Doris L. Bergen, and Zygmunt Bauman. "The Holocaust: A Colonial Genocide? A Scholars' Forum." *Dapim: Studies on the Holocaust* 27, no. 1 (2013): 40–73.

Perry, Samuel. "President Trump and Charlottesville: Uncivil Mourning and White Supremacy." *Journal of Contemporary Rhetoric* 8, nos. 1–2 (2018): 57–71.

Pfeifer, Michael J. "At the Hands of Parties Unknown? The State of the Field of Lynching Scholarship." *Journal of American History* 101, no. 3 (December 2014): 832–46. At https://doi.org/10.1093/jahist/jau640.

Phelps, Jess R., and Jessica Owley. "Etched in Stone: Historic Preservation Law and Confederate Monuments." *Florida Law Review* 71 (2019): 627–87.

Pinar, William F. "The N.A.A.C.P. and the Struggle for Antilynching Federal Legislation, 1917–1950." *Counterpoints* 163 (2001): 683–752.

Powell, Kimberly A. "The Association of Southern Women for the Prevention of Lynching: Strategies of a Movement in the Comic Frame." *Communication Quarterly* 43, no. 1 (1995): 86–99. At https://doi.org/10.1080/01463379509369958.

Rable, George C. "The South and the Politics of Antilynching Legislation, 1920–1940." *Journal of Southern History* 51, no. 2 (1985): 201–20. At https://doi.org/10.2307/2208825.

Raiford, Leigh. "Photography and the Practices of Critical Black Memory." *History and Theory* 48, no. 4 (December 2009): 112–29.

Rice, Anne. "How We Remember Lynching." *Nka: Journal of Contemporary African Art*, no. 20 (Fall 2006): 32–43.

Rigby, David, and Charles Seguin. "The Racial Position of European Immigrants, 1883–1941: Evidence from Lynching in the Midwest." *Social Currents* 5, no. 5 (2018): 438–57.

Rothberg, Michael. "Against Zero-Sum Logic: A Response to Walter Benn Michaels." *American Literary History* 18, no. 2 (Summer 2006): 303–11.

Rothberg, Michael. "Between Auschwitz and Algeria: Multidirectional Memory and the Counterpublic Witness." *Critical Inquiry* 33, no. 1 (August 2006): 158–84.

Rothberg, Michael. "From Gaza to Warsaw: Mapping Multidirectional Memory." *Criticism* 53, no. 4 (Fall 2011): 523–48.

Rothberg, Michael. "W. E. B. Du Bois in Warsaw: Holocaust Memory and the Color Line, 1949–1952." *Yale Journal of Criticism* 14, no. 1 (March 2001): 169–89.

Saad, Megan. "Mass Incarceration as a Contemporary Racial Project in North America and Its Stratification across Racialized and Gendered Lines." *Prandium* 1, no. 1 (Fall 2017): 1–11.

Sanchez, James Chase. "Trump, the KKK, and the Versatility of White Supremacy Rhetoric." *Journal of Contemporary Rhetoric* 8, nos. 1–2 (2018): 44–56.

Schuyler, George S. "Scripture for Lynchers." *The Crisis* 42, no. 1 (1935): 12.

Seguin, Charles, and David Rigby. "National Crimes: A New National Data Set of Lynchings in the United States, 1883 to 1941." *Socius: Sociological Research for a Dynamic World* 5 (January 2019): 1–9. At https://doi.org/10.1177/2378023119841780.

Squires, David. "Outlawry: Ida B. Wells and Lynch Law." *American Quarterly* 67, no. 1 (March 2015): 141–63.

Stevenson, Bryan. "Crime, Punishment, and Executions in the Twenty-First Century." *Proceedings of the American Philosophical Society* 147, no. 1 (March 2003): 24–29.

Steyn, Melissa. "The Ignorance Contract: Recollections of Apartheid Childhoods and the Construction of Epistemologies of Ignorance." *Identities: Global Studies in Culture and Power* 19, no. 1 (January 2012): 8–25. At https://doi.org/10.1080/1070289X.2012.672840.

Stob, Paul. "'Terministic Screens,' Social Constructionism, and the Language of Experience: Kenneth Burke's Utilization of William James." *Philosophy and Rhetoric* 41, no. 2 (2008): 130–52.

Stoler, Ann Laura. "On Archiving as Dissensus." *Comparative Studies of South Asia, Africa, and the Middle East* 38, no. 1 (May 2018): 43–56.

Sturken, Marita. "Reenactment, Fantasy, and the Paranoia of History: Oliver Stone's Docudramas." *History and Theory* 46, no. 4 (December 1997): 64–79.

Thomas, Brook. "The Unfinished Task of Grounding Reconstruction's Promise." *Journal of the Civil War Era* 7, no. 1 (March 2017): 16–38. At https://doi.org/10.1353/cwe.2017.0011.

Tolnay, Stewart E., and E. M. Beck. "'Racialized Terrorism' in the American South: Do Completed Lynchings Tell an Accurate Story?" *Social Science History* 42, no. 4 (Winter 2018): 677–701.

Tucker, Mark. "'You Can't Argue with Facts': Monroe Nathan Work as Information Officer, Editor, and Bibliographer." *Libraries and Culture* 26, no. 1 (Winter 1991): 151–68.

Vinitzky-Seroussi, Vered, and Chana Teeger. "Unpacking the Unspoken: Silence in Collective Memory and Forgetting." *Social Forces* 88, no. 3 (March 2010): 1103–22.

Vivian, Bradford. "Witnessing Time: Rhetorical Form, Public Culture, and Popular Historical Education." *Rhetoric Society Quarterly* 44, no. 3 (2014): 204–19.

Waldrep, Christopher. "War of Words: The Controversy over the Definition of Lynching, 1899–1940." *Journal of Southern History* 66, no. 1 (February 2000): 75–100. At https://doi.org/10.2307/2587438.

Wallace, Michele Faith. "The Good Lynching and 'The Birth of a Nation': Discourses and Aesthetics of Jim Crow." *Cinema Journal* 43, no. 1 (Autumn 2003): 85–104.

Warner, Michael. "Publics and Counterpublics." *Public Culture* 14, no. 1 (Winter 2002): 49–90.

Watson, Martha Solomon. "Mary Church Terrell vs. Thomas Nelson Page: Gender, Race, and Class in Anti-Lynching Rhetoric." *Rhetoric and Public Affairs* 12, no. 1 (Spring 2009): 65–89.

Watts, Eric King. "Postracial Fantasies, Blackness, and Zombies." *Communication and Critical/Cultural Studies* 14, no. 4 (2017): 317–33. At https://doi.org/10.1080/14791420.2017.1338742.

Weisberger, Bernard A. "The Dark and Bloody Ground of Reconstruction Historiography." *Journal of Southern History* 25, no. 4 (November 1959): 427–47. At https://doi.org/10.2307/2954450.

White, Walter. "The Costigan-Wagner Bill." *The Crisis* 42, no. 1 (January 1935): 10–11, 29.

Wiegman, Robyn. "The Anatomy of Lynching." *Journal of the History of Sexuality* 3, no. 3 (January 1993): 445–67.

Woodruff, Nan Elizabeth. Review of *The NAACP Crusade against Lynching, 1909–1950*, by Robert L. Zangrando. *Science and Society* 48, no. 1 (Spring 1984): 123–24.

Worger, William H. "Convict Labour, Industrialists and the State in the US South and South Africa, 1870–1930." *Journal of Southern African Studies* 30, no. 1 (2004): 63–86. At https://doi.org/10.1080/0305707042000223942.

Young, Harvey. "The Black Body as Souvenir in American Lynching." *Theatre Journal* 57, no. 4 (2005): 639–57.

Young, James E. "The Counter-Monument: Memory against Itself in Germany Today." *Critical Inquiry* 18, no. 2 (Winter 1992): 267–96. At https://doi.org/10.1086/448632.

Zackodnik, Teresa. "Ida B. Wells and 'American Atrocities' in Britain." *Women's Studies International Forum* 28, no. 4 (July–August 2005): 259–73.

Zelizer, Barbie. "Reading the Past against the Grain: The Shape of Memory Studies." *Critical Studies in Mass Communication* 12, no. 2 (June 1995): 214–39.

POPULAR MAGAZINE ARTICLES

Ajudua, Christine. "How Alabama's New Memorial to Victims of Lynching Could Change America." *AFAR*, July 31, 2018. At https://www.afar.com/magazine/how-alabamas-new-memorial-to-victims-of-lynching-could-change-america.

Alexander, Neta. "A Haunting Legacy of Racial Terror: The Thousands of Lynchings That Changed America." *Ha'aretz*, November 3, 2017. At https://www.haaretz.com/us-news/.premium.MAGAZINE-how-racial-terror-permanently-altered-americas-demographics-1.5462682.

Anapol, Avery. "Alabama Governor Defends Confederate Monuments: We Don't Need 'Out-of-State Liberals' Telling Us What to Do." *The Hill*, April 17, 2018. At https://thehill.com/

homenews/state-watch/383616-alabama-governor-defends-confederate-monuments-we-dont-need-out-of-state.
Avins, Jenni. "The NAACP's 'A Man Was Lynched Yesterday' Flag Has Been Reprised and Hangs in New York City." *Quartz*, July 10, 2016. At https://qz.com/727602/the-naacps-a-man-was-lynched-yesterday-flag-has-been-reprised-and-hangs-in-new-york-city/.
Ayisi, Erica. "Lynching Memorial: Ghanaian Artist Hopes Sculpture Captures Shared Pain between African Americans and the Motherland." *The Root*, May 7, 2018. At https://www.theroot.com/lynching-memorial-ghanian-artist-hopes-sculpture-captu-1825817044.
Bliss, Laura. "A Comprehensive Map of American Lynchings." CityLab, January 17, 2017. At https://www.citylab.com/equity/2017/01/a-comprehensive-map-of-american-lynchings/513293/?utm_source=SFTwitter.
Boissoneault, Lorraine. "The Deadliest Massacre in Reconstruction-Era Louisiana Happened 150 Years Ago." *Smithsonian Magazine*, September 28, 2018. At https://www.smithsonianmag.com/history/story-deadliest-massacre-reconstruction-era-louisiana-180970420/.
Bump, Philip. "Study: Cops Tend to See Black Kids as Less Innocent Than White Kids." *Atlantic*, March 2014. At https://www.theatlantic.com/national/archive/2014/03/cops-tend-to-see-black-kids-as-less-innocent-than-white-kids/383247/.
Bunn, Curtis. "Death Row Lawyer Bryan Stevenson Plans a Lynching Memorial in Alabama." *The Undefeated*, April 11, 2017. At https://theundefeated.com/features/death-row-lawyer-bryan-stevenson-plans-a-lynching-memorial-in-alabama/.
Capps, Kriston. "Hanged, Burned, Shot, Drowned, Beaten." *Atlantic*, November 2017. At https://www.theatlantic.com/magazine/archive/2017/11/a-national-monument-to-america-s-known-victims-of-lynching/540663/.
Cheney-Rice, Zak. "Bryan Stevenson on His 'Not Entirely Rational' Quest for Justice." *New York Magazine*, June 25, 2019. At http://nymag.com/intelligencer/2019/06/bryan-stevensons-not-entirely-rational-quest-for-justice.html.
Cole, David. "The Disgrace of Our Criminal Justice." *New York Review of Books*, December 4, 2014. At https://www.nybooks.com/articles/2014/12/04/disgrace-our-criminal-justice/.
Conley Kevin. "Bryan Stevenson Is Working to Transform How Society's Most Vulnerable Access Legal Aid." *Town and Country*, May 2, 2016. At https://www.townandcountrymag.com/society/politics/a5602/bryan-stevenson-equal-justice-initiative/.
Couric, Katie. "The Blood of Lynching Victims Is in This Soil." *National Geographic*, April 2018. At https://www.nationalgeographic.com/magazine/2018/04/race-lynching-museum-katie-couric-alabama/.
Dabney, Virginius. "Dixie Rejects Lynching." *The Nation*, November 27, 1937.
Dilawar, Arvind. "A New Way to Memorialize Racial Violence." *The Nation*, November 14, 2019. At https://www.thenation.com/article/race-riot-chicago/.
Eschner, Kat. "Some States Celebrate MLK Day and Robert E. Lee's Birthday on the Same Day." *Smithsonian Magazine*, January 16, 2017. At https://www.smithsonianmag.com/smart-news/some-states-celebrate-mlk-day-and-robert-e-lees-birthday-same-day-180961772/.
Feldblum, Sammy. "In Montgomery, a Harrowing, Beautiful Reckoning with Racial Terror." *Scalawag*, May 8, 2018. At https://www.scalawagmagazine.org/2018/05/in-montgomery-a-harrowing-beautiful-reckoning/.

Foretek, Jared. "Seeking Peace and Justice, Montgomery Plans a Lynching Memorial." CityLab, August 21, 2017. At https://www.citylab.com/equity/2017/08/seeking-peace-and-justice-montgomery-plans-a-lynching-memorial/536637/.

Goodkind, Nicole. "Texas Confederate Monuments Debate Invokes Talk of Statues of Lynching, Tearing Down Auschwitz." *Newsweek*, April 10, 2019. At https://www.newsweek.com/texas-confederate-monuments-lynching-auschwitz-1392438.

Harriot, Michael. "Court Rules Alabama Town's School Segregation Too Racist . . . Even for Alabama." *The Root*, February 13, 2018. At https://www.theroot.com/court-rules-alabama-towns-school-segregation-too-racist-1822976807.

Hobbs, Allyson, and Nell Freudenberger. "A Visit to Montgomery's Legacy Museum." *New Yorker*, July 17, 2018. At https://www.newyorker.com/culture/personal-history/a-visit-to-montgomerys-legacy-museum.

Jackson, Jenn M. "Lynching in the United States, Explained." *Teen Vogue*, October 2, 2017. At https://www.teenvogue.com/story/lynching-in-the-united-states-explained.

Johnson, James Weldon. "The Practice of Lynching: A Picture, the Problem, and What Shall Be Done about It." *Century Magazine*, November 1927, 65–70.

Kelley, Robin D. G. "Memory and Politics." *The Nation*, October 3, 1994.

Kelman, Ari Y. "At the National Memorial for Peace and Justice in Alabama, a Lesson in Memory and Responsibility." *Tablet*, May 1, 2018. At https://www.tabletmag.com/scroll/260961/at-the-national-memorial-for-peace-and-justice-in-alabama-a-lesson-in-memory-and-responsibility.

Kersey, Paul. "New Lynching Memorial Celebrates White Guilt." *Unz Review*, May 7, 2018. At https://www.unz.com/article/new-lynching-memorial-celebrates-white-guilt/.

Klein, Ezra. "Bryan Stevenson Explains How It Feels to Grow Up Black amid Confederate Monuments." *Vox*, May 24, 2017. At https://www.vox.com/2017/5/24/15675606/bryan-stevenson-confederacy-monuments-slavery-ezra-klein.

Leonard, David J. "White Anti-Racists Must Be 'Stone Catchers' for Oppressed People." *The Root*, November 15, 2016. At https://www.theroot.com/white-anti-racists-must-be-stone-catchers-for-oppress-1790857731.

Levin, Kevin M. "The Pernicious Myth of the 'Loyal Slave' Lives On in Confederate Memorials." *Smithsonian Magazine*, August 17, 2017. At https://www.smithsonianmag.com/history/pernicious-myth-loyal-slave-lives-confederate-memorials-180964546/.

Lockhart, P. R. "After More Than 200 Attempts, the Senate Has Finally Passed Anti-Lynching Legislation." *Vox*, December 21, 2018. At https://www.vox.com/identities/2018/12/21/18151805/senate-lynching-legislation-hate-crimes-booker-harris-scott.

Lockhart, P. R. "A New Lynching Memorial Highlights America's Grim Legacy of Racial Terrorism." *Vox*, April 26, 2018. At https://www.vox.com/identities/2018/4/26/17286236/lynching-victims-memorial-alabama-equal-justice-initiative.

Lopez, German. "Mississippi Lawmaker: Leaders Taking Down Confederate Monuments 'Should Be LYNCHED.'" *Vox*, May 22, 2017. At https://www.vox.com/identities/2017/5/22/15675604/confederate-monuments-karl-oliver.

Marler, Scott. "Removing the Confederate Monuments in New Orleans Was Only a First Step Toward Righting the Wrongs of History." *The Nation*, June 14, 2017. At https://www

.thenation.com/article/archive/removing-the-confederate-monuments-in-new-orleans-was-only-a-first-step-toward-righting-the-wrongs-of-history/.

McWilliams, James. "Bryan Stevenson on What Well-Meaning White People Need to Know about Race." *Pacific Standard*, February 6, 2018, updated February 18, 2019. At https://psmag.com/magazine/bryan-stevenson-ps-interview.

Mock, Brentin. "Why Memorializing America's History of Racism Matters." CityLab, July 6, 2015. At https://www.citylab.com/design/2015/07/why-memorializing-americas-history-of-racism-matters/397781/.

Olmstead, Molly. "How Did an Alabama County Just Open Its First Integrated School? Nearly 65 Years after the *Brown v. Board* Ruling." *Slate*, August 15, 2018. At https://slate.com/news-and-politics/2018/08/alabama-county-opens-first-integrated-school-in-2018-heres-why-it-took-so-long.html.

Owens, Donna M. "Inspiration behind 'Just Mercy' Hopes Film 'Motivates' Viewers 'to Get Involved' in Criminal Justice System." *Essence*, January 13, 2020. At https://www.essence.com/entertainment/only-essence/bryan-stevenson-just-mercy/.

Patterson, Margot. "The Fleeting Satisfaction of Pulling Down Confederate Monuments." *America: The Jesuit Review*, September 18, 2017. At https://www.americamagazine.org/politics-society/2017/09/18/fleeting-satisfaction-pulling-down-confederate-monuments.

Rothman, Joshua. "When Bigotry Paraded through the Streets." *Atlantic*, December 4, 2016. At https://www.theatlantic.com/politics/archive/2016/12/second-klan/509468/.

Segura, Liliana. "The Stepchild of Lynching: Alabama's Lynching Memorial and the Legacy of Racial Terror in the South." *The Intercept*, June 17, 2018. At https://theintercept.com/2018/06/17/lynching-museum-alabama-death-penalty/.

Simien, Evelyn M. "Lynching Memorial Shows Women Were Victims, Too." *The Conversation*, April 24, 2018. At https://theconversation.com/lynching-memorial-shows-women-were-victims-too-95029.

Sisson, Patrick. "New Memorial for Lynching Victims Reaches for Truth and Reconciliation." *Curbed*, April 24, 2018. At https://www.curbed.com/2018/4/24/17275094/montgomery-slavery-lynching-museum-eji.

Smith, Clint. "The Meaning of Life without Parole." *New Yorker*, February 8, 2016. At https://www.newyorker.com/news/news-desk/the-meaning-of-life-without-parole.

Smith, Jamil. "On a Hill in Alabama, the Lynched Haunt Us." *Rolling Stone*, May 6, 2018. At https://www.rollingstone.com/politics/politics-features/on-a-hill-in-alabama-the-lynched-haunt-us-629262/.

Solly, Meilan. "Brooklyn Museum's 'Legacy of Lynching' Exhibition Confronts Racial Terror." *Smithsonian Magazine*, August 7, 2017. At https://www.smithsonianmag.com/smart-news/brooklyn-museums-legacy-lynching-exhibition-confronts-racial-terror-180964288/.

Solnit, Rebecca. "The Monument Wars." *Harper's Magazine*, January 2017. At https://harpers.org/archive/2017/01/the-monument-wars/.

Speri, Alice. "'I Don't Think We're Free in America': An Interview with Bryan Stevenson." *The Intercept*, January 2, 2017. At https://theintercept.com/2017/01/02/i-dont-think-were-free-in-america-an-interview-with-bryan-stevenson/.

Stevenson, Bryan. "A Presumption of Guilt." *New York Review of Books*, July 13, 2017. At https://www.nybooks.com/articles/2017/07/13/presumption-of-guilt/.

Tayleur, Eleanor. "The Negro Woman: Social and Moral Decadence." *Outlook* 75 (January 10, 1904): 266–71.
Toobin, Jeffrey. "The Legacy of Lynching, on Death Row." *New Yorker*, August 22, 2016. At https://www.newyorker.com/magazine/2016/08/22/bryan-stevenson-and-the-legacy-of-lynching.
Williams, Patricia J. "Ida B. Wells-Barnett Deserves a Bigger Statue." *The Nation*, May 2, 2018. At https://www.thenation.com/article/archive/ida-b-wells-barnett-deserves-a-bigger-statue/.
Winkler, Adam. "'Corporations Are People' Is Built on an Incredible 19th-Century Lie." *Atlantic*, March 5, 2018. At https://www.theatlantic.com/business/archive/2018/03/corporations-people-adam-winkler/554852/.
Zorthian, Julia. "President Trump Says It's 'Sad' to See U.S. Culture 'Ripped Apart' by Removing Confederate Statues." *Time*, August 17, 2017. At https://time.com/4904510/donald-trump-twitter-confederate-statues/.

LAW REVIEW ARTICLES

Alfieri, Anthony V. "Lynching Ethics: Toward a Theory of Racialized Defenses." *Michigan Law Review* 95, no. 5 (February 1997): 1063–104.
Baldus, David C., Charles Pulaski, and George Woodworth. "Comparative Review of Death Sentences: An Empirical Study of the Georgia Experience." *Journal of Criminal Law and Criminology* 74, no. 3 (Fall 1983): 661–753.
Bell, Jeannine. "The Hangman's Noose and the Lynch Mob: Hate Speech and the Jena Six." *Harvard Civil Rights–Civil Liberties Law Review* 44, no. 2 (Summer 2009): 329–60.
Bright, Stephen B. "Discrimination, Death and Denial: The Tolerance of Racial Discrimination in Infliction of the Death Penalty." *Santa Clara Law Review* 35, no. 2 (1995): 433–84.
Capers, Bennett. "Critical Race Theory and Criminal Justice." *Ohio State Journal of Criminal Law* 12, no. 1 (2014): 1–8.
Chin, Gabriel Jackson. "The *Plessy* Myth: Justice Harlan and the Chinese Cases." *Iowa Law Review* 82 (1996): 151–82.
Delgado, Richard. "A Comment on Rosenberg's New Edition of *The Hollow Hope*." *Northwestern University Law Review Colloquy* 103 (2008): 147–52.
Delgado, Richard. "The Law of the Noose: A History of Latino Lynching." *Harvard Civil Rights–Civil Liberties Law Review* 44, no. 2 (Summer 2009): 297–312.
Dudziak, Mary L. "Desegregation as a Cold War Imperative." *Stanford Law Review* 41, no. 1 (November 1988): 61–120.
Golub, Mark. "'Plessy as 'Passing': Judicial Responses to Ambiguously Raced Bodies in *Plessy v. Ferguson*." *Law and Society Review* 39, no. 3 (September 2005): 563–600.
Haney-López, Ian F. "Post-Racial Racism: Racial Stratification and Mass Incarceration in the Age of Obama." *California Law Review* 98 (2010): 1023–73.
Harris, Angela P. "On Doing the Right Thing: Education Work in the Academy." *Vermont Law Review* 15, no. 1 (Summer 1990): 125–38.
Harris, Angela P. "Race and Essentialism in Feminist Legal Theory." *Stanford Law Review* 42, no. 3 (February 1990): 581–616.
Harris, Cheryl I. "Whiteness as Property." *Harvard Law Review* 106, no. 8 (June 1993): 1707–91.

Hickman, Christine B. "The Devil and the One Drop Rule: Racial Categories, African Americans, and the U.S. Census." *Michigan Law Review* 95, no. 5 (March 1997): 1161–265.

Holden-Smith, Barbara. "Lynching, Federalism, and the Intersection of Race and Gender in the Progressive Era." *Yale Journal of Law and Feminism* 8, no. 1 (1996): 31–78.

Hutchinson, Darren Lenard. "Who Locked Us Up: Examining the Social Meaning of Black Punitiveness." *Yale Law Journal* 127, no. 8 (June 2018): 2388–447.

Kennedy, Randall. "Reconstruction and the Politics of Scholarship." *Yale Law Journal* 98, no. 3 (January 1989): 521–40.

Kerr, Lisa. "How to End Mass Imprisonment: The Legal and Cultural Strategies of Bryan Stevenson." *University of Toronto Law Journal* 67 (Winter 2017): 104–23.

Killeen, Erin. "The Increased Criminalization of African American Girls." *Georgetown Law*, April 17, 2019. At https://www.law.georgetown.edu/poverty-journal/blog/the-increased-criminalization-of-african-american-girls/.

Manganello, Zachary. "Sociological Materials in Vermont Constitutional Interpretation." *Vermont Law Review* 32 (2008): 607–31.

Matsuda, Mari J. "Dissent in a Crowded Theater." *Southern Methodist University Law Review* 72, no. 3 (2019): 431–56.

Pillsbury, Albert E. "A Brief Inquiry into a Federal Remedy for Lynching." *Harvard Law Review* 15, no. 9 (May 1902): 707–13.

Post, Deborah Waire. "Reflections on Identity, Diversity and Morality." *Berkeley Women's Law Journal* 6, no. 1 (1990–1991): 136–66.

Roberts, Dorothy E. "Punishing Drug Addicts Who Have Babies: Women of Color, Equality, and the Right of Privacy." *Harvard Law Review* 104, no. 7 (May 1991): 1419–82.

Stevenson, Bryan A. "Confronting Mass Imprisonment and Restoring Fairness to Collateral Review of Criminal Cases." *Harvard Civil Rights–Civil Liberties Law Review* 41, no. 2 (Summer 2006): 339–68.

LEGAL CASES

Chesapeake, o. B S.W. R.R. v. Wells, 1887. 4 S.W. 5 (Tenn.).
Collins v. Collins, 510 U.S. 1141 (1994).
Oliver Brown et al. v. Board of Education of Topeka et al., 347 U.S. 483 (1954).
Plessy v. Ferguson, 163 U.S. 537 (1896).
Powell v. Alabama, 287 U.S. 45 (1932).
Smith v. Allright, 321 U.S. 649 (1944).
United States v. Cruikshank, 92 U.S. 542 (1876).
United States v. Harris, 106 U.S. 629 (1883).
Williams v. New York City Housing Authority, 154 F. Supp. 2d 820, 824 (S.D.N.Y. 2001).

DISSERTATIONS AND PRESENTED PAPERS

Balthrope, Robin Bernice. "Lawlessness and the New Deal: Congress and Anti-Lynching Legislation, 1934–1938." PhD diss., Ohio State University, 1995.

Bright, Stephen B. "Imposition of the Death Penalty upon the Poor, Racial Minorities, the Intellectually Disabled, and the Mentally Ill." Paper presented at the Program of the High Commissioner for Human Rights of the United Nations, New York, April 24, 2014. At http://www.law.nyu.edu/sites/default/files/upload_documents/Bright-Death-Penalty-UN-April-2014.pdf.

Minor, Wanda Madison. "The Rhetorical Construction of White Supremacy in Alabama's 1901 Constitution: A Critical-Historical Study." PhD diss., University of Alabama, 2008.

INDEX

Page numbers in **bold** refer to illustrations.

Abbeville, South Carolina, 158
Abbeville Press and Banner, 158
activism, 6, 9, 11–12, 44–45, 47, 49, 59–60, 72, 77, 81, 84, 87–112, 117, 126, 181, 189, 205, 210
Adams, Tim, 117, 135
African Americans: artists, 88; communities, 6, 11, 43, 72, 81, 89–90, 101–2, 118, 128, 193; predatory male sexuality, 24, 26–27, 30–31, 42, 52–53, 56–59, 61, 67, 83, 93, 102, 105, 119, 121, 130, 177; social equality, 23, 25–26, 33, 42, 93, 99; soldiers, 22–23, 28, 68, 92–93, 115, 211; women, 57, 59, 72, 115, 149, 194
Afro-American, 71
Afro-American League, 47
Agamben, Giorgio, 60
Akoto-Bamfo, Kwame, 162, **163**, 164
Alabama, 53, 64, 71, 118, 125–27, 131, 137–38, 141, 144–48, 153–57, 183, 184–85, 189, 200, 206, 212–13; Confederate memorials, 137–38, 141–45, **141, 142, 143**; state capitol, 141, 143, 146, 183. *See also individual cities*
Alabama Memorial Preservation Act, 137–38
Alexander, Elizabeth, 18
Alfieri, Anthony, 101–2
Allen, Gerald, 137
Allen, James, 91, 102–4, 106–12
American Civil Liberties Union, 95
Ames, Jessie Daniel, 61, 72–73, 98–99
"Amour et Dévouement, A Miss Ida B. Wells," 56
Angelou, Maya, 203
anti-lynching legislation, 3–4, 11, 17, 29, 31, 34, 37, 42–44, 47–49, 52–53, 55, 57–58, 61–62, 83–86, 87–89, 91–92, 94–95, 99–100, 104, 107, 111, 113, 126, 156, 178, 195, 206–7, 209–10; 1930s legislative attempts, 74–82; prior to 1935, 63–72
apartheid, 6, 17, 154
Arkansas, 7, 82, 126; executions, 133; riots, 81. *See also individual cities*
Arlington Confederate Memorial Association, 35
Arlington National Cemetery, 35
Arnold, Jennifer, 174
"Art Commentary on Lynching, An," 75–76, 103, 109
Associated Negro Press, 71
Association of Southern Women for the Prevention of Lynching (ASWPL), 11, 36, 62, 65, 72–74, 85, 98–99, 217
Atlanta Journal-Constitution, 41, 175
atonement, 8, 114, 176, 178, 205
Austin-Hillery, Nicole, 202
Ayers, Edward, 33

Bacon, Jacqueline, 12–13
Baker, Ray Stannard, 46, 57–58
Bakk-Hansen, Heidi, 178
Balfour, Lawrie, 59
Balthrop, V. William, 148, 151–52
Bancroft, Hubert, 46
Bankhead, John, 79
Barrett, Will, 49
Barry, Marion, 216
Barthes, Roland, 105
Bates, Beth, 89
Beck, E. M., 6, 62, 116
"Behold the Corpse," 110
Bell, Jeannine, 102
Benjamin, Walter, 14–15, 100, 185, 200, 210
Berg, Manfred, 46
Bethune, Mary McLeod, 75, 99

Biddle, Francis, 93
Birmingham, Alabama, 32–33, 147, 177–78, 188
Birmingham Daily Post, 55
Birth of a Nation, The, 67
Black, Hugo L., 79
Black Girls Matter, 10
Black Lives Matter, 10, 17, 182, 184
Blackman, Harry, 135–36
Block, Julius, 75
Blood of Emmett Till, The, 97
Blue Lives Matter, 17
Booker, Cory, 3–4, 86
Bracey, John H., 91
Bright, Stephen, 118
"British Anti-Lynchers," 57
Brown, DeNeen L., 60
Brown, Henry Billings, 44–45
Brown, Tessa, 72
Brown, Will, 7
Brownsville, Tennessee, 87
Brown v. Board of Education (1954), 29, 85, 95, 98, 111, 147, 192
Brundage, W. Fitzhugh, 94, 139, 165, 209–10
Bryant, Carolyn, 95–97
Bryant, Roy, 96–97
Bunn, Curtis, 200
Burdett, Winston, 75
Butts County, Georgia, 127

Capeci, Dominic, Jr., 93
Capehart, Jonathan, 173, 199
capital punishment, 28, 82–83, 85, 89, 101, 114–18, 119–28, 130–36, 186–87, 189, 193–94, 196–97, 200, 202, 203–4, 206–8, 210, 212–13, 215–17; in Alabama, 125–26; in Arkansas, 133; in Louisiana, 127
carceral systems, 17, 114, 120, 123, 127, 129, 135, 147, 185, 188, 191, 195, 205–6, 211–12, 214–15, 217; convict leasing, 31–33, 119–20; mass incarceration, 13–14, 16–18, 20, 28, 37–38, 89, 101, 115–16, 118, 124–25, 129, 131–32, 135, 186–88, 193–94, 197, 201–2, 203–8, 210–12, 214–17; prison abuses, 31–32, 186; prison-industrial complex, 5, 101, 132, 206, 214; prison statistics, 209; sentencing, 3, 82, 135, 188, 193–94, 196, 203, 206–8, 212–13; stonecatchers, 132–33, 135, 213, 217; superpredators, 132, 193, 210; treatment of children and youths, 125, 131–32, 193, 206, 212–13; treatment of mentally disabled, 131–32, 135, 145, 196; wrongful convictions, 131–32, 208
Chadbourn, James Harmon, 68, 84
Charleston, South Carolina, 137–38, 144, 148
Charlottesville, Virginia, 73, 113, 139, 144, 149–50, 152
Cheney-Rice, Zak, 212
Chesnutt, Charles, 34–35
Chicago, Illinois, 43, 51
Chicago Conservator, 48
Chicago Defender, 68, 82
Chicago Tribune, 62, 65, 85
Circumstantial Evidence, 132
civil rights, 9–12, 20–21, 29, 33–34, 40, 42, 44–47, 56, 59–60, 69, 72, 81, 83–85, 87–112, 145, 159, 181, 183, 185–86, 188–90, 192, 194, 197–99, 201, 204–5, 208, 216
Civil Rights Act of 1964, 111, 194
Civil Rights Committee, 91
Civil Rights Memorial, 161, 190
Civil War, 22–28, 32, 34, 79–80, 119, 148, 152, 155, 190
Clarke, Charles, 27
Clayton, Elias, 177
Clayton Jackson McGhie Memorial, 178, **178**
Coker, Fred, 170
Coker, Hillary, 86
Cold War, 88–92, 94, 98–100, 109, 112, 122, 147
Cole, Ernest, 181–82
Cole, Grant, 170
Collins, Winfield, 68
Collins v. Collins (1994), 135–36
colorblindness, 44, 46, 72, 85, 88, 90–91, 95, 97, 100–101, 118, 126, 140, 147, 180, 190, 194, 196

color lines, 47, 49, 52, 54, 81, 100, 120
Commission on Interracial Cooperation, 78–79
Communists, 11, 71, 81–83, 86, 87, 89, 119, 217
Confederate flag, 137–38, 144, 146, 151, 157–58
Confederate Memorial Day, 144, 147
Confederate statuary and memorials, 17, 34–35, 137–59, **141, 142, 143**, 161, 179, 183, 200–201, 204, 207, 209, 211, 217; preservation acts, 137–40, 150, 153, 155. *See also* memorialization
Costigan, Edward, 76, 79
Costigan-Wagner bill, 63, 76–79, 84
Cox, Karen, 35
Crawford, Anthony, 158
criminal justice system, 115, 119, 127, 132, 152, 179, 197, 214, 217
critical genealogical studies, 13–18, 97, 99, 103, 105, 110, 133, 159, 167, 179, 182–83, 185–86, 200–201, 203, 206–7
critical legal studies (CLS) movement, 101–2
critical race theory (CRT) movement, 13, 60, 76, 91, 101–3, 112, 114, 120, 192, 201, 206, 208, 213–14, 216
cultural amnesia, 5, 9, 28, 60, 86, 88, 91, 94, 97, 107, 109, 111, 153, 180, 182–83, 185, 187
Cutler, James Elbert, 30, 64–65

Daniels, Josephus, 85
Davis, Angela, 58–59
Davis, Jefferson, 35, **142**, 143, 144, 151, 155, 199
Death (Lynched Figure), 75
Decatur, Georgia, 161, 175
DeKalb County, Georgia, 175
Delaney, Brigid, 134
Deleuze, Gilles, 175
Delgado, Richard, 101
DeLuca, Kevin, 12, 110
Demnig, Gunter, 153
Dennis, Reuben, 166
Derrida, Jacques, 16
Dilawar, Arvind, 9

Dixie monumentalism, 34–35, 115, 137–59, 185
Donegan, William, 170
Donham, Carolyn. *See* Bryant, Carolyn
Doubt, 195
Douglass, Frederick, 54, 114, 217
Dred Scott decision, 214
drug laws, 124, 129, 216; war on drugs, 186, 193, 210
Du Bois, W. E. B., 5, 31, 40, 81, 99–100, 103, 111, 114, 122, 185, 217
Duke, David, 149
Duluth, Minnesota, 116, 177–78, **178**
Duncan, Horace, 170
Dvorak, Petula, 96
Dyer, Leonidas, 68
Dyer Anti-Lynching Bill, 68–69, 71, 74, 78

Earley, Pete, 132
Edelman, Marian Wright, 201
Edgemon, Erin, 196
Ehrenhaus, Peter, 12, 51, 104, 108, 110
Eighth Amendment, 128
Eisenman, Peter, 167
Elaine, Arkansas, 65, 82
Emanuel African Methodist Episcopal Church, 144
Emberton, Carole, 22, 24
End of American Lynching, The, 62
Eng, David, 98
Equal Justice Initiative (EJI), 4–9, 13–18, 20–22, 26, 28–29, 31–32, 34–38, 39–40, 42–43, 48, 54–55, 58–60, 61, 63, 69, 72, 85–86, 87–88, 91, 94, 98, 100, 103, 107, 109, 111, 112, 113–18, 120–28, 132–35, 137–38, 140–42, 144–45, 147–48, 150, 153–58, 160–65, 167, 172, 175–76, 179, 183, 184–202, 203–17
Espy, Watt, 128
Executive Order 8802, 92–93
Eyerman, Ron, 19
Ezekiel, Moses, 35

FBI, 94, 97
Feldblum, Sammy, 18, 197

Ferris, William, 140
Fifteenth Amendment, 20–21, 23, 27–29, 32, 40–41, 46, 69, 95, 119–20, 190–91, 209
Fisk, Clinton, 24
Flood, Chris, 140
Foley, Malcolm, 161
Following the Color Line, 46, 57–58
Foner, Eric, 19
Foote, Kenneth, 5
Forman, James, 216
Forrest, Nathan Bedford, 26–27, 35
Fort Mill, South Carolina, 35
Foucault, Michel, 13–14, 39–40, 56, 59, 88, 114, 117, 172, 185, 200, 210
Fourteenth Amendment, 20–21, 23, 27–28, 32, 40–41, 46, 69–70, 81, 95, 119–20, 190–91, 209
Francis, Willie, 127–28
Frank, Leo, 205
Franklin, Robert M., Jr., 166–67
Freedman's Bureau, 23, 25
Fults, Kenneth, 127
Fuoss, Kirk, 4

Garnett, Clarence, 166
Garrett, Finis, 70
gender, 27, 30, 32, 41, 43–44, 49, 59, 70, 120, 130, 181, 212. *See also* women
genocide, 138, 153–54, 176, 186–88, 192, 197–202, 204, 210
Georgia, 105, 114, 165. *See also individual cities and counties*
Germany, 153, 167, 200
Goffney, Gladys, 166
Gone with the Wind, 80
Goodkind, Nicole, 107
Grant, Ulysses S., 25
Great Britain, 47–48, 55–56
Great Depression, 20, 66, 73, 74
Great Migration, 9, 16, 50, 118, 122, 157, 191–92, 197–202
Gregory, Vanessa, 105, 109
Griffin, Ms., 27
Grindy, Matthew, 12

Gross, Terry, 106
Guattari, Félix, 175
Guided by Justice, 180, **181**
guns, 47, 49, 52, 60, 201

Hampson, Rick, 147, 151
Harding, Warren G., 69
Harlan, John Marshall, 45–46
Harold, Christine, 12, 110
Harpaz, Beth, 156
Harper's Magazine, 24
Harris, Kamala, 3–4, 86
Harvard Civil Rights–Civil Liberties Law Review, 102
Harvard Law School, 125, 131
hate crimes, 3, 121, 144, 148
Hayes, Robert, 158–59
Hayes, Rutherford B., 28
Haywood, Harry, 83
Heim, Joe, 149
Helena, Arkansas, 81–82
Henderson, Nia-Malika, 166
Herbert, Hilary, 35
Heyer, Heather, 149
Hinds County, Mississippi, 31
Hinshaw, Wendy, 108–10
Hitler, Adolf, 91, 153, 200
Hodes, Martha, 24, 26–27
Holder, Eric, 216
Holocaust, 12, 45, 99–100, 103, 123, 138, 153, 186–87, 189, 196–97, 200, 202, 205; African American, 110, 167, 186–87, 191, 197–202, 204
hooks, bell, 110
Hopkins, Francis Pauline, 43
Hose, Sam, 41
Houck, Davis, 12
Houston, Charles Hamilton, 98
Houston, Kerr, 181–82
Howard, Oliver, 24
Howard-Hassmann, Rhoda, 12–13
"How We Remember Lynching," 39
Hughey, Randall, 156
Huston, Lewis, 177

identity, 146, 151; civic, 10–11; cultural, 11;
    formation, 144; politics, 152, 211; racial,
    101–2
Ifill, Sherrilyn, 107
Illuminations, 14
Indianapolis Freeman, 48
International Labor Defense (ILD), 62, 65,
    82–85
Ivey, Kay, 137, 154–55

Jackson, Elmer, 177
Jackson, Jesse, 43
Jackson, Mahalia, 96
Jackson, Stonewall, 35, 149–50
Jefferson County Memorial Project, 177
Jefferson Davis Memorial Association, 35
Jena, Louisiana, 102
Jet magazine, 96
Jewish Life, 99
Jezebel, 86
Jim Crow laws, 7, 28–34, 38, 40, 42, 52, 56,
    66, 83, 86, 89, 101, 118, 120–21, 139, 165,
    181, 188, 191–92, 195–96, 203, 208
Johnson, Elihu, 65
Johnson, Gibson, 65
Johnson, James Weldon, 4, 66, 70–71, 111
Johnson, Jarvis, 207–8
Johnson, Joe Spinner, 71
Johnson, Leroy, 65
Johnson, Louis, 65
Johnson, Lyndon, 181
Jones, Marion, 78
Judge Lynch, 22–28, 41, 47, 58–59, 209
justice, 10, 54, 90, 96, 104, 133, 135, 162,
    173–74, 203, 208–14; historical, 178;
    racial, 161; restorative, 12, 17–18, 116, 123,
    145, 204; social, 10, 91, 118, 178, 217
Justice for Victims of Lynching Act, 3–5, 86
Just Mercy, 28, 104, 113, 115, 118, 129–34,
    145–46, 188, 193, 211–13, 215, 217

Kaphar, Titus, 195
Kazanjian, David, 98
Keenan, Mikki, 185

Kendi, Ibram, 152
Kennedy, John Fitzgerald, 181
Kennedy, Robert, 181
Kennicott, Philip, 165, 167, 176, 184
Kentucky, 104–5, 166
Kerr, Lisa, 217
Kersey, Paul, 184
Killers of the Dream, 94
King, Dana, 180, **181**
King, Martin Luther, Jr., 12, 86, 100, 114, 144,
    162, 181, 201, 209, 212–13
Kirschke, Amy, 12
Klein, Ezra, 140
Korean War Veterans Memorial, 180
Ku Klux Klan, 6, 20–21, 24–27, 29, 34, 37,
    40, 43, 44, 67–68, 74, 84, 86, 102, 109–10,
    120, 138, 149, 188, 195, 211

labor abuses, 44, 119–20, 146, 162, 186, 189
Lamar County, Texas, 7–8, 14–15
Landrieu, Mitch, 150
Lawrence, Elizabeth, 195
Lee, Harper, 130
Lee, Robert E., 35, 144, 149–51
Legacies of Lynching, 108
Legacy Museum, 4–6, 9, 13–18, 26, 34,
    37–38, 39–40, 42–43, 59–60, 61, 63, 69,
    103, 109, 111, 112, 113, 115–18, 125, 128, 131,
    134, 137, 141, 144–45, 148, 150, 154–59,
    160–83, 184–202, 203–4, 206, 208, 210,
    212–13, 216–17
Legal Defense Fund (LDF), 95, 107
Lennon, John, 161
"Letter from Duluth," 177
Levin, Kevin, 34
Levin, Sam, 155–56
Lezak, Michael, 167
linkages, 12, 32, 34, 38, 54, 70, 79, 89, 99, 101,
    111, 119–20, 123–25, 128, 176, 188, 193, 196,
    199–201, 208, 211
Littlefield, John, 91
Lockhart, P. R., 178–79
Locking Up Our Own, 216
Lombardo, Anthony, 12–13

Lost Cause narrative, 21, 34–35, 80, 139–40, 144, 146–48, 151, 154, 156, 159
Louisiana, 44, 127, 150–51, 153. *See also* Jena, Louisiana
Lowther, Henry, 26
Lurleen B. Wallace Office Building, 141, **141**
Lynch, Charles, 22
Lyncher in Me, The, 177
"Lynchers in Congress," 73
lynching: archives, 8, 13, 16, 20, 36–38, 50, 54, 56–59, 62, 65, 72, 78, 83, 85, 90, 101, 111, 114–16, 127–28, 158, 160, 175, 185, 191, 200–202, 210, 216; cultures, 48, 101–2; definition, 11, 36, 61–66, 69, 71–74, 86, 107, 121–22, 165; great forgetting, 11, 97–101, 108, 112, 124, 127, 204, 212; histories, 5, 7, 12, 14, 86, 101, 113, 119, 139, 175, 178, 197, 207–9, 211, 214–16; historiographies, 9, 16, 103; legacies, 4–5, 12, 14, 36–38, 39, 94, 98, 101–3, 111–12, 114–15, 117, 122, 125, 148, 185–86, 193, 204–5, 208, 211, 214; legality, 22, 30–32, 42, 47–48, 57, 82, 85, 98, 101, 120, 123–24, 128, 133, 191, 196; markers, 7–8, 13, 106, 175, 205, 207; mass, 47, 53, 58, 93, 102, 110, 176, 186, 195, 211; memorials, 116, 138, 155; memories, 88, 103, 111, 112, 183, 211; photographs, 7–8, 15, 52–53, 59, 62, 75, 80, 89, 91, 95–96, 99, 103–12, 174, 191, 203, 209–10; postcards and mementos, 7, 53, 103, 105–8, 174, 191, 209; as public spectacles, 7, 12, 15, 53, 109, 112, 165, 174, 186, 204, 208; purported end, 37, 62, 73, 75, 84–86, 87–88, 93, 98–99, 116, 120–21, 123–26, 186; reenactments, 11, 172; soil from sites, 13, 16, 172, 178, 195, 204, 206; statistics, 62, 64–66, 74, 85, 99, 109, 112, 113, 122, 123, 160, 167, 195, 204, 212; studies, 10, 64, 89, 91, 98
Lynching: Violence, Rhetoric, and American Identity, 10
"Lynching Ethics," 101–2
Lynching Memorial. *See* National Memorial for Peace and Justice
"Lynching's Long Shadow, A," 109

Lynch Justice at Work, 81
Lynch-Law, 30, 64
"Lynch Law," 53

Major, Brian, 157
Malcolm X, 181
marginalization, 46, 48, 59, 87, 89, 128, 146
Markovitz, Jonathan, 12, 108
Marsh, Richard, 75
Marshall, Eugene, 166
Marshall, Thurgood, 73, 76–77, 85, 98, 114, 205
Martin, Trayvon, 10
MASS Design Group, 160
Massey, Jim, 156
Massey, Mary, 156
Masur, Louis, 5
McDowell, Calvin, 49–52
McFadden, Jane, 6–7, 9, 32
McGee, Michael, 211
McGhie, Isaac, 177
McIlherron, Jim, 71
McIntosh, Dawn Marie, 208
McKerrow, Raymie, 14
McMillian, Walter, 129–30, 132
Meier, August, 91
memorialization, 9, 14, 17, 40, 108, 116, 138, 140, 144, 146, 149, 151–53, 158–59, 161, 165, 176–77, 185, 187, 194, 209, 216; countermemorialization, 18, 54, 183. *See also* Confederate statues and memorials
memory, 7, 16, 56, 58, 86, 103, 109–10, 138, 143, 152, 159, 163–64, 168, 183, 194, 197, 200, 204; collective, 19, 39; competitive, 14, 16, 44, 148, 154, 197, 202; countermemories, 14, 39, 54, 59, 109–10, 185; cultural, 13; local, 19; lynching, 88, 103, 111, 112, 183, 211; multidirectional, 14, 16, 100, 117, 148, 149, 154, 159, 196–97, 202; public, 9, 12, 37, 44, 61, 110, 128, 148, 160, 183, 209; studies, 123
Memphis, Tennessee, 49–52, 177
Memphis Daily Commercial, 50
Memphis Free Speech and Headlight, 49–51

mercy, 17–18, 114, 131, 146, 188, 193–94, 203–7, 209–15
Middleton, Michael, 161, 180
Milam, J. W., 96–97
Miners' Physical Check, 181–82
Mirzoeff, Nicholas, 158
Mississippi, 12, 118. *See also individual cities and counties*
Money, Misissippi, 95–97
Monroeville, Alabama, 130
Montgomery, Alabama, 5–6, 16–17, 40, 43, 60, 63, 87–88, 112, 114, 116–17, 124–25, 137–38, 140–43, **141, 142, 143**, 145, 148, 156–59, 160–62, 170, 183, 184–89, 193, 195, 202, 208–9, 214; bus boycott, 180, 208; sites of memory, 6, 15, 17, 60, 113, 158–59, 160–62, 184, 197–98, 200–201, 205, 209–11, 217; spaces and places, 6–7, 14, 17, 39, 113, 116, 143, 145, 160–61, 164, 166, 174, 177, 181, 183, 184, 186, 188, 203–4
Montgomery Advertiser, 200, 208
Moon, Dreama, 208
Moore, Quess, 152
Moores, Merrill, 68
Moore v. Dempsey (1923), 82
Morrison, Ronda, 130
Moss, Thomas, 49–52
Murphree, Gaen, 105
Myers, Joe, 106

Nakayama, Thomas, 208
National Association for the Advancement of Colored People (NAACP), 3–4, 11–12, 36, 42, 46, 47–48, 62, 64–66, 68–69, 71–77, 79–86, 87–92, 94–95, 98–99, 101–2, 107, 109, 111, 116, 128, 155, 158, 195, 204, 209–10, 212, 217
National Memorial for Peace and Justice, 5–6, 9, 13, 15–16, 18, 26, 39, 60, 63, 80, 103, 109, 111, 113, 117, 124–25, 127–28, 134, 138, 140–41, 144–45, 148, 150, 154–59, 160–83, **168, 169, 171, 172, 173, 181**, 186, 188, 196–200, 202, 203–4, 206, 208, 211, 214, 216–17; Monument Park, 173–83, **176**,

179; participatory dimensions, 148, 160, 168, 175–76, 179–80, 183, 186
National Museum of African American History and Culture (NMAAHC), 6, 39
National September 11 Memorial and Museum, 187, 198
Nazis, 84, 91–93, 98, 99, 150, 153, 187
Neal, Claude, 77
"Negro and the Warsaw Ghetto, The," 99–100
Negro Motorist Green Book, The, 180
Neiman, Susan, 153
Nelson, Laura, 217
New Age, 47
New Deal, 20, 74–76, 79, 84, 86
New Reconstruction, 4, 115, 117, 145, 164, 176, 203, 206, 212
New South, 32, 35
New York Times, 57, 60, 78, 86, 98, 105, 109, 140, 170, 177, 183
Nietzsche, Friedrich, 14, 16, 39, 144–45, 200, 210
Nixon, Richard, 193
Nkyinkyim installation, 162–65, **163**, 182
Noguchi, Isamu, 75

Obama, Barack, 11, 114, 118
Offett, William, 52
Ohl, Jessy, 12, 109–10
Oliver, Karl, 150–51
Olmstead, Molly, 147
Olufani, Masud, 164–65
Omaha, Nebraska, 7
On the Courthouse Lawn, 107
oral histories, 20, 160, 196
Order of Things, The, 88
Ore, Ersula, 10–11, 24, 41, 67, 105
Owen, Susan, 12, 51, 104, 108, 110

Page, Thomas Nelson, 11, 34
Paris, Texas, 7–8, 14–15
Park, Marlene, 4, 88
Parker, Dennis, 95–96
Parks, Rosa, 12, 86, 114, 180, 201, 209

participatory critical rhetoric (PCR), 14, 161–62, 165–66, 168, 173–74, 176, 182, 186, 193, 203, 214
Patterson, Margot, 152
Patterson, Wade, 166
peonage, 33, 38, 44, 48, 81, 120, 146, 201
People's Grocery, 49
Peters, John Durham, 100
Pfeifer, Michael, 19, 37, 101
Pilkington, Ed, 8
Pinar, William, 68, 94
Plessy, Homer, 44–45
Plessy v. Ferguson (1896), 44–45, 98
police, 49, 63, 65, 69–70, 72, 78, 81–84, 93, 99, 110, 111, 114, 119, 146, 194, 216; harassment, 146; profiling, 101, 113; undue force, 10, 152, 164–65, 202
politics, 14, 24, 36, 41–43, 49, 52, 59, 63, 65, 76, 91, 93–94, 112, 113, 115, 124, 130, 132–33, 147, 152, 155, 181, 183, 200, 209; culture of, 19; myths of, 11; power of, 13; pressures of, 175; rights of, 20, 27; traditions of, 11
populism, 41, 51
Porter, Ray, 53
post-Reconstruction period, 20–22, 28–34, 36–37, 40–41, 64, 78–80, 145, 147, 186, 193, 207
Potter, Jennifer, 12, 109–10
Powell, Kimberly, 11, 72
"Presumption of Guilt, A," 120–22
Progressive Era, 20, 41–42, 46–48, 54, 58, 63, 65
Pulliam, Sam, 166

Rable, George, 68, 84
racial hierarchies, 17, 20, 25, 33, 40, 44–45, 100, 190–91
racism, 3, 5, 9, 12, 24, 27, 29–33, 38, 39–60, 63, 67, 81, 83, 85, 88–95, 99–100, 102, 116–17, 121, 123–25, 129, 136, 139, 144, 151–52, 155–56, 180–81, 196, 204, 208, 215
radicalism, 48, 57–60, 83–84, 86, 87, 90, 92–93, 103, 108–12, 114, 116, 118, 135, 181, 201–2, 204–6, 208

Radical Republicans, 19–20, 22–26, 28–29, 119–20, 147
Raiford, Leigh, 42
Rainey, Joseph, 27
Raise Up, 181–82, **182**
Randolph, A. Philip, 81, 90, 92
Raper, Arthur, 74–75, 127
Read, Warren, 177
reconciliation, 4, 8, 36, 60, 86, 116, 138, 145, 157, 159, 177, 183, 186–87, 199–200, 205–6, 208–14
Reconstruction, 15, 19–28, 31, 33–34, 37–38, 39–41, 63, 79–80, 118–21, 146–47, 166, 184, 186, 193, 207, 209
Reconstruction Acts of 1867, 20
redemption, 22, 32, 42, 104, 114, 203
Red Record, The, 42–43, 53–54, 59, 64
Red Summer, 68
Reflector, 73
religion, 3, 12, 21, 51, 55, 114; Christianity, 22, 54, 67, 82, 104, 167; Judaism, 12, 92, 99–100, 149, 153, 167, 202, 205, 210
Renkl, Margaret, 157
reparations, 4, 12–13, 18, 59, 69, 116, 123, 145, 187, 192, 201, 204, 206, 211
rhetorical culture, 4, 13, 24, 94, 115, 162, 178–79
Rhodes, Tommy, 156
Rice, Anne, 39, 109, 116
Richardson, Herbert, 134
Rillieux, Victor-Ernest, 56
Robertson, Campbell, 140, 170
Rochelle, Fred, 170
Roessner, Lori Amber, 43, 60
Rogers, James, 166
Roof, Dylann, 144, 149
Roosevelt, Eleanor, 77–78
Roosevelt, Franklin D., 75, 78, 84, 86, 92–93
Rope and Faggot, 64
Rothberg, Michael, 100, 148, 154, 197
Rothman, Joshua, 67
Royster, Jacqueline Jones, 10, 42
Rushdy, Ashraf H. A., 11, 62
Rwanda, 153–54, 186, 197–98, 200

Sanchez, James, 149
Savage, Kirk, 138
Schmidt, Jalane, 141
Schneider, Abigail, 177
Scott, Tim, 3
Scottsboro Boys, 11, 81–84, 86, 87, 123–24, 131, 217
"Scottsboro Decision, The," 83
segregation, 28–29, 32–34, 44–45, 47–48, 58–59, 66, 68, 82–84, 88–92, 94–95, 99, 144, 147–48, 151, 181, 184, 186, 188–89, 192, 196, 198, 202, 207, 214
Segura, Liliana, 125–29
Selma, Alabama, 26–27, 188
separate but equal doctrine, 28–29, 44–46, 88–89, 98, 192
Sharecroppers' Union, 71–72
sharecropping, 40, 55, 71, 119, 122, 202
Shipp, J. Thomas, 217
Siegel, Robert, 133
Silber, Nina, 63, 80
Simelton, Benard, 155
Simmons, William J., 67
Sims, James Marion, 143, **143**
60 Minutes, 214–15
Slater, Brady, 178
Slaughter-House Cases, 70
slavery, 9–10, 12–13, 19, 22–27, 29–31, 35, 37, 39–40, 43, 55, 70, 117, 119–21, 134, 140, 143, 145–46, 148, 150–54, 162–65, 176, 179, 181, 183, 184, 186–93, 195, 197–202, 206–7, 214
Smith, Ellison "Cotton Ed," 79
Smith, Henry, 7–9, **8**, 14–15, 18, 99, 217
Smith, Jamil, 43
Smith, Lillian, 94
Smith, Shawn Michelle, 53
Smith, Theophus, 108
Smith v. Allwright (1944), 95
social change, 5, 24, 40, 44, 57, 79, 95, 105, 110, 188
social class, 20, 23, 25, 27, 35, 41, 43–45, 49, 52, 70, 72, 75, 81, 83, 120, 130
Social Darwinism, 30, 33, 44, 66, 192
Sons of Confederate Veterans, 156

Souls of Black Folk, The, 99
South Africa, 17, 32, 154, 181, 186, 200
South Carolina, 131, 144, 146; state capitol, 144, 146. *See also individual cities*
Southern Commission on the Study of Lynching, 74
Southern Democrats, 21, 24–26, 34, 43, 69, 74–75, 84, 85
Southern Horrors and Other Writings, 10, 59, 61
Southern Poverty Law Center, 138, 147, 184
Spingarn, Arthur, 92
Squires, David, 42, 46, 50–51, 57–58
Stacy, Rubin, 78–79
Staples, Brent, 107–8
Steim, Tyler, 151–52, 157–58
stereotypes, 57–58, 80, 155
Stevenson, Alabama, 83
Stevenson, Bryan, 4–6, 9, 13–18, 21, 28, 31–32, 34, 37–38, 43, 53, 60, 63, 86, 100, 103–4, 110–11, 112, 113–36, 137, 140–41, 144–47, 153–54, 157, 160, 162, 166, 176, 179, 185–88, 192–94, 196, 198–202, 204–8, 210–17; TED Talk, 115, 117, 135, 188
Stewart, Henry, 49–52
Steyn, Melissa, 17
Stinney, George, 131–32
Stoler, Ann, 13–14, 21, 185, 210
Stoll, Philip H., 131
Stone Mountain, Georgia, 67
Strange, Todd, 208–9
Sturgeon, Grace, 93
Sturken, Marita, 7–8
suffrage, 19–20, 27, 30, 33, 34, 46, 57, 72, 92, 191
Sullivan, Joe, 135
SuperSoul Sunday, 133

"Take 'Em Down in Louisiana," 152
Tayleur, Eleanor, 57
Taylor, Jennifer Rae, 120
Teeger, Chana, 153
Teen Vogue, 21
Tennessee, 50, 52, 70–71, 195. *See also individual cities*

Terrell, Mary Church, 11, 43
Thirteenth Amendment, 20–21, 23, 27–28, 32, 40–41, 46, 69, 119–20, 145, 190–91, 209
Thirty Years of Lynching in the United States, 1889–1918, 66
This Is Her First Lynching, 75
Thomas, Hank Willis, 181–82, **182**
Till, Emmett, 12, 91, 95–97, 105, 111, 206
Till-Mobley, Mamie Elizabeth, 95
To Kill a Mockingbird, 130
Tolnay, Stewart, 6, 62, 116
Toobin, Jeffrey, 134–35
Tourgée, Albion, 46
tourism, 15, 116, 143, 154, 156–57, 161–63, 183, 195, 197; dark, 6, 162, 183, 187
Tragedy of Lynching, The, 74, 127
transgenerational pasts, 7, 14, 39, 123, 147, 202, 210
"True Justice: Bryan Stevenson's Fight for Equality," 214, 217
Truman, Harry, 90–91, 94
Trump, Donald, 3–4, 17, 115, 118, 133, 149, 150, 205
truth, 4, 6, 8, 40, 42, 52, 56, 59–60, 82, 85–86, 115, 145, 158, 179, 183, 186, 200, 205–6, 208, 210–11, 213–15
Tubman, Harriet, 189
Turner, Mary, 161, 217
Tuskegee Institute, 36, 42, 62, 65, 71, 85, 99, 113, 116, 143, 158
Tutu, Desmond, 117
Tydings, Millard Evelyn, 76
Tyson, Timothy, 97

Underwood, Mrs. J., 52
UNESCO, 45, 90
United Daughters of the Confederacy (UDC), 35
United States v. Cruikshank (1875), 191
"United We Lynch," 109
US Department of Justice, 77, 95, 97, 206
US Holocaust Memorial Museum (USHMM), 187, 192, 198, 210

Vance, Myrtle, 7, **8**
Vardaman, James K., 30
Vietnam Veterans Memorial, 161, 180
Vinitzky-Seroussi, Vered, 153
violence, 10, 12, 17, 19–20, 22–31, 34, 39–40, 47, 49, 57–58, 60, 62, 67–68, 71–75, 79, 82–84, 88, 93–95, 100–101, 104, 107–8, 116, 121, 124, 133, 145–46, 149, 159, 160, 174, 184–85, 191–92, 197, 201, 206, 210
Virginia, 73, 150, 165. *See also* Charlottesville, Virginia
visualities, 5, 7, 11, 14, 24, 38–40, 53, 62, 75, 80, 88–89, 103–4, 106–13, 115, 117, 137, 144, 155, 158, 161, 164, 180, 182–83, 188–89, 194, 201, 203, 210–11, 217
Völkischer Beobachter, 92
Voting Rights Act of 1965, 95, 194

Wagner, Robert F., 76, 78–79
Waldrep, Christopher, 47, 61–63
Walker, David, 170
Wallace, George, 141, 192, 195
Walton County, Georgia, 93
Warren, Earl, 29, 98
Washington, Booker T., 79
Washington, Jesse, 106
Washington County, Texas, 166
Washington Post, 79, 93, 96
Watson, Martha Solomon, 11, 66–67
Weizman, Eyal, 189
Wells-Barnett, Ida B., 5–6, 10, 17, 36, 40, 41–44, 46–60, 61, 63–66, 81–82, 86, 87, 90, 99, 100, 102, 109, 111, 114, 116, 119, 122, 174, 181, 185, 201, 204–5, 212–13, 217
White, George H., 34
White, Walter Francis, 4–5, 64, 66, 71, 75–77, 80, 93–94, 103, 105, 109, 122, 174, 185, 195, 217
White, William, 205
white supremacy, 4, 20–21, 24–25, 27, 29, 31, 33, 35, 37, 40, 48, 53–54, 63, 67, 85, 89, 102, 106, 114, 119, 121–22, 138–41, 144–45, 149, 153, 184, 189, 191, 193–94, 197, 204, 208, 212, 215

Wiegman, Robyn, 22
Wieland, Bob, 155
Wilberforce, William, 55
Willard, Charlie, 152
Williams, Elbert, 87
Williams, Eugene, 131
Williams, Kenneth, 127
Williams, Patricia, 60
Wilkins, Roy, 89
Wilson, Cynthia, 108
Winfrey, Oprah, 133, 214–15
Winnie Davis Hall, 151
Winston, J. T., 30
Without Sanctuary, 91, 103–12; photography exhibit, 12, 91, 103–4, 109, 217
women, 10, 26, 41, 44, 47–48, 51, 55, 57–59, 66, 72, 83, 115, 143, 180–81, 194; African American, 57, 59, 72, 115, 149, 194; protection of white women, 26–27, 30–31, 35, 42, 48, 51–54, 66–68, 70, 83, 95, 105, 119, 122, 130–31, 166, 170, 177, 195, 209. *See also* gender

Women, Race and Class, 58
Wood, Amy Louise, 12
Work, Monroe N., 64–65, 85, 113
World War I, 24, 67–68, 211
World War II, 9, 18, 45–46, 63, 66–67, 84, 86, 87–95, 98–99, 103, 111, 138, 147, 166, 189, 197, 200, 202, 211
Wright, Cleo, 93
Wright, Roy, 131
Wright, Walter Francis, 75

Yamakawa, James, 178
Yawn, Andrew, 176
Young, James, 148

Zackodnik, Teresa, 48
Zangrando, Robert, 85, 92
Zimmerman, George, 10

ABOUT THE AUTHORS

Marouf A. Hasian Jr. is distinguished professor of communication at the University of Utah. He is the author of *Restorative Justice, Humanitarian Rhetorics, and Public Memories of Colonial Camp Cultures*.

Nicholas S. Paliewicz is associate professor in the Department of Communication at the University of Louisville. His work has appeared in such publications as *Environmental Communication: A Journal of Nature and Culture*, *Southern Communication Journal*, and *Popular Communication: The International Journal of Media and Culture*.

www.ingramcontent.com/pod-product-compliance
Lightning Source LLC
Chambersburg PA
CBHW030336240426
43661CB00052B/1649